Kaplan Publishing are constantly finding r … make a
difference to your studies and our excitin … lly do
offer something different to students loo

This book comes with free MyKaplan or … n
study anytime, anywhere. **This free on**
separately and is included in the price of the

Having purchased this book, you have access to the following online study materials:

CONTENT	ACCA (including FBT, FMA, FFA)		FIA (excluding FBT, FMA, FFA)	
	Text	Kit	Text	Kit
Electronic version of the book	✓	✓	✓	✓
Knowledge checks with instant answers	✓		✓	
Material updates	✓	✓	✓	✓
Latest official ACCA exam questions*		✓		
Pocket Notes (digital copy)	✓		✓	
Study Planner	✓			
Progress Test including questions and answers	✓		✓	
Syllabus recap Videos		✓		✓
Revision Planner		✓		✓
Question Debrief and Walkthrough Videos		✓		
Mock Exam including questions and answers		✓		

* Excludes BT, MA, FA, FBT, FMA, FFA; for all other papers includes a selection of questions, as released by ACCA

How to access your online resources

Received this book as part of your Kaplan course?
If you have a MyKaplan account, your full online resources will be added automatically, in line with the information in your course confirmation email. If you've not used MyKaplan before, you'll be sent an activation email once your resources are ready.

Bought your book from Kaplan?
We'll automatically add your online resources to your MyKaplan account. If you've not used MyKaplan before, you'll be sent an activation email.

Bought your book from elsewhere?
Go to **www.mykaplan.co.uk/add-online-resources**
Enter the ISBN number found on the title page and back cover of this book.
Add the unique pass key number contained in the scratch panel below.
You may be required to enter additional information during this process to set up or confirm your account details.

This code can only be used once for the registration of this book online. This registration and your online content will expire when the examinations covered by this book have taken place. Please allow one hour from the time you submit your book details for us to process your request.

Please scratch the film to access your unique code.

Please be aware that this code is case-sensitive and you will need to include the dashes within the passcode, but not when entering the ISBN.

KAPLAN
PUBLISHING

ACCA

Applied Skills

Financial Management (FM)

EXAM KIT

KAPLAN PUBLISHING

British Library Cataloguing-in-Publication Data

A catalogue record for this book is available from the British Library.

Published by:

Kaplan Publishing UK

Unit 2 The Business Centre

Molly Millar's Lane

Wokingham

Berkshire

RG41 2QZ

ISBN: 978-1-83735-003-2

Printed and bound in Great Britain.

Acknowledgements

The past ACCA examination questions are the copyright of the Association of Chartered Certified Accountants. The original answers to the questions from June 1994 onwards were produced by the examiners themselves and have been adapted by Kaplan Publishing.

We are grateful to the Chartered Institute of Management Accountants and the Institute of Chartered Accountants in England and Wales for permission to reproduce past examination questions. The answers have been prepared by Kaplan Publishing.

CONTENTS

Key features in this edition

In addition to providing a wide ranging bank of real past exam questions, we have also included in this edition:

- An analysis of all of the recent examinations.
- Exam-specific information and advice on exam technique.
- Our recommended approach to make your revision for this particular subject as effective as possible.
- This includes step-by-step guidance on how best to use our Kaplan material (Study text, pocket notes and exam kit) at this stage in your studies.
- Enhanced tutorial answers packed with specific key answer tips, technical tutorial notes and exam technique tips from our experienced tutors.
- Complementary online resources including full tutor debriefs to point you in the right direction when you get stuck.

You will find a wealth of other resources to help you with your studies on the following sites:

www.mykaplan.co.uk

https://www.accaglobal.com/gb/en/student/exam-support-resources/fundamentals-exams-study-resources/f9.html

Quality and accuracy are of the utmost importance to us so if you spot an error in any of our products, please send an email to mykaplanreporting@kaplan.com with full details, or follow the link to the feedback form in MyKaplan.

Our Quality Co-ordinator will work with our technical team to verify the error and take action to ensure it is corrected in future editions.

INDEX TO QUESTIONS AND ANSWERS

INTRODUCTION

Following the introduction of the revised exam format, all previous ACCA constructed response (long) exam questions within this kit have been adapted.

The specimen exam is included at the end of the kit.

KEY TO THE INDEX

EXAM ENHANCEMENTS

We have added the following enhancements to the answers in this exam kit:

Key answer tips

All answers include key answer tips to help your understanding of each question.

Tutorial note

Many answers include more tutorial notes to explain some of the technical points in more detail.

Top tutor tips

For selected questions, we 'walk through the answer' giving guidance on how to approach the questions with helpful 'tips from a top tutor', together with technical tutor notes.

These answers are indicated with the 'footsteps' icon in the index.

Within the questions in the exam kit you will see the following icons, shown in the question requirements:

= word processing

= spreadsheet

The icons highlighting the constructed response workspace tool alongside some of the questions are for guidance only – it is important to recognise that each question is different and that the answer space provided by ACCA in the exam is determined by both the technical content of the question as well as the quality assurance processes ACCA undertakes to ensure the student is provided with the most appropriate type of workspace.

ONLINE ENHANCEMENTS

Answer debrief

For selected questions, we recommend that they are to be completed in full exam conditions (i.e. properly timed in a closed book environment).

In addition to the examining team's technical answer, enhanced with key answer tips and tutorial notes in this exam kit, online you can find an answer debrief by a top tutor that:

- works through the question in full
- explains key elements of the answer
- ensures that the easy marks are obtained as quickly as possible.

These questions are indicated with the 'video' icon in the index.

Answer debriefs will be available on MyKaplan at:

www.mykaplan.co.uk

BUSINESS FINANCE AND COST OF CAPITAL – EXAM STYLE QUESTIONS

ANALYSIS OF PAST EXAMS

The table below summarises the key topics that have been tested within the constructed response questions in the examinations to date. A much wider range of topics will now be examined following the introduction of objective test questions. Only selected questions are released by ACCA every six months.

	S20/ D20	M21/ J21	S21/ D21	M22/ J22	S22/ D22	M23/ J23	S23/ D23	M24/ J24	S24/ D24
Working capital management									
Elements and importance (including cash operating cycle)			✓		✓				✓
Overtrading									
Inventories			✓		✓				
Receivables			✓						
Payables									
Cash									✓
Working capital needs and funding strategies									
Investment appraisal									
Appraisal process			✓						
Non-discounted techniques		✓		✓	✓				
NPV with tax									
NPV with tax and inflation	✓			✓		✓	✓	✓	✓
IRR									
Risk and uncertainty						✓	✓	✓	✓
Lease or buy			✓						
Asset replacement	✓	✓			✓				
Capital rationing									

	S20/ D20	M21/ J21	S21/ D21	M22/ J22	S22/ D22	M23/ J23	S23/ D23	M24/ J24	S24/ D24
Business finance and cost of capital									
Sources of short term finance									
Sources of long term finance	✓			✓		✓		✓	
Internal sources and dividend policy									
Gearing and capital structure		✓				✓		✓	
Small and medium enterprises									
Islamic financing						✓		✓	
Sources and relative costs		✓		✓			✓		
Estimating cost of equity		✓							
CAPM	✓	✓					✓		
Cost of debt									
Overall cost of capital				✓			✓		
Gearing theories				✓					
Impact of cost of capital on investments									
Forecasting after capital issue									
Dividend theory									

EXAM TECHNIQUE

GENERAL COMMENTS

- Read the examination questions carefully.
- **Divide the time** you spend on questions in proportion to the marks on offer:
  - one suggestion for this examination is to allocate 1.8 minutes to each mark available, so a 20 mark question should be completed in approximately 36 minutes.
  - within that, try to allow time at the end of each question to review your answer and address any obvious issues.

  Whatever happens, always keep your eye on the clock and **do not over run on any part of any question!**
- If you **get completely stuck** with a question:
  - flag the question and
  - **return to it later**.
- Stick to the question and **tailor your answer** to what you are asked.
  - Pay particular attention to the verbs in the question.
  - Try to apply your comments to the scenario where possible.
- If you do not understand what a question is asking, **state your assumptions**.

  Even if you do not answer in precisely the way the examiner hoped, you should be given some credit, if your assumptions are reasonable.
- You should do everything you can to make things easy for the marker.

  The marker will find it easier to identify the points you have made if your **answers are well laid out and well labelled, with references made to workings for calculation questions**.

OBJECTIVE TEST QUESTIONS

- Decide whether you want to attempt these at the start of the exam or at the end.
- No credit for working will be given in these questions, the answers will either be correct (2 marks) or incorrect (0 marks).
- Read the question carefully, as any alternative answer choices will be given based on common mistakes that could be made in attempting the question.
- If a question looks particularly difficult or time consuming, then miss it out first time through (make sure you flag it) and come back to it later. You may wish to enter a guess on the first run through in case you don't get time to return to the question.

CONSTRUCTED RESPONSE (LONG) QUESTIONS

- **Written elements:**

  Your answer should have:

  – a clear structure

  – short paragraphs containing short, succinct sentences

  Be concise.

  Brief points that are correct and answer the question are likely to pick up one mark. Well-developed points may pick up two marks.

  Where possible, try to relate comments to the specific context given rather than your answer looking like it was simply copied out of the textbook.

- **Computations:**

  It is essential to include all your workings in your answers.

COMPUTER-BASED EXAMS – ADDITIONAL TIPS

- Do not attempt a CBE until you have **completed all study material** relating to it.
- On the ACCA website there is a CBE demonstration. It is **ESSENTIAL** that you attempt this before your real CBE. You will become familiar with how to move around the CBE screens and the way that questions are formatted, increasing your confidence and speed in the actual exam.
- Be sure you understand how to use the **software** before you start the exam. If in doubt, ask the assessment centre staff to explain it to you.
- Questions are **displayed on the screen** and answers are entered using keyboard and mouse.
- In addition to the traditional multiple choice question type, CBEs will also contain other types of questions, such as number entry questions, formulae entry questions, multiple correct answers (select two or more), matching labels to targets, stem questions with multiple parts and written questions requiring text entry.
- You need to be sure you **know how to answer questions** of these types before you sit the exam, through practise.
- Functions are available in the spreadsheet software for NPV and IRR calculations. If you wish to use these, make sure that you familiarise yourself with them in advance as, unlike Microsoft Excel, the software will not give you any guidance on how to complete the formula you are writing.
- For NPV calculations, the syntax is:

  =NPV(rate,cash flows from time period 1 onwards)

  The rate can be entered as a percentage (e.g. 10%) or as a decimal (e.g. 0.1). Include the total net cash flows for each year as values, excluding the year zero figure. The year 0 cash flow should be deducted separately from the formula result. It is easiest to have the values for each year in consecutive columns and then highlight them all together when writing the formula.

- For IRR calculations, the syntax is:

  =IRR(values)

  Unlike the NPV formula, the total net cash flow values in the IRR formula should include those for all time periods. It makes no difference if the total cash flows are laid out in columns are in rows, as long as each year is in the cell next to the previous one.

EXAM-SPECIFIC INFORMATION

THE EXAM

FORMAT OF THE EXAM

The exam will be in **THREE sections**, and will be a mix of narrative and computational answers.

All questions are compulsory.

		Number of marks
Section A:	Fifteen objective test questions of 2 marks each	30
Section B:	Three objective test case studies	
	– five questions per case study of 2 marks each	30
Section C:	Two constructed response (long) questions, mainly from the syllabus areas of working capital management, investment appraisal and business finance:	
	Question 1	20
	Question 2	20
		100

Total time allowed: 3 hours (plus 10 minutes to read the exam instructions).

Note that:

- the Financial Management exam will have both a discursive and computational element. The objective test questions and the objective test case study questions will therefore include a mix of calculation-based and explanation-based questions.
- there is likely to be a discussion element included in the constructed response questions in Section C.

PASS MARK

The pass mark for all ACCA Qualification examination exams is 50%.

APPROACH TO THIS EXAM

Financial Management is divided into three different sections, requiring the application of different skills to be successful.

Section A

Stick to the timing principle of 1.8 minutes per mark. This means that the 15 OT questions in section A (30 marks) should take 54 minutes.

Work steadily. Rushing leads to careless mistakes and the OT questions are designed to include answers which result from careless mistakes.

If you don't know the answer, eliminate those options you know are incorrect and see if the answer becomes more obvious.

Remember that there is no negative marking for an incorrect answer. After you have eliminated the options that you know to be wrong, if you are still unsure, guess.

Section B

There is likely to be a significant amount of information to read through for each case. You should begin by reading the OT questions that relate to the case, so that when you read through the information for the first time, you know what it is that you are required to do.

Each OT question is worth two marks. Therefore, you have 18 minutes (1.8 minutes per mark) to answer the five OT questions relating to each case. It is likely that all of the cases will take the same length of time to answer, although some of the OT questions within a case may be quicker than other OT questions within that same case.

Once you have read through the information, you should first answer any of the OT questions that do not require workings and can be quickly answered. You should then attempt the OT questions that require workings utilising the remaining time for that case.

All of the tips for section A are equally applicable to each section B question.

Section C

The constructed response questions in section C will require a written response rather than being OT questions. Therefore, different techniques need to be used to score well.

Unless you know exactly how to answer the question, spend some time planning your answer. Stick to the question and tailor your answer to what you are asked. Pay particular attention to the verbs in the question e.g. 'Calculate', 'State', 'Explain'.

As stated earlier, if you **get completely stuck** with a question, leave space in your answer and return to it later.

If you do not understand what a question is asking, state your assumptions. Even if you do not answer in precisely the way the examining team hoped, you should be given some credit, provided that your assumptions are reasonable.

You should do everything you can to make things easy for the marker. The marker will find it easier to identify the points you have made if your answers are well laid out.

Computations: It is essential to include all your workings in your answers. Many computational questions require the use of a standard format. Be sure you know these formats thoroughly before the examination and use the layouts that you see in the answers given in this book and in model answers.

Remember, you can use the spreadsheet function to help you with the layout and calculation of your answers. Markers are able to see the formulae you are using.

Adopt a logical approach and cross reference workings to the main computation to keep your answers tidy and make it easier for the marker to find your calculations.

All sections

Don't skip parts of the syllabus. The FM exam has 32 different questions so the examination can cover a very broad selection of the syllabus each sitting.

Spend time learning the rules and definitions.

Practise plenty of questions to improve your ability to apply the techniques and perform the calculations.

Spend the last five minutes reading through your answers and making any additions or corrections.

Always keep your eye on the clock and do not over run on any part of any question!

DETAILED SYLLABUS, STUDY GUIDE AND CBE SPECIMEN EXAM

The detailed syllabus and study guide written by the ACCA, along with the specimen exam, can be found at:

www.accaglobal.com/financial-management

KAPLAN'S RECOMMENDED REVISION APPROACH

QUESTION PRACTICE IS THE KEY TO SUCCESS

Success in professional examinations relies upon you acquiring a firm grasp of the required knowledge at the tuition phase. In order to be able to do the questions, knowledge is essential.

However, the difference between success and failure often hinges on your exam technique on the day and making the most of the revision phase of your studies.

The **Kaplan Study Text** is the starting point, designed to provide the underpinning knowledge to tackle all questions. However, in the revision phase, poring over text books is not the answer.

MyKaplan knowledge check tests help you consolidate your knowledge and understanding and are a useful tool to check whether you can remember key topic areas.

Kaplan pocket notes are designed to help you quickly revise a topic area. However, you then need to practise questions. There is a need to progress to full exam standard questions as soon as possible, and to tie your exam technique and technical knowledge together.

The importance of question practice cannot be over-emphasised.

The recommended approach below is designed by expert tutors in the field, in conjunction with their knowledge of the examiner and their recent real exams.

The approach taken for the fundamental exams is to revise by topic area. However, with the professional stage exams, a multi topic approach is required to answer the scenario based questions.

You need to practise as many questions as possible in the time you have left.

OUR AIM

Our aim is to get you to the stage where you can attempt exam standard questions confidently, to time, in a closed book environment, with no supplementary help (i.e. to simulate the real examination experience).

Practising your exam technique on real past examination questions, in timed conditions, is also vitally important for you to assess your progress and identify areas of weakness that may need more attention in the final run up to the examination.

In order to achieve this, we recognise that initially you may feel the need to practise some questions with open book help and exceed the required time.

The approach below shows you which questions you should use to build up to coping with exam standard question practice, and references to the sources of information available should you need to revisit a topic area in more detail.

Remember that in the real examination, all you have to do is:

- attempt all questions required by the exam
- only spend the allotted time on each question, and
- get them at least 50% right!

Try and practise this approach on every question you attempt from now to the real exam.

EXAMINER COMMENTS

We have included the examiner's comments to the specific new syllabus examination questions in this kit for you to see the main pitfalls that students fall into with regard to technical content.

However, too many times in the general section of the report, the examiner comments that students had failed due to:

- 'misallocation of time'
- 'running out of time' and
- showing signs of 'spending too much time on earlier questions and clearly rushing the answer to a subsequent question'.

Good exam technique is vital.

ACCA SUPPORT

For additional support with your studies please also refer to the ACCA Global website.

THE KAPLAN FINANCIAL MANAGEMENT REVISION PLAN

Stage 1: Assess areas of strengths and weaknesses

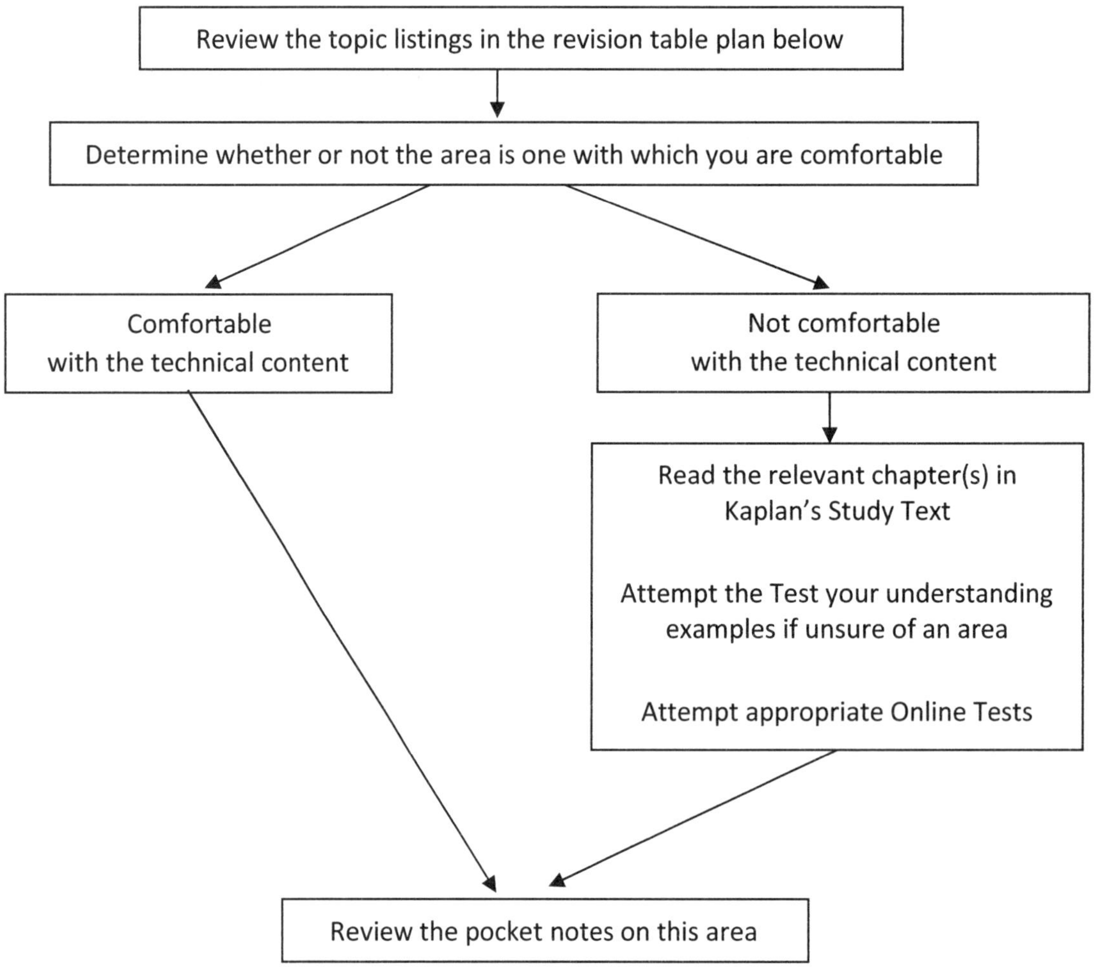

Stage 2: Practice questions

Follow the order of revision of topics as recommended in the revision table plan below and attempt the questions in the order suggested.

Try to avoid referring to text books, notes and the model answer until you have completed your attempt.

Try to answer the question in the allotted time.

Review your attempt with the model answer and assess how much of the answer you achieved in the allocated exam time.

Fill in the self-assessment box below and decide on your best course of action.

Comfortable with question attempt

↓

Only revisit when comfortable with questions on all topic areas

Not comfortable with question attempts

↓

Focus on these areas by:

- Reworking test your understanding examples in Kaplan's Study text
- Revisiting the technical content from Kaplan's pocket notes
- Working any remaining questions on that area in the exam kit
- Reattempting an exam standard question in that area, on a timed, closed book basis

Note that:

The 'footsteps questions' give guidance on exam techniques and how you should have approached the question.

Stage 3: Final pre-exam revision

We recommend that you **attempt at least one three hour mock examination** containing a set of previously unseen exam standard questions.

It is important that you get a feel for the breadth of coverage of a real exam without advanced knowledge of the topic areas covered – just as you will expect to see on the real exam day.

Ideally this mock should be sat in timed, closed book, real exam conditions and could be:

- a mock examination offered by your tuition provider, and/or
- the specimen exam in the back of this exam kit, and/or
- the last real examination (available shortly afterwards on MyKaplan with 'enhanced walk through answers' and a full 'tutor debrief').

THE KAPLAN FINANCIAL MANAGEMENT REVISION PLAN

Topic	Study Text Chapter	Pocket note Chapter	Questions to attempt	Tutor guidance	Date attempted	Self-assessment
Investment appraisal	2 and 3	2 and 3	102, 103, 107, 117, 118	Start with the basics – remind yourself of the four techniques (ROCE, payback, NPV, IRR) and ensure you can compare and contrast between them. Start with some short questions on the basic topics before moving to detailed NPV calculations.		
– Further aspects of discounted cash flows	4	4	287 (a), 285, 291	Most section C NPV questions will include tax and inflation. Start with question 287 part (a) (Hebac). Then attempt question, 285 (OKM), which involves identifying errors (which are commonly made in the exam) and 291 (Pinks) which is a slightly more complex question on this area.		
– Risk and uncertainty	6	6	286 (a) and (b), 290, 298	This is an aspect that is often examined alongside the more complex areas of discounted cash flow techniques. Work through questions 286 parts (a) and (b) (Hraxin), 290 (Copper) and 298 (Gini)		
– Asset investment decisions and capital rationing	5	5	292, 293 and 297	Recap these techniques using these three questions, 292 (Dink), 293 (Crocket) and 297 (Clover)		

Topic	Study Text Chapter	Pocket note Chapter	Questions to attempt	Tutor guidance	Date attempted	Self-assessment
Working capital management	7	7	280	Begin by recapping on the key ratio calculations relating to working capital management and the calculation of the cash operating cycle. Question 280 (Pumice) is a good recent example of a question on this area. Leave part (b) ii until you have revised working capital funding.		
– Receivables and payables	9	9	278 (a) and (b), 275 (a), 233 (a)	Questions on working capital management will often draw upon several different elements. Work through question 278 parts (a) and (b) (Oscar) and 275 part (a) (KXP) to cover receivables and 233 part (a) (Jeeps) for a payables calculation.		
– Inventory	8	8	279 (a), 282 (a)	Inventory calculations are common as parts of section C questions but rarely for 20 marks. Work through 279 part (a) (Dusty) and 282 part (a) (Purdy)		
– Cash and funding strategies	10	10	280 (b) ii, 279 (b), 277 (a)–(d), 275 (c)	Now you can go back to question 280 (Pumice) and do part (b) ii and part (b) of 279 (Dusty) to cover working capital financing. 277 parts (a) to (d) (Flit) relate to cash management and forecasting. Also look at 275 (c) (KXP) to go over the similarities and differences between working capital investment and financing policies.		

Topic	**Study Text Chapter**	**Pocket note Chapter**	**Questions to attempt**	**Tutor guidance**	**Date attempted**	**Self-assessment**
Financial management function	1	1	Section A questions	Now is a good point to visit some of the less widely examined areas of the syllabus. Use the questions on this area in section A to revise the topic area.		
The economic environment for business	11	11	230	Question 230 (Arkwright) reflects how this topic could be examined.		
Financial markets and the treasury function	12	12	Section A questions	Use the questions on this area in section A to revise the topic area.		
Sources of finance	15	15	310, 313, 315	Questions 310 (Spine) and 313 (Graffham) are good examples of how this area is often tested through the use of forecasts, ratios and interpretation of the results. Graffham also includes the commonly tested topic of Islamic finance. Question 315 (Gamgee) also uses the calculation of ratios to help determine a financing decision.		
The cost of capital	17	17	308, 314	This is another popular exam topic. As well as reviewing the Study Text and the pocket notes, ensure you download and review the examiner's series of articles relating to CAPM. Use questions 308 (Tufa) and 314 (Marble).		

Topic	Study Text Chapter	Pocket note Chapter	Questions to attempt	Tutor guidance	Date attempted	Self-assessment
Capital structure	18	18	307, 311 (c) and (d)	This is a tricky topic. Be sure to work carefully through the pocket notes, perhaps attempting the test your understandings within the Study Text before attempting the exam standard questions. Then work 307 (Card), particularly part (d). Also do question 311 (Zeddemore) parts (c) and (d)		
Business valuations and market efficiency	20	20	259, 262, 263	Testable in sections A and B, you must be able to apply each of the main methods of business valuation and consider the impact on prices of the level of market efficiency present. Work through questions 259 (Bluebell), 262 (Light) and 263 (Fuchsia)		
Dividend policy	16	16	247, 303	This small topic is often examined alongside business valuations or sources of finance. Work through 247 (empire) and 303 (Pavlon).		
Foreign exchange risk	13	13	264, 272	Another topic that students often find difficult. This area won't be tested in a section C question. Work through questions 264 (Mallett) and 272 (Marigold).		
Interest rate risk	14	14	267, 271	This area won't be tested in a section C question. Work through questions 267 (H Co) and 271 (Peony).		

Note that not all of the questions are referred to in the programme above. We have recommended an approach to build up from the basic to exam standard questions. The remaining questions are available in the kit for extra practise for those who require more questions on some areas.

MATHEMATICAL TABLES AND FORMULAE SHEET

Economic order quantity

$$= \sqrt{\frac{2C_oD}{C_H}}$$

Miller-Orr Model

$$\text{Return point} = \text{Lower limit} + \left(\frac{1}{3} \times \text{spread}\right)$$

$$\text{Spread} = 3\left(\frac{\frac{3}{4} \times \text{Transaction cost} \times \text{Variance of cash flows}}{\text{Interest rate}}\right)^{\frac{1}{3}}$$

The Capital Asset Pricing Model

$$E(r)_j = R_f + \beta_j (E(r_m) - R_f)$$

The asset beta formula

$$\beta_a = \left(\frac{V_e}{(V_e + V_d(1-T))}\beta_e\right) + \left(\frac{V_d(1-T)}{(V_e + V_d(1-T))}\beta_d\right)$$

The Growth Model

$$P_0 = \frac{D_0(1+g)}{(r_e - g)} \qquad r_e = \frac{D_0(1+g)}{(P_0)} + g$$

Note: $D_0(1+g)$ may be replaced by D_1

Gordon's growth approximation

$$g = br_e$$

The weighted average cost of capital

$$\text{WACC} = \left(\frac{V_e}{V_e + V_d}\right)k_e + \left(\frac{V_d}{V_e + V_d}\right)k_d(1-T)$$

The Fisher formula

$$(1 + i) = (1 + r)(1 + h)$$

Purchasing power parity and interest rate parity

$$S_1 = S_0 \times \frac{(1+h_c)}{(1+h_b)} \qquad F_0 = S_0 \times \frac{(1+i_c)}{(1+i_b)}$$

Present Value Table

Present value of 1 i.e. $(1 + r)^{-n}$

Where r = discount rate

n = number of periods until payment

Periods **Discount rates (r)**

(n)	1%	2%	3%	4%	5%	6%	7%	8%	9%	10%	
1	0.990	0.980	0.971	0.962	0.952	0.943	0.935	0.926	0.917	0.909	**1**
2	0.980	0.961	0.943	0.925	0.907	0.890	0.873	0.857	0.842	0.826	**2**
3	0.971	0.942	0.915	0.889	0.864	0.840	0.816	0.794	0.772	0.751	**3**
4	0.961	0.924	0.888	0.855	0.823	0.792	0.763	0.735	0.708	0.683	**4**
5	0.951	0.906	0.863	0.822	0.784	0.747	0.713	0.681	0.650	0.621	**5**
6	0.942	0.888	0.837	0.790	0.746	0.705	0.666	0.630	0.596	0.564	**6**
7	0.933	0.871	0.813	0.760	0.711	0.665	0.623	0.583	0.547	0.513	**7**
8	0.923	0.853	0.789	0.731	0.677	0.627	0.582	0.540	0.502	0.467	**8**
9	0.914	0.837	0.766	0.703	0.645	0.592	0.544	0.500	0.460	0.424	**9**
10	0.905	0.820	0.744	0.676	0.614	0.558	0.508	0.463	0.422	0.386	**10**
11	0.896	0.804	0.722	0.650	0.585	0.527	0.475	0.429	0.388	0.350	**11**
12	0.887	0.788	0.701	0.625	0.557	0.497	0.444	0.397	0.356	0.319	**12**
13	0.879	0.773	0.681	0.601	0.530	0.469	0.415	0.368	0.326	0.290	**13**
14	0.870	0.758	0.661	0.577	0.505	0.442	0.388	0.340	0.299	0.263	**14**
15	0.861	0.743	0.642	0.555	0.481	0.417	0.362	0.315	0.275	0.239	**15**

(n)	11%	12%	13%	14%	15%	16%	17%	18%	19%	20%	
1	0.901	0.893	0.885	0.877	0.870	0.862	0.855	0.847	0.840	0.833	**1**
2	0.812	0.797	0.783	0.769	0.756	0.743	0.731	0.718	0.706	0.694	**2**
3	0.731	0.712	0.693	0.675	0.658	0.641	0.624	0.609	0.593	0.579	**3**
4	0.659	0.636	0.613	0.592	0.572	0.552	0.534	0.516	0.499	0.482	**4**
5	0.593	0.567	0.543	0.519	0.497	0.476	0.456	0.437	0.419	0.402	**5**
6	0.535	0.507	0.480	0.456	0.432	0.410	0.390	0.370	0.352	0.335	**6**
7	0.482	0.452	0.425	0.400	0.376	0.354	0.333	0.314	0.296	0.279	**7**
8	0.434	0.404	0.376	0.351	0.327	0.305	0.285	0.266	0.249	0.233	**8**
9	0.391	0.361	0.333	0.308	0.284	0.263	0.243	0.225	0.209	0.194	**9**
10	0.352	0.322	0.295	0.270	0.247	0.227	0.208	0.191	0.176	0.162	**10**
11	0.317	0.287	0.261	0.237	0.215	0.195	0.178	0.162	0.148	0.135	**11**
12	0.286	0.257	0.231	0.208	0.187	0.168	0.152	0.137	0.124	0.112	**12**
13	0.258	0.229	0.204	0.182	0.163	0.145	0.130	0.116	0.104	0.093	**13**
14	0.232	0.205	0.181	0.160	0.141	0.125	0.111	0.099	0.088	0.078	**14**
15	0.209	0.183	0.160	0.140	0.123	0.108	0.095	0.084	0.074	0.065	**15**

Annuity Table

Present value of an annuity of 1 i.e. $\frac{1-(1+r)^{-n}}{r}$

Where r = discount rate

n = number of periods

Periods — **Discount rates (r)**

(n)	1%	2%	3%	4%	5%	6%	7%	8%	9%	10%	
1	0.990	0.980	0.971	0.962	0.952	0.943	0.935	0.926	0.917	0.909	1
2	1.970	1.942	1.913	1.886	1.859	1.833	1.808	1.783	1.759	1.736	2
3	2.941	2.884	2.829	2.775	2.723	2.673	2.624	2.577	2.531	2.487	3
4	3.902	3.808	3.717	3.630	3.546	3.465	3.387	3.312	3.240	3.170	4
5	4.853	4.713	4.580	4.452	4.329	4.212	4.100	3.993	3.890	3.791	5
6	5.795	5.601	5.417	5.242	5.076	4.917	4.767	4.623	4.486	4.355	6
7	6.728	6.472	6.230	6.002	5.786	5.582	5.389	5.206	5.033	4.868	7
8	7.652	7.325	7.020	6.733	6.463	6.210	5.971	5.747	5.535	5.335	8
9	8.566	8.162	7.786	7.435	7.108	6.802	6.515	6.247	5.995	5.759	9
10	9.471	8.983	8.530	8.111	7.722	7.360	7.024	6.710	6.418	6.145	10
11	10.37	9.787	9.253	8.760	8.306	7.887	7.499	7.139	6.805	6.495	11
12	11.26	10.58	9.954	9.385	8.863	8.384	7.943	7.536	7.161	6.814	12
13	12.13	11.35	10.63	9.986	9.394	8.853	8.358	7.904	7.487	7.103	13
14	13.00	12.11	11.30	10.56	9.899	9.295	8.745	8.244	7.786	7.367	14
15	13.87	12.85	11.94	11.12	10.38	9.712	9.108	8.559	8.061	7.606	15

(n)	11%	12%	13%	14%	15%	16%	17%	18%	19%	20%	
1	0.901	0.893	0.885	0.877	0.870	0.862	0.855	0.847	0.840	0.833	1
2	1.713	1.690	1.668	1.647	1.626	1.605	1.585	1.566	1.547	1.528	2
3	2.444	2.402	2.361	2.322	2.283	2.246	2.210	2.174	2.140	2.106	3
4	3.102	3.037	2.974	2.914	2.855	2.798	2.743	2.690	2.639	2.589	4
5	3.696	3.605	3.517	3.433	3.352	3.274	3.199	3.127	3.058	2.991	5
6	4.231	4.111	3.998	3.889	3.784	3.685	3.589	3.498	3.410	3.326	6
7	4.712	4.564	4.423	4.288	4.160	4.039	3.922	3.812	3.706	3.605	7
8	5.146	4.968	4.799	4.639	4.487	4.344	4.207	4.078	3.954	3.837	8
9	5.537	5.328	5.132	4.946	4.772	4.607	4.451	4.303	4.163	4.031	9
10	5.889	5.650	5.426	5.216	5.019	4.833	4.659	4.494	4.339	4.192	10
11	6.207	5.938	5.687	5.453	5.234	5.029	4.836	4.656	4.486	4.327	11
12	6.492	6.194	5.918	5.660	5.421	5.197	4.988	4.793	4.611	4.439	12
13	6.750	6.424	6.122	5.842	5.583	5.342	5.118	4.910	4.715	4.533	13
14	6.982	6.628	6.302	6.002	5.724	5.468	5.229	5.008	4.802	4.611	14
15	7.191	6.811	6.462	6.142	5.847	5.575	5.324	5.092	4.876	4.675	15

Section 1

OBJECTIVE TEST QUESTIONS – SECTION A

Each question is worth two marks.

FINANCIAL MANAGEMENT FUNCTION

1 **In relation to the financial management of a company, which of the following provides the best definition of a firm's primary financial objective?**

A To achieve long-term growth in earnings

B To maximise the level of annual dividends

C To maximise the wealth of its ordinary shareholders

D To maximise the level of annual profits

2 **Indicate, by clicking in the relevant boxes, whether the following objectives are financial or non-financial objectives of a company.**

Objective	**Financial**	**Non-financial**
Maximisation of market share		
Earnings growth		
Sales revenue growth		
Achieving a target level of customer satisfaction		
Achieving a target level of return on capital employed		

3 **Which THREE of the following are the main types of decision facing the financial manager in a company?**

A Income decision

B Investment decision

C Dividend decision

D Financing decision

E Appraisal decision

F Budget decision

4 Which TWO of the following are examples of financial objectives that a company might choose to pursue?

A Dealing honestly and fairly with customers on all occasions

B Provision of good working conditions and industrial relations

C Earning above a particular level of return on capital employed

D Producing environmentally friendly products

E Restricting the level of gearing to below a specified target level

5 Value for money is an important objective for not-for-profit organisations.

Which of the following actions is consistent with increasing value for money?

A Using a cheaper source of goods and thereby decreasing the quality of not-for-profit organisation services

B Searching for ways to diversify the finances of the not-for-profit organisation

C Decreasing waste in the provision of a service by the not-for-profit organisation

D Focusing on meeting the financial objectives of the not-for-profit organization

6 Which of the following is LEAST likely to fall within financial management?

A The dividend payment to shareholders is increased

B Funds are raised to finance an investment project

C Surplus assets are sold off

D A report is produced comparing actual results to budget

7 Indicate, by clicking in the relevant boxes, whether the following statements are true or false.

Statement	**True**	**False**
Financial management is concerned with the long-term raising of finance and the allocation and control of resources		
Management accounting is concerned with providing information for the more day-to-day functions of control and decision-making		
Financial accounting is concerned with providing information about the historical results of past plans and decisions		

8 Which of the following tasks would typically be carried out by a member of the financial management team?

A Evaluating proposed expansion plans

B Review of overtime spending

C Depreciation of non-current assets

D Apportioning overheads to cost units

9 Which TWO of the following are examples of internal stakeholders in a firm?

A Company directors

B Customers

C Suppliers

D Employees

E Finance providers

10 What is the main purpose of corporate governance?

A To separate ownership and management control of organisations

B To maximise shareholder value

C To facilitate effective management of organisations and to make organisations more visibly accountable to a wider range of stakeholders

D To ensure that regulatory frameworks are adhered to

11 The agency problem is a driving force behind the growing importance attached to sound corporate governance.

In this context, who are the agents?

A Customers

B Shareholders

C Managers

D Auditors

12 Which TWO of the following statements are correct?

1 Maximising market share is an example of a financial objective

2 Shareholder wealth maximisation is the primary financial objective for a company listed on a stock exchange

3 Financial objectives should be quantitative so that their achievement can be measured

4 Three E's are used as a performance measure to assess value of money in not for profit organisations. The three E's stand for economy, efficiency and environment

13 **Which TWO of the following are 'efficiency' targets that a not for profit organisation might put in place?**

A Reduction of wastage of paper

B Pay rates for staff of appropriate levels of qualification

C Staff utilisation

D Customer satisfaction ratings

14 Managerial reward schemes should help ensure managers take decisions that are consistent with the objectives of shareholders.

Which THREE of the following are characteristics of a carefully designed remuneration package?

A Linking of rewards to changes in shareholder wealth

B Matching of managers' time horizons to shareholders' time horizons

C Possibility of manipulation by managers

D Encouragement for managers to adopt the same attitudes to risk as shareholders

E Motivational to primarily achieve short-term goals

15 **Indicate, by clicking in the relevant boxes, which of the following are typical criticisms of executive share option schemes (ESOPs)?**

Statement	**Is a criticism**	**Is NOT a criticism**
When directors exercise their options, they tend to sell the shares almost immediately to cash in on their profits		
If the share price falls when options have been awarded, and the options have no value, they cannot act as an incentive		
Directors may distort reported profits to protect the share price and the value of their share options		

16 The directors of Portico Co have recently engaged a firm of consultants to negotiate standard terms of trade for one of its strategic business units. This includes the agreement by Portico Co to pay a 5% penalty on any late invoice settlement.

This policy is an illustration of the company's concern for which major stakeholder?

A Lenders

B Suppliers

C Customers

D Trade unions

17 Under the terms of the UK Corporate Governance Code, what are the only type of directors permitted to sit on a company's audit committee?

A Independent non-executive directors

B Non-executive directors

C Executive directors

D Directors with financial experience

18 Which of the following would you expect to be the responsibility of financial management?

A Producing annual accounts

B Producing monthly management accounts

C Advising on investment in non-current assets

D Deciding pay rates for staff

19 Indicate, by clicking in the relevant boxes below, whether the following statements are true or false.

Statement	**True**	**False**
Value for money is usually taken to mean economy, efficiency and engagement		
Cum dividend means the buyer of the share is entitled to receive the dividend shortly to be paid		
The dividend payout ratio compares the dividend per share with the market price per share		
The agency problem means that shareholder wealth is not being maximised		

20 Increasing which TWO of the following would be associated with the financial objective of shareholder wealth maximisation?

A Share price

B Dividend payment

C Reported profit

D Earnings per share

E Weighted average cost of capital

21 ARP is a charity providing transport for people visiting hospitals.

Which of the following performance measures would BEST fit with efficiency in a value for money review?

A Percentage of members who re-use the service

B Cost per journey to hospital

C A comparison of actual operating expenses against the budget

D Number of communities served

22 A state funded hospital has the objective of providing value for money. It measures the achievement of this objective using the three E's (economy, effectiveness and efficiency).

Which of the following performance indicators measures the hospital's economy?

A Number of patients admitted per year

B Total medical staff salary cost

C Cost per successfully treated patient

D Average waiting time for patient admission to hospital

23 BeachLitter is a charity that was set up with the objective of cleaning litter from all beaches within the local area.

Which TWO of the following performance measures would best fit with effectiveness in a value for money audit?

A Average hours worked to clean each beach

B Number of beaches awarded the government's clean beach certification

C Average annual expenditure on each successfully cleaned beach

D Average hours worked by each volunteer per month

E Amount of litter cleared each year measured in tonnes

FINANCIAL MANAGEMENT ENVIRONMENT

24 Which of the following is/are among the elements of fiscal policy?

1 Government actions to raise or lower taxes

2 Government actions to raise or lower the size of the money supply

3 Government actions to raise or lower the amount it spends

A 1 only

B 1 and 3 only

C 2 and 3 only

D 1, 2 and 3

25 Which TWO of the following statements are correct?

1 Securitisation is the conversion of illiquid assets into marketable securities

2 The reverse yield gap refers to equity yields being higher than debt yields

3 Disintermediation arises where borrowers deal directly with lending individuals

4 Demand-pull inflation will occur when there are increases in production costs independent to the state of demand

26 Indicate, by clicking in the relevant boxes, whether the following statements are true or false.

Statement	**True**	**False**
Coupon bearing securities have a fixed maturity and a specified rate of interest		
In the discount market, funds are raised by issuing bills at a discount to their eventual redemption or maturity value		

27 The principal objectives of macroeconomic policy include which of the following?

1 Full employment of resources

2 Price stability

3 Economic growth

4 Balancing the government budget

A 1 and 2 only

B 1 and 3 only

C 1, 2 and 3 only

D 1, 2, 3 and 4

28 Governments have a number of economic targets as part of their fiscal policy.

Which TWO of the following government actions relate predominantly to fiscal policy?

A Decreasing interest rates in order to stimulate consumer spending

B Reducing taxation while maintaining public spending

C Using official foreign currency reserves to buy the domestic currency

D Borrowing money from the capital markets and spending it on public works

E Regulating foreign exchange rates

29 Which THREE of the following are key roles played by money markets?

A Providing short-term liquidity to companies, banks and the public sector

B Providing short term trade finance

C Allowing an organisation to manage its exposure to foreign currency risk and interest rate risk

D Dealing in long-term funds and transactions

E Allowing companies to issue shares to raise money

30 Which of the following are money market instruments?

1 Certificates of deposit

2 Corporate bond

3 Commercial paper

4 Treasury bill

A 1, 2 and 4 only

B 1 and 3 only

C 1, 3 and 4 only

D 1, 2, 3 and 4

31 Which THREE of the following are common roles of the treasury function within a firm?

A Short-term management of resources

B Long-term maximisation of shareholder wealth

C Long-term maximisation of market share

D Risk management

E Management of accounts receivable

F Management of financial reporting

32 Which of the following is a difference between primary and secondary capital markets?

A Primary capital markets relate to the sale of new securities, while secondary capital markets are where securities trade after their initial offering

B Both primary and secondary capital markets relate to where securities are traded after their initial offering

C Both primary and secondary capital markets relate to the sale of new securities

D Primary markets are where stocks trade and secondary markets are where loan notes trade

33 Changes in monetary policy will influence which of the following factors?

1 The level of exchange rates

2 The cost of finance

3 The level of consumer demand

4 The level of inflation

A 1 and 2 only

B 2 and 3 only

C 2, 3 and 4 only

D 1, 2, 3 and 4

34 Which of the following is/are usually seen as forms of market failure where regulation may be a solution?

1 Imperfect competition

2 Social costs or externalities such as pollution

3 Suppliers agree between themselves to set minimum sales prices

A 1 only

B 1 and 2 only

C 2 and 3 only

D 1, 2 and 3

35 There are two main types of financial market: capital and money markets, and within each of these are primary and secondary markets.

Which TWO of the following statements are true?

A Primary markets allow the realisation of investments before their maturity date by selling them to other investors

B Primary markets deal in new issues of loanable funds

C Capital markets consist of stock markets for shares and loan bond markets

D Money markets provide long-term debt finance and investment

36 Indicate, by clicking in the relevant boxes, whether the following statements are true or false.

Statement	**True**	**False**
Interest rate smoothing is the policy of some central banks to move official interest rates in a sequence of relatively small steps in the same direction, rather than waiting until making a single larger step		
If governments wish to influence the amount of money held in the economy or the demand for credit, they may attempt to influence the level of interest rates		

37 A variety of Corporate Governance rules have been introduced in different countries but what are the principles, common to all, that they typically include?

1 The chairperson and chief executive officer should not be the same individual

2 Non-executive directors on the board should prevent the board from being dominated by the executive directors

3 The audit committee should consist solely of executive directors

4 A remuneration committee should be established to decide on the remuneration of executive directors

A 1 and 2 only

B 1, 2 and 3 only

C 1, 2 and 4 only

D 1, 2, 3 and 4

38 Which of the following statements is correct?

A Direct taxes are levied on one set of individuals or organisations but may be partly or wholly passed on to others and are largely related to consumption not income

B Indirect taxes are levied directly on income receivers whether they are individuals or organisations

C A balanced budget occurs when total expenditure is matched by total taxation

D A deficit budget occurs when total expenditure is less than total taxation income

39 Indicate, by clicking in the relevant boxes, whether the following statements are true or false.

Statement	True	False
Demand-pull inflation might occur when excess aggregate monetary demand in the economy and hence demand for particular goods and services enable companies to raise prices and expand profit margins		
Cost-push inflation will occur when there are increases in production costs independent of the state of demand e.g. rising raw material costs or rising labour costs		

40 Which THREE of the following are true, in relation to certificates of deposit?

A They are evidence of a deposit with an issuing bank

B They are not negotiable and therefore unattractive to the depositor as they do not ensure instant liquidity

C They provide the bank with a deposit for a fixed period at a fixed rate of interest

D They are coupon-bearing securities

E They are not tradeable

41 Which of the following is least likely to be a reason for seeking a stock market listing?

A Enhancement of the company's image

B Transfer of capital to other users

C Improving existing owners' control over the business

D Access to a wider pool of finance

42 Which of the following is NOT typically a principal objective of macroeconomic policy?

A To achieve full employment of resources

B To achieve economic growth

C To achieve a balance of payments deficit

D To achieve an appropriate distribution of income and wealth

43 Which THREE of the following are advantages of having a centralised treasury department in a large international group of companies?

A No need for treasury skills to be duplicated throughout the group

B Necessary borrowings can be arranged in bulk, at keener interest rates than for smaller amounts

C The group's foreign currency risk can be managed much more effectively since they can appreciate the total exposure situation

D Local operating units should have a better feel for local conditions than head office and can respond more quickly to local developments

E Divisional managers will be motivated by having less responsibility for cash management

44 Investing in a small or medium sized business (SME) is inherently more risky than investing in a larger company due to lack of business history and a lower level of public scrutiny over accounts and records. What is the frequently used term to describe the difficulty SMEs can often face when raising finance?

A Maturity gap

B Funding gap

C Duration gap

D Equity gap

45 Indicate, by clicking in the relevant boxes, which market the following financial instruments would be traded on.

Statement	**Money market**	**Stock market**
Commercial paper		
Convertible loan notes		
Treasury bills		
Certificates of deposit		

46 Which of the following government actions would lead to an increase in aggregate demand?

1 Increasing taxation and keeping government expenditure the same

2 Decreasing taxation and increasing government expenditure

3 Decreasing money supply

4 Decreasing interest rates

A 1 only

B 1 and 3

C 2 and 4 only

D 2, 3 and 4

47 Which TWO of the following activities are carried out by a financial intermediary?

A Transforming interest rates

B Transforming foreign exchange

C Transforming maturity

D Transforming risk

48 Indicate, by clicking in the relevant boxes, whether the following statements are true or false.

Statement	**True**	**False**
A prospective merger would need to result in a company having a market share greater than 80% before it can be described as a monopoly		
A government may intervene to weaken its country's exchange rate in order to eliminate a balance of payments deficit		
A relatively high rate of domestic inflation will lead to a strengthening currency		
Government fiscal policy involves the management of interest rates		

49 Which of the following statements relating to money market instruments is/are correct?

1 Discounted instruments do not pay coupon interest

2 Commercial paper is secured on assets of the issuing company

A 1 only

B 2 only

C Both 1 and 2

D Neither 1 nor 2

50 A listed company is to enter into a sale and repurchase agreement on the money market.

The company has agreed to sell \$10m of treasury bills for \$9.6m and will buy them back in 50 days' time for \$9.65m.

Assume a 365-day year.

What is the implicit annual interest rate in this transaction (to the nearest 0.1%)?

[ ] %

51 Which of the following statements relating to disintermediation is/are correct?

1 Disintermediation allows investors to conduct transactions directly but at increased risk when compared to the use of intermediaries

2 Disintermediation requires the use of cryptocurrencies for settlement of transactions

A 1 only

B 2 only

C Both 1 and 2

D Neither 1 nor 2

52 Which of the following statements relating to Security Token Offerings (STOs) is/are correct?

1 The value of STOs comes from being tied to assets with a real monetary value

2 STO transactions are recorded on a blockchain ledger

A 1 only

B 2 only

C Both 1 and 2

D Neither 1 nor 2

53 A large, listed company is to issue 90-day commercial paper with a nominal value of $10m. Each paper will have a nominal value of $100,000. The annual required rate of return is 4% assuming a 360-day year.

What will be the issue price of each paper?

A $99,024

B $96,154

C $99,014

D $96,000

54 **Which FOUR of the following descriptions relate to the main macroeconomic policy objectives?**

A Ensuring minimum amounts of price increases

B Increasing national income and living standards

C Ensuring a balanced ratio of imports to exports

D Maintaining interest rates at minimum levels

E Balancing government spending with tax receipts

F Ensuring a stable and fully employed labour force

55 **Select the type of financial market appropriate to each of the company's needs.**

Amby Co needs to convert foreign currency into domestic currency	Foreign exchange market	Euro currency market
Benji Co needs to issue new ordinary shares	Primary capital market	Secondary capital market
Carlo Co needs to purchase short-term over-the-counter derivatives	Primary money market	Secondary money market
Dill Co needs to issue new long-term loan notes	Capital market	Money market

56 A company is planning a major investment in a new manufacturing unit in the next year. Due to recent concerns that the economy may be growing too slowly, the government has unexpectedly announced a decrease in interest rates.

Which of the following statements concerning the impact of the government's decision is TRUE?

A The company’s cost of capital will increase

B The company's shareholders will require higher returns

C Demand for the company's products will increase

D The NPV of the investment will be lower than initially expected

WORKING CAPITAL MANAGEMENT

57 Thrifty Co's cash budget highlights a short-term surplus in the near future.

Which of the following actions would be appropriate to make use of the surplus?

A Pay suppliers earlier to take advantage of any prompt payment discounts

B Buy back the company's shares

C Increase payables by delaying payment to suppliers

D Invest in a long term deposit bank account

58 **Indicate, by clicking in the relevant boxes, whether the following statements are true or false.**

Statement	**True**	**False**
Working capital should increase as sales increase		
An increase in the cash operating cycle will lead to an increase in working capital funding costs		
Overtrading is also known as under-capitalisation		

59 **Which of the following might be associated with a shortening working capital cycle?**

A Lower net operating cash flow

B Increasing tax-allowable depreciation expenditure

C Slower inventory turnover

D Taking longer to pay suppliers

60 The following information has been calculated for D Co:

Trade receivables collection period	10 weeks
Raw material inventory turnover period	6 weeks
Work in progress inventory turnover period	2 weeks
Trade payables payment period	7 weeks
Finished goods inventory turnover period	6 weeks

What is the length of the working capital cycle?

[ ] weeks

61 A company sells inventory for cash to a customer, at a selling price which is below the cost of the inventory items.

How will this transaction affect the current ratio and the quick ratio immediately after the transaction? Indicate, by clicking in the relevant boxes, whether each ratio will increase or decrease.

Ratio	**Increase**	**Decrease**
Current ratio		
Quick ratio		

62 A company has the following summarised Statement of Financial Position at 31 December 20X4:

	$000	$000
Non-current assets		1,000
Current assets		
Inventories	200	
Receivables	150	
Cash	100	
	450	
Current liabilities		
Payables	200	
Net current assets		250
		1,250

Over the next year the company should double its sales. The company does not plan to invest in any new non-current assets, but inventories, receivables and payables should all move in line with sales.

What cash balance in one year's time would this imply if the non-current assets were all land, no new capital was raised and all profits were paid out as dividends?

A $100,000 cash in hand

B $200,000 cash in hand

C $50,000 overdraft

D $100,000 overdraft

63 Goldstar has an accounts receivables turnover of 10.5 times, an inventory turnover of 4 times and payables turnover of 8 times.

What is Goldstar's cash operating cycle to the nearest day (assume 365 days in a year)?

[ ] days

64 The cash operating cycle is equal to which of the following?

A Accounts receivable collection period plus inventory holding period minus accounts payable payment period

B Inventory holding period minus accounts receivable collection period minus accounts payable payment period

C Accounts receivable collection period plus inventory holding period plus accounts payable payment period

D Accounts receivable collection period minus accounts payable payment period minus inventory holding period

65 A company has annual credit sales of $27 million and related cost of sales of $15 million. The company has the following targets for the next year:

Accounts receivable collection period	50 days
Inventory holding period	60 days
Accounts payable payment period	45 days

Assume there are 360 days in the year.

What is the net investment in working capital required for the next year?

A $8,125,000

B $4,375,000

C $2,875,000

D $6,375,000

66 A cash budget was drawn up as follows:

	October	November	December
	$	$	$
Receipts			
Credit Sales	20,000	11,000	14,500
Cash Sales	10,000	4,500	6,000
Payments			
Suppliers	13,000	4,200	7,800
Wages	4,600	2,300	3,000
Overheads	3,000	1,750	1,900
Opening cash	500		

What is the closing cash balance for December budgeted to be?

A $20,550 overdraft

B $21,050 overdraft

C $22,450 deposit

D $24,950 deposit

67 **Which TWO of the following would be key aspects of a company's accounts receivable credit policy?**

A Assessing creditworthiness

B Checking credit limits once a year

C Invoicing promptly and collecting overdue debts

D Delaying payments to obtain a 'free' source of finance

68 A company is preparing its cash flow forecast for the next financial period.

Which THREE of the following items should be included in the calculations?

A A corporation tax payment

B A dividend receipt from a short term investment

C The loss made on the disposal of an item of machinery

D A bad debt written off

E An increase in a provision

F The receipt of funding for the purchase of a new vehicle

69 **Which of the following is NOT usually associated with overtrading?**

A An increase in the current ratio

B A rapid increase in revenue

C A rapid increase in the volume of current assets

D Most of the increase in current assets being financed by credit

70 Generally, increasing the accounts payable payment period suggests advantage is being taken of available credit but there are risks involved.

Which of the following is unlikely to be one of the risks involved in increasing the accounts payable payment period?

A Customer bargaining power increasing

B Losing supplier goodwill

C Losing prompt payment discounts

D Suppliers increasing the price to compensate

71 **Which TWO of the following are aims of a Just in Time system of inventory control?**

A Reduction in capital tied up in inventory

B Creation of an inflexible production process

C Elimination of all activities performed that do not add value

D Lowering of inventory ordering costs

72 Although cash needs to be invested to earn returns, businesses need to keep a certain amount readily available.

Which TWO of the following are reasons for holding cash?

A Movement motive

B Transactions motive

C Precautionary motive

D Asset motive

73 Andrew Co is a large listed company financed by both equity and debt.

In which of the following areas of financial management will the impact of working capital management be smallest?

A Liquidity management

B Interest rate management

C Management of relationship with the bank

D Dividend policy

74 Crag Co has sales of $200m per year and the gross profit margin is 40%. The finished goods inventory holding period varies throughout the year within the following range:

	Maximum	**Minimum**
Inventory holding period (days)	120	90

All purchases and sales are made on a cash basis and no inventory of raw materials or work in progress is carried. Crag Co intends to finance permanent current assets with equity and fluctuating current assets with its overdraft.

In relation to finished goods inventory and assuming a 360-day year, how much finance will be needed from the overdraft?

[ ] million

75 **Which of the following is an advantage of implementing just-in-time inventory management?**

A Quality control costs will be eliminated

B Monthly finance costs incurred in holding inventory will be kept constant

C The frequency of raw material deliveries is reduced

D The amount of obsolete inventory will be minimised

76 Dev Co is a large multinational company which expects to have a $10m cash deficit in one month's time. The deficit is expected to last no more than two months. Dev Co wishes to resolve its short-term liquidity problem by issuing an appropriate instrument on the money market.

Which of the following instruments should Dev Co issue?

A Commercial paper

B Interest rate futures

C Corporate loan notes

D Treasury bills

77 Mile Co is looking to change its working capital policy to match the rest of the industry. The following results are expected for the coming year:

	$000
Revenue	20,500
Cost of sales	(12,800)
Gross profit	7,700

Revenue and cost of sales can be assumed to be spread evenly throughout the year.

The working capital ratios of Mile Co, compared with the industry, are as follows:

	Mile Co	**Industry**
Accounts receivable collection period	50	42
Inventory holding period	45	35
Accounts payable payment period	40	35

Assume there are 365 days in each year.

If Mile Co matches its working capital cycle with the industry, what will be the decrease in its net working capital?

A $624,600

B $730,100

C $835,600

D $975,300

78 Swap Co is due to receive goods costing $2,500. The terms of trade state that payment must be received within three months. However, a discount of 1.5% will be given for payment within one month.

Which of the following is the annual percentage cost of ignoring the discount and paying within three months?

A 6.23%

B 9.34%

C 6.14%

D 9.49%

79 Will Co incurs costs of $65 every time it places an order with its raw materials supplier. It orders 300,000 units of product each year. The cost of holding one unit of inventory for a month is $2.50. Will Co keeps a buffer inventory at all times of 25,000 units of material.

Calculate the economic order quantity (EOQ) that will optimise the business's inventory costs to the nearest 10 units.

[ ] units

80 **Which TWO of the following statements are true about cash management models?**

A The Baumol model is more suitable when cash flows are steady and predictable

B Both models assume that cash is either held in a current account or in long-term investments

C In the Miller Orr model the upper limit for the current account balance is set by management

D Both models take into account the transaction costs of switching between current accounts and investments

E The Miller Orr model aims to keep cash balances as close to the return point at all times

81 A company has erratic daily cash movements with a standard deviation of $3,000 per day. It costs $25 to move cash between its current account and its short-term deposit account. The deposit account earns an interest rate of 7.3% per year. There are 365 days in a year.

Calculate, to the nearest $000, the spread between the upper and lower limits that should be set for the current account using the Miller Orr cash management model.

$ [ ]

82 A company has sales revenue of $30 million and its customers take an average of 75 days to pay. The company offers a 1% discount to customers who pay in 30 days.

Calculate, to the nearest hundred thousand dollars, the new anticipated receivables balance if 60% of customers take up the offer of the discount and the rest carry on paying in 75 days. Assume 360 days in a year.

$ [ ]

83 **Which of the following is/are true?**

1 A conservative working capital investment policy implies a higher proportion of permanent current assets to fluctuating current assets

2 Long-term finance is generally cheaper than short-term finance

A 1 only is correct

B 2 only is correct

C 1 and 2 are correct

D 1 and 2 are incorrect

84 **Which of the following statements is consistent with an aggressive working capital funding policy?**

A Most current assets are financed with long-term funding rather than short-term funding, despite long-term funding being more expensive

B Most current assets are funded with debt rather than equity, as it is cheaper

C Most current assets are financed with short-term funding rather than long-term funding, despite the higher risk involved

D Most current assets are funded by secured funding to enable the financial manager to focus on managing the working capital balances

85 Two companies, Acacia and Birch, have the following average levels of working capital:

Working capital level ($m)	Acacia	Birch
Maximum	10	12
Minimum	6	9

Acacia's working capital is financed with $4m of long-term debt and Birch's working capital is financed with $9m of long-term debt.

The balance of finance is from short-term sources.

Identify, by clicking on the relevant boxes in the table, which type of working capital funding strategy each company is employing.

Working capital funding strategy	Aggressive	Matching	Conservative
Acacia			
Birch			

86 **Which of the following is/are true?**

1 An aggressive working capital funding policy implies a lower value of current assets and a higher value of current liabilities than a conservative working capital funding policy

2 Long-term debt finance is riskier for the lender than short-term debt finance

A 1 only is correct

B 2 only is correct

C 1 and 2 are correct

D 1 and 2 are incorrect

87 The inventory ordering policy of ZAR Co is to order 100,000 units when the inventory level falls to 20,000 units. The cost of placing and processing an order is $200, while the cost of holding inventory is $0.50 per unit per year. Orders are received one week after being placed with the supplier. The production requirement for the next year (50 weeks) is 600,000 units.

What is the cost of ZAR Co's inventory ordering policy?

$ ________

88 For the coming year, a company has budgeted sales of \$2m per month, 80% of which will be on credit. It expects its accounts receivable payment period to be three months.

Forecast average inventory and average accounts payable for the coming year are \$10m and \$4m respectively.

What is the company's working capital requirement (calculated as receivables plus inventory less payables) for the coming year (in \$m to one decimal place)?

\$ [ ] m

89 **Match the characteristic below with the appropriate working capital strategy.**

Characteristic	**Working capital strategy**
Relatively high level of current assets	Conservative investment strategy
Relatively low level of current assets	Aggressive financing strategy
Relatively large amounts of short-term finance	Aggressive investment strategy
Relatively small amounts of short-term finance	Conservative financing strategy

90 Directive Co finances its working capital with an overdraft at a cost of 7% per year. Its major supplier offers a discount of 0.5% for settlement of invoices after 10 days rather than the usual 30 days.

Assume 365 days in a year.

Which statement correctly explains what Directive Co should do?

A Pay in 10 days because at 9.5% per year the benefit of the discount exceeds the cost of the overdraft

B Pay in 30 days because at 9.5% per year the discount is more expensive than the overdraft

C Pay in 30 days because at 6.3% per year the benefit of the discount is less than the cost of the overdraft

D Pay in 10 days because at 6.3% per year the discount is cheaper than the overdraft

91 The following information relates to Blanc Co's inventory:

	Units
Annual demand	400,000
Order quantity	70,000
Reorder level	30,000
Lead time	3 weeks

Assume 50 weeks in the year.

What is the buffer (safety) level of inventory?

A 6,000 units

B 40,000 units

C 30,000 units

D 24,000 units

92 The following are extracts from the financial statements of Inci Co:

	$m
Revenue	2,780
Cost of sales	1,612
Inventories	226
Trade receivables	417
Trade payables	198

10% of Inci Co's sales, by value, are on cash terms.

Purchases for the year totalled $1,451m.

Assume a 365-day year.

Calculate Inci Co's inventory holding period, trade receivables collection period and trade payables payment period (all calculations should be to the nearest day).

Inventory holding period (days)	
Trade receivables collection period (days)	
Trade payables payment period (days)	

INVESTMENT APPRAISAL

93 A company is considering investing in a two-year project. Machine set-up costs will be $125,000, payable immediately. Working capital of $4,000 is required at the beginning of the contract and will be released at the end.

Given a cost of capital of 10%, what is the minimum acceptable contract price (to the nearest thousand dollar) to be received at the end of the contract?

$ ______

94 **Which TWO of the following statements are correct?**

A Tax allowable depreciation is a relevant cash flow when evaluating borrowing to buy compared to leasing as a financing choice

B Asset replacement decisions require relevant cash flows to be discounted by the after-tax cost of debt

C If capital is rationed, divisible investment projects can be ranked by the profitability index when determining the optimum investment schedule

D Government restrictions on bank lending are associated with hard capital rationing

95 A company has 31 December as its accounting year-end. On 1 January 20X5, a new machine costing $2,000,000 is purchased. The company expects to sell the machine on 31 December 20X6 for $350,000.

The rate of corporation tax for the company is 30% and tax is paid at the end of the year in which it is incurred. Tax-allowable depreciation is obtained at 25% on the reducing balance basis, and a balancing allowance is available on disposal of the asset. The company makes sufficient profits to obtain relief for tax-allowable depreciation as soon as they arise.

If the company's cost of capital is 15% per year, what is the present value of the tax savings from the tax-allowable depreciation at 1 January 20X5 (to the nearest thousand dollars)?

A $391,000

B $248,000

C $263,000

D $719,000

96 An investment project has a cost of $12,000, payable at the start of the first year of operation. The possible future cash flows arising from the investment project have the following present values and associated probabilities:

PV of Year 1 cash flow ($)	Probability	PV of Year 2 cash flow ($)	Probability
16,000	0.15	20,000	0.75
12,000	0.60	(2,000)	0.25
(4,000)	0.25		

What is the expected value (EV) of the net present value of the investment project?

$ ☐

97 A company has a 'money' cost of capital of 21% per year. The general rate of inflation is currently estimated at 8% per year.

What is the 'real' cost of capital (to the nearest whole number)?

☐ %

98 A company is considering a project that has an initial outflow followed by several years of cash inflows, with a cash outflow in the final year.

How many internal rates of return could there be for this project?

A Either zero or two

B Either one or two

C Zero, one or two

D Only two

99 A project consists of a series of cash outflows in the first few years followed by a series of positive cash inflows. The total cash inflows exceed the total cash outflows. The project was originally evaluated assuming a zero rate of inflation.

If the project were re-evaluated on the assumption that the cash flows were subject to a positive rate of inflation, what would be the effect on the payback period and the internal rate of return? Indicate, by clicking in the relevant boxes, whether the payback period and internal rate of return would increase or decrease.

Method	**Increase**	**Decrease**
Payback period		
Internal rate of return		

100 **The lower risk of a project can be recognised by increasing which of the following?**

A The cost of the initial investment of the project

B The estimates of future cash inflows from the project

C The internal rate of return of the project

D The required rate of return of the project

101 A company has the following pattern of cash flow for a project:

Year	**Cash flow**
	$
0	(100,000)
1	40,000
2	20,000
3	30,000
4	5,000
5	40,000

The company uses a discount rate of 10%. In what year does discounted payback occur?

Year

102 Sudan Co wishes to undertake a project requiring an investment of $732,000 which will generate equal annual inflows of $146,400 in perpetuity.

If the first inflow from the investment is a year after the initial investment, what is the IRR of the project?

A 20%

B 25%

C 400%

D 500%

103 **Which THREE of the following are advantages of the IRR?**

A Considers the whole life of the project

B Uses cash flows not profits

C It is a measure of absolute return

D It is an accurate calculation

E It is useful when liquidity is poor

F It considers the time value of money

104 Jones Ltd plans to spend $90,000 on an item of capital equipment on 1 January 20X2. The expenditure is eligible for 25% tax-allowable depreciation, and Jones pays corporation tax at 30%. Tax is paid at the end of the accounting period concerned. The equipment will produce savings of $30,000 per year for its expected useful life deemed to be receivable every 31 December. The equipment will be sold for $25,000 on 31 December 20X5. Jones has a 31 December year-end and has a 10% post-tax cost of capital.

What is the present value at 1 January 20X2 of the tax savings that result from the tax-allowable depreciation?

A $13,170

B $15,828

C $16,018

D $19,827

105 Four projects, P, Q, R and S, are available to a company that is facing shortages of capital over the next year but expects capital to be freely available thereafter.

	P	Q	R	S
	$000	$000	$000	$000
Total capital required over life of project	20	30	40	50
Capital required in next year	20	10	30	40
Net present value of project at company's cost of capital	60	40	80	80

In what sequence should the projects be selected if the company wishes to maximise net present values?

A P, R, S, Q

B Q, P, R, S

C Q, R, P, S

D R, S, P, Q

106 Alicia is contemplating purchasing for $280,000 a machine that she will use to produce 50,000 units of a product per year for five years. These products will be sold for $10 each and unit variable costs are expected to be $6. Incremental fixed costs will be $70,000 per year for production costs and $25,000 per year for selling and administration costs. Alicia has a required return of 10% per year.

By how many units must the estimate of production and sales volume fall for the project to be regarded as not worthwhile?

[ ] units

107 **The payback period is the number of years that it takes a business to recover its original investment from net returns. Select the correct items from the drop down choices.**

It is calculated **before/after** depreciation and **before/after** taxation

108 Data of relevance to the evaluation of a particular project are given below.

Cost of capital in real terms	10% per year
Expected general inflation rate	8% per year
Expected increase in the project's annual cash inflow	6% per year
Expected increase in the project's annual cash outflow	4% per year

Which of the following sets of adjustments will lead to the correct NPV being calculated?

	Cash inflow	**Cash outflow**	**Discount percentage**
A	Unadjusted	Unadjusted	10.0%
B	6% per year increase	4% per year increase	18.8%
C	6% per year increase	4% per year increase	10.0%
D	8% per year increase	8% per year increase	18.8%

109 Spotty Ltd plans to purchase a machine costing $18,000 to save labour costs through efficiency savings. Labour savings would be $9,000 in the first year and would increase in the second year by 10%. The estimated general annual rate of inflation is 8% and the company's real cost of capital is estimated at 12%. The machine has a two-year life with an estimated actual salvage value of £5,000 receivable at the end of year 2. All cash flows occur at the year-end.

What is the negative NPV (to the nearest $10) of the proposed investment?

A $50

B $270

C $380

D $650

110 A company buys a machine for $10,000 and sells it for $2,000 at time 3. Running costs of the machine are: time 1 = $3,000; time 2 = $5,000; time 3 = $7,000.

If a series of machines are bought, run and sold on an infinite cycle of replacements, what is the equivalent annual cost of the machine if the discount rate is 10%?

A $22,114

B $8,892

C $8,288

D $7,371

111 A company has four independent projects available:

	Capital needed at time 0	NPV
	$	$
Project 1	10,000	30,000
Project 2	8,000	25,000
Project 3	12,000	30,000
Project 4	16,000	36,000

If the company has $32,000 to invest at time 0, and each project is infinitely divisible, but none can be delayed, what is the maximum NPV that can be earned?

A $85,000

B $89,500

C $102,250

D $103,000

112 A project has an initial outflow at time 0 when an asset is bought, then a series of revenue inflows at the end of each year, and then finally sales proceeds from the sale of the asset. Its NPV is £12,000 when general inflation is zero % per year.

If general inflation were to rise to 7% per year, and all revenue inflows were subject to this rate of inflation, but the initial expenditure and resale value of the asset were not subject to inflation, what would happen to the NPV?

A The NPV would remain the same

B The NPV would rise

C The NPV would fall

D The NPV could rise or fall

113 Which TWO of the following statements about the investment appraisal methods of return on capital employed (ROCE) and payback are true?

A Both methods are affected by changes in the cost of capital

B The ROCE does not take account of returns over the entire life of the project

C The payback method is based on the project's cash flows

D A requirement for an early payback can increase a company's liquidity

114 Indicate, by clicking in the relevant boxes, whether the following statements in relation to a simulation exercise are true or false.

Method	True	False
It considers the effect of changing one variable at a time		
It considers the impact of many variables changing at the same time		
It points directly to the correct investment decision		
It assesses the likelihood of a variable changing		

115 When considering standard deviation as a statistical measure, which of the following statements is true?

A Standard deviation is a measure of the variability of a distribution around its mean

B The tighter the distribution, the higher the standard deviation will be

C The wider the dispersion, the less risky the situation

D Standard deviation is the weighted average of all the possible outcomes

116 In relation to a long-term lease, which of the following statements is NOT correct?

A All the risks and rewards of ownership transfer to the lessee

B The asset and lease obligation will be recorded in the statement of financial position

C The lease period will cover almost all of the leased asset's useful economic life

D The lessor will be responsible for repairs and maintenance of the leased asset

117 Peach Co's latest results are as follows:

	$000
Operating profit	2,500
Profit before income taxes	2,250
Profit for the year	1,400

In addition, extracts from its latest statement of financial position are as follows:

	$000
Equity	10,000
Non-current liabilities	2,500

What is Peach Co's return on capital employed (ROCE)?

[ ] %

118 A company undertakes a project that involves purchasing machinery at a cost of $65,000. The machinery is used on the project for four years, generating operating cash inflows of $20,000 per year. It is sold at the end of the project for $10,000. Taxation is charged at a rate of 30%.

Calculate the initial return on capital employed (ROCE) for the project, to the nearest whole percentage.

[ ] %

119 A company is appraising a three-year project which requires an initial outlay on 1 January 20X4 of $30,000. The project is expected to give the following cash inflows on 31 December of each year:

20X4 $10,000

20X5 $20,000

20X6 $25,000

All of the above cash flows are before taking account of specific annual inflation of 5% per year. The real cost of capital is 4% and the nominal cost of capital is 14%.

Using a nominal approach and the discount tables provided, what is the NPV of the project on 1 January 20X4 (to the nearest dollar)?

$ [ ]

120 In relation to the return on capital employed (ROCE) investment appraisal method, which of the following statements is correct?

A ROCE leads to better investment decisions since it uses accounting profit rather than estimated cash flows

B Investment projects with a ROCE greater than the weighted average cost of capital should be accepted

C Investment projects with a ROCE less than the current ROCE of an organisation should be rejected

D ROCE takes into account all years of operation of an investment project

121 Togue Co is investigating how often it should replace its company car fleet. It is considering replacement every two, three, four or five years. Cash flow estimates have been compiled and the following negative NPVs have been obtained, based on Togue Co's cost of capital of 11%:

Years to replacement	Negative NPV
	$
2	149,308
3	209,142
4	254,893
5	310,860

Using the annuity tables provided, if Togue Co adopts the optimal replacement cycle, what will be the equivalent annual cost (to the nearest dollar)

$ ________

122 A machine costing $450,000 has a useful life of six years, after which time its estimated present value of resale will be $25,800. The present value of the total running costs over the next six years is $82,280.

The company's cost of capital is 10%.

What is the equivalent annual cost of using the machine if it were bought and replaced every six years in perpetuity (to the nearest dollar)?

$ ________

BUSINESS FINANCE AND COST OF CAPITAL

123 The equity shares of Nice Co have a beta value of 0.80. The risk free rate of return is 6% and the market risk premium is 4%. Corporation tax is 30%.

What is the required return on the shares of Nice Co (to one decimal place)?

[ ] %

124 **Which TWO of the following statements are correct?**

A A bonus issue can be used to raise new equity finance

B A share repurchase scheme can increase both earnings per share and gearing

C Miller and Modigliani argued that the financing decision is more important than the dividend decision

D Shareholders usually have the power to increase dividends at annual general meetings of a company

E Offering new shares for tender may mean that not enough funding is raised from the share issue

125 Four companies are identical in all respects, except for their capital structures, which are as follows:

	A Co	**B Co**	**C Co**	**D Co**
	%	%	%	%
Equity as a proportion of total market capitalisation	70	20	65	40
Debt as a proportion of total market capitalisation	30	80	35	60

The equity beta of A Co is 0.89 and the equity beta of D Co is 1.22.

Within which ranges will the equity betas of B Co and C Co lie?

A The beta of B Co and the beta of C Co are both higher than 1.22

B The beta of B Co is below 0.89 and the beta of C Co is in the range 0.89 to 1.22

C The beta of B Co is above 1.22 and the beta of C Co is in the range 0.89 to 1.22

D The beta of B Co is in the range 0.89 to 1.22 and the beta of C Co is higher than 1.22

126 **Which TWO of the following statements concerning profit are correct?**

1 Accounting profit is not the same as economic profit

2 Profit takes account of risk

3 Accounting profit can be manipulated by managers

4 Gross profit margin is calculated as gross profit divided by shareholder's funds

127 A company issued its 12% irredeemable loan notes at 95. The current market price is 92. The company is paying corporation tax at a rate of 30%.

What is the current net cost of capital per year of these loan notes (to one decimal place)?

[ ] %

128 Ingham Co's capital structure is as follows:

	$m
50c ordinary shares	12
8% $1 preference shares	6
12.5% loan notes 20X6	8
	26

The loan notes are redeemable at nominal value in 20X6. The current market prices of the company's securities are as follows.

50c ordinary shares	250c
8% $1 preference shares	92c
12.5% loan notes 20X6	$100

The company is paying corporation tax at the rate of 30%. The cost of the company's ordinary equity capital has been estimated at 18% per year.

What is the company's weighted average cost of capital (to the nearest whole %) for capital investment appraisal purposes?

A 10%

B 14%

C 16%

D 17%

129 Indicate, by clicking in the relevant boxes, whether the following statements are true or false.

	True	False
An increase in the cost of equity leads to a fall in share price		
Investors faced with increased risk will expect increased return as compensation		
The cost of debt is usually lower than the cost of preference shares		

130 A company has just declared an ordinary dividend of 25.6p per share; the cum-div market price of an ordinary share is 280p.

Assuming a dividend growth rate of 16% per year, what is the company's cost of equity capital (to one decimal place)?

[ ] %

131 Which TWO of the following would be implied by a decrease in a company's operating gearing ratio?

A The company is less profitable

B The company is less risky

C The company has a lower proportion of costs that are variable

D The company has profits which are less sensitive to changes in sales volume

132 Which of the following statements is part of the traditional theory of gearing?

A There must be taxes

B There must exist a minimum WACC

C Cost of debt increases as gearing decreases

D Cost of equity increases as gearing decreases

133 Which of the following statements is true of a scrip issue with perfect information?

A Decreases earnings per share

B Decreases the debt/equity ratio (calculated on a market value basis) of the company

C Increases individual shareholder wealth

D Increases the market price of the share

134 A company incorporates increasing amounts of debt finance into its capital structure, while leaving its operating risk unchanged.

Assuming that a perfect capital market exists, with corporation tax (but without personal tax), which of the following correctly describes the effect on the company's costs of capital and total market value? Indicate, by clicking in the relevant boxes, whether the cost of equity, weighted average cost of capital and total market value would increase, decrease or be unaffected.

	Increase	**Decrease**	**Unaffected**
Cost of equity			
Weighted average cost of capital			
Total market value			

135 If, for a given level of activity, a firm's ratio of variable costs to fixed costs were to fall and, at the same time, its ratio of debt to equity were also to fall, what would be the effect on the firm's financial and operating risk? Indicate, by clicking in the relevant boxes, whether financial risk and operating risk would increase or decrease.

	Increase	**Decrease**
Financial risk		
Operating risk		

136 A security's required return can be predicted using the CAPM using the formula:

$r_i = r_f + \beta_i (r_m - r_f)$

Security X has a beta value of 1.6 and provides a return of 12.0%

Security Y has a beta value of 0.9 and provides a return of 13.0%

Security Z has a beta value of 1.2 and provides a return of 13.2%

Security Z is correctly priced.

The risk free return is 6%.

What does this information indicate about the pricing of securities X, Y? Fill in the gaps in the statements below.

Security X is ....

Security Y is ....

Choose from the following:

underpriced

overpriced

137 The following are extracts from the statement of financial position of a company:

	$000	$000
Equity		
Ordinary shares	8,000	
Reserves	20,000	
		28,000
Non-current liabilities		
Bonds	4,000	
Bank loans	6,200	
Preference shares	2,000	
		12,200
Current liabilities		
Overdraft	1,000	
Trade payables	1,500	
		2,500
Total equity and liabilities		42,700

The ordinary shares have a nominal value of 50 cents per share and are trading at $5.00 per share. The preference shares have a nominal value of $1.00 per share and are trading at 80 cents per share. The bonds have a nominal value of $100 and are trading at $105 per bond.

What is the market value based gearing of the company, defined as prior charge capital/ equity?

A 15.0%

B 13.0%

C 11.8%

D 7.3%

138 Fill in the gaps in the statements below.

Risk that cannot be diversified away can be described as ....

Risk that increases as a company gears up is described as ....

Choose from the following:

Business risk

Financial risk

Systematic risk

Unsystematic risk

139 An all equity company issues some irredeemable loan notes to finance a project that has the same risk as existing projects. The company operates in a tax-free environment under conditions of perfect capital markets. Indicate, by clicking in the relevant boxes, whether the following statements are true for the company.

	True	**False**
The cost of equity will fall		
The weighted average cost of capital will rise		

140 Which TWO of the following are most likely to result in a company's financial gearing being high?

A Low taxable profits

B High tax rates

C Inexpensive share issue costs

D Intangible assets being a low proportion of total assets

141 Compared to ordinary secured loan notes, which of the following statements is true when considering convertible secured loan notes?

A Likely to be more expensive to service because of their equity component

B Likely to be less expensive to service because of their equity component

C Likely to be more expensive to service because converting to equity requires the holders to make additional payments

D Likely to be less expensive to service because they must rank after ordinary secured loan stock

142 Which of the following is the best statement of the conclusion of Modigliani and Miller on the relevance of dividend policy?

A Shareholders in any type of market are indifferent between receiving dividend income and capital gains

B Increase in retentions results in a higher growth rate

C Discounting the dividends is not an appropriate way to value the firm's equity

D The value of the shareholders' equity is determined solely by the firm's investment selection criteria

143 If a company that currently pays its workforce on a piece rate system were to automate its production line, which of the following responses would it expect of operating gearing?

A Decrease

B Increase

C Remain the same

D Increase or decrease depending on the nature of the production process

144 If a geared company's asset beta is used in the CAPM formula (ri = rf + ßi (rm – rf)) what will ri represent?

A The WACC of the company

B The ungeared cost of equity

C The geared cost of equity

D The market premium

145 Which of the following ratios is used to measure a company's liquidity?

A Current ratio

B Interest cover

C Gross profit margin

D Return on capital employed

146 In relation to preference shares as a source of capital for a company, fill in the gaps below to complete the sentence.

Preference shares are a form of .... capital which carry .... risk from the company point of view than ordinary shares.

Choose from the following:

equity

loan

lower

higher

147 What is the dividend cover ratio a measure of?

A How many times the company's earnings could pay the dividend

B The interest or coupon rate expressed as a percentage of the market price

C The returns to the investor by taking about of dividend income and capital growth

D How much of the overall dividend pay-out the individual shareholders are entitled to

148 In relation to long-term leases, which TWO of the following statements are true?

A The lease agreement cannot be cancelled

B Many leases can be offered in sequence to cover the whole of useful life of the asset

C The lessor retains the risks and rewards of ownership

D The lessee is responsible for repairs and maintenance

149 In relation to an irredeemable security paying a fixed rate of interest, which of the following statements is correct?

A As risk rises, the market value of the security will fall to ensure that investors receive an increased yield

B As risk rises, the market value of the security will fall to ensure that investors receive a reduced yield

C As risk rises, the market value of the security will rise to ensure that investors receive an increased yield

D As risk rises, the market value of the security will rise to ensure that investors receive a reduced yield

150 Drumlin Co has $5m of $0.50 nominal value ordinary shares in issue. It recently announced a 1 for 4 rights issue at $6 per share. Its share price on the announcement of the rights issue was $8 per share.

What is the theoretical value of a right per existing share?

A $1.60

B $0.40

C $0.50

D $1.50

151 Small and medium-sized entities (SMEs) can have difficulty raising finance due to the maturity gap.

Which of the following is the best explanation of the maturity gap?

A The lack of available funds from shareholders

B Venture capitalists need an exit route for their investment within a specific time period

C The business finds it difficult to obtain short-term funding but easier to obtain long-term funding secured against its non-current assets

D The lack of business history makes borrowing more risky for lenders

152 Frost Co is planning a 1 for 4 rights issue with an issue price at a 10% discount to the current share price.

The EPS is currently $0.50 and the shares of Frost Co are trading on a price/earnings ratio of 20 times. The market capitalisation of the company is $50m.

What is the theoretical ex rights price per share (to two decimal places)?

$ [ ]

153 **Select the correct term to complete the below sentence.**

Small and medium-sized entities (SMEs) have restricted access to capital markets. The difference between the finance required to operate an SME and the amount obtained is known as the

A Forecasted gap

B Maturity gap

C Funding gap

D Asset gap

154 Green Co, a listed company, had the following share prices during the year ended 31 December 20X5:

At start of 20X5	$2.50
Highest price in the year	$3.15
Lowest price in the year	$2.40
At end of 20X5	$3.00

During the year, Green Co paid a total dividend of $0.15 per share.

What is the total shareholder return for 20X5?

A 26%

B 22%

C 32%

D 36%

155 Carp Co has announced that it will pay an annual dividend equal to 55% of earnings. Its earnings per share is $0.80 and it has ten million shares in issue. The return on equity of Carp Co is 20% and its current cum dividend share price is $4.60.

What is the cost of equity of Carp Co?

A 19.4%

B 20.5%

C 28.0%

D 22.7%

156 The following are extracts from the statement of profit or loss for Champ Co:

	$
Sales income	180,000
Cost of sales	(100,000)
Operating profit	80,000
Interest expense	(25,000)
Profit before income taxes	55,000
Tax	(15,000)
Profit for the year	40,000

70% of the cost of sale is variable costs.

What is the operational gearing (measured as contribution/operating profit) of Champ Co to one decimal place?

[ ] **times**

157 Yan Co is planning a 1 for 4 rights issue. The value of rights has been calculated as $0.40 per existing share. Simon Co's market price is currently $7.00 per share.

What is the theoretical ex rights price (TERP) per share and the rights issue price per share? Select the correct items from the drop down choices.

TERP: **$5.00/$5.40/$6.20/$6.60/$7.00/$7.40/$8.60**

Rights issue price: **$5.00/$5.40/$6.20/$6.60/$7.00/$7.40/$8.60**

158 Small and medium sized entities (SMEs) often face a funding gap problem.

Indicate, whether the following statements about SMEs are TRUE or FALSE, by selecting the correct answer next to the relevant statement.

Statement	**True**	**False**
SMEs will often experience a funding gap, due to them being seen as a higher risk investment than a larger company		
Founding shareholders of an SME will often have to sacrifice limited liability in order to obtain bank finance		
A lack of suitable, sufficient, non-current assets increases the funding gap problem for an SME		

159 The following information is available for a listed company:

Dividend recently paid	$0.10 per share
Dividend cover	4 times
Price earnings ratio	5 times
Estimated future growth in dividends	8%

Using the dividend growth model, what is the cost of equity for this company (to one decimal place)?

[ ] %

160 A listed company has a dividend yield of 9%, based on its most recent dividend of $0.35 per share. What is the value of the share price in relation to these values?

What is the value of the share price in relation to these values (in cents, to the nearest whole cent)?

[ ] cents

161 Beaver Co has 100 million equity shares in issue and has just reported a profit, after tax, of $55m. A new issue of 50 million equity shares at an issue price of $1.50 is being considered. All proceeds would be used to redeem a bank loan with an annual cost of 8%. Beaver Co pays corporation tax at a rate of 20%.

Assume that operating profit (profit before interest and tax) remains constant.

If the equity issue goes ahead and the bank loan is redeemed, what will be the new earnings per share figure?

A $0.399

B $0.367

C $0.598

D $0.388

BUSINESS VALUATIONS

162 Mrs Mays has been left $30,000 which she plans to invest on the Stock Exchange in order to have a source of capital should she decide to start her own business in a few years' time. A friend of hers who works in the City of London has told her that the London Stock Exchange shows strong form market efficiency.

If this is the case, which of the following investment strategies should Mrs Mays follow?

A Study the company reports in the press and try to spot under-valued shares in which to invest

B Invest in two or three blue chip companies and hold the shares for as long as possible

C Build up a good spread of shares in different industry sectors

D Study the company reports in the press and try to spot strongly growing companies in which to invest

163 A company has 7% loan notes in issue which are redeemable in seven years' time at a 5% premium to their nominal value of $100 per loan note. The before-tax cost of debt of the company is 9% and the after-tax cost of debt of the company is 6%.

What is the current market value of each loan note (to two decimal places)?

$ [ ]

164 TKQ Co has just paid a dividend of 21 cents per share and its share price one year ago was $3.10 per share. The total shareholder return for the year was 19.7%.

What is the current share price (to two decimal places)?

$ [ ]

165 Compton Co has announced a 1 for 4 rights issue at a subscription price of $2.50. The current cum-rights price of the shares is $4.10.

What is the new ex-rights market value of the shares?

A $3.78

B $2.82

C $3.55

D $1.32

166 An investor believes that they can make abnormal returns by studying past share price movements.

In terms of capital market efficiency, to which of the following does the investor's belief relate?

A Fundamental analysis

B Operational efficiency

C Technical analysis

D Semi-strong form efficiency

167 Supa Co has 50 million shares in issue, and its capital structure has been unchanged for many years.

Its dividend payments in the years 20X1 to 20X5 were as follows.

End of year	**Dividends**
	$000
20X1	2,200
20X2	2,578
20X3	3,108
20X4	3,560
20X5	4,236

Dividends are expected to grow at the same average rate into the future.

According to the dividend valuation model, what should be the market price per share (to the nearest ten cents) at the start of 20X6 if the required return on the shares is 25% per year?

$ [ ]

168 The following data relates to an all equity financed company.

Dividend just paid	$50m
Earnings retained and invested	70%
Return on investments	15%
Cost of equity	25%

What is the market value of the company (to the nearest million dollars)?

A $381m

B $200m

C $221m

D $218m

169 The following information relates to two companies, Alpha Co and Beta Co.

	Alpha Co	**Beta Co**
Earnings after tax	$210,000	$900,000
P/E ratio	16	21

Beta Co's management estimate that if they were to acquire Alpha Co they could save $100,000 annually after tax on administrative costs in running the new joint company. Additionally, they estimate that the P/E ratio of the new company would be 18.

On the basis of these estimates, what is the maximum that the shareholders of Beta Co should pay for the entire share capital of Alpha Co?

A $1.1m

B $2.9m

C $4.2m

D $2.0m

170 The shares of Fencer Co are currently valued on a P/E ratio of 8. The company is considering a takeover bid for Seed Limited, but the shareholders of Seed have indicated that they would not accept an offer unless it values their shares on a P/E multiple of at least 10.

Which TWO of the following are reasons which might justify an offer by Fencer Co for the shares of Seed on a higher P/E multiple?

A Fencer has better growth prospects than Seed

B Seed has better-quality assets than Fencer

C Seed has a higher gearing ratio than Fencer

D Seed is in a different country from Fencer, where average P/E ratios are higher

171 Fill in the gap at the end of the following sentence.

An investor, who bases all his/her investment decisions on information he/she has gathered from published statements and comments on company plans and performance, is acting as if he/she believed that the maximum level of efficiency of the capital market is .... form efficient.

Choose from the following:

Strong

Semi-strong

Weak

Zero

172 The following data relate to an all-equity financed company.

Dividend just paid	$200,000
Earnings retained and invested	40%
Return on investments	15%
Cost of equity	23%

What is the market value (to the nearest $1,000)?

$ ☐

173 Indicate, by clicking in the relevant boxes, whether the following statements are true or false.

Statement	**True**	**False**
The existence of projects with positive expected net present values contradicts the idea that the stock market is strong-form efficient		
The existence of information content in dividends contradicts the idea that the stock market is strong-form efficient		

174 Peter Co has made an offer of one of its shares for every three of Baker Co. Synergistic benefits from the merger would result in an increase in after-tax earnings of $4m per year. Extracts from the latest accounts of both companies are as follows:

	Peter Co	**Baker Co**
Profit for the year	$120m	$35m
Number of shares	400 million	90 million
Market price of shares	250c	120c

Assume that the price of Peter Co's shares rises by 50c after the merger and that Peter issues new shares as consideration.

What will be the price-earnings ratio of the group?

A 6.76

B 8.11

C 9.07

D 10.75

175 Spanner Co has paid the following dividends per share in recent years:

Year	**20X3**	**20X2**	**20X1**	**20X0**
Dividend (cents per share)	36.0	33.8	32.8	31.1

The dividend for 20X3 has just been paid and SKV Co has a cost of equity of 16%.

Using the historical dividend growth rate and the dividend growth model, what is the market price of Spanner Co shares to the nearest cent on an ex dividend basis?

$ [ ]

176 **Asset-based business valuations using net realisable values are useful in which of the following situations?**

A When the company is being bought for the earnings/cash flow that all of its assets can produce in the future

B For asset stripping

C To identify a maximum price in a takeover

D When the company has a highly skilled workforce

177 For a company, let

EPS	= Earnings per share
PPS	= Price per share
VPS	= Value per share
EY	= Earnings yield
TE	= Total earnings

Which of the following is the best expression for the total value of the company?

A TE × [1/EY]

B EPS × [1/EY]

C EPS/PPS

D PPS/EPS

178 A company has just paid an ordinary share dividend of 32.0 cents and is expected to pay a dividend of 33.6 cents in one year's time. The company has a cost of equity of 13%.

What is the market price of the company's shares to the nearest cent on an ex dividend basis?

$ [ ]

179 Toggle Co has in issue 6% loan notes which are redeemable at their nominal value of $100 in three years' time. Alternatively, each loan may be converted on that date into 30 ordinary shares of the company.

The current ordinary share price of Toggle Co is $3.50 and this is expected to grow at 4% per year for the foreseeable future.

Toggle Co has a pre-tax cost of debt of 5% per year.

What is the current market value of each $100 convertible loan note?

A $102.12

B $107.06

C $115.74

D $118.46

180 The owners of a private company wish to dispose of their entire investment in the company. The company has an issued share capital of $1m of $0.50 nominal value ordinary shares. The owners have made the following valuations of the company's assets and liabilities.

Non-current assets (book value)	$30m
Current assets	$18m
Non-current liabilities	$12m
Current liabilities	$10m

The net realisable value of the non-current assets exceeds their book value by $4m. The current assets include $2m of accounts receivable, which are thought to be irrecoverable.

What is the minimum price per share that the owners should accept for the company?

$ [ ]

181 A company has annual after-tax operating cash flows of $2 million per year that are expected to continue in perpetuity. The company has a cost of equity of 10%, a before-tax cost of debt of 5% and an after-tax weighted average cost of capital of 8% per year. Corporation tax is 20%.

What is the theoretical value of the company?

A $20m

B $40m

C $50m

D $25m

182 Lane Co has in issue 3% convertible loan notes, which are redeemable in five years' time at their nominal value of $100 per loan note. Alternatively, each loan note can be converted in five years' time into 25 Lane Co ordinary shares.

The current share price of Lane Co is $3.60 per share and future share price growth is expected to be 5% per year. The before-tax cost of debt of these loan notes is 10% and corporation tax is 30%.

What is the current market value of a Lane Co convertible loan note, to the nearest whole $?

$ [ ]

183 **Indicate, by clicking on the relevant boxes, whether the following statements are true or false in relation to business valuation.**

Statement	**True**	**False**
The earnings yield method and the dividend growth model should give similar values for a company		
Market capitalisation represents the maximum value for a company		
The price/earnings ratio is the reciprocal of the earnings yield		
The price/earnings ratio should be increased if the company being valued is riskier than the valuing company		

184 **In relation to capital markets, which of the following statements is true?**

A The return from investing in larger companies has been shown to be greater than the average return from all companies

B Weak form efficiency arises when investors tend not to make rational investment decisions

C Allocative efficiency means that transaction costs are kept to a minimum

D Research has shown that, over time, share prices appear to follow a random walk

185 In relation to behavioural finance, which TWO of the following are terms used to explain why investors in shares do not always make rational decisions?

A Herding

B Fishing

C Simulation

D Noise traders

E Bubble

186 In relation to behavioural finance, which of the following is an explanation of the market paradox?

A Rising share prices may lead to a continued rise in prices

B Shares that have performed poorly are bought by speculative investors

C Unethical insider trading in shares can boost the efficiency of the stock market

D Investors must believe that stock markets are inefficient in order for the markets to act in an efficient manner

187 Bilbo Co is an unlisted company with 800,000 issued shares. Seema is one of the founders and owns 20% of the issued shares.

Bilbo Co has just paid its annual dividend of $0.30 per share. It is expected that next year's dividend will be $0.32 per share. After that it is expected that dividends will grow indefinitely at 2% per year.

Shareholders expect a 12% return from their investment.

Using the dividend valuation model, calculate the value of Seema's shareholding.

A $512,000

B $522,240

C $489,600

D $480,000

188 The efficient markets hypothesis refers to the way in which the prices of traded financial securities reflect relevant information.

Which TWO of the following are true for a weak-form efficient market?

A Share prices fully and fairly represent past information

B Share prices fully and fairly represent private information

C Share prices appear to follow a 'random walk'

D The market does not provide enough information to make good buying and selling decisions

189 Black Co has in issue 5% irredeemable loan notes, nominal value of $100 per loan note, on which interest is shortly to be paid. Black Co has a before-tax cost of debt of 10% and corporation tax is 30%.

What is the current market value of one loan note?

A $55

B $50

C $76

D $40

190 Tryde Co is a listed company which has 800 million ordinary shares in issue. Yesterday the ordinary share price closed at $6.00. Two days earlier, the board of directors approved the launch of two new innovative products, but this has not been publicly announced.

Product A has an NPV of $40m. The decision to launch product A will be announced publicly tomorrow.

Product B has an NPV of $160m. The decision to launch product B will be announced publicly this morning.

Assume all other things are equal and that the capital markets believe the projected NPVs. Both products will be financed using internally generated funds.

What will the ordinary share price be at the end of today if the capital market is (1) semi-strong form efficient and (2) strong form efficient? Select the correct items from the drop down choices.

Semi-strong form efficient market:	**$6.00/$6.05/$6.20/$6.25**
Strong form efficient market:	**$6.00/$6.05/$6.20/$6.25**

191 Abrar Co has 6% convertible loan notes in issue with a floor value of $106.20 per $100 loan note. Each loan note can be converted into 15 ordinary shares at any time or redeemed in five years' time at nominal value:

What is the minimum share price at which investors would convert their loan notes (to two decimal places)?

$ [ ]

192 A financial manager believes that if information regarding his organisation is made public, it will not affect the share price as this information is already reflected in the current share price.

In terms of capital market efficiency, to which of the following does the financial manager's belief relate?

A Weak form efficiency

B No efficiency

C Strong form efficiency

D Semi-strong form efficiency

193 Which of the following is an implication of the semi-strong form of the efficient markets hypothesis?

A Security price movements should be predictable

B Security prices should fully and fairly reflect all available information, whether public or private

C Security prices should move when a takeover is announced

D There would be no need to ban insider dealing

194 Alfreda Co is an unlisted company with 200 million $1 ordinary shares in issue. It has earnings attributable to ordinary shareholders of $90m, of which $30m was distributed to shareholders as an ordinary dividend.

Otis Co is a listed company with 550 million ordinary shares in issue. Its earnings per share ratio is $0.25 and its market capitalisation is $2,750m.

What is the value of an ordinary share in Alfreda Co using Otis Co's price/earnings ratio, in $, to two decimal places?

$ [ ]

RISK MANAGEMENT

195 What does the term 'matching' refer to?

A The coupling of two simple financial instruments to create a more complex one

B The mechanism whereby a company balances its foreign currency inflows and outflows

C The adjustment of credit terms between companies

D Contracts not yet offset by futures contracts or fulfilled by delivery

196 A company whose home currency is the dollar ($) expects to receive 500,000 pesos in six months' time from a customer in a foreign country. The following interest rates and exchange rates are available to the company:

Spot rate	15.00 pesos = $1
Six-month forward rate	15.30 peso = $1

	Home country	**Foreign country**
Borrowing interest rate	4% per year	8% per year
Deposit interest rate	3% per year	6% per year

Working to the nearest $100, what is the six-month dollar value of the expected receipt using a money-market hedge?

A $32,500

B $33,700

C $31,800

D $31,900

197 Edted Co has to pay a Spanish supplier 100,000 euros in three months' time. The company's Finance Director wishes to avoid exchange rate exposure, and is looking at four options.

Indicate, by clicking in the relevant boxes, whether the following would provide cover or not against the exchange rate exposure that Edted would otherwise suffer.

Statement	Would provide cover	Would not provide cover
Do nothing for three months and then buy euros at the spot rate		
Pay in full now, buying euros at today's spot rate		
Buy euros now, put them on deposit for three months, and pay the debt with these euros plus accumulated interest		
Arrange a forward exchange contract to buy the euros in three months' time		

198 **Indicate, by clicking in the relevant boxes, whether the following statements concerning currency risk are true or false.**

Statement	True	False
Lagging is a method of hedging transaction exposure		
Matching receipts and payments is a method of hedging translation exposure		

199 A UK company has just despatched a shipment of goods to Sweden. The sale will be invoiced in Swedish kroner, and payment is to be made in three months' time. Neither the UK exporter nor the Swedish importer uses the forward foreign exchange market to cover exchange risk.

If the pound sterling were to weaken substantially against the Swedish kroner, what would be the foreign exchange gain or loss effects upon the UK exporter and the Swedish importer? Indicate, by clicking in the relevant boxes, which effect would be seen.

	Gain	Loss	No effect
UK exporter			
Swedish importer			

200 A UK company will purchase new machinery in three months' time for \$7.5m. The forward exchange rate is \$2.0383 – \$2.0390 = £1.

What is the appropriate three-month forward rate at which the company should hedge this transaction (to four decimal places)?

[ ] \$/£

201 The current spot exchange rate between sterling and the euro is €1.4415 = £1. The sterling annual interest rate is 5.75% per year and the euro annual interest rate is 4.75% per year.

What should the three month €/£ forward rate be (to four decimal places)?

[ ] €/£

202 **Fill in the gap in the sentence below.**

The difference between the price of a futures contract and the spot price on a given date is known as ....

Choose from the following:

the initial margin

basis

hedge efficiency

the premium

203 **Which of the following statements is correct?**

A Once purchased, currency futures have a range of close-out dates

B Currency swaps can be used to hedge exchange rate risk over longer periods than the forward market

C Banks will allow forward exchange contracts to lapse if they are not used by a company

D Currency options are paid for when they are exercised

204 The following options are held by Frances Co at their expiry date:

1 A call option on £500,000 in exchange for US$ at an exercise price of £1 = $1.90.

The exchange rate at the expiry date is £1 = $1.95.

2 A put option on £400,000 in exchange for Singapore $ at an exercise price of £1 = $2.90.

The exchange rate at the expiry date is £1 = $2.95.

Indicate, by clicking in the relevant boxes, which choice should be undertaken by the company for each option.

	Exercise	**Let it lapse**
Call option		
Put option		

205 Eady Co is a UK company that imports furniture from a Canadian supplier and sells it throughout Europe. Eady Co has just received a shipment of furniture, invoiced in Canadian dollars, for which payment is to be made in two months' time. Neither Eady Co nor the Canadian supplier use hedging techniques to cover their exchange risk.

If the pound sterling were to weaken substantially against the Canadian dollar, what would be the foreign exchange gain or loss effects upon Eady Co and the Canadian supplier? Indicate the effect by clicking in the relevant boxes.

	Gain	**Loss**	**No effect**
Eady Co			
Canadian supplier			

206 **Indicate, by clicking in the relevant boxes, whether the following statements are true or false about the impact of a fall in the value of a country's currency.**

Statement	**True**	**False**
Exports will be given a stimulus		
The rate of domestic inflation with rise		

207 **Which of the following statements is true of a put option?**

A It is the right to sell an asset at a fixed price

B It is an obligation to sell an asset at a fixed price

C It is the right to buy an asset at a fixed price

D It is an obligation to buy an asset at a fixed price

208 **The following statements refer to interest rate risk. Are each of the following statements true or false?**

Statement 1: The aim of a forward rate agreement (FRA) is to lock the company into a target interest rate and hedge both adverse and favourable interest rate movements.

Statement 2: An interest rate guarantees (IRG) is more expensive than an FRA as one has to pay for the flexibility to be able to take advantage of favourable interest rate movements.

	Statement 1	**Statement 2**
A	True	True
B	False	True
C	True	False
D	False	False

209 The following statements refer to interest rate futures. Are each of the following statements true or false?

Statement 1: If you sell a futures contract you have a contract to lend money.

Statement 2: Each contract is for a standardised amount with a set maturity date. A whole number of contracts must be dealt with.

	Statement 1	Statement 2
A	True	True
B	False	True
C	True	False
D	False	False

210 The shape of the yield curve at any point in time is the result of three theories acting together.

Which of the following theories does NOT influence the yield curve?

A Liquidity preference theory

B Expectations theory

C Flat yield theory

D Market segmentation theory

211 Which of the following is shown by a yield curve?

A The relationship between liquidity and bond interest rates

B The relationship between time to maturity and the return to bond investors

C The relationship between risk and bond interest rates

D The relationship between bond interest rates and bond prices

212 Which of the following measures will allow a UK company to enjoy the benefits of a favourable change in exchange rates for their Euro receivables contract while protecting them from unfavourable exchange rate movements?

A A forward exchange contract

B A put option for Euros

C A call option for Euros

D A money market hedge

213 Which of the following statements is correct?

A Governments may choose to raise interest rates so that the level of general expenditure in the economy will increase

B The normal yield curve slopes upward to reflect increasing compensation to investors for being unable to use their cash now

C The yield on long-term loan notes is lower than the yield on short-term loan notes because long-term debt is less risky for a company than short-term debt

D Expectations theory states that future interest rates reflect expectations of future inflation rate movements

214 Interest Rate Parity Theory generally holds true in practice. However, it suffers from several limitations.

Which of the following is NOT a limitation of Interest Rate Parity Theory?

A Government controls on capital markets

B Controls on currency trading

C Intervention in foreign exchange markets

D Future inflation rates are only estimates

215 **Which of the following are descriptions of basis risk?**

1 It is the difference between the spot exchange rate and currency futures exchange rate

2 It is the possibility that the movements in the currency futures price and spot price will be different

3 It is the difference between fixed and floating interest rates

4 It is one of the reasons for an imperfect currency futures hedge

A 1 only

B 1 and 3

C 2 and 4 only

D 2, 3 and 4

216 The following data is available:

Country Y currency	Dollar
Country X currency	Peso
Country Y interest rate	1% per year
Country X interest rate	3% per year
Country X expected inflation rate	2% per year
Spot exchange rate in Country Y	1.60 peso per $1

What is the current six-month forward exchange rate in Country Y (to two decimal places)?

[ ] **peso per $1**

217 **Indicate, by clicking in the relevant boxes, whether the following statements about interest rate risk hedging are correct or incorrect.**

Statement	Correct	Incorrect
An interest rate floor can be used to hedge an expected increase in interest rates		
The cost of an interest rate floor is higher than the cost of an interest rate collar		
The premium on an interest rate option is payable when it is exercised		
The standardised nature of interest rate futures means that over- and under-hedging can be avoided		

218 Brass Co has produced a cash forecast that predicts a cash shortage of 5 months, starting in 4 months' time. It has noted the following forward rate agreements available from its bank:

3-8 FRA 3.8% – 4.0%

4-5 FRA 3.8% – 4.0%

5-9 FRA 3.8% – 4.0%

4-9 FRA 3.8% – 4.0%

Indicate which FRA would be used and which rate would be fixed if Brass Co took on the most appropriate FRA to cover its position.

	3-8	**4-5**	**5-9**	**4-9**
FRA used				
	3.8%	**4.0%**	**3.9%**	**7.8%**
Rate fixed				

219 Plum Co, a company based in New Zealand, has entered into a contract with a Japanese company to purchase an item of machinery. The cost in Japanese Yen, is Yen 400,000 and is due to be paid in six months. Plum Co decides to enter into a forward exchange contract with its bank, who has offered a contract at the following six-month rates:

Japanese yen 77.2 – 78.2 = 1 New Zealand dollar

Calculate, to the nearest dollar, the value of New Zealand dollars that would be needed to settle the purchase invoice if the forward exchange contract is used.

[ ] **NZD**

220 The expected future spot rate in one year is 1.4505 euro per $1. The predicted inflation rates for the year ahead are:

Eurozone	**Dollar**
2% per year	3.5% per year

What is the current spot rate (to four decimal places)?

[ ] euro per $1

221 **Which TWO of the following statements concerning the interest rate risk management method of smoothing are true?**

A The debt portfolio will consist of a mixture of fixed and floating rate debt

B Interest payments will still increase if the interest rate rises

C Investments with a fixed cash flow will be financed with fixed rate debt

D Full benefit will be obtained from a fall in interest rates

E The net effect will be an interest payment which is fixed overall

222 A company that has a $14m loan, with a variable rate of interest, has acquired a forward rate agreement (FRA) with a financial institution that offered a 4-11, 2.85% – 2.35% spread.

What would be the amount received from the financial institution, under the terms of the FRA, if the actual rate of interest was 3.75% (to the nearest dollar)?

$ ☐

223 Which TWO of the following derivative instruments are characterised by a standard contract size?

A Forward contract

B Forward rate agreement

C Futures contract

D Swap

E Over-the-counter option

F Exchange tradable option

224 Which of the following is a description of gap exposure?

A The difference between short-term and long-term interest rates

B The difference between the amounts of interest-sensitive assets and liabilities

C The difference between spot interest rates and futures interest rates

D The difference between fixed and floating interest rates

225 Which of the following statements about an over-the-counter interest rate option are correct?

1 It is an agreement with a financial institution

2 It can be traded

3 An immediate premium is payable

4 It must be exercised

A 1 and 2 only

B 1 and 3

C 3 and 4

D 1, 2 and 4

226 Which TWO of the following hedging techniques can be used by an investor to protect against a fall in interest rates?

A Money market hedge

B Interest rate collar

C Interest rate cap

D Interest rate floor

227 Kaya Co is expecting to borrow $25m in three months' time. The loan will be for a four month period. Kaya Co is concerned that interest rates could rise over the next three months, so it wants to fix the rate of interest now with a forward rate agreement (FRA) and has obtained the following quotes:

3 v 4 4.6% – 4.9%

3 v 7 4.7% – 5.0%.

Assuming the interest rate is 5.3% in three months' time, what will be the financial settlement under the FRA?

A $25,000

B £33,333

C $50,000

D $75,000

228 Shadow Co, which has a home currency of dollars, orders goods from a foreign supplier. A payment of £400,000 is due to the supplier in four months' time. The financial manager is concerned that the cost of the goods may rise in dollar terms and has decided to hedge the foreign currency risk of the payment due.

The following information has been provided by the company's bank:

Spot rate (£ per $)	0.790 – 0.795
Four month forward rate (£ per $)	0.775 – 0.783

What is the amount payable, in dollars, using a forward market hedge (to the nearest dollar)?

$ [ ]

Section 2

OBJECTIVE TEST CASE STUDY QUESTIONS – SECTION B

Each objective test case question is worth 10 marks.

FINANCIAL MANAGEMENT FUNCTION AND ENVIRONMENT

229 The following are extracts from the last Board meeting at Y Co, a quoted high street retailer based in Country A. Y Co sources some products, such as food and clothing, from third party suppliers but also makes some of its own products, such as furniture. The context of the discussion is a plan to close a domestic furniture factory and build a new one in a cheaper country.

CEO: I think we should be more cautious about going ahead with plans to build a new factory in Country B, as I've looked at their forecast inflation rates and they are higher than expected. This would send our costs sky high when the reason we want to build it is to save money. However, if we cannot boost profits, then I fear we will have to cut the next dividend, something that will be disastrous for our shareholders, many of whom will then sell their shares.

Director A: Surely the exchange rate will move to compensate for the difference in inflation, so it won't make a huge difference?

Director B: I think the key issue is improving reported profit – that is the main way we can keep our shareholders happy, which is, after all, our job. Sacking people in Country A will only result in a boost to the share price due to the cost savings – as long as we keep shareholders informed, that is.

Director C: I think we should be more worried about what is happening in our own country – the Government is talking about restricting the money supply to control excessive cost-push inflation.

Director D: I have some good news – the government has blocked a proposed merger between W Co and X Co (two rivals of Y Co) on competition grounds.

(a) Which TWO dividend concepts/theories are consistent with the CEO's fears over the cut in dividend?

A Modigliani and Miller dividend irrelevancy

B Clientele effect

C Residual theory

D Dividend signalling

(b) What theory is consistent with Director A's view on exchange rates?

A Interest rate parity

B Purchasing power parity

C Liquidity preference theory

D Market segmentation theory

(c) Which TWO statements concerning Director B's comments are true?

A Increasing profit is always in shareholders' best interests

B Directors have a fiduciary duty to put shareholder interests first

C Sacking staff will have no impact on the share price, other than as a result of the cost savings that result

D In a semi-strong form market, the share price of Y Co will react when news about the new factory and any redundancies is made public

(d) Which of the following statements concerning Director C's comments is/are true?

(i) Restricting growth in the money supply will have more impact on 'demand-pull' inflation than 'cost-push' inflation.

(ii) Restricting the money supply may result in smaller businesses struggling to raise finance.

(iii) Restricting the money supply is part of a government's fiscal policy.

A (i), (ii) and (iii)

B (i) and (ii) only

C (ii) and (iii) only

D (ii) only

(e) Which of the following is NOT a reason governments seek to limit monopoly power of companies?

A Output is produced at a higher price than necessary

B Reduced incentive to innovate

C Reduced price discrimination

D High prices to limit new market entrants

230 The senior management team of Arkwright Co are concerned that an imminent general election will mean a change in government. The two primary political parties have quite different economic policies.

The CEO has stated:

"If the other party comes to power, then there will be a shift from managing the economy using monetary policy to managing it via fiscal policy. Each policy uses quite different methods to manage the budget deficit that the country currently has. The new potential government has also stated that it will use taxation as a way of controlling externalities. We need to understand these policies in order to determine how Arkwright Co will be affected by any change."

In addition, the FD has stated:

"Our shareholders use common measures such as earnings per share and return on capital employed to evaluate the performance of the company. One major shareholder's only real concern is that we maintain a consistent rate of dividend growth. We need to make sure that we evaluate the effect of any political changes, particularly if the corporation tax rate rises under the new government."

Arkwright Co's dividends over the past five years have been as follows:

20X3	$0.15 per share
20X4	$0.16 per share
20X5	$0.18 per share
20X6	$0.19 per share
20X7	$0.21 per share

(a) Calculate the equivalent annual percentage growth rate in dividends over the past five years, as a percentage, to one decimal place.

[ ] %

(b) Which TWO of the following statements about monetary and fiscal policy are correct?

A Monetary policy is solely concerned with controlling the economy using interest rates

B Fiscal policy involves managing the economy using taxation and government spending

C If a government feels that inflation is too high due to rising aggregate demand levels it may choose to lower interest rates to try and reduce demand

D The use of increasing government borrowing to stimulate the economy can lead to 'crowding out' of private investment

(c) If a country's government budget deficit is increasing, which of the following could represent the situation?

A An increase in government spending has outweighed an increase in taxation income, leading to increased government borrowing

B An increase in government spending has been outweighed by an increase in taxation income, leading to decreased government borrowing

C An increase in interest rates leading to increased government borrowing

D A decrease in interest rates lasing to decreased government borrowing

(d) If the new government chooses to increase the rate of corporate taxation levels, which TWO of the following would represent the initial direct effects on earnings per share (EPS) and return on capital employed (ROCE)?

A EPS would rise

B EPS would fall

C There would be no effect on EPS

D ROCE would rise

E ROCE would fall

F There would be no effect on ROCE

(e) The following statements have been made about externalities.

1 Externalities do not directly affect the consumer of the product that causes them.

2 The existence of externalities suggests that there is a misallocation of resources.

Which of these statements is/are correct?

A 1 only

B Both 1 and 2

C 2 only

D Neither 1 nor 2

WORKING CAPITAL MANAGEMENT

231 Green Co is a furniture manufacturer whose auditors have pointed out that its working capital position is far from satisfactory. The main problem is the high level of inventory, which has led to the company building up a larger and larger bank overdraft. Managers at Green Co have been to numerous public lectures discussing various types of inventory control systems and technologies, but have felt that most of them are impractical.

(a) **Indicate, by clicking in the relevant boxes, whether the following are or are not assumptions behind the traditional economic order quantity (EOQ) formula,**

EOQ = $\sqrt{(2 \times C_o \times D \div C_h)}$.

Statement	Is an assumption	Is not an assumption
Constant demand		
Zero lead time		

(b) The production manager has established the following information about a major inventory item.

Purchase price per unit	\$480
Annual demand	4,000
Supplier's delivery costs per order	\$10
Chief buyer's salary per year	\$30,000
Total number of orders placed per year*	1,000
Annual storage costs per unit	\$2
Cost of capital	10% per year

*Relates to all product lines, not just this one.

What is the economic order quantity for this inventory item?

[ ] units

(c) Green Co adopts the EOQ as its order quantity for that item of inventory and it takes one week for an order to be delivered. Green Co does not wish to hold any buffer inventory.

How much inventory will Green Co have on hand when the order is placed? Assume there are 52 weeks in a year.

[ ] units

(d) The following statements refer to different types of inventory control systems and procedures.

1 In moving from an economic order quantity (EOQ) model of inventory control to a just in time (JIT) model, total annual inventory holding costs would be expected to fall and total annual inventory ordering costs would be expected to rise.

2 Periodic review means ordering inventory when it falls below the designated safety inventory level.

3 Use of the economic order quantity model means that holding and ordering costs should be the same.

Which of the above statements is/are correct?

A 1 only

B 1 and 3 only

C 2 and 3 only

D 1, 2 and 3

(e) The following possible benefits have been attributed to just-in-time systems.

1 Reduced inventory levels

2 Less waste

3 Reduced production times

4 Improved quality of output

Which of these claims can be justified?

A 1 only

B 1 and 2

C 1, 2 and 3

D 1, 2, 3 and 4

232 Hall Co is a retail organisation that buys goods from abroad for cash and sells them locally to both individuals and businesses. It has grown rapidly since its formation on 1 January 20X1 with results summarised below.

Year	**20X1**	**20X2**	**20X3**	**20X4**	**20X5** (forecast)
	$000	$000	$000	$000	$000
Sales	200	400	800	1,200	1,600
Cost of sales	(100)	(200)	(400)	(600)	(800)
Gross profit	100	200	400	600	800
Administration costs	(50)	(60)	(200)	(500)	(640)
Operating profit ($000)	50	140	200	100	160

In the first year, sales were made on a purely cash basis, then credit sales were introduced for businesses. However, Hall Co has now found that its working capital position has deteriorated as business customers take longer and longer to pay. When making decisions that affect the company's finances, a discount rate of 10% is used, which is the best estimate of the cost of capital. Assume credit sales equal business sales.

(a) Indicate, by clicking in the relevant boxes, whether the following would influence or would not influence Hall Co's credit policy for accounts receivable:

Statement	**Would influence**	**Would not influence**
Competitors' terms		
Risk of irrecoverable debts		
Financing costs		
Suppliers' terms		

(b) During the period up to and including 20X5, the expected accounts receivable collection period has been maintained. However, by 20X5, the actual business proportion of sales has grown from 50% to 60%. Credit periods are as follows: 40% of customers take 1 month's credit, 40% of customers take 2 months' credit and 20% of customers take 3 months' credit.

What is the annual cost in $ of financing 20X5 receivables?

$ [ ]

(c) If Hall were to offer customers 1.5% discount for payments within one month, what would be the annual cost of that in respect of receivables who currently take two months or three months to pay?

	2-month receivables	**3-month receivables**
A	19.89%	9.49%
B	9.49%	4.64%
C	4.64%	9.49%
D	9.49%	19.89%

(d) Hall is considering the use of debt factoring or invoice discounting. The following statements have been made in relation to these services.

1 It is apparent in both instances that someone else is collecting your debts.

2 The debts remain an asset of Hall Co under factoring.

Which of these statements are correct?

A 1 only

B Both 1 and 2

C 2 only

D Neither 1 nor 2

(e) Which of the following is NOT a function of a credit control department?

A Advising existing customers on payment terms

B Determining whether to accept cash discounts

C Giving credit references to third parties

D Investigating potential customers' creditworthiness

233 Jeeps Co is concerned about its cash position and has taken to delaying payments to some suppliers in order to ease that problem. Each month the purchase ledger department splits the total value of invoices for that month into three categories, A, B and C, depending on their importance.

Category A invoices, amounting to $2,000,000, are urgent and paid after 30 days

Category B invoices, amounting to $3,000,000, are less urgent and paid after 60 days; and

Category C invoices, amounting to $4,000,000, are least urgent and paid after 90 days.

Several suppliers have reacted to this by offering Jeeps Co a 2% cash discount if the accounts are settled within 15 days. Jeeps Co is currently considering whether or not to accept this. Another supplier, who Jeeps Co now waits 90 days to pay, has been threatening legal action over the $300,000 currently owed. Jeeps Co feels that some sort of compromise might be needed.

Jeeps Co's cost of capital is 12% per year.

Assume that there are 30 days in a month and that purchases accrue evenly over the 360-day year.

(a) Jeeps Co is considering the advantage of the early settlement discount from those it currently pays after:

1 60 days

2 90 days

From which payables should Jeeps take the 2% cash discount?

A 1 only

B Both 1 and 2

C 2 only

D Neither 1 nor 2

(b) **What is Jeeps Co's accounts payable payment period (to the nearest day)?**

[ ] days

(c) **Which of the following is NOT a feature of overtrading?**

A Rapid increase in the level of current assets

B Increase in shareholders' funds

C Increase in accounts receivable collection period

D Rapid increase in revenue

(d) To avoid court action, Jeeps Co is considering offering to repay the creditor it owes $300,000 to in instalments as follows (all figures in $000):

Now	**1 month**	**2 months**	**3 months**	**4 months**	**5 months**
75	45	45	45	45	45

How much will Jeeps Co save, in present value terms, if the creditor accepts the instalment offer instead of Jeeps having to pay in full immediately (to the nearest $00)?

$ [ ]

(e) A company can make decisions that affect its level of investment in working capital. These can be described as either aggressive or conservative policies.

Indicate, by clicking in the relevant boxes, whether the following policies are aggressive or conservative.

Statement	**Aggressive**	**Conservative**
Holding high levels of inventory to avoid long lead times for its customers		
Delay paying creditors (payables) for as long as possible		

234 King Co is a decentralised organisation whose different divisions have approached the matter of cash control in different ways, partly because of their different circumstances. Assume 365 days in a year.

The Western division is facing a two-year major capital investment programme for which significant funds need to be raised to meet the steady demand for cash. The division intends to use the 'Baumol model' to decide when to raise funds, which will be done by selling off investments currently earning 5% per year. The transaction cost of these sales will be $500 per transaction and the total amount needed over the two years is $2,000,000.

The Alpine division has no significant investment plans but finds itself regularly having to either sell investments to make funds available or invest surplus cash. This is because of the considerable variation in daily cash inflows, which has been quantified as having a standard deviation of $7,000. As a result, the division uses the 'Miller-Orr model' to determine when to invest and when to make sales, using the same transaction cost and investment rate as the Western division.

The Southern division has just been created to manufacture a product used by other divisions but mainly sold to outside customers. The coming month, Month 1, will be spent converting and equipping existing corporate premises at a total cash cost of $800,000. Production will start in Month 2 and sales in Month 3. Planned sales volumes are as follows.

Month	**3**	**4**	**5**	**6**	**7**
Sales volume (000s)	10	11	13	16	20

The product will sell for $24 per unit. 20% of sales will be for cash. Of the credit sales, 25% of credit customers (including other divisions) pay in the month following the sale, 50% will pay one month later and 25% after another month.

(a) How much finance should the Western division raise in a single tranche according to the Baumol model?

A $14,142

B $20,000

C $141,421

D $200,000

(b) What does the Miller-Orr model suggest is the spread between the upper and lower limits of cash levels that the Alpine division should maintain?

A $1,123

B $8,028

C $21,489

D $153,569

(c) What will be the Southern division's cash receipts from sales in Month 5?

$ [ ]

(d) It is important to distinguish between a cash budget and a cash forecast. What is the validity of the following statements?

Statement 1: A cash forecast is an estimate of cash receipts and payments for a future period under existing conditions before taking account of possible actions to modify cash flows, raise new capital, or invest surplus funds.

Statement 2: A cash budget is a commitment to a plan for cash receipts and payments for a future period after taking any action necessary to bring the preliminary cash forecast into conformity with the overall plan of the business.

Drag and drop the relevant statements to indicate whether they are true or false.

(e) Which of the following is NOT an advantage to King Co of having a centralised treasury function?

A Better foreign currency risk management

B Borrowing can be made at more advantageous rates

C Increases individual division's responsibility for cash

D The treasury function can be run as a profit centre to raise additional profits

235 Grumpy Co sells stress-relieving toys and is happy with the progress it is making financially, as it is growing and is profitable. There are, however, issues about its cash flow.

An extract from the accounting records for the most recent financial period (a year) is as follows:

	$
Credit sales	480,000
Cash sales	80,000
Trade receivables	85,000
Other receivables	12,000
Credit purchases	212,000
Cash purchases	21,000
Trade payables	30,000
Other payables including VAT	26,000
Finished goods inventory at start of year	45,000
Finished goods inventory at end of year	52,000

In one typical cycle of trade (cycle X), goods were ordered on 17/1/15 and delivered 21 days later, the supplier was paid on 25/2/15. The goods remained in inventory for 62 days. At which point these goods were sold on credit terms of 60 days. Grumpy was eventually paid 68 days after the sale was made. Assume there are 365 days in the year.

(a) What is the accounts receivable collection period from the table data?

A 68 days

B 65 days

C 55 days

D 74 days

(b) What is the accounts payable payment period, in days, to the nearest whole day, from the table data?

[ ] days

(c) What is the inventory holding period at the year end?

A 81 days

B 84 days

C 90 days

D 73 days

(d) For cycle X, what is length, in days, of the cash operating cycle?

[ ] days

(e) **Indicate, by clicking in the relevant boxes, whether the following statements about a cash operating cycle are true or false.**

Statement	True	False
A long operating cycle is more serious in a period of strong growth		
Operating cycles tend to be longer in brand new businesses compared to established businesses		

236 Amax Co is a multinational company which has been reviewing its working capital management.

Inventory	Unit price
Component X	$25

Trade payables	$000
Bard Co	1,000
Colix Co	3,200

Amax Co has received an offer of a discount for bulk purchase from Bard Co, one of its major suppliers. Bard Co has offered a 0.5% discount on orders of 60,000 units or more of Component X. Amax Co currently consumes 240,000 units of Component X each year and places orders of 20,000 units at the end of each month. The holding cost for Component X is $1 per unit per year and ordering costs are $250 per order. Amax Co does not maintain any buffer inventory of Component X.

Colix Co, a major supplier of Component M to Amax Co, has offered a 1% early settlement discount for payment within 30 days. Amax Co currently takes 72 days to settle outstanding invoices with Colix Co.

Amax Co has a cost of short-term finance of 6% through an overdraft and no surplus cash. Assume that there are 360 days in each year.

Amax Co currently has decentralised treasury operations, but is considering implementing a centralised treasury department.

(a) **Using months as a basis, what is the financial consequence of accepting the bulk purchase discount?**

A Benefit of $8,000 per year

B Benefit of $12,000 per year

C Cost of $13,000 per year

D Cost of $8,000 per year

(b) **Using days as a basis, what is the financial consequence of accepting the early settlement discount?**

A Benefit of $48,000 per year

B Cost of $32,000 per year

C Cost of $80,000 per year

D Benefit of $80,000 per year

(c) In relation to managing foreign accounts receivable, which of the following statements is correct?

A Companies expecting to receive foreign currency from foreign accounts receivable will be concerned about the risk of the foreign currency appreciating against the domestic currency

B The safest way to conduct business with foreign accounts receivable is by making a sale where goods are shipped and delivered before payment is due (open account)

C There is no need to assess the creditworthiness of foreign customers if a company has export credit insurance for foreign accounts receivable

D Discounting bills of exchange can reduce foreign accounts receivable default risk

(d) In relation to Amax Co's proposed change to treasury management operations, which of the following statements is correct?

A Local management will be incentivised to maximise profitability

B Amax Co will be more responsive to localised needs for currency hedging

C Amax Co will suffer a loss of autonomy at a local level

D The change should increase the cost of hedging foreign currency risk for Amax Co

(e) In relation to working capital funding strategy, which of the following statements is correct?

A An aggressive strategy seeks to maximise liquidity at the expense of profitability

B Short-term finance has a higher cost than long-term finance

C Fluctuating current assets should be financed from a short-term source

D A moderate or matching strategy finances current assets from a short-term source

INVESTMENT APPRAISAL

237 Bell Co has decentralised its operations and divisional managers are allowed to make their own investment decisions, subject to confirmation by the main company board. Because each of the three divisions (Ding, Dong and Merrily) are subject to different levels of risk, it has been thought appropriate to use different discount rates in each division.

Ding has been told that its real discount rate is 5%. The general rate of inflation, based on an index that uses a very wide range of prices, is 2%. In the industry in which Ding operates, a number of prices are seen to be inflating at 3%.

Dong is assessing a project in which the first of four annual lease payments has been agreed at $120,000. This is payable in one year's time and subsequent payments will rise by 4% per year. Dong's nominal (money) cost of capital is 8%.

Merrily is considering investing $1,000,000 in a project, which will produce the following annual outflows and inflows:

Year	1	2	3
Outflows ($000)	1,800	2,500	1,500
Inflows ($000)	2,000	3,000	2,000

The cash flows, which arise at the end of each year, are stated in current terms. It is expected that outflows will rise by 3% per year and inflows by 2% per year. The nominal (money) cost of capital of the Merrily Division is 9%.

(a) What is Ding's nominal (money) discount rate?

A 7.1%

B 4.0%

C 1.9%

D 1.1%

(b) What is the present value of Dong's last payment that will be made in four years' time (to the nearest $000)?

$ [ ] ,000

(c) What is the net present value of Merrily's project (to the nearest $000)?

A $252,000

B $(10,000)

C $(39,000)

D $(61,000)

(d) When considering risk in project appraisal, what is the main advantage of using simulations to assist the appraisal?

A A clear decision rule

B More than one variable can change at a time

C Statistically more accurate than other methods

D Being diagrammatic is easier to understand

(e) Is it possible to have a negative real discount rate to apply to the cash flow estimates made in current terms when making investment decisions?

From the below, select yes or no and then select your reason

Answer:

Yes

No

Reason:

The calculation of a present value won't work if the discount rate is negative

Negative interest rates never happen in the real world

It will happen in deflationary times

It will happen if the rate of inflation exceeds the money cost of capital

238 Care Co needs to replace a major piece of office equipment that is in constant use and for which there is expected to continue to be use for the foreseeable future. Two types of machine are available with different capital costs, useful lives, scrap values and annual running costs.

Machine 1 will initially cost $480,000, have a life of four years, scrap value of $60,000 and annual running costs of $72,000.

Machine 2 will initially cost $540,000, have a life of three years, scrap value of $120,000 and annual running costs of $47,000.

Care Co's cost of capital is 10%. Assume all cash flows, except the initial capital cost, occur at the end of the relevant year and assume that taxation and inflation can be ignored.

(a) **What is the equivalent annual cost of machine 2 (to the nearest $000)?**

$ [ ] ,000

(b) **Drag and drop the relevant statements to indicate whether they are true or false.**

1 The equivalent annual cost calculation assumes the same type of machine is going to be used into the foreseeable future.

2 The equivalent annual cost calculation assumes the capabilities of Machine 1 and Machine 2 are identical.

(c) It is now felt that the final scrap value of the machines depends on two factors: whether or not a new supplier enters the market (which would reduce the likely scrap value) and the strength of the dollar against other currencies (since sales of used machines will be made abroad and invoiced in the foreign currency). Adverse effects will each reduce the scrap value by 10% of the figure used in the investment appraisal. The relevant probabilities are as follows.

New supplier	Probability	Strong $	Probability
Yes	0.4	Yes	0.3
No	0.6	No	0.7

What is now the expected value of the scrap proceeds from machine 2?

A $106,800

B $109,000

C $111,600

D $113,000

(d) To overcome the difficulties of incorporating probabilities into the investment appraisal calculations, one of Care Co's directors suggests performing a simulation exercise to help reach a decision.

Drag and drop to indicate whether the following statements, relating to simulation, are true or false.

1 It eliminates the effects of risk associated with various estimates.

2 It requires probabilities of estimates subject to risk to be known.

(e) Which of the following statements about Care Co's replacement decision are true?

1 The decision between machine 1 and machine 2 could be found by calculating total NPV of each machine over a 12-year period.

2 The replacement analysis model assumes that Care Co replaces like with like each time it needs to replace an existing asset.

A 1 only

B Both 1 and 2

C 2 only

D Neither 1 nor 2

239 Easter Co is about to hold its annual strategic planning meeting and a number of capital investment projects will be discussed. A summary of the projects' cash flows is shown below.

Project	**NPV**	**Investment**
	$000	$000
A	4,900	3,200
B	7,400	9,300
C	5,900	7,300
D	7,500	5,200
E	9,000	5,600

The investments will need to be made at the start of the coming year; no projects can be delayed and none are divisible. The funds available for these projects are limited to $10,000,000.

(a) Indicate, by clicking in the relevant boxes, whether the following statements about capital rationing are true or false.

Statement	**True**	**False**
Both hard and soft capital rationing are the result of external factors		
Both hard and soft capital rationing are the result of internal policies		
Hard rationing is the result of external factors, soft rationing is the result of internal policies		
Soft rationing is the result of external factors, hard rationing is the result of internal policies		

(b) From the list below, select which TWO projects should be accepted, based on the circumstances described?

A project A

B project B

C project C

D project D

E project E

(c) What projects would be accepted if it were found that projects A and E were mutually exclusive?

A A and D

B A and E

C A, D and E

D D and E

(d) What projects, and fractions of projects, would be accepted if a partner could be found to invest in a proportion of one of the projects, making them effectively infinitely divisible (ignoring the mutually exclusive limitation)?

A A, D and 2/7 E

B A, E and 3/13 D

C A, D and E

D D and E

(e) A sixth project, Project F, is causing considerable confusion, particularly among those members of the board of Easter Co whose sole means of appraising projects is to find an internal rate of return (IRR) using the spreadsheet function on their computers. The summarised cash flows of Project F are as follows.

Time 0	Invest	$4.00m
Time 1	Receive	$8.80m
Time 2	Spend	$4.83m

The spreadsheet function requires you to enter the cash flows of a project and also enter a guess for the IRR. The directors are struggling to guess the IRR for this sixth project.

Which TWO of the following statements represent likely causes of confusion over project F?

A It has a negative NPV when undiscounted

B It never earns a positive NPV

C It has no real IRRs

D It has one positive and one negative IRR

E It may have more than one IRR

240 Ace Co is considering a new project. Ace currently installs burglar alarms, putting contact points on access portals and movement sensors in general areas of a property. The new project is in the fire alarm business, a business considered to be similar in many ways to what Ace currently does.

A junior member of the finance team has estimated the cash flows for the project as follows:

Time	**Description**	**Cash flow** $
0	Loose tools	(6,000)
1–4	Contribution	25,000
1–4	Allocated overheads	(8,000)
2–5	Tax @ 25% of profit	(4,250)

No tax-allowable depreciation is available for loose tools.

Ace is entirely equity financed with a cost of equity correctly calculated as 12%.

(a) **What is the NPV of the above project to the nearest $100?**

A $28,700

B $53,000

C $58,400

D $34,100

(b) **The IRR of the above project has been correctly calculated as 26%. Which of the following statements are true?**

1 The IRR is not a measure of absolute profitability and linear interpolation provides only an estimate of the IRR.

2 If the IRR of the project is higher than its cost of capital then the project is always acceptable regardless of the pattern of the cash flows.

A Both statements are true

B Both statements are false

C Statement 1 only

D Statement 2 only

(c) **If the loose tools became allowable for tax-allowable depreciation which of the following statements would be true?**

1 Reported profit before income taxes would rise.

2 The NPV of the project would rise.

3 Assuming that one of the answers to the NPV calculation in part (a) above is correct, then the decision to proceed would alter.

A 1 and 2

B 2 and 3

C 2 only

D 1 only

(d) One of the directors thinks that calculating the payback period would be a useful addition. What is the project's payback period in months to one decimal place?

[ ] months

(e) Indicate, by clicking in the relevant boxes, whether the following statements about the payback period calculation are true or false.

Statement	True	False
It normally ignores time value		
It is a risk-focussed approach in decision-making		
There is clear advice once it is calculated		

241 The following information relates to an investment project, which is being evaluated by the directors of Fence Co, a listed company. The initial investment, payable at the start of the first year of operation, is $3.9 million.

Year	**1**	**2**	**3**	**4**
Net operating cash flow ($000)	1,200	1,500	1,600	1,580
Scrap value ($000)				100

The directors believe that this investment project will increase shareholder wealth if it achieves a return on capital employed greater than 15%. As a matter of policy, the directors require all investment projects to be evaluated using both the payback and return on capital employed methods. Shareholders have recently criticised the directors for using these investment appraisal methods, claiming that Fence Co ought to be using the academically-preferred net present value method.

The directors have a remuneration package which includes a financial reward for achieving an annual return on capital employed greater than 15%. The remuneration package does not include a share option scheme.

(a) What is the payback period of the investment project, in years to 2 decimal places?

[ ] years

(b) Based on the average investment method, what is the percentage return on capital employed of the investment project, to one decimal place?

[ ] %

(c) Which TWO of the following statements about investment appraisal methods are correct?

A The return on capital employed method considers the time value of money

B Return on capital employed must be greater than the cost of equity if a project is to be accepted

C Riskier projects should be evaluated with shorter payback periods

D Payback period calculations ignore the timing of cash flows within the payback period

(d) **Which of the following statements about Fence Co is/are correct?**

1 Managerial reward schemes of listed companies should encourage the achievement of shareholder objectives.

2 Requiring investment projects to be evaluated with return on capital employed is an example of dysfunctional behaviour encouraged by performance-related pay.

3 Fence Co has an agency problem as the directors are not acting to maximise the wealth of shareholders.

A 1 and 2 only

B 1 only

C 2 and 3 only

D 1, 2 and 3

(e) **Which of the following statements about the Fence Co directors' remuneration package is/are correct?**

1 Directors' remuneration should be determined by senior executive directors.

2 Introducing a share option scheme would help bring directors' objectives in line with shareholders' objectives.

3 Linking financial rewards to a target return on capital employed will encourage short-term profitability and discourage capital investment.

A 2 only

B 1 and 3 only

C 2 and 3 only

D 1, 2 and 3

242 Link Co has been prevented by the competition authorities from buying a competitor, Twist Co, on the basis that this prevents a monopoly arising. Link Co has therefore decided to expand existing business operations instead, and as a result the finance director has prepared the following evaluation of a proposed investment project for the company.

	$000
Present value of sales revenue	6,657
Present value of variable costs	(2,777)
Present value of contribution	**3,880**
Present value of fixed costs	(1,569)
Present value of operating cash flow	**2,311**
Initial capital investment	(1,800)
Net present value	**511**

The project life is expected to be four years and the finance director has used a discount rate of 10% in the evaluation. The investment project has no scrap value.

The finance director is considering financing the investment project by a new issue of debt.

(a) What is the percentage change in sales volume which will bring the NPV to zero, calculated to one decimal place?

[ ] %

(b) Which of the following statements relating to sensitivity analysis is/are correct?

1 Although critical factors may be identified, the management of Link Co may have no control over them.

2 A weakness of sensitivity analysis is that it ignores interdependency between project variables.

3 Sensitivity analysis can be used by Link Co to assess the risk of an investment project.

A 1 and 2 only

B 1 only

C 2 and 3 only

D 1, 2 and 3

(c) Using the average investment method and assuming operating cash flows of $729,000 per year, what is the return on capital employed of the investment project?

A 16%

B 28%

C 31%

D 64%

(d) Which of the following statements relating to debt finance is correct?

A Link Co can issue long-term debt in the euro currency markets

B The interest rate which Link Co pays on its new issue of debt will depend on its weighted average cost of capital

C A new issue of loan notes by Link Co will take place in the primary market

D Link Co will not be able to issue new debt without offering non-current assets as security

(e) Indicate, by clicking in the relevant boxes, whether the following statements relating to competition policy are correct or incorrect.

Statement	**Correct**	**Incorrect**
Scale economies are an advantage of monopoly and oligopoly		
Social cost or externalities are an example of economic inefficiency arising from market failure		
Monopoly is discouraged because it can lead to inefficiency and excessive profits		

243 Gaimett Co has some surplus cash that it wishes to invest in long-term projects. The market it operates in is in recovery from a recession and more potential projects are becoming available on a regular basis.

The finance director wishes to ensure that the best use is made of the available cash. A list of potential projects currently available has been made. All projects are divisible and must be started immediately.

Project	NPV $000	Investment value $000
A	125	375
B	240	800
C	80	400
D	40	50
E	150	600

(a) **If the surplus cash available is $1.5 million, calculate the optimum combination of projects that Gaimett Co should undertake.**

A B, E and 26.7% of A

B C, E and 62.5% of B

C A, D, E, C and 9.4% of B

D A, B, D and 45.8% of E

(b) Before the decision on the projects is made, project A becomes unavailable and it is realised that the remaining projects are actually indivisible.

Under the new circumstances, calculate the optimum combination of projects that Gaimett Co should undertake.

A B, C and D

B C, D and E

C B, D and E

D B, C, D and E

(c) **Which TWO of the following would be reasons why managers may reduce the amount that they are willing to invest as part of soft capital rationing?**

A The company's bank has refused to provide available funds

B A debt covenant forbids the issue of new shares to raise cash

C Managers believe that better quality projects will shortly be available

D The precautionary motive

E A stock market crash discourages shareholders from investing further

(d) The managers have decided that they will hold on to $600,000 of the available investment cash for 3 months, as they know that another very good project will become available at that time.

Which TWO of the following investments would be suitable to make use of this cash over this period?

A Certificates of deposit

B Listed company shares

C Unlisted company shares

D Instant access bank deposit account

E Listed company debt

(e) **Which of the following should NOT be included in a cash flow forecast?**

A Payment of a one-off dividend

B Receipt from an insurance company to cover the value of stolen inventory

C Tax allowable depreciation allowed in relation to a new asset purchase

D Buy back of shares

BUSINESS FINANCE AND COST OF CAPITAL

244 Brash Co can buy a new piece of sophisticated machinery for $500,000 by borrowing under a secured loan at 8%. It has also researched the possibility of leasing the asset.

The company's finance director (FD) is a little rusty on leasing issues as the business has never leased before and he/she has worked in Brash Co for 20 years. The FD said 'I studied leasing years ago but I think leasing is cheaper than borrowing because the lease company has access to greater amounts of finance and so benefits from economies of scale on that front'.

The managing director (MD) is sceptical, arguing that leasing companies are commercial and so each deal must be assessed on its merits. The MD commented: 'We have to careful here, I know the lease companies are always responsible for the maintenance but that can't be free!'

The lease offer is as follows:

The lease will be over 5 years with lease payments of $146,000 annually in advance (at the start of each accounting period). Tax is payable 1 year after the accounting year-end and the corporation tax rate is 25%. Maintenance is payable by the lessor and costs $20,000 per year payable at the end of each year, including the last year in preparation for sale. The residual value is expected to be $40,000 (the expected tax written down value at the end of the lease) and the lessor will retain that.

(a) **Indicate, by clicking in the relevant boxes, whether the statements made by the finance director and the managing director are true or false.**

Statement	**True**	**False**
Statement by the finance director		
Statement by the managing director		

(b) In a calculation to compare the cost of leasing with cost of borrowing to buy the asset above, which TWO of the following items are not relevant?

A The interest cash flows saved on borrowing

B The saving on maintenance

C The residual value

D The cash benefits arising from use of the machinery

E The tax-allowable depreciation

(c) What is the present value of the maintenance cash flows, after tax?

A $63,180

B $64,380

C $84,240

D $103,047

(d) What is the present value of the tax relief on the lease payments, after tax, to the nearest $000?

$ [ ]

(e) Indicate, by clicking in the relevant boxes, whether the following statements about the potential effects of taking on a lease are true.

Statement	**True**	**False**
The use of leasing as opposed to purchasing an asset could turn a negative NPV project into a positive NPV one		
If shareholders see that there is a significant lease in place then they may perceive an increase in risk		

245 Kelvin Co is considering an extensive rights issue to raise new finance. It currently has 4 million shares and has been very successful over a prolonged period.

The terms of the deal are as follows:

- One new share for every 4 held at a price of 90% of the existing market value per share
- The existing market value is $20 per share (the cum rights price).

One of the directors is unhappy with offering any discounts to existing shareholders. He/she claims that the company's past success should be enough to encourage shareholders to increase their investment.

(a) What is the theoretical ex rights price (TERP) per share in $?

$ [ ]

(b) What would be the effect on the TERP value if the new shares were offered at a 20% discount level whilst raising the same total amount of finance?

A The TERP value would not change since the total amount raised would be the same

B The TERP would increase

C The TERP would fall

D The TERP would fall to a level unacceptable to existing shareholders

(c) Indicate, by clicking in the relevant boxes, whether the following statements about discounts on a rights issue are true or false.

Statement	True	False
The level of discount is simply not relevant to the wealth of a shareholder as long as they accept the right. It is ignorance of the theory that encourages the offer of a discount in most cases		
The bigger the discount the more likely a shareholder is to accept the rights offer in most cases		

(d) Which of the following actions by shareholders would be the worst thing that they could do in relation to a rights issue as far as shareholder wealth is concerned?

A Accept the rights offer without negotiation

B Renounce their rights and sell them on the open market

C Save their investment and do nothing

D Sell 50% of their rights on the open market whilst ignoring the rest

(e) Which of the following actions will result in the least dilution of control for existing shareholders?

A Accept the rights offer without negotiation

B Renounce their rights and sell them on the open market

C Save their investment and do nothing

D Sell 50% of their rights on the open market

246 Dominance Co is considering raising some new finance but there is disagreement at board level how best to proceed.

The managing director thinks that the company should retain control in the hands of the existing and loyal shareholders. The finance director feels that the gearing level should be allowed to increase to benefit from the tax relief allowed on interest.

The existing equity is quoted at $4.20 cum div with an imminent dividend of 16c due any day. The company earnings have grown at a fairly steady rate of 8% over recent years, but expectations are for growth to be 2% points better in the future.

The company's debt is 4% irredeemable bonds, which were issued at a 5% discount of $95. They have a nominal value of $100 but are currently quoted at $80 with the interest having just been paid. The corporation tax rate is 25%.

(a) Assuming the business wants to retain control in the hands of the existing shareholders, how should it seek to raise the new finance?

A A placing of new shares via a loyal broker

B A further public offering of shares

C A rights issue where it is expected that 95% of the existing shareholders will accept the offer

D Issue new debt

(b) Assuming the business wants to maximise the tax shield on the new finance, how should it raise the money?

A A placing of new shares and $10,000,000 of preference shares

B Accepting a VC offer which includes $5,000,000 of 4% redeemable bonds and some shares

C Sell redeemable debt with a market value $12,700,000 (nominal value $12,000,000) with interest at 5%. The redemption value will make up 25% of the market value

D Sell 120,000 irredeemable loan notes at nominal value with interest at 5.25%

(c) What is the percentage cost of equity to one decimal place?

[ ] %

(d) What is the after tax cost of debt, as a percentage to two decimal places?

[ ] %

(e) The cost of equity for Dominance Co is significantly greater than the cost of debt. The main reason for this is:

A The total risk level in the business

B The specific risk in the business

C The tax shield

D The level of systematic risk in the business

247 The board of Empire Co are discussing their dividend policy and there have been various statements made by the directors.

Director A: "Our shareholders rely on the level of dividend we pay and we cannot ignore that. We must pay out a dividend as expected, otherwise our shareholders will be forced to sell shares or invest elsewhere."

Director B: "I know that when I was young that if I got a rise in my allowance in a particular week then I was more likely to get it again. It was expected. We must pay what is expected."

Director C: "What matters is the underlying value of the projects that we are doing now and that we will do in the future. We should stop wasting time discussing this."

Director D: "What matters is what we can afford in cash. If we are short of money, then it should be the end of the discussion – a lower or even no dividend should be paid. What we could then do is issue more shares instead – I think that is called a scrip dividend."

(a) Which director supports the dividend irrelevancy theory?

A Director A

B Director B

C Director C

D Director D

(b) Which director supports the signalling effect of dividends?

A Director A

B Director B

C Director C

D Director D

(c) Which director supports the dividend dependency theory?

A Director A

B Director B

C Director C

D Director D

(d) Which director is more concerned about company liquidity than dividend policy?

A Director A

B Director B

C Director C

D Director D

(e) Once the discussion about dividend policy was finalised there was another discussion about scrip issues. Indicate, by clicking on the relevant boxes, whether the following statements are true or false.

Statement	True	False
In a scrip issue a shareholder will end up with more shares, this means there will be a gain to them		
Scrip issues serve the purpose of reducing market values in return for more shares. This can make the shares more marketable		

248 The board of a major bank is discussing their investment appraisal methodology as they have a new project under consideration. They have agreed that using the CAPM approach is sensible as they feel it likely that most of their shareholders will have a well-diversified shareholding in the stock market as a whole.

There has been some dispute about which risks constitute specific risks in the bank and which risks are more systematic in nature, partly driven by the nature of the bank's operations. Equally, no one seems quite sure what the required return derived from the CAPM formula actually represents.

The finance director has produced the following data relating to the bank itself, the financial market and the new project it is considering.

Data

Required return on existing debt	6.0%
Cost of existing debt to the bank	4.8%
Return on short-dated government securities	5.2%
Return in the stock market	12.8%
Equity beta of the bank	1.35
Beta of the new project	1.52
Asset beta of the bank	1.15

(a) **Which TWO of the following risks could be correctly described as systematic risks in this case?**

A The interest rates set by the bank

B The risk of default by the banks customers on loans made

C The recessionary pressures in the country in which the bank operates

D The demand for loans made to the bank

E A change in government after a general election

(b) **In the CAPM what would be the value to use for the risk-free rate of return (Rf), from the data above?**

A 6.0%

B 4.8%

C 5.2%

D 4.16% (the after-tax return on short dated government securities)

(c) In the CAPM formula R = Rf + βj(Rm – Rf) where βj represents the project beta, R represents **the cost of equity capital/the required return on the new project** and the market risk premium is represented by **(Rm – Rf)/Rm.**

Pick the correct answers to complete the sentences.

(d) **What is the percentage required return on the new project as derived from the CAPM formula above, to two decimal places?**

[ ] %

(e) **What is the meaning of a beta value of 1?**

A The investment is risk free

B The investment has the same level of risk as the bank

C The investments total risk is as risky as the market

D The investment has the same level of systematic risk as the market

249 The board of Freedling Co are in discussion about the various risk types that face the business. It is evident that there is considerable confusion and disagreement.

Operating risk

Some of the directors feel that given the increasing volume of trade having fixed costs is the best thing to do. 'How can it be risky to have fixed costs when we know how much they are and that they don't change overly much from one year to the next' was one comment.

Gearing risk

The directors were more aware in this area, with some favouring a more traditional view of gearing and others remembering Modigliani and Miller (M&M) fondly from their studies.

(a) **Indicate, by clicking in the relevant boxes, whether the following statements on operating gearing are true or false?**

Statement	**True**	**False**
Given the level of fixed costs do not change considerably from one year to the next, having a lot of fixed cost in Freedling's cost structure would mean that they had low levels of operating risk		
Variable costs are risky because they change as volume changes. Given Freedling is growing, the year-on-year variable cost level has changed a lot as well		

(b) **In relation to changing the gearing of Freedling, which of the following statements are true?**

1 As debt is more risky for the company, it is more expensive than equity and including a higher proportion of debt in the capital structure will therefore increase the WACC.

2 Equity holders respond to the increased risk when a company includes more debt in its capital structure by increasing the return they demand from the company.

A Both statements are true

B Both statements are false

C Only statement 1 is true

D Only statement 2 is true

(c) **Assuming the board were considering raising more debt, indicate, by clicking in the relevant boxes, whether the assertion that the WACC of the business would fall holds true or not in the following models.**

Statement	**Holds true**	**Does not hold true**
Under the M&M "no tax" theory		
Under the M&M "with corporation tax" theory		
At low levels of gearing under the traditional theory of gearing		

(d) Under the M&M "no tax" theory on capital structure, which of the following statements are true?

1 It does not matter how a business raises finance.

2 Shareholders, given the M&M assumptions, will recognise the level of risk inherent in any extra debt and compensate themselves by a commensurate increase in required return to leave the company WACC unaltered and without any inherent gain.

A Both statements are true

B Both statements are false

C Only statement 1 is true

D Only statement 2 is true

(e) In diagrams of the traditional theory of capital structure, the cost of debt line is often drawn with a slight tail, arcing upwards at very high levels of gearing. Indicate, by clicking in the relevant boxes, whether the following statements are true or false.

Statement	True	False
The rising tail represents an increased risk to debt holders		
Tax exhaustion can increase the cost of borrowing at high levels of gearing		
In practice, businesses rarely reach this point as banks refuse to lend despite the high interest rates possible		

250 Tulip Co is a large company with an equity beta of 1.05. The company plans to expand existing business by acquiring a new factory at a cost of $20m. The finance for the expansion will be raised from an issue of 3% loan notes, issued at nominal value of $100 per loan note. These loan notes will be redeemable after five years at nominal value or convertible at that time into ordinary shares in Tulip Co with a value expected to be $115 per loan note.

The risk-free rate of return is 2.5% and the equity risk premium is 7.8%.

Tulip Co is seeking additional finance and is considering using Islamic finance and, in particular, would require a form which would be similar to equity financing.

(a) What is the cost of equity of Tulip Co using the capital asset pricing model, calculated to 1 decimal place?

[ ] %

(b) Using estimates of 5% and 6%, what is the cost of debt of the convertible loan notes?

A 3.0%

B 5.2%

C 6.9%

D 5.7%

(c) In relation to using the capital asset pricing model to value Tulip Co, which of the following statements is correct?

A The model assumes that all shareholders of Tulip Co have the same required rate of return

B The model assumes a constant share price and a constant dividend growth for Tulip Co

C The model assumes that capital markets are semi-strong form efficient

D The model assumes that Tulip Co's interim dividend is equal to the final dividend

(d) Which TWO of the following statements about equity finance are correct?

A Equity finance reserves represent cash which is available to a company to invest

B Additional equity finance can be raised by rights issues and bonus issues

C Retained earnings are a source of equity finance

D Equity finance includes both ordinary shares and preference shares

E Cutting a dividend provides a source of equity finance

(e) Regarding Tulip Co's interest in Islamic finance, which of the following statements is/are correct?

1 Murabaha could be used to meet Tulip Co's financing needs.

2 Mudaraba involves an investing partner and a managing or working partner.

A 1 only

B 2 only

C Both 1 and 2

D Neither 1 nor 2

251 Nolciln Co needs to raise more capital and wants to identify the most appropriate capital structure to maximise its shareholders' wealth. The company has approached you for advice on aspects of its financial and operational gearing.

The following has been extracted from Nolciln Co's 20X9 financial statements:

Time	$000
Revenue	9,540
Operating profit	1,590
Profit for the year	1,072
Dividends paid	500
Ordinary shares (nominal value $1)	7,800
8% loan notes	3,125

Detailed analysis has shown that variable costs are equal to 60% of Nolciln Co's revenue. You have been informed that it is company policy to calculate operational gearing as:

Operational gearing = Contribution/operating profit

The directors of Nolciln Co are also seeking advice on the optimal capital structure. They are aware of the Modigliani and Miller models but seek further information, in particular in respect of what is meant by market imperfections.

(a) What was Nolciln Co's operational gearing in 20X9 (to one decimal place)?

times

(b) What was Nolciln Co's interest cover in 20X9 (to one decimal place)?

times

(c) Which TWO of the following are consistent with traditional capital structure theory?

A There is no optimal capital structure

B The value of the company remains unchanged with increased gearing

C The cost of equity is higher when there is a high proportion of debt capital

D There is a point at which the weighted average cost of capital is minimised

(d) Responding to the directors' request for advice, which of the following is consistent with Modigliani and Miller's with-tax model?

A The value of Nolciln Co decreases with increased gearing

B The weighted average cost of capital remains constant with increased gearing

C The optimal capital structure is made up almost entirely of debt

D The cost of equity remains constant with increased gearing

(e) In relation to capital structure, which TWO of the following are valid statements about market imperfections?

A Tax exhaustion occurs when there is a very high proportion of equity capital

B Debtholders may impose restrictive covenants in loan agreements

C Agency costs, tax exhaustion and bankruptcy risk encourage very high gearing levels

D When a company's gearing creates a high risk of bankruptcy the weighted average cost of capital will be higher

BUSINESS VALUATIONS

252 Kevin Dutton is an investor who specialises in buying corporate debt at discounted values and aims to make gains either by selling bonds at a higher value later or by receiving redemption payments. Kevin is currently evaluating the following investments:

Last year Kevin bought $1m nominal value of unquoted 5% bonds in Company A at a price of $500,000. The bonds are to be redeemed at nominal value of $100 each in 5 years' time but **Company A** is showing signs of financial distress. To value the bonds Kevin has estimated that a return of 30% is appropriate here to compensate for the risks of non-payment.

Company B, a forestry company, is looking to raise $5 million through the issue of 6 year deep discounted zero coupon bonds. The issue price has been set at a 40% discount to nominal value. Kevin may invest but is looking for a return of 10% per year to do so. The bonds will be redeemed at nominal value upon redemption.

Kevin also owns fixed rate bonds in **Company C**. These bonds are traded on major bond markets. Kevin is thinking of selling them now as he believes that interest rates are going to increase shortly resulting in a drop in the bond price.

All three companies mentioned pay tax at 25%.

(a) **What is the estimated current market value of Kevin's investment in the bonds in company A, to the nearest $1,000?**

A $293,000

B $360,000

C $391,000

D $500,000

(b) **Calculate the annual return to the investor on the deep discounted bonds (the average annual growth rate of the bond value). Give your answer as a percentage to 1 decimal place.**

[ ] %

(c) **Calculate the discount required so that the deep discounted bonds give a return to the investor of 10%. Give your answer to the nearest whole percent.**

A 40%

B 42%

C 44%

D 46%

(d) **Indicate, by clicking in the relevant boxes, whether the following statements concerning deep discounted bonds are true or false.**

Statement	**True**	**False**
It is illegal for companies to issue bonds at a discount		
Deep discount bonds can help Company B's cash flow		
Investors' required returns will generally be lower with deep discounted bonds		

(e) Which TWO of the following statements concerning bond prices are true?

A The price of bonds with fixed coupon rates will not be affected by changes in interest rates

B Changes in expected inflation levels will not affect bond prices

C Changes in bond values will result in changes in the return required by investors in those bonds

D Bond prices typically fall as interest rates rise

E The market price of the bond may not be the same as the theoretical price

253 Loki Co is a growing company specialising in making accessories for mobile phones and tablets. The company is currently all-equity financed with 2 million ordinary shares in issue. The existing shareholders are mainly family members and friends. The directors of Loki need to raise finance to fund a new factory and are considering a range of options including flotation and venture capital. Future growth is anticipated to be the following:

Earnings next year = $0.25m, expected then to grow at 7% pa

Dividend next year = $0.14m, expected then to grow at 4% pa

Flotation

Q Co, a listed company with similar business activities to Loki has a P/E ratio of 9, an equity beta of 1.2 and gearing, measured as Debt:Equity of 1:2. Loki is expected to grow faster than Q Co, at least in the short term.

If flotation is approved, then the issue share price would be set at a 15% discount to fair value. The directors of Loki do not believe that an asset valuation is of much use here.

Venture capital

The directors of Loki have been in discussion with 4Ts, a listed venture capital company. As well as contributing equity, 4Ts would seek to spread the risk of their investment by also investing in the form of 4-year 5% secured redeemable bonds as well as convertible preference shares. The risk adjusted return on similar bonds has been estimated at 6%.

Corporation tax is currently 30%.

(a) Which of the following statements, concerning the usefulness of asset based methods of business valuation, is correct?

A Replacement cost normally represents the minimum price that should be accepted for the sale of a business as a going concern.

B Break-up value should provide a measure of the maximum amount that any purchaser should pay for the business.

C Book value will normally be a meaningless figure as it will be based on historical costs.

D Asset based methods give consideration to non statement of financial position intangible assets such as a highly skilled workforce and a strong management team.

(b) Calculate the value of Loki Co's equity beta to 2 dp.

(c) Calculate the issue price of Loki shares for the flotation to the nearest cent using the dividend valuation model with a cost of equity of 14%.

A $0.60

B $0.70

C $1.19

D $1.24

(d) What is the market value per bond of the redeemable bonds, in $, to two decimal places?

$ [ ]

(e) Which TWO of the following statements concerning 4Ts' perspective are true?

A 4Ts' investment in the preference shares will have the lowest risk out of the three methods of finance offered due to the option to convert

B 4Ts will accept a lower level of dividends on the convertible preference shares compared to normal preference shares

C 4Ts are likely to prefer to use CAPM in valuing Loki shares

D The current shareholders of Loki would be willing to sell a majority equity stake to 4Ts

254 Davina McNabb is a fund manager within M Inc, a global stock-market listed investment company. She has recently identified the following potential acquisition targets:

Company A is an unquoted, property development company with a portfolio of over two hundred houses at various stages of renovation. It has been loss making for the last two years due to the economic downturn. Davina believes that new government legislation will bring a welcome boost to the housing market.

Company B is an unquoted shoe manufacturer. It has also suffered in the recent recession, but the directors are confident that the company is past the worst and growth lies ahead:

- Earnings are expected to be $12.5 million next year and expected to grow at 2% per year
- Dividends will be $5 million for each of the next three years and then expected to grow at 3% thereafter.

Davina has located a similar listed company that has an earnings yield of 12% and a cost of equity of 14%.

Company C is a quoted fashion retailer. Davina believes that the current share price of $2.58 undervalues the company significantly, making it a suitable target. She is also interested in Company C as she feels it would have a good fit with her existing fund portfolio and would diversify away some risk.

(a) Which of the following valuation methods is most suitable for valuing Company A?

A P/E ratio × earnings

B Dividend valuation model (DVM)

C Net realisable value of assets

D Market capitalisation

(b) Calculate the value of Company B by reference to its predicted earnings, in millions of dollars, to one decimal place.

$ [ ] m

(c) Calculate the value of company B using the dividend valuation model.

A $35.71m

B $43.21m

C $46.82m

D $47.32m

(d) Which of the following statements concerning Davina's opinion that Company C is undervalued is true?

A Davina believes that the stock market is strong form efficient and she has access to secret inside information.

B Davina believes that the stock market is semi-strong form efficient and she has access to secret inside information.

C Davina believes that the stock market is semi-strong form efficient and she has analysed financial statements and press releases to form this opinion.

D Davina believes that the stock market is weak form efficient and she has produced graphs of historic share prices to form her opinion.

(e) Indicate, by clicking in the relevant boxes, whether the following statements concerning whether Davina should buy Company C to diversify away portfolio risk are true or false.

Statement	**True**	**False**
The shareholders of M Inc. are unlikely to value such diversification		
Davina should always try to reduce the average beta of her portfolio		
Davina should seek to diversify away any systematic risk in her portfolio		

255 Pike Co, a listed conglomerate, is looking to buy Minnow Co, an advertising company owned and run by Freda Minnow. Freda has agreed to the sale and has insisted on cash consideration as she wishes to retire. Pike Co is considering issuing bonds to generate the cash required.

The following information is available:

Statement of financial position for Minnow Co

• Net book value of assets	$12.8m
• Net realisable value of assets	$13.7m
• Replacement cost of assets	$17.8m
• Bank loan	$2.5m

Statement of profit or loss

- Minnow Co made a profit for the year (after tax) of $7m last year. This expected to grow by 3% next year.
- Despite owning and running the company, Freda Minnow does not take a salary, preferring to take money out of the business via high dividends. Pike Co estimates that it will need to offer a salary of $100,000 to replace Freda when she leaves.

Cash flow

- Pike Co anticipates that, after making a number of changes, Minnow Co will generate free cash flow of $6m next year. This is expected to grow by 4% per year thereafter.

Other information

- Trout and Co, a quoted advertising agency with similar gearing and growth prospects to Minnow Co, has a P/E ratio of 7, a WACC of 12% and a cost of equity of 15%.
- Minnow Co pays corporation tax at 30%.

(a) **Based on asset values, what is the minimum amount Freda should accept for the equity of Minnow Co?**

A $10.3m

B $11.2m

C $13.7m

D $15.3m

(b) **Calculate the market value of Minnow Co using earnings. Give your answer to the nearest $million.**

$ [ ] m

(c) **Calculate the market value of the equity of Minnow Co using discounted cash flows.**

A $72.5m

B $75.0m

C $75.5m

D $78.0m

(d) **Which TWO of the following statements about the proposed acquisition are true?**

A Freda probably prefers to take dividends due to tax considerations.

B A major risk faced by Pike Co is that customers will be loyal to Freda rather than the company, so may leave when she retires.

C If the stock market that Pike Co is listed on is strong form efficient, then the share price of Pike Co will only react to the acquisition when the confirmation is published.

D The directors of Pike Co should only be concerned about the unsystematic risks of Minnow Co.

(e) **Which of the following statements concerning the use of different valuation methods for Minnow Co is true?**

(i) Asset valuations are unlikely to give a good indicator of market value.

(ii) Theoretically, discounted cash flow approaches are the best method.

(iii) Dividend valuation model using historic dividend information would give a fair market valuation for the company.

A (i), (ii) and (iii)

B (i) and (ii) only

C (i) only

D (iii) only

256 It is now 1/1/20X6. Predator Co is looking to make a bid for the entire share capital of Prey Co, a small family-owned company that makes specialist gears for high performance racing bikes. Prey Co's products have had a niche but loyal customer base for many years, but demand started to soar in early 20X4 when it was revealed that all the gold medal winners in the cycling events at the Olympics were using a new revolutionary gear type developed and patented by Prey Co. The sale has been agreed in principle, but a valuation still needs to be agreed for Prey Co. The following information is available:

Prey Co – Statement of Financial Position

	Note	$000s
Non-current assets	1	400
Current assets	2	50
Total assets		**450**
Share capital (50 cent ords.)		100
Reserves		170
Bank Loans – repayable 20X8		140
Current liabilities		40
Total equity and liabilities		**450**

Note 1: Included in non-current assets is specialist machinery that has a NBV of $100,000, would cost $500,000 to replace but would only be able to be sold for scrap of $25,000 if disposed of.

Note 2: Current assets have a net realisable value of $40,000.

Prey Co – Summary statements of financial position

$000s	**20X1 (audited)**	**20X2 (audited)**	**20X3 (audited)**	**20X4 (audited)**	**20X5 (unaudited)**	**20X6 (forecast)**
Profit for the year	(10)	20	40	130	140	156
Dividends paid	–	10	20	65	70	78

A similar quoted company has been found that has a cost of equity of 15% and a quoted P/E ratio of 10.

(a) **Calculate the asset value of Prey Co's shares using net realisable value, in $s, to the nearest $000.**

$ [ ] ,000

(b) **Calculate the asset value of Prey Co's shares using replacement cost.**

A $270,000

B $500,000

C $670,000

D $770,000

(c) **Indicate, by clicking in the relevant boxes, whether the following statements concerning the use of asset valuations for Prey Co with the information given are true or false.**

Statement	**True**	**False**
The replacement cost valuation is a good indication of corporate value as Prey Co operates in a capital intensive industry		
The replacement cost valuation is likely to be a poor indication of corporate value as Prey Co's most valuable asset is likely to be its brand name		
Net book value is an indicator of the minimum amount the current owners will want for their company		

(d) **Calculate the share price of Prey Co using earnings**

A $7.00

B $7.80

C $14.00

D $15.60

(e) **What growth rate should be used if estimating the value of Prey Co using the dividend valuation model? Give your answer as a percentage to 1 dp.**

[ ] %

257 Ring Co has in issue ordinary shares with a nominal value of $0.25 per share. These shares are traded on an efficient capital market. It is now 20X6 and the company has just paid a dividend of $0.450 per share. Recent dividends of the company are as follows:

Year	**20X6**	**20X5**	**20X4**	**20X3**	**20X2**
Dividend per share	$0.450	$0.428	$0.408	$0.389	$0.370

Ring Co also has in issue loan notes which are redeemable in seven years' time at their nominal value of $100 per loan note and which pay interest of 6% per year.

The finance director of Ring Co wishes to determine the value of the company.

Ring Co has a cost of equity of 10% per year and a before-tax cost of debt of 4% per year. The company pays corporation tax of 25% per year.

(a) Using the dividend growth model, what is the market value of each ordinary share, in dollars, to two decimal places?

$ [ ]

(b) What is the market value of each loan note?

A $109.34

B $112.01

C $116.57

D $118.68

(c) The finance director of Ring Co has been advised to calculate the net asset value (NAV) of the company.

Which TWO of the following formulae calculate correctly the NAV of Ring Co?

A Total assets less current liabilities

B Non-current assets plus net current assets

C Non-current assets plus current assets less total liabilities

D Net current assets plus non-current assets less long-term liabilities

E Non-current assets less net current assets less non-current liabilities

(d) Which of the following statements about valuation methods is true?

A The earnings yield method multiplies earnings by the earnings yield

B The equity market value is number of shares multiplied by share price, plus the market value of debt

C The dividend valuation model makes the unreasonable assumption that average dividend growth is constant

D The price/earnings ratio method divides earnings by the price/earnings ratio

(e) Indicate, by clicking in the relevant boxes, whether the following statements about capital market efficiency are correct or incorrect.

Statement	Correct	Incorrect
Insider information cannot be used to make abnormal gains in a strong form efficient capital market		
In a weak form efficient capital market, Ring Co's share price reacts to new information the day after it is announced		
Ring Co's share price reacts quickly and accurately to newly-released information in a semi-strong form efficient capital market		

258 The finance director of Coral Co has been asked to provide values for the company's equity and loan notes. Coral Co is a listed company and has the following long-term finance:

	$m
Ordinary shares	7.8
7% Convertible loan notes	8.0
	15.8

The ordinary shares of Coral Co have a nominal value of $0.25 per share and are currently trading on an ex dividend basis at $7.10 per share. An economic recovery has been forecast and so share prices are expected to grow by 8% per year for the foreseeable future.

The loan notes are redeemable after six years at their nominal value of $100 per loan note, or can be converted after six years into 10 ordinary shares of Coral Co per loan note. The loan notes are traded on the capital market.

The before-tax cost of debt of Coral Co is 5% and the company pays corporation tax of 20% per year.

(a) What is the equity market value of Coral Co (to two decimal places)?

$ [ ] m

(b) Assuming conversion, what is the market value of each loan note of Coral Co?

A $110.13

B $112.67

C $119.58

D $125.70

(c) Which of the following statements about the equity market value of Coral Co is/are true?

1 The equity market value will change frequently due to capital market forces.

2 If the capital market is semi-strong form efficient, the equity market value will not be affected by the release to the public of insider information.

3 Over time, the equity market value of Coral Co will follow a random walk.

A 1 only

B 1 and 3 only

C 2 and 3 only

D 1, 2 and 3

(d) Indicate, by clicking in the relevant boxes, whether the following are assumptions that are made by the dividend growth model.

Statement	**Is an assumption**	**Is not an assumption**
Investors make rational decisions		
Dividends show either constant growth or zero growth		
The dividend growth rate is less than the cost of equity		

(e) **Why might valuations of the equity and loan notes of Coral Co be necessary?**

1 The company is planning to go to the market for additional finance.

2 The securities need to be valued for corporate taxation purposes.

3 The company has received a takeover bid from a rival company.

A 1 and 2 only

B 1 and 3 only

C 3 only

D 1, 2 and 3

259 Extracts from the financial statements of Bluebell Co, a listed company, are as follows:

	$m
Operating profit	238
Interest expense	(24)
Profit before income taxes	214
Corporation tax	(64)
Profit for the year	150

	$m
Assets	
Non-current assets	
Property, plant and equipment	768
Goodwill (internally generated)	105
	873
Current assets	
Inventories	285
Trade receivables	192
	477
Total assets	1,350
Equity and liabilities	
Total equity	688
Non-current liabilities	
Long-term borrowings	250
Current liabilities	
Trade payables	312
Short-term borrowings	100
Total current liabilities	412
Total liabilities	662
Total equity and liabilities	1,350

A similar size competitor company has a price/earnings ratio of 12.5 times.

This competitor believes that if Bluebell Co were liquidated, property, plant and equipment would only realise $600m, while 10% of trade receivables would be irrecoverable and inventory would be sold at $30m less than its book value.

Separately, Bluebell Co is considering the acquisition of Dandelion Co, an unlisted company which is a supplier of Bluebell Co.

(a) What is the value of Bluebell Co on a net realisable value basis?

A $140.8 million

B $470.8 million

C $365.8 million

D $1,027.8 million

(b) What is the value of Bluebell Co using the earnings yield method?

$ [ ] **million**

(c) When valuing Bluebell Co using asset-based valuations, which of the following statements is correct?

A An asset-based valuation would be useful for an asset-stripping acquisition

B Bluebell Co's workforce can be valued as an intangible asset

C Asset-based valuations consider the present value of Bluebell Co's future income

D Replacement cost basis provides a deprival value for Bluebell Co

(d) Which of the following is/are indicators of market imperfections?

1 Low volume of trading in shares of smaller companies.

2 Overreaction to unexpected news.

A 1 only

B 2 only

C Both 1 and 2

D Neither 1 nor 2

(e) Which TWO of the following statements are correct?

A Dandelion Co is easier to value than Bluebell Co because a small number of shareholders own all the shares

B Bluebell Co will have to pay a higher price per share to take control of Dandelion Co than if it were buying a minority holding

C Scrip dividends decrease the liquidity of shares by retaining cash in a company

D Dandelion Co's shares will trade at a premium to similar listed shares because it will have a lower cost of equity

E If Bluebell's shares are traded on a market that is semi-strong form efficient, there will be opportunities for insider trading on the shares

260 GWW Co is a listed company which is seen as a potential target for acquisition by financial analysts. The value of the company has therefore been a matter of public debate in recent weeks and the following financial information is available:

Year	**20X3**	**20X4**	**20X5**	**20X6**
Operating profit ($m)	12.6	13.8	14.9	15.7
Profit for the year ($m)	8.5	8.9	9.7	10.1
Total dividends ($m)	5.0	5.2	5.6	6.0

Statement of financial position for 20X6:

	$m	$m
Non-current assets		91.0
Current assets:		
Inventory	3.8	
Trade receivables	4.5	8.3
Total assets		99.3
Equity finance:		
Ordinary shares	20.0	
Reserves	47.2	67.2
Non-current liabilities:		
8% bonds		25.0
Current liabilities		7.1
Total liabilities		99.3

The shares of GWW Co have a nominal (par) value of $0.50 per share and a market value of $4.00 per share. The cost of equity of the company is 9% per year. The business sector of GWW Co has an average price/earnings ratio of 17 times. The 8% bonds are redeemable at nominal (par) value of $100 per bond in seven years' time and the before-tax cost of debt of GWW Co is 6% per year.

The expected net realizable values of the non-current assets and inventory are $86.0m and $4.2m respectively. In the event of liquidation, only 80% of the trade receivables are expected to be collectible.

(a) **Calculate the market capitalisation (equity market value) of GWW Co to the nearest $ million.**

$ [ ] **million**

(b) Calculate the value of GWW Co using a net asset value (liquidation) basis, in $ millions to one decimal place.

$ [ ] **million**

(c) Calculate the value of GWW Co using the price/earnings ratio method?

A $90.9 million

B $141.3 million

C $171.7 million

D $266.9 million

(d) Calculate the value of GWW Co using the dividend growth model with growth calculated using the average historic dividend growth rate, to the nearest $5 million.

$ [ ] **million**

(e) Calculate the value of growth to be used in the dividend growth model using the Gordon's growth approximation. Use the figures from the most recent year in your calculations.

A 4.4%

B 6.1%

C 6.9%

D 8.9%

261 The following financial information relates to Dazvin Co, a company that is listed on a large stock market:

	$m
Revenue	35.5
Cost of sales	(20.0)
Other expenses	(8.4)
Interest expense	(1.4)
Profit before income taxes	**5.7**
Corporation tax (30%)	(1.7)
Profit for the year	**4.0**

Equity and liabilities	$m
Ordinary share capital	26.0
Preference share capital	10.0
Retained earnings	21.5
Total equity	**57.5**
Non-current liabilities:	
Long-term borrowings	18.0
Current liabilities:	
Trade payables	11.1
Total liabilities	**29.1**
Total equity and liabilities	**86.6**

The preference share capital consists of irredeemable 6% preference shares with a nominal value of $0.50 per share. The cost of capital of the preference shares is 8%.

The ordinary shares have a nominal value of $1.00 per share. Dazvin Co has a price/earnings ratio of 12 times. Future share price growth on the stock market is expected to be 6% per year.

The long-term borrowings consist of 7.5% convertible loan notes with a nominal value of $100 per loan note. These loan notes can be converted at the end of six years into 40 ordinary shares of Dazvin Co, or redeemed on the same date at their nominal value of $100 per loan note. Dazvin Co has a before-tax cost of debt of 6%.

(a) What is the market value of the preference shares of Dazvin Co?

A $7.50m

B $5.25m

C $3.75m

D $10.71m

(b) Using the price/earnings ratio method, what is the value of Dazvin Co, in millions of dollars, to one decimal place?

$ [ ] m

(c) Based on a current ordinary share price of $2.00 per share, what is the market value of the convertible debt of Dazvin Co?

A $19.0m

B $19.3m

C $21.0m

D $20.1m

(d) In relation to information requirements for valuing shares, which of the following statements is correct?

A Only information on the market values of tangible assets should be used in valuing shares

B Shares are likely to be mispriced where managers and investors have different levels of information (information asymmetry)

C Details of key personnel are not relevant to the market capitalisation of a listed company

D Since companies do not release information that undermines their competitive advantage, most of the published information about a company is not relevant to placing a value on its shares

(e) In relation to behavioural finance, which of the following statements is/are correct?

1 When investors believe that recent share price increases will continue, this can lead to irrational investment decisions by uninformed investors.

2 Informed investors can contribute to speculative stock market bubbles.

A 1 only

B 2 only

C Both 1 and 2

D Neither 1 nor 2

262 Light Co has the following capital structure.

	$m
Equity and reserves	
Ordinary shares	55
9% preference shares	10
Reserves	433
	498
Long-term liabilities	
6% loan notes	22
8% loan notes	35
	57
Current liabilities	92
Total equity and liabilities	**647**

The ordinary shares of Light Co have a nominal value of $0.25 per share and a current ex dividend market price of $6.75 per share. Ordinary share prices are expected to grow by 5%, per year, for the foreseeable future.

The 9% preference shares of Light Co are irredeemable and have a nominal value of $1.00 per share. The cost of capital of the preference shares is 9.5%.

The 6% loan notes are irredeemable and have a nominal value of $100 per loan note. The before-tax cost of debt of these loan notes is 7%.

The 8% loan notes are convertible, after seven years, into 15 ordinary shares of Light Co per $100 loan note. If not converted, the loan notes will be redeemed at nominal value after eight years. The before-tax cost of debt of these loan notes is 9%.

Light Co pays corporation tax of 25%.

(a) What is the total market value of the 6% loan notes (to one decimal place)?

$ ________ **m**

(b) What is the market value of each 8% loan note?

A $94.48

B $118.20

C $131.87

D $119.38

(c) In relation to valuing preference shares, which of the following statements is correct?

A The market value, of an irredeemable preference share, is calculated by multiplying the dividend by one, minus the tax rate and then dividing by the cost of the preference shares

B Preference shares are a tax-efficient way of raising finance

C Preference shares can be difficult to value when they pay a variable rate of dividend

D Redeemable preference shares are classed as equity in the statement of financial position

(d) In relation to practical considerations in valuing shares and businesses, which of the following statements is correct?

A The share price of a company can rise even when it has cut its dividend

B The marketability of ordinary shares can be improved with a share buyback scheme

C Investors will always act rationally in response to good news from a company

D Random walk theory suggests that share price movements can be forecast in a weak form efficient market

(e) Considering behavioural finance, which of the following statements is correct?

A Behavioural finance supports the view that stock market bubbles result from rational investment decisions

B Noise traders make investment decisions by using software to analyse real-time share price data

C Share price anomalies do not undermine the perfect capital market theory

D The momentum effect suggests that investors can buy shares in the belief that a recent rise in share prices will continue

263 Fuchsia Co is a listed company with a cost of equity of 10%, which plans to achieve dividend growth of 5% per year for the foreseeable future. Fuchsia Co operates in an industry with an average price/earnings ratio of 11 times. The ordinary shares of the company have a nominal value of $0.50 per share. Extracts from the financial statements of the company are as follows:

	$m
Operating profit	278
Interest expense	(14)
Profit before income taxes	**264**
Taxation at 25%	(66)
Profit for the year	**198**
Ordinary dividends	(110)
Retained profit	**88**

	$m
Equity and liabilities	92
Share capital	90
Reserves	726
Total equity	**816**
Non-current liabilities	
Long-term borrowings	300
Current liabilities	364
Total liabilities	**664**
Total equity and liabilities	**1,480**

The long-term borrowings consist of loan notes paying interest of 8% per year, which are redeemable in five years' time at a 4% premium to their nominal value of $100 per loan note. The before-tax cost of debt of Fuchsia Co is 7% per year.

(a) What is the value of Fuchsia Co using the price/earnings ratio method?

A $968m

B $3,058m

C $2,178m

D $2,265m

(b) What is the value of Fuchsia Co using the dividend valuation model?

A $2,310m

B $2,200m

C $1,925m

D $1,100m

(c) What is the market value of the loan notes of Fuchsia Co?

A $308.3m

B $312.3m

C $320.9m

D $296.3m

(d) Which of the following statements relating to capital market efficiency is/are correct?

1 Share prices take several days to respond to new information if a capital market is weak form efficient.

2 In a weak form capital market, technical analysis cannot produce abnormal gains.

A 1 only

B 2 only

C Both 1 and 2

D Neither 1 nor 2

(e) Which of the following statements about noise traders is/are correct?

1 They generally overreact to good news and bad news.

2 They make rational decisions based on fundamental data.

A 1 only

B 2 only

C Both 1 and 2

D Neither 1 nor 2

RISK MANAGEMENT

264 Mallett Co is an Australian firm currently manufacturing a large item of machinery, which is due to be exported shortly to the United States. The sale has been priced in US dollars, the client is expected to pay 850,000 USD.

This is Mallett Co's first sale to an American client since most of its exports normally go to Asia. The client has agreed to pay Mallett Co three months from now. The following relevant additional information is available.

Spot rate	0.7233 US dollars to the Australian dollar
US dollar interest rate	3.3% per year
Australian dollar interest rate	2.9% per year

(a) What will be the Australian dollar receipt, to the nearest thousand dollars, if the transaction is hedged using the money market?

[ ] **AUD**

(b) Which of the following relationships suggests that current long-term interest rates can be used to predict future short-term interest rates?

A Expectations theory

B Fisher effect

C Interest rate parity

D Purchasing power parity

(c) What is the 3-month forward exchange rate, to four decimal places?

[ ] **US dollars to the Australian dollar**

(d) One risk that a company which exports and imports may face is that of exchange losses when accounting results of its foreign branches or subsidiaries are converted into home currency.

What is the name usually given to this type of risk?

A Economic risk

B Political risk

C Transaction risk

D Translation risk

(e) Why is a currency option a particularly suitable device to reduce exposure to currency movements when tendering for a contract priced in a foreign currency?

A Cheapest means of achieving a hedge

B Least risky means of achieving a hedge

C Least unfavourable effect in the published accounts

D You may not get the contract and therefore the currency

265 Noon Co, a company based in Centreland whose home currency is the Centreland Colon (CC), has been regularly buying components from and selling finished products to businesses in Flyland, where the currency is the Flyland Franc (FF).

One particular payment of 3,000,000 Flyland Francs has to be made by Noon Co to a supplier in Flyland in three months' time. The following information is available.

Spot rate	6.170 – 6.210 Flyland Francs to the Centreland Colon
Three-month forward rate	6.321 – 6.362 Flyland Francs to the Centreland Colon

Interest rates that can be used by Noon Co are as follows.

	Borrow	**Deposit**
Flyland Franc interest rate	18.0% per year	13.5% per year
Centreland Colon interest rate	8.1% per year	6.3% per year

(a) What is the cost in Centreland Colons of a forward market hedge?

A 471,550 CC

B 474,608 CC

C 483,092 CC

D 486,224 CC

(b) Which of the following relationships attempt to explain the difference between forward and spot rates of exchange between two currencies and the relative rates of interest in the countries of origin of the two currencies?

A Expectations theory

B Fisher effect

C Interest rate parity

D Purchasing power parity

(c) What is the cost in Centreland Colons of a money market hedge?

A 428,391 CC

B 463,091 CC

C 470,349 CC

D 479,874 CC

(d) Indicate, by clicking in the relevant boxes, whether the following statements on the characteristics of interest rate futures are true or false.

Statement	True	False
Amounts and periods are standardised		
They are legally binding contracts		
They can be bought and sold on a secondary market		
They can be used both to hedge risks and to speculate on interest rate movements		

(e) If inflation is currently running at 3.8% per year in Centreland, what (to the nearest 1%) is the implied inflation rate in Flyland?

[ ] %

266 PZK Co, whose home currency is the dollar, trades regularly with customers in a number of different countries. The company expects to receive €1,200,000 in six months' time from a foreign customer. Current exchange rates in the home country of PZK Co are as follows:

Spot exchange rate:	4.1780 – 4.2080 euros per $
Six-month forward exchange rate:	4.2302 – 4.2606 euros per $
Twelve-month forward exchange rate:	4.2825 – 4.3132 euros per $

The interest rate in the home country of PZK Co is 4% per year.

As well as considering the use of derivatives to hedge the risk exposure presented by the receipt, the treasurer of PZK is looking at 'internal' methods such as invoicing in dollars and leading and lagging.

(a) What type of risk exposure is PZK Co exposed to due to the foreign receipt?

A Transaction risk

B Economic risk

C Translation risk

D Political risk

(b) Calculate, to the nearest dollar, the loss compared to its current dollar value which PZK Co will incur by taking out a forward exchange contract on the future euro receipt.

$ [ ]

(c) Calculate the annual interest rate in the foreign customer's country implied by the spot exchange rate and the twelve-month forward exchange rate.

A 1.5%

B 3.9%

C 4.1%

D 6.6%

(d) If PZK instead chooses to use leading/lagging to manage the foreign currency receipt, which of the following statements concerning whether PZK Co should 'lead' or 'lag' is true?

A The $ is expected to weaken against the €, so PZK should lead

B The $ is expected to weaken against the €, so PZK should lag

C The $ is expected to strengthen against the €, so PZK should lead

D The $ is expected to strengthen against the €, so PZK should lag

(e) Indicate, by clicking in the relevant boxes, whether the following statements concerning whether PZK Co should invoice in dollars are true or false.

Statement	True	False
Invoicing in dollars will eliminate all foreign exchange risk that PZK is exposed to		
Invoicing in dollars will pass exchange rate risk to the customer		
Invoicing in dollars may not be commercially acceptable to foreign customers		

267 H Company, a large manufacturer, is planning to sell an existing subsidiary and use the funds to buy land and build a new factory. The proceeds of the sale are likely to be delayed, so the directors have estimated that $10 million will be needed in 3 months' time for a period of 6 months. Given this, the directors have decided that a bank loan would be appropriate as a form of finance rather than equity sources.

After checking that interest rate yield curves in the financial press are normal rather than inverted, the treasurer is now looking to hedge the interest rate exposure. Traditionally H Company has used forward rate agreements (FRAs) for hedging interest rate risk exposure but the treasurer is now considering using interest rate futures, although he/she is concerned that futures will not be as good a hedge as the FRAs.

H Company's bank have offered an FRA on the following terms:

3v9 FRA 7.2 – 7.8%

(a) Which TWO of the following are possible reasons why the Directors decided that a bank loan was preferable to equity in this case?

A The factory will act as security on the loan

B They believe Modigliani and Miller's theory of gearing with taxation

C All equity sources have higher issue costs than the loan

D The servicing cost of the debt will be lower

(b) Which of the following would NOT be a possible explanation for the normal yield curve observed?

A Expectations theory

B Liquidity preference theory

C Market segmentation theory

D An expected rise in interest rates

(c) Select, from the drop down list, which represents the payment/receipt payable on the FRA if the reference interest rate moves to 7.6% in 3 months' time?

$10,000 payment / $10,000 receipt / $20,000 payment / $20,000 receipt

(d) Which THREE of the following are reasons why futures are not always a perfect hedge?

A Futures contracts are in standard sizes which may not coincide with how much H Company wants to borrow

B Futures have standardised contract dates, which may not coincide with when H Company wants to take out the loan

C Basis risk

D Interest rates are hard to predict

(e) Which of the following statements concerning FRAs and interest rate futures is/are true?

(i) In both cases Company H stills needs to borrow the money at the market rate in three months' time.

(ii) Both have standardised contract sizes.

(iii) Both result in a net gain or loss that can be offset against the loss or gain on the associated real world borrowing.

A (i), (ii) and (iii)

B (i) and (ii) only

C (i) and (iii) only

D (i) only

268 It is now the 31st of January. The treasurer of F Company is reviewing cash forecasts and funding requirements and has identified the need for the following transactions:

Transaction 1:

F Company will have a surplus of $1 million from 1st of May for 3 months, which will need to be deposited to earn additional interest. The treasurer has seen inverted interest rate yield curves in the financial press, so is considering using a 3v6 FRA quoted at 5% – 5.6% to hedge the interest rate risk exposure. He/she is also considering the use of interest rate options as an alternative strategy.

Transaction 2:

F Company also needs to borrow $20 million longer term debt to finance expansion. The treasurer would prefer to borrow at a floating rate but does not feel that the company can obtain competitive rates. He/she is thus considering the possibility of borrowing fixed and entering into a swap arrangement. F Company's advisors have identified G Company as a possible counter party. Details of the current borrowing rates that each company can achieve are as follows:

Company	Best fixed rate	Best variable rate
F	7%	base rate + 3%
G	6%	base rate + 1%

(a) Which TWO predictions are normally associated with an inverted yield curve?

A An expected fall in interest rates

B An expected rise in interest rates

C A rise in inflation

D A downturn of the economy into a recession

(b) What is the payment/receipt payable on the FRA if the reference interest rate moves to 5.5% on the 1st May?

$250 payment / $250 receipt / $1,250 payment / $1,250 receipt

(c) Which of the following best describes an interest rate option?

A A right but not an obligation to buy or sell interest rate futures

B An obligation to obtain a loan at an agreed interest rate at a future date

C A right but not an obligation to obtain a loan (or deposit) at a future date

D A right but not an obligation to enter into a forward rate agreement

(d) With reference to interest rate swaps, which of the following statements is true?

A It allows the company a period of time during which it has the option to buy a forward rate agreement at a set price

B It locks the company into an effective interest rate

C It is an agreement whereby the parties to the agreement exchange interest rate commitments

D It involves the exchange of principal

(e) **Indicate, by clicking in the relevant boxes, whether the following statements concerning the swap are true or false.**

Statement	True	False
G company has been offered lower interest rates due to having a better credit rating		
Under the swap loan principals are exchanged		
If G defaults on the loan it has taken out, then F would also be liable under the swap		

269 Herd Co is based in a country whose currency is the dollar ($). The company expects to receive €1,500,000 in six months' time from Find Co, a foreign customer. The finance director of Herd Co is concerned that the euro (€) may depreciate against the dollar before the foreign customer makes payment and he/she is looking at hedging the receipt.

Herd Co has in issue loan notes with a total nominal value of $4 million which can be redeemed in 10 years' time. The interest paid on the loan notes is at a variable rate linked to the central bank base rate. The finance director of Herd Co believes that interest rates may increase in the near future.

The spot exchange rate is €1.543 per $1. The domestic short-term interest rate is 2% per year, while the foreign short-term interest rate is 5% per year.

(a) **What is the six-month forward exchange rate predicted by interest rate parity, to three decimal places?**

€ [ ] **per $1**

(b) **As regards the euro receipt, what is the primary nature of the risk faced by Herd Co?**

A Transaction risk

B Economic risk

C Translation risk

D Business risk

(c) **Which TWO of the following hedging methods will NOT be suitable for hedging the euro receipt?**

A Forward exchange contract

B Money market hedge

C Currency futures

D Forward rate agreement

E Currency swap

(d) Which of the following statements support the finance director's belief that the euro will depreciate against the dollar?

1 The dollar inflation rate is greater than the euro inflation rate.

2 The dollar nominal interest rate is less than the euro nominal interest rate.

A 1 only

B 2 only

C Both 1 and 2

D Neither 1 nor 2

(e) As regards the interest rate risk faced by Herd Co, which TWO of the following statements are correct?

A In exchange for a premium, Herd Co could hedge its interest rate risk by buying interest rate options.

B Buying a floor will give Herd Co a hedge against interest rate increases.

C Herd Co can hedge its interest rate risk by selling interest rate futures now in order to buy them back at a future date.

D Taking out a variable rate overdraft will allow Herd Co to hedge the interest rate risk through matching.

270 Park Co is based in a country whose currency is the dollar ($). The company regularly imports goods denominated in Euro (€) and regularly sells goods denominated in dinars. Two of the future transactions of the company are as follows:

Three months:	Paying €650,000 for imported goods
Six months:	Receiving 12 million dinars for exported capital goods

Park Co has the following exchange rates and interest rates available to it:

Spot exchange rate (dinars per $1):	57.31	–	57.52
Six-month forward rate (dinars per $1):	58.41	–	58.64
Spot exchange rate (€ per $1):	1.544	–	1.552
Three-month forward rate (€ per $1):	1.532	–	1.540

Six-month interest rates:

	Borrow	**Deposit**
Dinars	4.0%	2.0%
Dollars	2.0%	0.5%

The finance director of Park Co believes that the upward-sloping yield curve reported in the financial media means that the general level of interest rates will increase in the future, and therefore expects the reported six-month interest rates to increase.

(a) What is the future dollar value of the dinar receipt using a money market hedge, in $, to the nearest $000?

$ [ ] ,000

(b) Indicate, by clicking in the relevant boxes, whether Park Co will find each of the following hedges to be effective or not effective in hedging the foreign currency risk of the two transactions.

Statement	**Effective**	**Not effective**
Leading the euro payment on its imported goods		
Taking out a forward exchange contract on its future dinar receipt		
Buying a tailor-made currency option for its future euro payment		

(c) Which hedging methods will assist Park Co in reducing its overall foreign currency risk?

1 Taking out a long-term Euro denominated loan.

2 Taking out a dinar-denominated overdraft.

A 1 only

B 2 only

C Both 1 and 2

D Neither 1 nor 2

(d) Indicate, by clicking in the relevant boxes, whether the following statements are correct or incorrect.

Statement	**Correct**	**Incorrect**
Purchasing power parity can be used to predict the forward exchange rate		
The international Fisher effect can be used to predict the real interest rate		

(e) Which of the following statements is consistent with an upward-sloping yield curve?

A The risk of borrowers defaulting on their loans increases with the duration of the lending.

B Liquidity preference theory implies that short-term interest rates contain a premium over long-term interest rates to compensate for lost liquidity.

C Banks are reluctant to lend short-term, while government debt repayments have significantly increased the amount of long-term funds available.

D The government has increased short-term interest rates in order to combat rising inflation in the economy.

271 Peony Co's finance director is concerned about the effect of future interest rates on the company and has been looking at the yield curve.

Peony Co, whose domestic currency is the dollar ($), plans to take out a $100m loan in three months' time for a period of nine months. The company is concerned that interest rates might rise before the loan is taken out and its bank has offered a 3 v 12 forward rate agreement at 7.10–6.85.

The loan will be converted into pesos and invested in a nine-month project which is expected to generate income of 580m pesos, with 200m pesos being paid in six months' time (from today) and 380m pesos being paid in 12 months' time (from today). The current spot exchange rate is 5 pesos per $1.

The following information on current short-term interest rates is available:

Dollars	6.5% per year
Pesos	10.0% per year

As a result of the general uncertainty over interest rates, Peony Co is considering a variety of ways in which to manage its interest rate risk, including the use of derivatives.

(a) In relation to the yield curve, which of the following statements is correct?

A Expectations theory suggests that deferred consumption requires increased compensation as maturity increases

B An inverted yield curve can be caused by government action to increase its long-term borrowing

C A kink (discontinuity) in the normal yield curve can be due to differing yields in different market segments

D Basis risk can cause the corporate yield curve to rise more steeply than the government yield curve

(b) If the interest rate on the loan is 6.5% when it is taken out, what is the nature of the compensatory payment under the forward rate agreement? Pick from each of the two drop down options.

Payment is made **from Peony Co to the bank/from the bank to Peony Co** of **$262,500/ $450,000**

(c) Using exchange rates based on interest rate parity, what is the dollar income received from the project, calculated in millions, to one decimal place?

$ ______ **million**

(d) In respect of Peony Co managing its interest rate risk, which of the following statements is/are correct?

1 Smoothing is an interest rate risk hedging technique which involves maintaining a balance between fixed-rate and floating-rate debt.

2 Asset and liability management can hedge interest rate risk by matching the maturity of assets and liabilities.

A 1 only

B 2 only

C Both 1 and 2

D Neither 1 nor 2

(e) In relation to the use of derivatives by Peony Co, which of the following statements is correct?

A Interest rate options must be exercised on their expiry date, if they have not been exercised before then

B Peony Co can hedge interest rate risk on borrowing by selling interest rate futures now and buying them back in the future

C An interest rate swap is an agreement to exchange both principal and interest rate payments

D Peony Co can hedge interest rate risk on borrowing by buying a floor and selling a cap

272 Marigold Co is based in a country which uses the dollar ($) as its home currency. Marigold Co has a wholly-owned subsidiary based in a country which uses the M shilling (MS) as its currency. The subsidiary's financial statements are prepared in MS.

Due to economic uncertainty in both countries, an exchange loss of $100,000 is expected to occur after consolidating the results of the subsidiary into Marigold Co's group accounts.

Marigold Co is expecting a receipt of MS300,000 from the subsidiary in three months which it wishes to protect against exchange rate movement. The following information is available:

Exchange rates	**MS per $1**
Spot rate	1.0950 – 1.1250
Three-month forward rate	1.0850 – 1.1125

Money market rates	**Annual deposit**	**Annual borrow**
Spot rate	%	%
MS	3.6	4.0
$	6.0	7.0

(a) What type of exchange rate risk would Marigold Co experience with the $100,000 loss in its consolidated financial statements?

A Economic

B Translation

C Transaction

D Political

(b) If Marigold Co uses the forward market to hedge the MS receipt, what amount will be received (to the nearest $)?

$ [ ]

(c) **Match the appropriate value to the relevant target in order to reflect what amount Marigold Co will borrow and deposit if it uses the money market to hedge the MS receipt.**

Amount to borrow: [ ]

Amount to deposit: [ ]

Pick from: MS288,461, MS289,575, MS297,030, MS297,324, $256,410, $263,435, $264,027, $271,260

(d) Marigold Co is now considering the use of an option to hedge the currency risk on the MS receipt. Its bank has offered an over-the-counter option with an exercise price of MS1.1250 per $.

Which TWO of the following statements concerning the option are TRUE?

A The option will be more expensive to set up compared with either the forward contract or money market hedge

B An imperfect hedge will result as the option will be for a standard amount of currency and only a whole number of contracts may be used

C If the $ was to strengthen against the MS, Marigold Co is likely to be worse off by using the option compared to either the forward contract or money market hedge

D Using an option hedge will mean that Marigold Co is obligated to exercise the option in three months irrespective of the spot rate on the day

(e) Marigold Co is unsure whether to use a forward contract or a money market hedge and is comparing the relative advantages and disadvantages of the two.

Which of the following statements is true?

A The forward contract has the advantage of being tailored precisely to Marigold Co's requirements, but the money market hedge will be a standardised instrument resulting in an imperfect hedge

B The forward contract will result in Marigold Co receiving the dollar equivalent of the MS receipt in three months' time, whereas the money market hedge will provide Marigold Co with dollar receipts today

C The forward contract will result in the effective rate of exchange being fixed whereas the money market hedge will allow Marigold Co to benefit from favourable movement in the exchange rate

D Marigold Co will be obligated to fulfil the forward contract in three months' time whereas the money market hedge could be traded on an exchange to another party before settlement

273 The home currency of Wren Co is the dollar ($) and the company has a supplier in a foreign country whose currency is the dinar (D). In six months' time, Wren Co must make a payment to the supplier, of D3 million, and the company is concerned about exchange rate risk.

Exchange rates:

Spot exchange rate:	2.00 dinars per dollar
Six-month forward exchange rate:	1.94 dinars per dollar

Six-month interest rates	**Borrowing**	**Deposit**
Dinars	4% per year	2% per year
Dollars	10% per year	8% per year

Wren Co wants to compare making a lead payment of D3 million now with taking out a forward exchange contract for D3 million, that can be exercised in six months' time. As the company is short of cash, it would need to borrow money for any exchange rate risk hedging.

Wren Co is considering raising $500,000 in three months' time in order to ease its cash flow problems. The company would borrow the money for a period of six months and it would hedge interest rate risk by using a forward rate agreement (FRA). Wren Co has been offered two different FRAs by its bank: a 3 v 9 FRA at 10.0 – 8.0 and a 3 v 6 FRA at 9.8 – 7.8, but the company is also considering interest rate derivative hedging.

(a) **In relation to interest rate derivatives, which of the following statements is correct?**

A Interest rate futures hedges can be closed out any time

B Forward rate agreements fix the interest rate on future long-term borrowing

C If interest rate options are allowed to lapse, there is no overall cost to the holder

D Buying both an interest rate cap and an interest rate floor is an example of an interest rate collar

(b) **Considering future values on the D3 million payment date, and comparing the lead payment with the forward exchange contract (FEC), select the correct items from the drop down choices.**

The FEC costs **$46,392/$28,608 more/less** than the lead payment

(c) **If Wren Co takes out the relevant FRA and borrows at a base rate of 10.5% per year, in three months' time, what is the company's net cost of borrowing?**

A $20,000

B $25,000

C $24,500

D $27,500

(d) **According to the four-way equivalence model, which of the following statements is correct?**

A If the exchange rate is 2.00 dinars per dollar, a relative increase in dollar interest rates will cause the dollar forward rate to appreciate against the dinar

B The international Fisher effect states that the expected change in the spot rate is equal to the expected difference in inflation rates

C Forward exchange rates reflect interest rate parity

D Purchasing power parity relates exchange rates and long-term interest rates

(e) In relation to foreign currency risk, which of the following statements is/are correct?

1 Economic risk is exchange rate risk that can be avoided by operating in domestic markets only.

2 Exchange rate risk arises because of changes in exchange rates that have not been anticipated.

A 1 only

B 2 only

C Both 1 and 2

D Neither 1 nor 2

274 A large manufacturing company, Tamunac Co, imports its raw material from a foreign country and sells its products in its home country only. To pay for its raw material purchases, the company generates suitable debt financing in the foreign country. The home country's currency is the $ while the foreign country's currency is the €.

A forward rate agreement (FRA) has been used on the borrowing for a recent raw material purchase of €10m. Before the purchase, a 3-6 4.00-3.60 FRA was acquired in the foreign country. The actual base rate applicable on borrowing the €10m was 3.2%.

Separately, Tamunac Co will receive a volume discount of €1.5m in three months' time. To protect against exchange rate volatility in relation to this receipt, the finance director has decided to set up a money market hedge for this amount.

The relevant financial information is as follows:

Spot rate: €1.16 = $1

Interest rate details:

	Borrowing	**Deposit**
	%	%
$ interest rates per year	4	2
€ interest rates per year	6	3

(a) The finance director is analysing the yield curve in the foreign country's market to select a suitable financing strategy. He observes that the yield curve has recently changed from a normal yield curve to become an inverted yield curve.

Which TWO of the following are true in this situation?

A Bonds with a long-term maturity term will have higher returns

B Tamunac Co is exposed to rising interest rates in the foreign country

C The change would have been beneficial for Tamunac Co if it had issued long-term variable rate debt before the inversion

D Raising Eurobond financing in the foreign country’s currency has become more attractive

(b) Which of the following best explains 'basis risk'?

A Interest rates changing before bonds are issued

B Foreign currency becoming more expensive to buy

C More funds needing to be raised due to increase in raw material costs

D The funds needed at maturity not being entirely hedged

(c) Which of the following is the correct transfer in relation to the FRA?

A €20,000 payable

B €80,000 payable

C €10,000 payable

D €100,000 payable

(d) How much will Tamunac Co expect to receive from the €1.5m volume discount?

A $1,244,307

B $1,305,970

C $1,337,694

D $1,280,364

(e) The finance director believes that in current market conditions of the foreign country, using an interest rate option could bring additional financial benefits.

Which TWO of the following are true about an over-the-counter interest rate option?

A It can be traded on a financial exchange

B It is an agreement with a financial institution

C It requires payment of an initial premium

D It must be exercised at its maturity date

Section 3

CONSTRUCTED RESPONSE (LONG) PRACTICE QUESTIONS – SECTION C

WORKING CAPITAL MANAGEMENT – EXAM STYLE QUESTIONS

275 KXP CO (DEC 12 – MODIFIED)

KXP Co is an e-business that trades solely over the internet. In the last year, the company had sales of $15 million. All sales were on 30 days' credit to commercial customers.

Extracts from the company's most recent statement of financial position relating to working capital are as follows:

	$000
Trade receivables	2,466
Trade payables	2,220
Overdraft	3,000

In order to encourage customers to pay on time, KXP Co proposes introducing an early settlement discount of 1% for payment within 30 days, while increasing its normal credit period to 45 days. It is expected that, on average, 50% of customers will take the discount and pay within 30 days, 30% of customers will pay after 45 days, and 20% of customers will not change their current paying behaviour.

KXP Co currently orders 15,000 units per month of Product Z, demand for which is constant. There is only one supplier of Product Z and the cost of Product Z purchases over the last year was $540,000. The supplier has offered a 2% discount for orders of Product Z of 30,000 units or more. Each order costs KXP Co $150 to place and the holding cost is 24 cents per unit per year.

KXP Co has an overdraft facility charging interest of 6% per year.

Required:

(a) **Calculate the net benefit or cost of the proposed changes in trade receivables policy and comment on your findings.** **(6 marks)**

(b) **Calculate whether the bulk purchase discount offered by the supplier is financially acceptable and comment on the assumptions made by your calculation.** **(6 marks)**

(c) **Critically discuss the similarities and differences between working capital policies in the following areas:**

(i) **Working capital investment**

(ii) **Working capital financing.** **(8 marks)**

(Total: 20 marks)

276 HGR CO (JUNE 09 – MODIFIED)

The following financial information relates to HGR Co:

Statement of financial position at the current date (extracts)

	$000	$000	$000
Non-current assets			48,965
Current assets			
Inventory		8,160	
Accounts receivable		8,775	
		16,935	
Current liabilities			
Overdraft	3,800		
Accounts payable	10,200		
		14,000	
Net current assets			2,935
Total assets less current liabilities			51,900

Cash flow forecasts from the current date are as follows:

	Month 1	**Month 2**	**Month 3**
Cash operating receipts ($000)	4,220	4,350	3,808
Cash operating payments ($000)	3,950	4,100	3,750
Six-monthly interest on traded bonds ($000)		200	
Capital investment ($000)			2,000

The finance director has completed a review of accounts receivable management and has proposed staff training and operating procedure improvements, which he/she believes will reduce the accounts receivable collection period to the average sector value of 53 days. This reduction would take six months to achieve from the current date, with an equal reduction in each month. He/she has also proposed changes to inventory management methods, which he/she hopes will reduce the inventory holding period by two days per month each month over a three-month period from the current date. He/she does not expect any change in the current level of accounts payable.

HGR Co has an overdraft limit of $4,000,000. Overdraft interest is payable at an annual rate of 6.17% per year, with payments being made each month based on the opening balance at the start of that month. Credit sales for the year to the current date were $49,275,000 and cost of sales was $37,230,000. These levels of credit sales and cost of sales are expected to be maintained in the coming year. Assume that there are 365 working days in each year.

Required:

(a) Discuss the working capital financing strategy of HGR Co. **(6 marks)**

(b) For HGR Co, calculate:

(i) the bank balance in three months' time if no action is taken; and

(ii) the bank balance in three months' time if the finance director's proposals are implemented.

Comment on the forecast cash flow position of HGR Co and recommend a suitable course of action. **(9 marks)**

(c) Discuss how risks arising from granting credit to foreign customers can be managed and reduced. **(5 marks)**

(Total: 20 marks)

277 FLIT CO (DEC 14 – MODIFIED)

Flit Co is preparing a cash flow forecast for the three-month period from January to the end of March for one of its divisions. The following sales volumes have been forecast:

	December	January	February	March	April
Sales (units)	1,200	1,250	1,300	1,400	1,500

Notes:

1 The selling price per unit is $800 and a selling price increase of 5% will occur in February. Sales are all on one month's credit.

2 Production of goods for sale takes place one month before sales.

3 Each unit produced requires two units of raw materials, costing $200 per unit. No raw materials inventory is held. Raw material purchases are on one months' credit.

4 Variable overheads and wages equal to $100 per unit are incurred during production, and paid in the month of production.

5 The opening cash balance at 1 January is expected to be $40,000.

6 A long-term loan of $300,000 will be received at the beginning of March.

7 A machine costing $400,000 will be purchased for cash in March.

Required:

(a) Calculate the cash balance at the end of each month in the three-month period. **(5 marks)**

(b) Calculate the forecast current ratio at the end of the three-month period. **(2 marks)**

(c) Assuming that Flit Co expects to have a short-term cash surplus during the three-month period, discuss whether this should be invested in shares listed on a large stock market. **(3 marks)**

Flit Co currently has total income of $30 million per year, of which 80% is from credit sales, and a net profit margin of 10%. Due to fierce competition, Flit Co has lost market share and is looking for ways to win back former customers and to keep the loyalty of existing customers. The sales director has pointed out that a major competitor of Flit Co currently offers an early settlement discount of 0.5% for settlement within 30 days, while Flit Co itself does not offer an early settlement discount. He/she suggests that if Flit Co could match this early settlement discount, annual income from credit sales would increase by 20%.

Credit customers of Flit Co take an average of 51 days to settle invoices. Approximately 0.5% of the company's credit sales have historically become bad debts each year and written off as irrecoverable. The finance director has been advised that offering an early settlement discount of 0.5% for payment within 30 days would increase administration costs by $35,000 per year, while 75% of credit customers would be likely to take the discount. The credit controller believes that bad debts would fall to 0.375% of credit sales if the early settlement discount were introduced.

Flit Co has an average short-term cost of finance of 4% per year. Assume that there are 360 days in each year.

(d) Evaluate whether Flit Co should offer the early settlement discount. **(6 marks)**

(e) Discuss TWO ways in which a company could reduce the risk associated with foreign accounts receivable. **(4 marks)**

(Total: 20 marks)

278 OSCAR CO (SEP/DEC 2018)

Oscar Co designs and produces tracking devices. The company is managed by its four founders, who lack business administration skills.

The company has revenue of $28m, and all sales are on 30 days' credit. Its major customers are large multinational car manufacturing companies that are often late in paying their invoices. Oscar Co is a rapidly growing company and revenue has doubled in the last four years. Oscar Co has focused in this time on product development and customer service, and managing trade receivables has been neglected.

Oscar Co's average trade receivables are currently $5.37m, and bad debts are 2% of credit sales revenue. Partly as a result of poor credit control, the company has suffered a shortage of cash and has recently reached its overdraft limit. The four founders have spent large amounts of time chasing customers for payment. In an attempt to improve trade receivables management, Oscar Co has approached a factoring company.

The factoring company has offered two possible options:

Option 1

Administration by the factor of Oscar Co's invoicing, sales accounting and receivables collection, on a full recourse basis. The factor would charge a service fee of 0.5% of credit sales revenue per year. Oscar Co estimates that this would result in savings of $30,000 per year in administration costs. Under this arrangement, the average trade receivables collection period would be 30 days.

Option 2

Administration by the factor of Oscar Co's invoicing, sales accounting and receivables collection on a non-recourse basis. The factor would charge a service fee of 1.5% of credit sales revenue per year. Administration cost savings and average trade receivables collection period would be as Option 1. Oscar Co would be required to accept an advance of 80% of credit sales when invoices are raised at an interest rate of 9% per year.

Oscar Co pays interest on its overdraft at a rate of 7% per year and the company operates for 365 days per year.

Required:

(a) **Calculate the costs and benefits of each of Option 1 and Option 2 and comment on your findings.** **(8 marks)**

(b) **Discuss reasons (other than costs and benefits already calculated) why Oscar Co may benefit from the services offered by the factoring company.** **(6 marks)**

(c) **Discuss THREE factors which determine the level of a company's investment in working capital.** **(6 marks)**

(Total: 20 marks)

279 DUSTY CO (SEP/DEC 2019)

Dusty Co wishes to improve its working capital management as part of an overall cost-cutting strategy to increase profitability. Two areas the company has been considering are working capital funding strategy and inventory management. Dusty Co currently follows a policy of financing working capital needs as much as possible from long-term sources of finance, such as equity. The company has been considering its inventory management and has been looking specifically at component K.

Current position

Dusty Co purchases 1,500,000 units of component K each year and consumes the component at a constant rate. The purchase price of component K is $14 per unit. The company places 12 orders each year. Inventory of component K in the financial statements of Dusty Co is equal to average inventory of component K.

The holding cost of component K, excluding finance costs, is $0.21 per unit per year. The ordering cost of component K is $252 per order.

Economic order quantity

Dusty Co wishes to investigate whether basing ordering of component K on the economic order quantity will reduce costs.

Bulk order discount

The supplier of component K has offered Dusty Co a discount of 0.5% on the purchase price of component K, provided the company orders 250,000 units per order.

Other information

Dusty Co has no cash but has access to short-term finance via an overdraft facility at an interest rate of 3% per year. This overdraft currently stands at $550,000.

Required:

(a) **(i)** **Calculate the annual holding and ordering costs of Dusty Co's current inventory management system.** **(1 mark)**

(ii) **Calculate the financial effect of adopting the Economic Order Quantity as the basis for ordering inventory.** **(4 marks)**

(iii) **Calculate the financial effect of accepting the bulk order discount.** **(4 marks)**

(iv) **Recommend, with justification, which option should be selected by Dusty Co.** **(1 mark)**

(b) **Discuss the key factors in determining working capital funding strategies.** **(10 marks)**

(Total: 20 marks)

280 PUMICE CO (MAR/JUL 2020)

Answer debrief

Pumice Co plans to expand its business operations by opening several new outlets at a cost of $8m, financed by an issue of loan notes. The company currently generates credit sales of $80.768m before cost of sales of $27.700m. All sales are on credit. The current statement of financial position of Pumice Co is as follows:

	$000
Assets	
Non-current assets	54,070
Current assets	
Inventories	4,000
Trade receivables	12,320
Cash and cash equivalents	800
	17,120
Total assets	**71,190**
Equity and liabilities	$000
Equity	6,000
Reserves	34,000
Total equity	40,000
Non-current liabilities	18,000
Current liabilities	
Trade payables	9,690
Overdraft	3,500
	13,190
Total equity and liabilities	**71,190**

Pumice Co expects that the expansion will increase credit sales by 18.7%, with cost of sales being 33% of credit sales and profit for the year (after tax) being $6.818m. Non-current assets will increase by 11%.

The bank has demanded that Pumice Co's overdraft be reduced to $3m and the company expects its cash balance to be $700,000 after the expansion.

Pumice Co has been receiving complaints from its suppliers about late payment and the company plans to improve its working capital management as part of the expansion. It expects that the following working capital ratios will result:

Inventory holding period	50 days
Trade receivables collection period	60 days
Trade payables payment period	60 days

The finance director of Pumice Co wishes to investigate how the expansion will change the following ratios:

(i) trade payables payment period

(ii) current ratio; and

(iii) revenue/net working capital ratio (defining net working capital as inventory plus trade receivables less trade payables).

Assume that there are 360 days in a year.

Required:

Using the information provided:

(a) (i) Prepare a forecast statement of financial position for Pumice Co; and (6 marks)

(ii) Calculate the effect of the proposed expansion on the working capital ratios listed by the finance director. (4 marks)

(b) Discuss the ways in which implementing the proposed changes in working capital represent:

(i) Changes in working capital investment policy for Pumice Co; and (5 marks)

(ii) Changes in working capital funding policy for Pumice Co. (5 marks)

(Total: 20 marks)

Calculate your allowed time, allocate the time to the separate parts

281 KANDY CO (SEP/DEC 2021)

Kandy Co purchases a number of different products from various manufacturers which it then sells on credit to a number of large retailers. Kandy Co is currently reviewing its working capital investment and two independent options are currently under consideration:

1 A bulk purchase discount from one of its biggest suppliers; and

2 Offering an early settlement discount to its customers.

Bulk purchase discount

One of Kandy Co's biggest selling items is the gimble. Kandy Co pays $30 for a gimble and annual sales demand is 18,000 units. At present, Kandy Co's order size is 1,000 gimbles and each order costs $75 to place excluding the purchase price. Annual holding costs are equivalent to 9% of the purchase price of a gimble. Due to the high level of demand for gimbles, Kandy Co always holds a buffer inventory sufficient to cover two days' demand.

Kandy Co has been offered a bulk purchase discount of 1.5% off the purchase price if the company increases its order size to 1,500 gimbles. Although this is 50% more than the size of the current order quantity, Kandy Co feels that it has sufficient storage capacity to accommodate this, but annual holding costs for the gimble would increase to 10% of the purchase price. Also, the increased size of the order would result in higher delivery costs, increasing the cost of placing an order by $25 per order. If accepted, Kandy Co would still maintain a buffer inventory sufficient to cover two days' demand.

Early settlement discount

Kandy Co has total credit sales of $45m per year and all of Kandy Co's customers are equal in terms of sales value. Although Kandy Co's credit terms require payment on 30 days, only 60% of its credit customers pay on time. The remaining 40% of customers pay on average on 40 days.

Kandy Co is considering the introduction of an early settlement discount of 0.5% for payment within 10 days. It expects that 50% of its customers will take advantage of the offer and pay in 10 days, 20% will still pay to terms and there will be 30% who will continue to pay on average on 40 days. Kandy Co finances in the short-term at a cost of 7% per year.

Note: Assume a 360 day-year for all calculations.

Required:

(a) (i) **Calculate the financial effect on Kandy Co of accepting the bulk purchase discount.** **(6 marks)**

(ii) **Calculate the financial effect on Kandy Co of offering the early settlement discount.** **(4 marks)**

(iii) **Using your results from (i) and (ii) above, comment on the financial acceptability to Kandy Co of each option.** **(2 marks)**

(b) **Discuss the working capital objectives of liquidity and profitability and the conflict between these objectives.** **(4 marks)**

(c) **Explain the cash operating cycle and discuss its relationship with the level of investment in working capital.** **(4 marks)**

(Total: 20 marks)

282 PURDY CO (SEP/DEC 2022)

Purdy Co uses 5 million litres of chemical X per year in its plastic manufacturing business. Chemical X costs Purdy Co $2.50 per litre per year to store and each order requires a quality check that costs Purdy Co $400 per order to perform.

Purdy Co currently purchases chemical X from a local supplier at a cost of $3.00 per litre. It uses the economic order quantity (EOQ) model to determine order size and carries a safety inventory of five days' usage to protect against variations in lead time demand.

Purdy Co has recently been approached by a company offering to supply chemical X at a cost of $2.25 per litre, if it will order in quantities of 1 million litres. The new supplier's credit terms are the same as the current supplier. Purdy Co estimates that its storage cost per litre and its quality check cost per order will be unchanged if it accepts this offer and that it will have sufficient storage space to cope with larger orders. However, it will need to increase its safety inventory to 15 days' usage if it accepts the new supplier's offer.

Purdy Co is under pressure from its bank to reduce its overdraft and its finance director is interested in the effect of the new supplier's offer on chemical X costs, working capital investment and the cash operating cycle.

Purdy Co operates for 365 days per year.

Required:

(a) **In relation to Purdy Co's potential change of supplier:**

(i) **Calculate the total annual costs relating to Chemical X for both the current and potential suppliers** **(7 marks)**

(ii) **Calculate the value of the average investment in Chemical X inventory for both the current and potential suppliers and** **(2 marks)**

(iii) **Recommend, with justification, whether Purdy Co should change its supplier.** **(1 mark)**

(b) **Discuss the conflict that exists between the objectives of liquidity and profitability in the management of working capital.** **(5 marks)**

(c) **Explain the cash operating cycle and its relationship with the level of investment in working capital.** **(5 marks)**

(Total: 20 marks)

283 GUILLERMO CO (SEP/DEC 2024)

Guillermo Co is a medium-sized company that manufactures a single product. The product should take two days to manufacture.

Figures from its most recent financial statements are as follows:

	$000
Revenue	6,000
Inventory – raw material	120
Inventory – work in progress	20
Inventory – finished goods	80
Trade receivables	850
Trade payables	162

Sales

Credit sales account for 75% of the total revenue and Guillermo Co's gross profit margin is 60%. Guillermo Co has a large number of credit customers but there is no separate credit control function and chasing of overdue debt is left to the relevant customer account manager. The finance manager considers this to be satisfactory to enable the finance department to concentrate on more important aspects of the business. Standard credit terms for credit customers is 30 days and no credit accounts are currently suspended. All customer account managers are paid a bonus based on the level of sales achieved.

Purchases

Raw material purchases in the year totalled $2,160,000 and 90% of this was purchased on credit. Raw material is the only supply Guillermo Co purchases on credit. Guillermo Co has always tried to maintain good supplier relations and the average credit term from suppliers is 35 days.

Cash management

The management of Guillermo Co has decided it wishes the minimum cash balance to be $40,000 but the cash balance is volatile with a daily standard deviation of $15,000.

If extra cash is needed then Guillermo Co will sell tradeable securities from an investment portfolio it owns. The transaction cost for a purchase is the same as for a sale at $55 per transaction.

Interest rates are currently 9% per year.

Assume a 360 day-year for ALL calculations.

Required:

(a) Calculate Guillermo Co's cash operating cycle. **(5 marks)**

(b) Discuss THREE ways in which Guillermo Co could reduce its cash operating cycle. **(6 marks)**

(c) Using the Miller-Orr model, calculate the target cash balance for Guillermo Co. **(3 marks)**

(d) Discuss the motives for a business to hold cash. **(6 marks)**

(Total: 20 marks)

INVESTMENT APPRAISAL – EXAM STYLE QUESTIONS

284 DUO CO (DEC 07 – MODIFIED) *Walk in the footsteps of a top tutor*

Duo Co needs to increase production capacity to meet increasing demand for an existing product, 'Quago', which is used in food processing. A new machine, with a useful life of four years and a maximum output of 600,000 kg of Quago per year, could be bought for $800,000, payable immediately. The scrap value of the machine after four years would be $30,000. Forecast demand and production of Quago over the next four years is as follows:

Year	**1**	**2**	**3**	**4**
Demand (kg)	1.4 million	1.5 million	1.6 million	1.7 million

Existing production capacity for Quago is limited to one million kilograms per year and the new machine would only be used for demand additional to this.

The current selling price of Quago is $8.00 per kilogram and the variable cost of materials is $5.00 per kilogram. Other variable costs of production are $1.90 per kilogram. Fixed costs of production associated with the new machine would be $240,000 in the first year of production, increasing by $20,000 per year in each subsequent year of operation.

Duo Co pays tax one year in arrears at an annual rate of 30% and can claim tax allowable depreciation (tax-allowable depreciation) on a 25% reducing balance basis. A balancing allowance is claimed in the final year of operation.

Duo Co uses its after-tax weighted average cost of capital when appraising investment projects. It has a cost of equity of 11% and a before-tax cost of debt of 8.6%. The long-term finance of the company, on a market-value basis, consists of 80% equity and 20% debt.

Required:

(a) Calculate the net present value of buying the new machine and advise on the acceptability of the proposed purchase (work to the nearest $1,000). (13 marks)

(b) Explain the difference between risk and uncertainty in the context of investment appraisal, and describe how sensitivity analysis and probability analysis can be used to incorporate risk into the investment appraisal process. (7 marks)

(Total: 20 marks)

285 OKM CO (JUNE 10 – MODIFIED)

The following draft appraisal of a proposed investment project has been prepared for the finance director of OKM Co by a trainee accountant. The project is consistent with the current business operations of OKM Co.

Year	**1**	**2**	**3**	**4**	**5**
Sales (units/yr)	250,000	400,000	500,000	250,000	
	$000	$000	$000	$000	$000
Contribution	1,330	2,128	2,660	1,330	
Fixed costs	(530)	(562)	(596)	(631)	
Depreciation	(438)	(438)	(437)	(437)	
Interest payments	(200)	(200)	(200)	(200)	
Taxable profit	162	928	1,427	62	
Taxation		(49)	(278)	(428)	(19)
Profit for the year	162	879	1,149	(366)	(19)
Scrap value				250	
After-tax cash flows	162	879	1,149	(116)	(19)
Discount at 10%	0.909	0.826	0.751	0.683	0.621
Present values	147	726	863	(79)	(12)

Net present value = 1,645,000 – 2,000,000 = ($355,000) so reject the project. The following information was included with the draft investment appraisal:

1 The initial investment is $2 million.

2 Selling price: $12/unit (current price terms), selling price inflation is 5% per year.

3 Variable cost: $7/unit (current price terms), variable cost inflation is 4% per year.

4 Fixed overhead costs: $500,000/year (current price terms), fixed cost inflation is 6% per year.

5 $200,000/year of the fixed costs are development costs that have already been incurred and are being recovered by an annual charge to the project.

6 Investment financing is by a $2 million loan at a fixed interest rate of 10% per year.

7 OKM Co can claim 25% reducing balance tax allowable depreciation on this investment and pays taxation one year in arrears at a rate of 30% per year.

8 The scrap value of machinery at the end of the four-year project is $250,000.

9 The real weighted average cost of capital of OKM Co is 7% per year.

10 The general rate of inflation is expected to be 4.7% per year.

Required:

(a) Identify and comment on any errors in the investment appraisal prepared by the trainee accountant. **(5 marks)**

(b) Prepare a revised calculation of the net present value of the proposed investment project and comment on the project's acceptability. **(10 marks)**

(c) Discuss the problems faced when undertaking investment appraisal in the following areas and comment on how these problems can be overcome:

(i) an investment project has several internal rates of return

(ii) the business risk of an investment project is significantly different from the business risk of current operations. **(5 marks)**

(Total: 20 marks)

286 HRAXIN CO (JUN 15 – MODIFIED)

Hraxin Co is appraising an investment project which has an expected life of four years and which will not be repeated. The initial investment, payable at the start of the first year of operation, is $5 million. Scrap value of $500,000 is expected to arise at the end of four years.

There is some uncertainty about what price can be charged for the units produced by the investment project, as this is expected to depend on the future state of the economy. The following forecast of selling prices and their probabilities has been prepared:

Future economic state	**Weak**	**Medium**	**Strong**
Probability of future economic state	35%	50%	15%
Selling price in current price terms	$25 per unit	$30 per unit	$35 per unit

These selling prices are expected to be subject to annual inflation of 4% per year, regardless of which economic state prevails in the future.

Forecast sales and production volumes, and total nominal variable costs, have already been forecast, as follows:

Year	**1**	**2**	**3**	**4**
Sales and production (units)	150,000	250,000	400,000	300,000
Nominal variable cost ($000)	2,385	4,200	7,080	5,730

Incremental overheads of $400,000 per year in current price terms will arise as a result of undertaking the investment project. A large proportion of these overheads relate to energy costs, which are expected to increase sharply in the future because of energy supply shortages, so overhead inflation of 10% per year is expected.

The initial investment will attract tax-allowable depreciation on a straight-line basis over the four-year project life. The rate of corporation tax is 30% and tax liabilities are paid in the year in which they arise. Hraxin Co has traditionally used a nominal after-tax discount rate of 11% per year for investment appraisal.

Required:

(a) Calculate the expected net present value of the investment project and comment on its financial acceptability. **(9 marks)**

(b) Critically discuss if sensitivity analysis will assist Hraxin Co in assessing the risk of the investment project. **(6 marks)**

(c) Describe the process that would be undertaken to decide whether to lease or buy an asset for a long-term investment. **(5 marks)**

(Total: 20 marks)

287 HEBAC CO (SEP 16)

Hebac Co is preparing to launch a new product in a new market which is outside its current business operations. The company has undertaken market research and test marketing at a cost of $500,000, as a result of which it expects the new product to be successful. Hebac Co plans to charge a lower selling price initially and then increase the selling price on the assumption that the new product will establish itself in the new market. Forecast sales volumes, selling prices and variable costs are as follows:

Year	**1**	**2**	**3**	**4**
Sales volume (units/year)	200,000	800,000	900,000	400,000
Selling price ($/unit)	15	18	22	22
Variable costs ($/unit)	9	9	9	9

Selling price and variable cost are given here in current price terms before taking account of forecast selling price inflation of 4% per year and variable cost inflation of 5% per year.

Incremental fixed costs of $500,000 per year in current price terms would arise as a result of producing the new product. Fixed cost inflation of 8% per year is expected.

The initial investment cost of production equipment for the new product will be $2.5 million, payable at the start of the first year of operation. Production will cease at the end of four years because the new product is expected to have become obsolete due to new technology. The production equipment would have a scrap value at the end of four years of $125,000 in future value terms.

Investment in working capital of $1.5 million will be required at the start of the first year of operation. Working capital inflation of 6% per year is expected and working capital will be recovered in full at the end of four years.

Hebac Co pays corporation tax of 20% per year, with the tax liability being settled in the year in which it arises. The company can claim tax-allowable depreciation on a 25% reducing balance basis on the initial investment cost, adjusted in the final year of operation for a balancing allowance or charge. Hebac Co currently has a nominal after-tax weighted average cost of capital (WACC) of 12% and a real after-tax WACC of 8.5%. The company uses its current WACC as the discount rate for all investment projects.

Required:

(a) **Calculate the net present value of the investment project in nominal terms and comment on its financial acceptability.** **(12 marks)**

(b) **Discuss how the capital asset pricing model can assist Hebac Co in making a better investment decision with respect to its new product launch.** **(8 marks)**

(Total: 20 marks)

288 DYSXA CO (DEC 2016)

Dysxa Co is looking to expand the capacity of an existing factory in its Alpha Division by 850,000 units per year in order to meet increased demand for one of its products. The expansion will cost $3.2 million.

The selling price of the unit is $3.10 per unit and variable costs of production are $1.10 per unit, both in current price terms. Selling price inflation of 3% per year and variable cost inflation of 6% per year are expected. Nominal fixed costs of production have been forecast as follows:

Year	**1**	**2**	**3**	**4**
Fixed costs ($)	110,000	205,000	330,000	330,000

Dysxa Co has a nominal after-tax weighted average cost of capital of 10% and pays corporation tax of 20% per year one year in arrears. The company can claim 25% reducing balance tax-allowable depreciation on the full cost of the expansion, which you should assume is paid at the start of the first year of operation.

Dysxa Co evaluates all investment projects as though they have a project life of four years and assumes zero scrap value at the end of four years.

Dysxa Co has limited the capital investment funds in its Delta division to $7 million. The division has identified five possible investment projects, as follows:

Project	Initial investment	Net present value
A	$3,000,000	$6,000,000
B	$2,000,000	$3,200,000
C	$1,000,000	$1,700,000
D	$1,000,000	$2,100,000
E	$2,000,000	$3,600,000

These projects are divisible and cannot be deferred or repeated. Projects C and E are mutually exclusive.

Required:

(a) **Calculate the net present value of the investment project and comment on its financial acceptability.** **(8 marks)**

(b) **Determine the net present value of the optimum investment schedule for Delta division.** **(3 marks)**

(c) **Discuss the reasons why hard and soft capital rationing occur.** **(5 marks)**

(d) **Discuss TWO ways in which the risk of a project can be assessed.** **(4 marks)**

(Total: 20 marks)

289 PELTA CO (SEP/DEC 2017)

The directors of Pelta Co are considering a planned investment project costing $25m, payable at the start of the first year of operation. The following information relates to the investment project:

	Year 1	Year 2	Year 3	Year 4
Sales volumes (units/year)	520,000	624,000	717,000	788,000
Selling price ($/unit)	30.00	30.00	30.00	30.00
Variable costs ($/unit)	10.00	10.20	10.61	10.93
Fixed costs ($/year)	700,000	735,000	779,000	841,000

This information needs adjusting to take account of selling price inflation of 4% per year and variable cost inflation of 3% per year. The fixed costs, which are incremental and related to the investment project, are in nominal terms. The year 4 sales volume is expected to continue for the foreseeable future.

Pelta Co pays corporation tax of 30% one year in arrears. The company can claim tax-allowable depreciation on a 25% reducing balance basis.

The views of the directors of Pelta Co are that all investment projects must be evaluated over four years of operations, with an assumed terminal value at the end of the fourth year of 5% of the initial investment cost. Both net present value and discounted payback must be used, with a maximum discounted payback period of two years. The real after-tax cost of capital of Pelta Co is 7% and its nominal after-tax cost of capital is 12%.

Required:

(a) (i) Calculate the net present value of the planned investment project. **(9 marks)**

(ii) Calculate the discounted payback period of the planned investment project. **(2 marks)**

(b) Discuss the financial acceptability of the investment project. **(3 marks)**

(c) Critically discuss the views of the directors on Pelta Co's investment appraisal. **(6 marks)**

(Total: 20 marks)

290 COPPER CO (MAR/JUN 2018)

Copper Co is concerned about the risk associated with a proposed investment and is looking for ways to incorporate risk into its investment appraisal process. The company has heard that probability analysis may be useful in this respect and so the following information relating to the proposed investment has been prepared:

Year 1		**Year 2**	
Cash flow ($)	**Probability**	**Cash flow** ($)	**Probability**
1,000,000	0.1	2,000,000	0.3
2,000,000	0.5	3,000,000	0.6
3,000,000	0.4	5,000,000	0.1

However, the company is not sure how to interpret the results of an investment appraisal based on probability analysis.

The proposed investment will cost $3.5m, payable in full at the start of the first year of operation. Copper Co uses a discount rate of 12% in investment appraisal.

Required:

(a) Using a joint probability table:

(i) Calculate the mean (expected) NPV of the proposed investment **(8 marks)**

(ii) Calculate the probability of the investment having a negative NPV **(1 mark)**

(iii) Calculate the NPV of the most likely outcome **(1 mark)**

(iv) Comment on the financial acceptability of the proposed investment. **(2 marks)**

(b) Discuss TWO of the following methods of adjusting for risk and uncertainty in investment appraisal:

(i) Simulation

(ii) Adjusted payback

(iii) Risk-adjusted discount rates. **(8 marks)**

(Total: 20 marks)

291 PINKS CO (MAR/JUN 2019)

Pinks Co is a large company listed on a major stock exchange. In recent years, the board of Pinks Co has been criticised for weak corporate governance and two of the company's non-executive directors have just resigned. A recent story in the financial media has criticised the performance of Pinks Co and claims that the company is failing to satisfy the objectives of its key stakeholders.

Pinks Co is appraising an investment project which it hopes will boost its performance. The project will cost $20m, payable in full at the start of the first year of operation. The project life is expected to be four years. Forecast sales volumes, selling price, variable cost and fixed costs are as follows:

Year	**1**	**2**	**3**	**4**
Sales (units/year)	300,000	410,000	525,000	220,000
Selling price ($/unit)	125	130	140	120
Variable cost ($/unit)	71	71	71	71
Fixed costs ($000/year)	3,000	3,100	3,200	3,000

Selling price and cost information are in current price terms, before applying selling price inflation of 5% per year, variable cost inflation of 3.5% per year and fixed cost inflation of 6% per year.

Pinks Co pays corporation tax of 26%, with the tax liability being settled in the year in which it arises. The company can claim tax-allowable depreciation on the full initial investment of $20m on a 25% reducing balance basis. The investment project is expected to have zero residual value at the end of four years.

Pinks Co has a nominal after-tax cost of capital of 12% and a real after-tax cost of capital of 8%. The general rate of inflation is expected to be 3.7% per year for the foreseeable future.

Required:

(a) (i) Calculate the nominal net present value of Pinks Co's investment project. **(8 marks)**

(ii) Calculate the real net present value of Pinks Co's investment project and comment on your findings. **(4 marks)**

(b) Discuss FOUR ways to encourage managers to achieve stakeholder objectives. **(8 marks)**

(Total: 20 marks)

292 DINK CO (SEP/DEC 2019)

Answer debrief

Dink Co is a small company that is finding it difficult to raise funds to acquire a new machine costing $750,000. Dink Co would ideally like a four-year loan for the full purchase price at a before-tax interest rate of 8.6% per year.

The machine would have an expected life of four years. At the end of this period the machine would have a residual value of $50,000. Tax-allowable servicing costs for the machine would be $23,000 per year. Tax-allowable depreciation on the full purchase price would be available on a 25% reducing balance basis.

A leasing company has offered a contract whereby Dink Co could have use of the new machine for four years in exchange for an annual lease rental payment of $200,000, payable at the start of each year. The contract states that the leasing company would undertake maintenance of the machine at no additional cost to Dink Co. At the end of four years the leasing company would remove the machine from the manufacturing facility of Dink Co.

Dink Co pays corporation tax of 30% one year in arrears.

Required:

(a) For the new machine:

(i) Calculate the present value of the cost of borrowing to buy. (6 marks)

(ii) Calculate the present value of the cost of leasing. (3 marks)

(iii) Recommend which option is more attractive in financial terms to Dink Co. (1 mark)

(b) (i) Discuss general reasons why investment capital may be rationed. (6 marks)

(ii) Discuss ways in which the external capital rationing experienced by Dink Co might be overcome. (4 marks)

(Total: 20 marks)

Calculate your allowed time, allocate the time to the separate parts

293 CROCKET CO (SEP/DEC 2020)

Crocket Co is a manufacturing company that has three investment decisions for the coming year.

Investment decision 1

Six investment projects are being considered with the following details:

Project	Initial Outlay	Net Present Value
	$000	$000
A	1,000	390
B	1,500	Not yet known
C	750	325
D	1,125	590
E	1,850	840
F	1,300	635

Project B is expected to generate the following cash flows:

Year	1	2	3	4
	$000	$000	$000	$000
Sales income	725	765	885	612
Costs	145	168	202	94

Project B cash flows are before allowing for inflation of 4% per year for sales income and 5% per year for costs. Crocket Co has a nominal cost of capital of 10%.

Due to management reluctance to raise new finance, capital for investment in the above projects is currently restricted to $5m. Projects A, B, D and F are all independent, but projects C and E are mutually exclusive. All of the above projects are divisible and none can be delayed or repeated.

Investment decision 2

A number of Crocket Co's employees have a company car. The entire company car fleet is now due for renewal and in the past, it has been replaced every four years. Management are not sure if this is the optimum length of time and feel that other fleet replacement cycles, such as every three or five years, should also be considered.

Investment decision 3

The management of Crocket Co are considering the financial viability of another project but as yet, no detailed financial information is available to perform an NPV appraisal. One of the reasons for this is that the various cash flows will be subject to a number of different rates of inflation that are very uncertain at present. For example, the selling price inflation may be no more than 2% per year whereas material cost inflation could be anything from 4% to 6% per year. The general rate of inflation is expected to differ from both of these. Management are not sure whether the appraisal could be performed by simply ignoring the inflation altogether.

Note: The $5m capital constraint outlined with investment decision 1 applies to that investment decision only and not to investment decisions 2 and 3.

Required:

(a) **For investment decision 1:**

(i) **Calculate the net present value of project B; and** **(4 marks)**

(ii) **Given the capital constraint, calculate the optimum investment combination and the resulting net present value.** **(6 marks)**

(b) **For investment decision 2, explain the approach Crocket Co should use to determine the optimum replacement cycle for the company car fleet.** **(4 marks)**

(c) **In relation to investment decision 3, describe the two approaches for dealing with inflation AND provide a reasoned recommendation as to which approach Crocket's management should follow.** **(6 marks)**

(Total: 20 marks)

294 CABRERAS CO (MAR/JUN 2021)

Cabreras Co is a construction company. It uses a large earth moving vehicle called the Beast to prepare foundations for buildings. It needs to decide whether the cheapest replacement interval for the Beast is three or four years.

The following details are available:

Cabreras Co purchases the Beast from a manufacturer for $800,000, payable one year after delivery. Its resale value will fall by 40% of the purchase price at the end of its first year of operation. The resale value will then reduce by 25% of its previous year's resale value for each further year of operation.

Yearly maintenance costs are $20,000 at the end of its first year of operations, rising by 5% per year. Maintenance must be provided in the year of sale. Yearly fuel costs are $28,000 in the first year rising by $5,000 for each extra year it is operated.

If the Beast is operated beyond three years it is subject to a government safety and carbon emissions test. The test would be paid for and would take place at the beginning of the fourth year of operation. Correction of any faults discovered by this test is mandatory. There is an 80% chance that the test and remedial work will cost Cabreras Co $50,000, and a 20% chance it will cost $120,000.

Cabreras Co's cost of capital is 8%.

Ignore taxation.

Required:

(a) **Calculate the equivalent annual cost of the three-year and four-year replacement intervals for the Beast and advise Cabreras Co which replacement interval to adopt.** **(11 marks)**

(b) **Discuss why replacement interval decisions should be based upon equivalent annual cost (EAC).** **(4 marks)**

(c) **Discuss why discounted cash flow methods of investment appraisal are considered superior to non-discounted cash flow methods.** **(5 marks)**

(Total: 20 marks)

295 HAWKER CO (SEP/DEC 2021)

Hawker Co is about to replace its existing delivery vehicle with a new design of vehicle that offers greater fuel economy. It estimates that replacing the existing vehicle will save running costs of $2,000 per year. There are two financing options:

Option 1

The vehicle could be purchased for $34,000 using a bank loan with an after-tax cost of borrowing of 4% per year. The vehicle would have a useful life of four years and would have a residual value of $14,000 at the end of that period. Straight-line tax-allowable depreciation is available on the vehicle. The vehicle would be subject to a government CO2 emissions tax of $600 at the end of each year of operation. Emissions tax expenses are corporation tax deductible.

Option 2

The vehicle could be leased for a period of four years for a payment of $6,000 per year, payable at the start of each year. The lessor will pay the CO2 emissions tax. Lease payments are a corporation tax deductible expense.

Hawker Co's after-tax weighted average cost of capital is 8%. It pays corporation tax at a rate of 20% one year in arrears.

Required:

(a) **Evaluate whether Hawker Co should use leasing or borrowing as a source of finance for the new vehicle.** **(10 marks)**

(b) **Discuss TWO reasons (other than possible after-tax cost advantages) why Hawker Co may choose to lease rather than buy the new delivery vehicle.** **(4 marks)**

(c) **Discuss THREE advantages of using NPV rather than IRR in investment appraisal.** **(6 marks)**

(Total 20 marks)

296 MELPLASH CO (MAR/JUN 2022)

Melplash Co manufactures motorcycles and is considering an investment in a new, high-performance model. The market for high-performance motorcycles is very competitive and Melplash Co's directors want to recover the costs of investment in the model quickly, before it is made obsolete by more advanced models at the end of four years. The directors also wish to show shareholders that the investment will be profitable.

The directors have therefore set a target payback period of two years and a target return on capital employed of 20% for the investment.

The directors have also asked the finance director to provide net present value (NPV) and internal rate of return (IRR) calculations for the investment. They plan to consider the results of these calculations if the investment fulfils the targets for payback and return on capital employed.

Melplash Co has prepared the following forecast of production and sales of the new model:

Year	**1**	**2**	**3**	**4**
Motorcycles	25,000	45,000	40,000	20,000

Melplash Co's finance director has prepared the following information relating to the investment proposal:

Initial investment	\$220m
Residual value at the end of four years	\$30m
Selling price (year 1 price terms)	\$20,000 per motorcycle
Expected selling price inflation	6% per year
Variable costs (year 1 price terms)	\$14,000 per motorcycle
Expected variable cost inflation	6% per year
Incremental fixed costs (year 1 price terms)	\$120m per year
Expected fixed cost inflation	10% per year
Nominal (money) discount rate	14%

Ignore taxation.

Required:

(a) For the proposed investment in the new motorcycle, calculate the following:

- **(i) Net present value** **(5 marks)**
- **(ii) Internal rate of return** **(2 marks)**
- **(iii) Payback period, and** **(1 mark)**
- **(iv) Return on capital employed (accounting rate of return) based on average investment.** **(3 marks)**

(b) Discuss the suitability of the techniques used in (a) for determining whether to undertake an investment and advise whether Melplash Co's proposed investment is financially acceptable. **(9 marks)**

(Total: 20 marks)

297 CLOVER CO (SEP/DEC 2022)

Clover Co must replace a machine which is essential to its production process. The company has identified two machines of identical capacity, but different technology, which would be suitable. Only one machine would be purchased in this mutually exclusive investment decision.

Machine 1

This machine would cost $2,000,000 and would need replacing after three years, when its residual value would be $200,000. Maintenance costs would be $52,000 per year in the first year of operation, increasing by 8% per year in each subsequent year. Annual operating costs, expected to be $300,000 in the first year of operation, would increase by 10% per year in each subsequent year.

Machine 2

This machine would cost $2,500,000 and would need replacing after five years, when its residual value would be $150,000. Maintenance costs are forecast to be $39,000 per year in the first year of operation, increasing by 6% per year in each subsequent year. Annual operating costs, expected to be $248,000 in the first year of operation, would increase by 12% per year in each subsequent year.

Other information

Clover Co believes that whether Machine 1 or Machine 2 is selected, future replacement machines would, in each case, be more advanced versions of the machines, with identical life cycles. Buying Machine 1 would therefore commit the company to a three-year replacement cycle, while buying Machine 2 would commit the company to a five-year replacement cycle.

The residual value of Machine 1 is a buyback price from the machine's seller that would be included in the contract of sale. The residual value of Machine 2 is an estimate made by Clover Co based on existing market information.

The technology used in each machine is expected to continue to develop in the future. While Clover Co thinks it is unlikely that Machine 1 would become obsolescent during its three-year life, the company thinks it is likely that Machine 2 could be affected by obsolescence towards the end of its life.

For both machines, all increases in costs are due to increasing age.

Clover Co uses a discount rate of 13% to appraise investment projects. Ignore taxation.

Required:

(a) (i) Calculate the equivalent annual cost of each machine's replacement cycle. **(10 marks)**

(ii) Discuss which machine should be selected by Clover Co. **(4 marks)**

(b) Discuss why discounted cash flow (DCF) investment appraisal methods are considered to be superior to non-DCF methods. **(6 marks)**

(Total: 20 marks)

298 GINI CO (MAR/JUN 2023)

Gini Co is a listed company that manufactures innovative products for the telecommunications industry. Gini Co has just developed a new product called the LP500, which is expected to have a project life of four years.

Gini Co's management has decided that the sales price for the LP500 will be $90 per unit, as anything higher than this will dramatically reduce the expected annual sales volume which is currently forecast to be 20,000 units per year.

The variable cost of the LP500 includes the cost of a bought-in component, the X22. The price of the X22 has been volatile due to supply problems with the manufacturers and consequently, the variable cost per unit is at present uncertain. The management of Gini Co has made the following estimates of the variable cost per unit, along with its associated probability:

Variable cost per unit	Probability
$	%
40	20
50	40
60	20
70	20

Incremental fixed costs will be $300,000 per year.

All of the above figures are expressed in current price terms. Sales price inflation is expected to be 5% per year. Variable cost per unit inflation and fixed cost inflation are both expected to be 3% per year.

New plant and equipment costing $1.5m will need to be purchased at the start of the first year of operation and is expected to have a residual value of $125,000, in nominal terms, at the end of year four. Gini Co pays corporation tax at a rate of 20% and tax is payable at the end of the year following the year to which it relates. The company can claim tax-allowable depreciation at a rate of 25% per year on a reducing balance basis with a balancing adjustment in the year of disposal.

Additional working capital totalling $100,000 will also be required at the start of the project. Working capital inflation is expected to be 3% per year.

Gini Co's nominal after-tax weighted average cost of capital for projects of this nature is 12%.

Required:

(a) Calculate the expected net present value of the LP500 project and comment on its financial acceptability. **(12 marks)**

(b) (i) Briefly discuss how your decision in part (a) will help Gini Co achieve their primary objective. **(2 marks)**

(ii) Discuss THREE limitations of using probability analysis in deciding whether or not to proceed with the LP500. **(6 marks)**

(Total: 20 marks)

299 PULOROUGH CO (SEP/DEC 2023)

Pulorough Co produces household electrical goods for its home country market and for markets in neighbouring countries. Pulorough Co is planning to make a major investment in new production facilities in order to produce an upgraded model of its cooker. Pulorough Co's finance director has assigned probabilities to a number of possible sales volumes of this new model, based on Pulorough Co's previous experience of launching product upgrades. He has calculated annual expected values for sales for the four-year time period over which the investment will be assessed.

However, after a number of years of strong economic growth, Pulorough Co's home country and its neighbours appear likely to enter a period of recession, meaning that consumers may be less willing to spend money on new kitchen goods.

The initial investment cost will be $39m. The finance director has assumed that there will be zero realisable value at the end of the four years. Working capital can be ignored.

The expected volumes of sales are:

Year	**1**	**2**	**3**	**4**
	60,000	150,000	140,000	80,000

The expected contribution from the upgraded cooker throughout the four years is $200 per cooker. This will not be affected by the rate of inflation.

Incremental fixed costs, excluding depreciation, are expected to be $2.5m in year 1. They will increase by the rate of inflation in each of years 2 to 4, which are predicted to be as follows:

Year	**2**	**3**	**4**
Inflation rate per year	6%	4%	3%

Pulorough Co pays corporation tax of 25% per year one year in arrears. No tax-allowable depreciation is available on the investment expenditure.

Pulorough Co currently uses 11% as the after-tax discount rate to appraise investments like this.

One of the other directors has commented that he thinks the level of contribution that the finance director has assumed is too high. He also wondered that, with the economic uncertainty, the cost of capital should be higher. The finance director has said that he will prepare sensitivity calculations, showing in relative terms the level of change in contribution and discount rate that would produce a nil net present value. He will assume that the contribution will be lower by the same percentage each year.

Another director has stated that she has heard that probability analysis can be helpful in decision-making, and wonders if this will be the same as the sensitivity analysis that the finance director is going to prepare.

Required:

(a) **Discuss the difference between risk and uncertainty in the context of investment decisions.** **(3 marks)**

(b) (i) **Calculate the nominal net present value of the investment project and comment on its financial acceptability** **(5 marks)**

(ii) **Calculate the sensitivity of the project's net present value to a change in the level of contribution per unit; and** **(3 marks)**

(iii) **Calculate the sensitivity of the project's net present value to a change in the discount rate.** **(3 marks)**

(c) **Compare and contrast sensitivity analysis and probability analysis as methods of assisting investment decisions when there is more than one possible outcome.** **(6 marks)**

(Total: 20 marks)

300 ELAAN CO (MAR/JUN 2024)

Elaan Co is a company appraising an investment project to purchase and operate a hotel. The hotel will offer basic accommodation, including its own restaurant, mainly for the business-traveller market. The hotel will be operated for a four-year period and then sold at the end of year four.

A suitable property has been located costing $5.5m but it will require new fittings which are expected to cost an additional $1.5m. It is expected that once the property is purchased, the fittings can be installed quickly so that the new hotel will be ready for business almost immediately after purchase. The hotel will have 50 rooms and be open for 365 days a year.

Forecasting assumptions are as follows:

Year	1	2	3	4
Room occupancy %	50	60	75	90

The daily room rate will be $85 for the first year and then increase by 6% per year afterwards. Restaurant revenue will be equivalent to 35% of the accommodation revenue.

Variable costs are expected to be equivalent to 20% of the total revenue. Incremental fixed costs are expected to be $433,000 for the first year and then increase by 4% per year afterwards.

Elaan Co pays corporation tax at 20% per year and tax is paid in the same year to which it relates. The purchase of the property is not eligible for tax relief, but the fittings will be eligible for tax allowable depreciation at 25% per year on a reducing balance basis.

Working capital equivalent to 5% of the total revenue will be required at the start of each year. Working capital will be released at the end of year four.

The expected sale value of the property at the end of year four is expected to be $7.5m after tax and the fixtures will be sold for an additional $100,000.

The real after-tax cost of capital for the project is 4.8% and the general rate of inflation is expected to be constant at 5% per year.

Elaan Co has never operated a hotel before, which has made the estimation of the above assumptions difficult. Also, inflation has been volatile in the country in which Elaan Co is undertaking the project.

Required:

(a) **Using a nominal-terms approach, calculate the net present value (NPV) of the project and comment on its financial acceptability to Elaan Co.** **(12 marks)**

(b) **Explain how the approach to the NPV appraisal in part (a) would change if a real-terms approach had been used.**

Note: Further calculations are NOT required. **(4 marks)**

(c) **Explain how simulation analysis could be used by Elaan Co in its appraisal of the hotel project AND the expected benefits of using simulation analysis.** **(4 marks)**

(Total: 20 marks)

301 GALLE CO (SEP/DEC 2024)

Galle Co is a company which manufactures car batteries.

Its latest project is a new battery called the G-Power Excel (GPE) which is a variation on an existing battery but uses less harmful materials in its construction. Due to technological advances, the GPE project is expected to have a life of only four years.

Sales for the first year are expected to be 10,000 units, but the remaining three years are more uncertain due to the risk of similar products being launched by competitors. Galle Co expects that sales volume will remain constant at 10,000 units per year for the final three years, but there is a 30% probability that volume could drop to only 5,000 units per year for years two, three and four.

The GPE has a selling price in current-price terms of $70 per unit, but sales price inflation is expected to be 4.5% per year. The variable cost per unit is $45 in current-price terms but variable cost inflation is expected to be 3% per year. Fixed costs will remain constant at $10,000 per year.

Manufacturing equipment costing $500,000 will be purchased at the start of the first year of production. The equipment will qualify for tax-allowable depreciation at 25% on a reducing balance basis and it is anticipated that the equipment will have zero residual value at the end of four years.

Working capital of $80,000 will be required at the start of the first year of production and working capital inflation is expected to be 3% per year. Working capital needs to be in place at the start of the year to which it relates and will be released at the end of the project.

Galle Co pays corporation tax at a rate of 20% and tax is paid at the end of the year to which it relates. Galle Co is profitable and can utilise any unused tax-allowable depreciation.

Galle Co uses a nominal after-tax cost of capital of 13% for appraising projects of this nature.

Required:

(a) **For the GPE project:**

(i) **Calculate the expected net present value; and** **(10 marks)**

(ii) **Comment on its financial acceptability.** **(2 marks)**

(b) **Discuss FOUR techniques for dealing with risk and uncertainty in an investment appraisal.** **(8 marks)**

(Total: 20 marks)

BUSINESS FINANCE AND COST OF CAPITAL – EXAM STYLE QUESTIONS

302 ECHO CO (DEC 07 – MODIFIED) *Walk in the footsteps of a top tutor*

The following financial information relates to Echo Co:

Statement of profit or loss information for the last year

	$m
Operating profit	12
Interest expense	3
Profit before income taxes	9
Income tax expense	3
Profit for the period	6
Dividends	2
Retained profit for the period	4

Statement of financial position information as at the end of the last year

	$m	$m
Ordinary shares, nominal value 50c	5	
Retained earnings	15	
Total equity		20
8% loan notes, redeemable in three years' time		30
Total equity and non-current liabilities		50

Average data on companies similar to Echo Co:

Interest coverage ratio	8 times
Long-term debt/equity (book value basis)	80%

The board of Echo Co is considering several proposals that have been made by its finance director. Each proposal is independent of any other proposal.

Proposal A

The current dividend per share should be increased by 20% in order to make the company more attractive to equity investors.

Proposal B

A bond issue should be made in order to raise $15 million of new debt capital. Although there are no investment opportunities currently available, the cash raised would be invested on a short-term basis until a suitable investment opportunity arose. The loan notes would pay interest at a rate of 10% per year and be redeemable in eight years' time at nominal value.

Proposal C

A 1 for 4 rights issue should be made at a 20% discount to the current share price of $2.30 per share in order to reduce gearing and the financial risk of the company.

Required:

(a) Analyse and discuss Proposal A. **(5 marks)**

(b) Evaluate and discuss Proposal B. **(8 marks)**

(c) Calculate the theoretical ex rights price per share and the amount of finance that would be raised under Proposal C. Evaluate and discuss the proposal to use these funds to reduce gearing and financial risk. **(7 marks)**

(Total: 20 marks)

303 PAVLON

(a) Pavlon Inc. has recently obtained a listing on the Stock Exchange. 90% of the company's shares were previously owned by members of one family but, since the listing, approximately 60% of the issued shares have been owned by other investors.

Pavlon's earnings and dividends for the five years prior to the listing are detailed below:

Year	Shares in issue	Earnings ($)	Dividend per share (cents)
20X6	21,333,333	1,800,000	3.6
20X7	21,333,333	2,400,000	4.8
20X8	26,666,667	3,850,000	6.16
20X9	26,666,667	4,100,000	6.56
20Y0	26,666,667	4,450,000	7.12
20Y1	40,000,000	5,500,000 (estimate)	3.16 (interim) +? (final)

The number of issued ordinary shares was increased by 25% three years ago and by 50% at the time of the listing. The company's authorised capital is currently $25,000,000 in 25¢ ordinary shares, of which 40,000,000 shares have been issued. The market value of the company's equity is $78,000,000.

The board of directors is discussing future dividend policy. An interim dividend of 3.16 cents per share was paid immediately prior to the listing and the finance director has suggested a final dividend of 2.34 cents per share.

The company's declared objective is to maximise shareholder wealth.

Required:

(i) **Calculate the actual/predicted dividend payout ratio for each year and comment upon the nature of the company's dividend policy prior to the listing. Discuss whether such a policy is likely to be suitable for a company listed on the Stock Exchange.** **(5 marks)**

(ii) **Discuss whether the proposed final dividend of 2.34 cents is likely to be an appropriate dividend:**

- **If the majority of shares are owned by wealthy private individuals; and**
- **If the majority of shares are owned by institutional investors such as pension funds.** **(10 marks)**

(b) By the end of 20Y1, the company is forecasting profit for the year (after tax) to grow by 15% per year for the next three years (20Y2–20Y4), and by 8% per year after that. Pavlon's cost of equity capital is estimated to be 12% per year. Dividends may be assumed to grow at the same rate as profits. Assume that the 20Y1 total dividend ended up as 7.12 cents and that all dividends will be paid at the end of the financial year.

Required:

Use the dividend valuation model to give calculations to indicate whether Pavlon's shares are currently under- or over-valued. **(5 marks)**

(Total: 20 marks)

304 GTK INC (JUNE 07 – MODIFIED) *Walk in the footsteps of a top tutor*

The finance director of GTK Inc. is preparing its capital budget for the forthcoming period and is examining a number of capital investment proposals that have been received from its subsidiaries. Details of one of these proposals is as follows:

Proposal 1

Division A has requested that it be allowed to invest $500,000 in solar panels, which would be fitted to the roof of its production facility, in order to reduce its dependency on oil as an energy source.

The solar panels would save energy costs of $700 per day but only on sunny days. The Division has estimated the following probabilities of sunny days in each year.

	Number of sunny days	Probability
Scenario 1	100	0.3
Scenario 2	125	0.6
Scenario 3	150	0.1

Each scenario is expected to persist indefinitely, i.e. if there are 100 sunny days in the first year, there will be 100 sunny days in every subsequent year. Maintenance costs for the solar panels are expected to be $2,000 per month for labour and replacement parts, irrespective of the number of sunny days per year. The solar panels are expected to be used indefinitely.

Other information

GTK Inc. is a profitable, listed company with several million dollars of shareholders' funds, a small overdraft and no long-term debt. For profit calculation purposes, GTK Inc. depreciates assets on a straight-line basis over their useful economic life. The company can claim tax-allowable depreciation on machinery on a 25% reducing balance basis and pays tax on profit at an annual rate of 30% in the year in which the liability arises. GTK Inc. has a before-tax cost of capital of 10% and an after-tax cost of capital of 8%.

Required:

(a) For the proposed investment in solar panels (Proposal 1), calculate:

(i) the net present value for each expected number of sunny days

(ii) the overall expected net present value of the proposal.

Comment on your findings. Ignore taxation in this part of the question.

(10 marks)

(b) Assuming GTK Inc. wishes to raise $1.1 million, discuss how equity finance or traded debt (bonds) might be raised, clearly indicating which source of finance you recommend and the reasons for your recommendation. **(10 marks)**

(Total: 20 marks)

305 THP CO (JUNE 08 – MODIFIED) *Walk in the footsteps of a top tutor*

THP Co is planning to buy CRX Co, a company in the same business sector, and is considering paying cash for the shares of the company. The cash would be raised by THP Co through a 1 for 3 rights issue at a 20% discount to its current share price.

The purchase price of the 1 million issued shares of CRX Co would be equal to the rights issue funds raised, less issue costs of $320,000. Earnings per share of CRX Co at the time of acquisition would be 44.8c per share. As a result of acquiring CRX Co, THP Co expects to gain annual after-tax savings of $96,000.

THP Co maintains a payout ratio of 50% and earnings per share are currently 64c per share. Dividend growth of 5% per year is expected for the foreseeable future and the company has a cost of equity of 12% per year.

Information from THP Co's statement of financial position:

Equity and liabilities	$000
Shares ($1 nominal value)	3,000
Reserves	4,300
	7,300
Non-current liabilities	
8% loan notes	5,000
Current liabilities	2,200
Total equity and liabilities	14,500

Further information:

THP Co

THP Co dividend per share = 32c per share

Share price of THP Co = $4.80

Market capitalisation of THP Co = $14.4m

Price earnings ratio of THP Co = 7.5

Required:

(a) **Assuming the rights issue takes place and ignoring the proposed use of the funds raised, calculate:**

(i) **the rights issue price per share**

(ii) **the cash raised**

(iii) **the theoretical ex rights price per share; and**

(iv) **the market capitalisation of THP Co.** **(5 marks)**

(b) **Using the price/earnings ratio method, calculate the share price and market capitalisation of CRX Co before the acquisition.** **(3 marks)**

(c) **Assuming a semi-strong form efficient capital market, calculate and comment on the post-acquisition market capitalisation of THP Co in the following circumstances:**

(i) **THP Co does not announce the expected annual after-tax savings; and**

(ii) **the expected after-tax savings are made public.** **(5 marks)**

(d) **Discuss the factors that THP Co should consider, in its circumstances, in choosing between equity finance and debt finance as a source of finance from which to make a cash offer for CRX Co.** **(7 marks)**

(Total: 20 marks)

306 GXG CO (JUNE 13 – MODIFIED)

GXG Co is an e-business that designs and sells computer applications (apps) for mobile phones. The company needs to raise $3,200,000 for research and development and is considering two financing options.

Option 1

GXG Co could suspend dividends for two years, and then pay dividends of 25 cents per share from the end of the third year, increasing dividends annually by 4% per year in subsequent years. Dividends in recent years have grown by 3% per year.

Option 2

GXG Co could issue $3,200,000 of bonds paying annual interest of 6%, redeemable after ten years at nominal value.

Recent financial information relating to GXG Co is as follows:

	$000
Operating profit	3,450
Interest expense	200
Profit before income taxes	3,250
Taxation	650
Profit for the year	2,600
Dividends	1,600

	$000
Ordinary shares (nominal value 50 cents)	5,000

Under both options, the funds invested would earn a before-tax return of 18% per year.

The profit tax rate paid by the company is 20% per year.

GXG Co has a cost of equity of 9% per year, which is expected to remain constant.

Required:

(a) Using the dividend valuation model, calculate the value of GXG Co under option 1, and advise whether option 1 will be acceptable to shareholders. (6 marks)

(b) Calculate the effect on earnings per share and interest cover of the proposal to raise finance by issuing new debt (option 2), and comment on your findings. (5 marks)

(c) Discuss the factors to be considered in choosing between traded bonds, new equity issued via a placing and venture capital as sources of finance. (9 marks)

(Total: 20 marks)

307 CARD CO (DEC 13 – MODIFIED)

Card Co has in issue 8 million shares with an ex-dividend market value of $7.16 per share. A dividend of 62 cents per share for 20X3 has just been paid. The pattern of recent dividends is as follows:

Year	**20X0**	**20X1**	**20X2**	**20X3**
Dividends per share (cents)	55.1	57.9	59.1	62.0

Card Co also has in issue 8.5% bonds redeemable in five years' time with a total nominal value of $5 million. The market value of each $100 bond is $103.42. Redemption will be at nominal value.

Card Co is planning to invest a significant amount of money into a joint venture in a new business area. It has identified a proxy company with a similar business risk to the joint venture. The proxy company has an equity beta of 1.038 and is financed 75% by equity and 25% by debt, on a market value basis.

The current risk-free rate of return is 4% and the average equity risk premium is 5%. Card Co pays profit tax at a rate of 30% per year and has an equity beta of 1.6.

Required:

(a) **Calculate the cost of equity of Card Co using the dividend growth model.** **(3 marks)**

(b) **Discuss whether the dividend growth model or the capital asset pricing model should be used to calculate the cost of equity.** **(5 marks)**

(c) **Calculate a project-specific cost of equity for Card Co for the planned joint venture.** **(4 marks)**

(d) **Discuss whether changing the capital structure of a company can lead to a reduction in its cost of capital and hence to an increase in the value of the company.** **(8 marks)**

(Total: 20 marks)

308 TUFA CO (SEP/DEC 2017)

The following statement of financial position information relates to Tufa Co, a company listed on a large stock market, which pays corporation tax at a rate of 30%.

	$m	$m
Equity and liabilities		
Share capital	17	
Retained earnings	15	
Total equity		32
Non-current liabilities		
Long-term borrowings	13	
Current liabilities	21	
Total liabilities		34
Total equity and liabilities		66

The share capital of Tufa Co consists of $12m of ordinary shares and $5m of irredeemable preference shares.

The ordinary shares of Tufa Co have a nominal value of $0.50 per share, an ex-dividend market price of $7.07 per share and a cum dividend market price of $7.52 per share. The dividend for 20X7 will be paid in the near future. Dividends paid in recent years have been as follows:

Year	**20X6**	**20X5**	**20X4**	**20X3**
Dividend ($/share)	0.43	0.41	0.39	0.37

The 5% preference shares of Tufa Co have a nominal value of $0.50 per share and an ex dividend market price of $0.31 per share.

The long-term borrowings of Tufa Co consist of $10m of loan notes and a $3m bank loan. The bank loan has a variable interest rate.

The 7% loan notes have a nominal value of $100 per loan note and a market price of $102.34 per loan note. Annual interest has just been paid and the loan notes are redeemable in four years' time at a 5% premium to nominal value.

Required:

(a) **Calculate the after-tax weighted average cost of capital of Tufa Co on a market value basis.** **(11 marks)**

(b) **Discuss the circumstances under which it is appropriate to use the current WACC of Tufa Co in appraising an investment project.** **(3 marks)**

(c) **Discuss THREE advantages to Tufa Co of using convertible loan notes as a source of long-term finance.** **(6 marks)**

(Total: 20 marks)

309 LAFORGE CO (MAR/JUL 2020)

Answer debrief

LaForge Co is a listed company which designs and manufactures air-conditioning units, which are then sold through third party retailers and distributors. Economic growth in a number of Asian countries has increased the demand for its products and LaForge Co wishes to target these markets in order to generate sales and profit growth.

To target these markets, LaForge Co needs new machinery which will require investment of $25.48m.

Two options for raising the finance are being considered:

1 A rights issue, at a discount of 30% on the current share price of $2.60 per share.

2 An issue of 6% loan notes, redeemable at nominal value of $100, in ten years' time.

LaForge Co's P/E ratio is 11 times and this is expected to remain unchanged, whichever financing option is chosen.

Extracts from LaForge Co's most recent financial statements are as follows:

	$m
Profit from operations	25.50
Profit for the year (after tax)	16.56
Share capital ($0.50 per share nominal)	35.00

Without the new investment, the forecast profit from operations for the coming year is expected to be the same as the previous year's actual result. If the investment is undertaken, the forecast profit from operations for the coming year is expected to increase by $4.5m.

LaForge pays tax at 20%.

Required:

(a) **For the rights issue, calculate the following:**

(i) **The theoretical ex-rights price per share; and** **(3 marks)**

(ii) **The value of a right per existing share.** **(1 mark)**

(b) **Assuming that the investment goes ahead, calculate LaForge Co's forecast earnings per share for the coming year AND the resulting share price, if it finances the investment using each of these alternatives:**

(i) **The rights issue; and** **(2 marks)**

(ii) **The loan notes.** **(3 marks)**

(c) Discuss the ways in which a company can issue new equity shares. **(5 marks)**

At a recent board meeting to discuss the financing options, one of the directors suggested reducing the forthcoming dividend. In the past few years, LaForge Co has consistently paid an annual dividend of $0.08 per share. Its shareholders include both financial institutions and individuals.

(d) Discuss and recommend whether LaForge Co should raise the finance it requires by reducing its annual dividend. **(6 marks)**

(Total: 20 marks)

Calculate your allowed time, allocate the time to the separate parts

310 SPINE CO (SEP/DEC 2020)

Spine Co is looking to spend $15m to expand its existing business. This expansion is expected to increase operating profit by 20%. Recent financial information relating to Spine Co can be summarised as follows:

	$000
Operating profit	13,040
Interest expense	240
Profit before income taxes	**12,800**
Taxation	3,840
Profit for the year (earnings)	**8,960**

Spine Co is not sure whether to finance the expansion with debt or with equity. If debt is chosen, the company will issue $15m of 8% loan notes at their nominal value of $100 per loan note. If equity is chosen, the company will have a 1 for 4 rights issue at a 20% discount to the current market price of $6.25 per share. Spine Co has 12 million shares in issue. The company pays corporation tax at 30%.

Required:

(a) Evaluate whether, on financial grounds, Spine Co should finance the expansion with debt or equity. **(10 marks)**

(b) Explain and discuss the relationship between systematic risk and unsystematic risk. **(5 marks)**

(c) Discuss the assumptions made by the capital asset pricing model. **(5 marks)**

(Total: 20 marks)

311 ZEDDEMORE CO (MAR/JUN 2021)

Zeddemore Co is a listed company in the house construction industry. Over the past five years results have been disappointing and as a result the share price has fallen from a high of $3.50 per share five years ago to only $1.05 per share today. This deterioration in the performance and share price has been accompanied by an increase in financial gearing to a high level.

Zeddemore Co's capital structure is as follows:

	$m
Equity:	
Share capital ($0.50 per share nominal value)	40
Retained earnings	35
Long-term liabilities:	
6.5% irredeemable loan notes ($100 per loan note nominal value)	250
7% bank loan	20

Zeddemore Co's loan notes are quoted at $65 per loan note and both the loan notes and the bank loan are secured. Zeddemore Co's equity beta is 2.3.

New venture

To improve performance, Zeddemore Co is considering the construction of commercial properties such as office blocks and industrial complexes. This is a new activity for Zeddemore Co and it is expected that the risks involved will be different from its current activity. The financial director has proposed that a project-specific discount rate should be used to appraise the new venture, but the commercial director does not believe this is necessary.

Winston Commercial Properties Co (WCP) undertakes commercial construction projects similar to those being considered by Zeddemore Co. WCP has an equity beta of 1.25. WCP has $100m of ordinary shares in issue, currently quoted at $2.60 per $1 nominal value ordinary share. The company also has $110m of loan notes in issue, currently quoted at $96 per $100 nominal value.

Both companies pay tax at 20%, the risk-free rate is 4% and the expected return on the market portfolio is 10%.

Required:

(a) (i) Using the Capital Asset Pricing Model, calculate Zeddemore Co's current cost of equity and a project-specific cost of equity suitable for the new venture. **(6 marks)**

(ii) Referring to your calculations above, comment briefly on the view of the commercial director. **(2 marks)**

(b) Discuss THREE problems Zeddemore Co may be facing as a result of its current high level of gearing. **(6 marks)**

(c) In respect of both equity and debt, discuss the risk-return relationship and how it affects Zeddemore Co's financing costs. **(6 marks)**

(Total: 20 marks)

312 TANZA CO (MAR/JUN 2022)

Tanza Co currently has the following sources of finance at 31 December 20X6. The capital structure and its nominal values have not changed for many years:

	Nominal value
	$m
Ordinary shares	50
6% convertible loan notes	150
4% bank loan	120

The ordinary shares are currently trading at $5.55 per share and have a nominal value of $0.50 per share. An ordinary dividend of $0.85 per share has recently been paid. The directors have indicated that a dividend of $0.90 will be paid on 31 December 20X7. Tanza Co's dividends and share price have grown steadily at 6% per year for several years and are expected to continue to do so.

Each loan note has a nominal value of $100 and is currently trading at $108.51. On 31 December 20X9, the investors holding the convertible loan notes may convert the loan notes into 20 ordinary shares. If they choose not to do so, the loan notes will be redeemed at nominal value on 31 December 20X9.

Tanza Co pays corporation tax at a rate of 15%.

Tanza Co needs to raise a further $200m of long-term finance and the directors have been discussing whether this should be borrowed (debt) or raised by issuing new share capital (equity). The finance is needed quickly for a new project.

During the discussion, Director A proposed the use of debt. She had heard that at high levels of gearing the company can make cost savings which improve the weighted average cost of capital.

Director B has pointed out that Tanza Co's capital gearing is amongst the lowest in the industry. 'Our competitors generally have higher gearing than we do and also have lower weighted average costs of capital (WACCs) than us. Although I do think when gearing gets high the WACC goes up again.'

Required:

(a) **Calculate the after-tax weighted average cost of capital for Tanza Co, at 31 December 20X6, on a market value basis.** **(10 marks)**

(b) (i) **Critically discuss, with reference to the relevant theory, the views of Director A and Director B on raising new finance.** **(6 marks)**

(ii) **Discuss TWO other factors for Tanza Co to consider in making the decision to raise debt finance or equity finance.** **(4 marks)**

(Total: 20 marks)

313 GRAFFHAM CO (MAR/JUN 2023)

Graffham Co's directors are planning to invest in a new project, which requires $18.9m of new finance to be raised. Graffham Co's directors have used a mix of debt and equity finance to finance recent investments, but have become concerned about the level of Graffham Co's gearing compared with the industry average. Therefore, they have decided not to use debt finance to fund the new project.

Graffham Co's finance director has proposed a 2 for 5 rights issue to existing shareholders at a 25% discount to the current share price of $8.40. The nominal value of the ordinary shares is $2.00 per share. However, Graffham Co's chairman has received objections from some small shareholders (shareholders owning less than 5% of issued share capital each) on the grounds that they do not have sufficient cash available to pay for the new shares.

Graffham Co's large shareholders (shareholders owning more than 10% of issued share capital each and 50% in total of issued share capital) will be happy to subscribe for a rights issue. However, they want the new project to earn at least the same operating profit margin in % terms as Graffham Co's current business does.

Operating profit margin is measured as ((operating profit /Revenue) × 100%).

Financial statement information prior to raising new finance:

	$000
Revenue	45,200
Operating profit	9,500
Ordinary shares	15,000
Retained earnings	27,875
Non-current liabilities: 8% loan notes	25,000
Total equity and liabilities	**67,875**

Corporation tax is payable at a rate of 16% per year. The nominal value of Graffham Co's loan notes is $100 per loan note and the market value is $110 per loan note. Graffham Co's price-earnings ratio can be assumed to be unchanged by undertaking the project.

The current industry average gearing figure at market values, measured as ((Non-current liabilities/(Non-current liabilities + Equity)) × 100%) is 25%.

The new project is expected to earn $20m revenue each year and have an operating profit margin of 18%. If the project is successful, there are expected to be opportunities to invest in further projects, offering higher operating profit margins.

Required:

(a) (i) **Calculate the theoretical ex rights price per share.** **(2 marks)**

(ii) **Calculate the current earnings per share before investment in the project.** **(2 marks)**

(iii) **Calculate the revised earnings per share and the share price after investment in the project, assuming the rights issue is successful.** **(3 marks)**

(iv) **Calculate the current gearing and the revised gearing after investment in the project, using market values and assuming the rights issue is successful.** **(2 marks)**

(v) **Discuss the views of the directors, and both the small and large shareholders, in relation to the new project and its financing.** **(5 marks)**

One of Graffham Co's non-executive directors has suggested using Islamic finance, either a mudaraba contract or a musharaka contract, as an alternative to the rights issue.

(b) **Discuss the use of a mudaraba or musharaka contract as possible alternative sources of finance for the project.** **(6 marks)**

(Total: 20 marks)

314 MARBLE CO (SEP/DEC 2023)

Marble Co wishes to calculate its current weighted average cost of capital, as part of a review of the company's performance in delivering shareholder value. Dividends per share paid to ordinary shareholders in recent years are as follows:

Year	**20X7**	**20X6**	**20X5**	**20X4**
Dividend ($/share)	0.80	0.78	0.73	0.69

The dividend for 20X8 of $0.84 per share is due to be paid shortly. Marble Co has, in issue, 226 million ordinary shares with a nominal value of $0.50 per share and a current cum dividend share price of $11.93 per share.

Marble Co also has, in issue, 20 million preference shares with a nominal value of $1.00 per share and a current ex dividend market price of $2.27 per share. A 25% per share preference dividend has just been paid.

Marble Co is partly financed by 6.5% convertible loan notes with a total nominal value of $94m. Interest on the loan notes has just been paid and the loan notes have an ex interest market value of $107.11 per $100 nominal value loan note. At the end of five years, the loan notes will either be redeemed at nominal value or converted into eight ordinary shares of Marble Co, per loan note. Future share price growth is expected to be 6% per year. The loan notes are secured on the non-current assets of Marble Co.

Marble Co pays corporation tax of 26%.

Required:

(a) **Using market values, calculate the after-tax weighted average cost of capital of Marble Co.** **(11 marks)**

(b) **Discuss the relative merits of the capital asset pricing model and the dividend growth model in calculating the cost of equity.** **(4 marks)**

(c) **Explain the connection between the creditor hierarchy and the relative costs of sources of finance.** **(5 marks)**

(Total: 20 marks)

315 GAMGEE CO (MAR/JUN 2024)

Gamgee Co is a large, listed company which has a diverse range of operations. Current information about Gamgee Co is as follows:

Current year operating profit (forecast)	\$177m
Debt (6% bank loan)	\$450m
Equity – number of issued shares (millions)	800
Corporation tax rate	20%
Current earnings per share (EPS)	\$0.15
Interest cover	6.6 times
P/E ratio	8
Total gearing (measured as debt/(debt + equity) using market values)	32.3%

Growth in profits has declined in recent years and Gamgee Co's large, institutional shareholders are insisting that the board of directors undertake an expansion plan.

Expansion plan

The board of directors has developed a plan which involves a project requiring a \$360m initial investment, earning an annual operating profit of \$64.8m.

Expansion finance

Gamgee Co does not have sufficient cash reserves to finance the project, therefore two financing options are under consideration:

Option 1: An issue of 5% loan notes for ten years, expected to trade at nominal value.

Option 2: A rights issue of equity at a 25% discount to the current share price.

Whichever finance option is chosen, the following are to be assumed:

– The finance will be raised and the investment undertaken in time for the project to be operational for the start of next year

– The P/E ratio will remain unchanged.

Required:

To aid its decision regarding which finance option to select, the board of directors wishes to see the impact of each financing option on the following three ratios for next year:

1 **Interest cover**

2 **EPS**

3 **Total gearing (debt/debt + equity using market values)**

(a) (i) Calculate the above three ratios for next year, assuming the project is financed by the loan note issue (option 1). **(4 marks)**

(ii) Calculate the above three ratios for next year, assuming the project is financed by the rights issue of equity (option 2). **(4 marks)**

(iii) Using the calculations from (i) and (ii), briefly comment on the results and recommend which source of finance Gamgee Co's board of directors should choose. **(3 marks)**

(b) Discuss the problems associated with high levels of financial gearing. **(5 marks)**

In a recent board meeting, the use of Islamic finance was mentioned as being another possible finance source, as the nature of the project and all of Gamgee Co's activities are eligible under Islamic finance principles. The board wishes to consider the use of Islamic finance, but a condition the board has agreed is that any Islamic finance arrangement should be similar to traditional debt with no profit sharing or management involvement from the investor/Islamic bank.

(c) Discuss TWO sources of Islamic finance that could satisfy Gamgee Co's needs for the project, taking into account the board's condition. **(4 marks)**

(Total: 20 marks)

Section 4

ANSWERS TO OBJECTIVE TEST QUESTIONS – SECTION A

FINANCIAL MANAGEMENT FUNCTION

1 C

The others are secondary objectives that could be used to help achieve the primary objective.

2 Statements 2, 3 and 5 are financial objectives

Achieving market share (a relative measure), or customer satisfaction (a qualitative measure), are non-financial objectives.

3 B, C and D

Financial management aims to ensure that the money is available to finance profitable projects and to select those projects that the company should undertake. Once profits have been made the decision then needs to be made about how much to distribute to the owners and how much to re-invest for the future. Income decisions are really sub-divisions of the investment decision. Appraisal decisions would be sub-divisions of the investment decision and budget decisions would be performed by management accountants.

4 C and E

C – ROCE is a financial objective. E – this is a financial objective that relates to the level of financial risk that the company is prepared to accept. The other objectives are non-financial.

5 C

Value for money relates to economy (value for money on inputs to the organisation), efficiency (vfm on converting inputs to outputs) and effectiveness (vfm on the outputs). Economy relates to keeping costs down without sacrificing quality, efficiency is about effective resource utilisation (such as decreasing waste levels) and effectiveness relates to the overall objectives of the organisation being achieved.

6 D

The management accountant would produce variance reports comparing actual to budget. All the others are common in the role of a financial manager. A relates to the dividend decisions and B and C relate to the financing decision.

7 True, True, True

8 A

A review of overtime spending and apportioning overheads to cost units is typically carried out by a member of the management accounting team. Depreciation of non-current assets is typically carried out by a member of the financial accounting team.

9 A and D

B, C and E are examples of connected stakeholders.

10 C

To facilitate effective management of organisations and to make organisations more visibly accountable to a wider range of stakeholders.

11 C

The separation of ownership and control creates a situation where managers act as the agents of the owners (shareholders).

12 Statements 2 and 3 are correct

The three E's in statement 4 should be economy, efficiency and effectiveness. Maximising market share may lead to financial gains, but is not directly a financial objective. It could, for example, be achieved by cutting prices and accepting lower profits.

13 A and C

Efficiency targets aim to make the most efficient use of the resources available. Paying rates for staff of appropriate levels of qualification is an 'economy' target (B). Customer satisfaction rating is an 'effectiveness' target (D).

14 A, B and D

Managerial reward schemes should be clearly defined and impossible to manipulate. Their targets should align with the aims of shareholders so should be focused on both long- and short-term goals.

15 Is a criticism, Is a criticism, Is a criticism

All three statements are typical criticisms of executive share option schemes.

16 B

Invoices are received from suppliers, not any of the other three stakeholders.

17 A

The Code clearly states that the requirement is for independent non-executive directors, but only one member of the committee (as a minimum) needs have recent and relevant financial experience, not all of them.

18 C

Advising on investments in non-current assets is a key role of financial management. Annual accounts are generally produced by financial accountants and management accounts by management accountants. The decision on pay rates varies from business to business but would normally include line managers and HR.

19 False, True, False, True

It is correct that the agency problem means that shareholder wealth is not being maximised and that cum dividend means the buyer of the share is entitled to receive the dividend shortly to be paid. Value for money means economy, efficiency and effectiveness. The dividend payout ratio compares the dividend to the profit before the dividend.

20 A and B

The sources of shareholder wealth are share prices and dividend payments, so increasing both of these would be associated with the objective of shareholder wealth maximisation.

Increasing profit and EPS are not directly correlated with shareholder wealth maximisation, although they can be used as secondary goals to help drive share prices up and generate cash for dividend payments. Reducing the WACC rather than increasing it would increase business value and therefore shareholder wealth.

21 B

Cost per journey to hospital is a measure of efficiency.

Percentage of members who re-use the service is a measure of effectiveness.

A comparison of actual operating expenses against the budget is an economy measure.

Number of communities served is an effectiveness measure.

22 B

Economy is the acquisition of resources of appropriate quantity and quality at minimum cost. Total medical staff salary cost is the only answer option that does this. Option C was incorrectly selected by a number of candidates, but this is a measure of efficiency (how well inputs are converted into outputs) as this looks at how well inputs are converted into outputs. Options A and D relate to effectiveness (whether outputs are achieved that match the predetermined objectives).

23 B and E

Effectiveness measures an organisation's success in meeting its objectives. The number of beaches awarded the government's clean beach kite mark and the amount of waste cleared each year are the only answer options that measure this. Answers A, C and D are measures of efficiency, which looks at how well inputs (hours used, money spent) are converted into outputs.

FINANCIAL MANAGEMENT ENVIRONMENT

24 B

Fiscal policy is implemented through the raising and lowering of taxes and through the raising and lowering of government spending. 1 only is not correct because there is another aspect to fiscal policy other than just taxation. 2 and 3 is not correct because government actions to raise or lower the size of the money supply is an aspect of monetary policy, not fiscal policy. 1, 2, and 3 is not correct because government actions to raise or lower the size of the money supply is an aspect of monetary policy, not fiscal policy.

25 Statements 1 and 3 are correct

A reverse yield gap is where the yield on debt is greater than that of equities. Statement 4 describes cost-push inflation.

26 Both statements are true

The 'coupon' is the defined rate of interest on the security. Examples of securities in the discount market are deep discounted bonds.

27 C

Governments may choose to run a surplus or a deficit as appropriate to meet their principal objectives.

28 B and D

Statements A, C and E relate to monetary policy.

29 A, B and C

Money markets provide short-term (< 1 year) debt financing and investment. Shares are long-term sources of finance.

30 C

Money markets focus on short term financial instruments. A corporate bond is a long-term source of finance, hence is a capital market instrument.

31 A, B and D

Short-term management of resources could relate to pooling of cash across a group to avoid any one division incurring an overdraft. Maximisation of shareholder wealth will always be a primary goal for managers in any part of the business. The treasury department may engage in, for example, hedging, to manage risk.

32 A

Primary capital markets relate to the sale of new securities, while secondary capital markets are where securities trade after their initial offering.

33 D

Monetary policy that increases the level of domestic interest rates is likely to raise exchange rates as capital is attracted into the country (statement 1). Any restrictions on the stock of money, or restrictions on credit, will raise the cost of borrowing, making fewer investment projects worthwhile and discouraging expansion by companies (statement 2). Periods of credit control and high interest rates reduce consumer demand (statement 3). Monetary policy is often used to control inflation (statement 4).

34 D

Imperfect competition can be addressed by a competition regulator to prevent consumers being taken advantage of, for instance by a firm with monopoly power or by the collusion of suppliers (a cartel) to prevent competitive pricing. Social costs or externalities such as pollution can be regulated against by imposing fines on firms that create them, for instance where a factory emits too many greenhouse gases.

35 B and C

It is the secondary market, not the primary market, that deals in 'second-hand' securities. Money markets provide short-term rather than long-term debt finance and investment.

36 Both statements are true

37 C

The audit committee should consist of non-executive directors.

38 C

A balanced budget occurs when total expenditure is matched by total taxation. The definitions for direct and indirect taxes have been reversed in A and B. A deficit budget occurs when the government is spending more than it is earning (government expenditure > taxation income).

39 Both statements are true

40 A, C and D

Certificates of deposits are fully negotiable and hence attractive to the depositor since they ensure instant liquidity if required and are tradeable.

41 C

A stock market listing is likely to involve a significant loss of control to a wider circle of investors.

42 C

One of the principal objectives of macroeconomic policy will typically be to achieve balance of payments (imports versus exports) equilibrium, not a deficit.

43 A, B and C

Local operating units (decentralised treasury function) should have a better feel for local conditions than head office and can respond more quickly to local developments. This is an advantage of decentralisation rather than centralisation. Divisional managers would be more motivated if they had more control over their cash resources.

44 B

A funding gap often arises when SMEs want to expand beyond their available funds but are not yet ready for a listing on the stock market.

45 Money market, stock market, money market, money market

Convertible loan notes are long-term finance and are traded on a stock market. The others are short-term and traded on a money market.

46 C

Decreasing taxation and increasing government expenditure would lead to increased aggregate demand. Decreasing interest rates reduces the incentive to save and so would lead to an increase in aggregate demand.

47 C and D

Financial intermediaries transform maturity and risk.

48 False, True, False, False

It is true that a government may intervene to weaken its country's exchange rate in order to eliminate a balance of payments deficit. A weak currency makes imports expensive and exports appear cheaper to foreign buyers. Reducing imports and stimulating exports would reduce a balance of payments deficit.

The other statements are false. A business would be a monopoly if it dominated the market it operated in, but this is not defined by a specific percentage market share. High inflation makes local product more expensive and less attractive to foreign buyers. This will weaken the home currency. Fiscal policy involves the levels of government spending and taxation. Management of interest rates is part of monetary policy.

49 A

Statement 1 only is correct.

Discounted instruments are originally sold for a price below their face value and do not pay interest.

Commercial paper is an unsecured money market instrument.

Remember, money markets deal in short-term instruments. Examples of discounted instruments are treasury bills, commercial bills, commercial papers and bankers acceptances. The difference between the issue price and redemption price implies an implicit interest rate, but no interest is paid.

50 3.9%

The calculation is as follows

Increase in value = \$9.65m – \$9.6m = \$0.05m

As a percentage of the original value = \$0.05m/\$9.6m = 0.52%

However, this gain has been achieved over a period of 50 days and we have been asked for the annual rate, so it needs to be annualised. We can calculate the annualised rate as:

$(1 + \text{interest rate expressed as a decimal})^{(365/\text{number of days over which interest is earned})} - 1$

Giving: $(1.0052)^{(365/50)} - 1 = 0.03865$ or 3.9% as a percentage to the nearest 0.1%

Note: previously, a calculation of 0.52% × 365/50 = 3.796% would have been allowed, but it has been clarified by ACCA that this approach should not be taken in the FM exam.

51 A

Statement 1 only is correct.

Disintermediation allows investors to conduct transactions directly, but they will do so without the professional expertise and advice of an intermediary, increasing the risk the investors face. There is no requirement to use cryptocurrencies for transactions where an intermediary is not used.

52 C

Both statements are correct.

STOs are tied to assets of real monetary value, such as shares, bonds and tangible assets. STO transactions are recorded on a blockchain ledger, making them secure.

53 A

A commercial paper will be issued at the issue price and redeemed at nominal value. This paper must earn a return of 4% on an annual basis, but is only being issued for a 90 day period. We need to calculate the 90 day return that it must earn, using the formula:

$(1+\text{annual rate in decimal form})^{\text{number of years in 90 days}} - 1$

The number of years in 90 days is 90/360, as we are working with a 360 day year. This calculates as 0.25, so the 90 day return calculates to:

$1.04^{0.25} - 1 = 0.0098534$

The issue price plus the return needs to add up to the nominal value of \$100,000.

Issue price × (1 + 0.0098534) = \$100,000

Issue price = \$100,000/1.0098534 = \$99,024

Note that you do not come to the same answer if you deduct the pro-rated 4% return from \$100,000. This is because a return on investment is based on what was paid for the investment (the issue price), not on its final value (the nominal value).

Also, be aware that if you round the return figure too much, your answer won't be exactly \$99,024. For instance, rounding it to 0.0099 would lead to a final value of \$99,020, which is still closest to answer A, but not exact. You may choose not to round it at all, perhaps by using your calculator's memory function.

54 A, B, C and F

A, B, C and F are all main macroeconomic policy objectives. A relates to price stability – low inflation. B relates to economic growth. C relates to maintaining a balance of payments equilibrium. F relates to full employment of resources.

Maintaining interest rates at minimum levels is instead a monetary policy objective and balancing government spending is a fiscal policy objective. Monetary and fiscal policies will be differently used by different governments in order to achieve the main objectives.

55

Amby Co needs to convert foreign currency into domestic currency	**Foreign exchange market**	
Benji Co needs to issue new ordinary shares	**Primary capital market**	
Carlo Co needs to purchase short-term over-the-counter derivatives	**Primary money market**	
Dill Co needs to issue new long-term loan notes	**Capital market**	

Foreign currency is sold on the **foreign exchange market** (euro currency market is a loan/deposit market for raising or investing short-term finance in a currency other than the home currency).

New shares are sold on the **primary capital market**. New shares and loan notes are issued on the primary market. If those shares and loan notes are subsequently sold between investors, this represents the use of the same market but as a secondary market.

Over-the counter derivatives are purchased on the **primary market**. As these are tailor made products, they do not have a secondary market for subsequent trading.

Long-term loan notes are sold on the **capital market**. The capital market is for long-term products, such as shares and loan notes. The money markets are for products that, generally, last for less than 1 year.

56 C

An interest rate decrease will result in lower shareholder required returns and a reduction in the cost of capital, which, in turn, will increase the investment's net present value. A reduction in interest rates is normally associated with an increase in spending and, assuming all other variables remain constant, this will increase the demand for the company's products.

WORKING CAPITAL MANAGEMENT

57 A

B and D are solutions for long-term cash surpluses. When the cash is needed again in the short-term, it would not be available if either of these options had been used. C would assist with a short-term shortage of cash, not a surplus.

58 All three statements are correct

Working capital will naturally increase with sales as more inventory is needed to satisfy demand and more credit is offered to more customers. Payables will also increase, reducing working capital but to a lower degree.

Lengthening of the operating cash cycle will lead to cash being out of the business for longer and more funding therefore needed to cover this.

Overtrading (undercapitalisation) is where the business doesn't have enough cash funding to sustain the level of trading activity.

59 D

Taking longer to pay trade payables would shorten the cash cycle as cash stays with company possession for a longer period of time. Lower net operating cash flows and slower inventory turnovers are signs of a lengthening cash cycle. Depreciation expenditure is a non-cash item and does not affect the cash cycle.

60 17 weeks

Add the asset periods and deduct the liability period

	Weeks
Raw materials	6
Payables	(7)
Production	2
Finished goods	6
Receivables	10
	17

61 Current ratio: decrease Quick ratio: increase

The current liabilities figures used as the denominator will stay the same in both cases. The total of the current assets will decrease because the reduction in the inventory value (cost value) will be greater than the increase in cash (sales value). Therefore, the numerator will decrease and the current ratio will decrease. The total of the liquid assets (current assets excluding inventory) used in the numerator of the quick ratio will increase because of the higher cash balance. Therefore, the quick ratio will increase.

62 C

As there is no new capital and all profits are paid out as dividends (so no retained earnings), the total of the SFP of 1,250 will not change. The cash balance is therefore a balancing figure to maintain this total after the other changes have been put through. As the non-current assets are land, they are not depreciated so their value stays the same.

	$000	$000		$000	$000
			Next year		
Non-current assets (no change)		1,000	→		1,000
Current assets					
Inventories (double)	200			400	
Receivables (double)	150			300	
Cash (balancing figure)	100			Nil	
	450			700	
Current liabilities					
Overdraft (balancing figure)				(50)	
Payables (double)		(200)		(400)	
Net current assets		250			250
		1,250			1,250
Capital		1,250			1,250

63 80

The cash operating cycle = receivables collection period + inventory holding period – payables payment period.

The receivables collection period = 365/average receivables turnover or 365/10.5 = 34.76. The inventory holding period = 365/inventory turnover or 365/4 = 91.25. The payables payment period = 365/payables turnover ratio = 365/8 = 45.63.

Putting it all together: cash operating cycle = 34.76 + 91.25 – 45.63 = 80.38 days or 80 to the nearest day.

64 A

Receivables collection period plus inventory holding period minus payables payment period.

65 B

Net investment in working capital = what working capital net balances will there be.

Inventory = 15,000,000 × 60/360 = $2,500,000

Trade receivables = 27,000,000 × 50/360 = $3,750,000

Trade payables = 15,000,000 × 45/360 = $1,875,000

Net investment required = 2,500,000 + 3,750,000 – 1,875,000 = $4,375,000

66 D

	October	November	December
	$	$	$
Total receipts	30,000	15,500	20,500
Total payments	(20,600)	(8,250)	(12,700)
Net cash flow	9,400	7,250	7,800
Balance b/f	500	9,900	17,150
Balance c/f	9,900	17,150	24,950

'Credit sales' under 'Receipts' implies receipts from credit customers.

67 A and C

Checking credit limits once a year is too specific and may not be appropriate, for example, if a customer is known to be struggling. Delaying payments to obtain a 'free' source of finance would be a key aspect of a company's accounts payable policy, not accounts receivable.

68 A, B and F

Bad debt write offs, changes in provisions and losses on disposal are non-cash items.

69 A

While overtrading can result in higher inventory and receivables (and payables), resulting in the current ratio increasing in the short term, over the longer term the inevitable drain on cash will result in falling liquidity ratios.

70 A

Customer bargaining power increasing is associated with an increased receivables collection period, not payables payment period.

71 A and C

The system aims to create a flexible production process that is responsive to the customer's requirements, not an inflexible process (B). With a Just in Time system, although inventory holding costs are close to zero, inventory ordering costs are high, not low as more frequent small deliveries of supplies will be needed (D).

72 B and C

Transactions motive is to have enough cash to pay for day-to-day transactions. Precautionary motive is to hold cash to pay for unexpected items, e.g. machine breakdown.

73 D

Working capital management may have an impact on dividend policy, but the other areas will be more significant.

74 10

As there is a minimum of 90 days' worth of inventory held, this element is classed as a permanent asset and would be financed with equity. Only the fluctuating element of the inventory balance will need to be financed with the overdraft, i.e. the difference between 120 days' worth and 90 days' worth of inventory – 30 days' worth.

Annual cost of inventory = $200m × 60% = $120m (at a 40% profit margin)

$120m × 30/360 = $10m

75 D

Obsolete inventory is minimised under just-in-time (JIT) inventory management. Quality control becomes more important under JIT as breakdowns/faulty goods become very costly when there is no buffer inventory. Finance costs of holding inventory will be minimised, not held constant. Raw materials will need to be delivered more frequently (in smaller loads to avoid holding large amounts of raw material inventory).

76 A

A commercial paper will be issued at a discount (money received by the company) and then repaid at nominal value on the settlement date. It is short term and traded on the money market. Interest rate futures would be used to hedge interest rate risk. Corporate loan notes are for long-term funding needs. Treasury bills are issued by the government, not by companies. Companies could decide to buy treasury bills if they have short-term cash surpluses.

77 A

For every day reduction, 1/365th less working capital will be needed. Receivables will reduce by 8 days, inventory by 10 days and payables by 5 days.

Reduced receivables = 8/365 × $20,500,000 = $449,300

Reduced inventory = 10/365 × $12,800,000 = $350,685

Reduced payables = 5/365 × $12,800,000 = $175,342

Total net working capital effect = –$449,300 – $350,685 + $175,342 = –$624,643 decrease.

Remember, the payables balance offsets the others as it is a liability.

78 D

If the discount is accepted, the company must pay $2,462.50 at the end of one month.

Alternatively, the company can effectively borrow the $2,462.50 for an additional two months at a cost of $37.50.

The two-month rate of interest is therefore $37.50/$2,462.5 × 100 = 1.5228%

The annual equivalent rate (AER) is therefore:

$(1 + 0.015228)^6 - 1 = 0.0949$ or 9.49%

Alternatively use the formula:

$(1 + \text{discount/amount left to pay})^{12/\text{months saved}} - 1$

$= (1 + (1.5/98.5))^{12/2} - 1 = 0.0949$ or 9.49%

79 1,140

The buffer inventory is not needed for the EOQ calculation (it would be included as part of the calculation for total inventory costs).

EOQ = √(2 × Co × D/Ch)

Co = $65, D = 300,000, Ch = $2.50 × 12 = $30 (the period of demand and of the holding costs must match, here both calculated as annual figures).

EOQ = √(2 × $65 × 300,000/$30) = 1,140 units

80 A and D

Statement A is true. The Baumol model assumes cash flows are steady and predictable. If cash flows are more erratic, then the Miller Orr model is better suited as a model. Statement B is false – they both assume that cash is held in either a current account or short-term investments and can easily be switched between the two. Statement C is false. It is the lower limit that is set by management. Statement D is true. Statement E is false. The current account balance is only taken back to the return point when either the higher or lower limit is hit. If these limits are not reached, no attempt will be made to adjust the balance.

81 $28,000

Spread = 3 × [3/4 × transaction cost × variance of cash flows/interest rate]$^{1/3}$

Transaction cost = $25

Variance = standard deviation squared = $3,000^2 = $9,000,000 per day

Interest (over a timescale that matches the variance, i.e. days) = 7.3/365 = 0.02% per day

Spread = 3 × [3/4 × $25 × $9,000,000/0.0002]$^{1/3}$ = $28,348 or $28,000 to the nearest $000

Note that to convert 0.02% to a decimal for use in the formula, an extra 2 zeros are needed after the decimal point.

82 $4,000,000

Receivables balance calculation = accounts receivable collection period × sales/360

Customers who don't take the discount (40%) and remain paying in 75 days

Receivables = 75 × $30m × 40%/360 = $2,500,000

Customers who take the discount (60%) and pay in 30 days but hold back 1% as discount

Receivables = 30 × $30m × 60% × 99%/360 = $1,485,000

Total new receivables balance = $2,500,000 + $1,485,000 = $3,985,000

If discount is ignored in calculation for those who take the discount:

Receivables = 30 × $30m × 60%/360 = $1,500,000

Total new receivables balance = $2,500,000 + $1,500,000 = $4,000,000

Under either calculation, balance to the closest hundred thousand is $4,000,000

83 D

A conservative working capital policy refers to a higher amount invested in working capital. It does not relate to the proportions of permanent to fluctuating current assets so statement 1 is incorrect.

Confusion may arise between the working capital investment policy and the working capital funding policy, which relates to the amount of long-term versus short-term finance used and is influenced by the levels of permanent and fluctuating current assets.

Long-term finance is not generally less expensive than short-term finance; it is more expensive as it is riskier for the lender (who demands a higher return for riskier investments), so statement 2 is also incorrect.

84 C

With an aggressive working capital funding policy, most current assets are financed with short-term funding rather than long-term funding, despite the higher risk involved. It is an aggressive policy because it aims to keep funding costs low (using short-term finance is generally cheaper than long-term), despite exposing the business to higher risk (short-term finance may be subject to renewal issues and changing costs).

85 Acacia = Aggressive, Birch = Matching

Acacia has $4m of long-term working capital finance, but permanent working capital of $6m. Therefore, it is using short-term finance for both fluctuating and some of its permanent working capital. This means its working capital funding strategy is aggressive.

Birch has $9m of long-term working capital finance and permanent working capital of $9m too. This means it is using short-term finance for fluctuating working capital and long-term finance for permanent working capital. Therefore, this is a matching strategy.

Neither company is using long-term finance for any of its fluctuating working capital, which would be a conservative approach.

86 B

An aggressive working capital funding policy refers to an organisation using short-term funding to finance most current assets, including those that permanently exist, such as buffer inventory. The policy of having low values of current assets and high values of current liabilities relates to an aggressive working capital investment policy, not a funding policy. Therefore, statement 1 is false.

Lenders who lend for longer face higher risk levels as their money is exposed to the fortunes of the company it is lent to for longer. Statement 2 is therefore true.

87 $30,200

Co = cost per order = $200

Ch = annual holding cost per unit = $0.50

D = annual demand = 600,000

Q = order quantity = 100,000

Annual ordering cost = Co × D/Q = $200 × (600,000/100,000) = $1,200 per year

Annual holding cost = Ch × (Q/2 + buffer inventory)

Buffer inventory will be the inventory till in the warehouse when the next order comes in. From the question info, there are 20,000 units remaining when the order is placed. It takes one week for the order to be received. If 600,000 units are used in 50 weeks, then (600,000/50) 12,000 units are used in one week.

Therefore, the buffer inventory will be 20,000 – 12,000 = 8,000 units

Holding cost = (100,000/2 + 8,000) × $0.50 = $29,000

Total costs of this inventory ordering policy = $1,200 + $29,000 = $30,200 per year.

88 $10.8M

Working capital = cash + receivables + inventory – payables

Accounts receivable collection period in months = receivables/credit sales × 12 (when working in months)

Therefore, receivables = accounts receivable collection months/12 × credit sales

Annual credit sales = $2m × 12 × 80% = $19.2m

Receivables = 3/12 × $19.2m = $4.8m

Cash is not mentioned, so ignore in the working capital calculation.

Working capital requirement = $4.8m + $10m – $4m = $10.8m.

89 The correct answers are:

Characteristic	Working capital strategy
Relatively high level of current assets	Conservative investment strategy
Relatively low level of current assets	Aggressive investment strategy
Relatively large amounts of short-term finance	Aggressive financing strategy
Relatively small amounts of short-term finance	Conservative financing strategy

A conservative investment policy involves carrying higher amounts of current assets. A conservative financing policy involves using more long-term finance than short-term finance.

Conservative strategies are lower risk strategies. Holding high levels of current assets is less risky than holding low levels as there is a lower chance of running out of inventory or of upsetting customers by chasing too quickly for receivables to be paid.

Using low levels of short-term finance implies that larger levels of long-term finance have been used. Long-term finance is less risky than short-term finance as it cannot be taken away at short notice.

90 A

Taking the discount will reduce the amount paid to the supplier and will benefit the company.

However, in paying the supplier earlier, the company will need to use its overdraft to replace the free funding that the supplier balance represented. This will cost the company 7% per annum.

To make a valid comparison, we must compare the **annual** benefit of the discount to this **annual** overdraft cost.

Annual benefit of taking the discount = $(1 + \text{discount/amount left to pay})^{(365/\text{number of days earlier payment is made})} - 1$

Discount/amount left to pay = 0.5%/(100% – 0.5%) = 0.5%/99.5% = 5.0% (use as 0.050 in the calculation)

Annual benefit of taking the discount = $(1 + 0.050)^{(365/20)} - 1 = 1.05^{18.25} - 1 = 9.5\%$

This is greater than the cost of overdraft and the discount should be taken.

The 6.3% used in answers C and D is an incorrect calculation of the benefit of the discount 1.005(365/30) –1 = 6.3

Note that you could have approximated the annual benefit of the discount as follows:

Benefit over (30 – 10) 20 day period = 0.5%

Benefit over 365 day period = 0.5%/20 × 365 = 9.125%

Using this approximate method will always underestimate the correct value, but would have allowed you to spot that the correct value will be 9.5% rather than 6.3%

91 A

The buffer represents the anticipated minimum level of inventory held. This will occur just before an order from the supplier is received.

To calculate it, we can look at how much inventory is held when an order is placed and deduct the value of inventory used while waiting for the order to arrive.

Inventory held when an order is placed = reorder level = 30,000 units

Inventory used per week = annual usage/number of weeks in the year = 400,000/50 = 8,000 units

Inventory used during lead time = usage per week × number of weeks lead time = 8,000 × 3 = 24,000 units

Minimum inventory = 30,000 – 24,000 = 6,000 units.

92 Inventory holding period 51 days, trade receivables collection period 61 days, trade payables payment period 50 days.

Inventory holding period = inventory/cost of sales × 365

Inventory holding period = ($226m/$1,612m) × 365 = 51 days

Trade receivables collection period = trade receivables/credit sales × 365

Trade receivables collection period = ($417m/(0.9 × $2,780m)) × 365 = 61 days

Trade payables payment period = trade payables/credit purchases × 365 = 50 days

Trade payables payment period = ($198m/$1,451m) × 365 = 50 days

Note that where the correct figure is not available, e.g. credit purchases, the most similar figure should be used, e.g. purchases.

INVESTMENT APPRAISAL

93 $152,000

PV of contract price should just cover the PV of the project costs to be acceptable.

Time	Flow	DF @ 10%	PV
0	(125,000)	1	(125,000)
0	(4,000)	1	(4,000)
2	4,000	0.826	3,304
			125,696

Therefore, contract price @ time 2 × 0.826 = 125,696

Price = 125,696/0.826 = $152,174 or $152,000 to the nearest $000.

94 C and D

It is the tax saving on the tax allowable depreciation that is the relevant cash flow, not the depreciation itself. The cost of capital is used for asset replacement decisions. The after tax cost of debt would be used in a lease vs buy decision. The profitability index can be used to rank divisible projects. Government restrictions on bank lending would represent hard capital rationing, which stems from sources external to the business that needs the capital.

95 A

The investment is made on 1 January 20X5, so tax-allowable depreciation can first be set off against profits for the accounting period ended 31 December 20X5, t1. As there is no delay in tax payments (and therefore in tax savings), the tax cash savings will therefore be at the same date as the tax-allowable depreciation.

Time	Date	$	Tax saved ($)	Payment time
0	1 January 20X5	2,000,000		
1	Tax-allowable depreciation	(500,000)	@ 30% = 150,000	1
		1,500,000		
2	31 December 20X6	(350,000)		
		1,150,000	@ 30% = 345,000	2

Present value = ($150,000 × 0.870) + ($345,000 × 0.756) = $391,320

96 $11,100

EV of PV of year 1 cash flow: $16,000 × 0.15 + $12,000 × 0.6 – $4,000 × 0.25 = $8,600

EV of PV of year 2 cash flow: $20,000 × 0.75 – $2,000 × 0.25 = $14,500

Total PV = ($12,000) + $8,600 + $14,500 = $11,100

97 12%

(1 + money rate) = (1 + real rate) × (1 + general inflation rate)

1.21 = (1 + real rate) × 1.08

Real rate= 12%

98 C

In general, it is possible for a project to have up to as many IRRs as there are sign changes in the cash flows. Since the project's cash flows have two sign changes there can be up to two IRRs. The NPV profile could take various forms depending on the relative magnitudes of the cash flows.

99 Payback period: decrease Internal rate of return: increase

The payback period will decrease and the IRR increase, because the outflow at time 0 is unaffected by inflation.

Consider a simple project.

Time	Cash flow	Inflation at, say, 10%	Revised cash flow
	$		$
0	(100)	1	(100)
1	(100)	1.1	(110)
2	100	1.1^2	121
3	100	1.1^3	133
4	100	1.1^4	146

Payback period 3 years to 2.7 years

IRR = approx. 17% to approx. 30%

100 B

The internal rate of return (C) and the cost of the initial investment (A) are independent of the risk of the project. The lower the risk of the project, the less (not greater) is the required rate of return (D).

101 Year 5

To work out discounted payback, cash flows must first be discounted at the company rate.

Year	Cash flow	Discount factor	Present value	Cumulative present value
	$		$	$
0	(100,000)	1	(100,000)	(100,000)
1	40,000	0.909	36,360	(63,640)
2	20,000	0.826	16,520	(47,120)
3	30,000	0.751	22,530	(24,590)
4	5,000	0.683	3,415	(21,175)
5	40,000	0.621	24,840	3,665

Discounted payback occurs in year 5.

102 A

Net initial investment = $732,000

The IRR is the interest rate at which the NPV of the investment is zero.

PV of perpetuity = $146,400/r

The IRR is where $146,400/r = $732,000

IRR = $146,400/$732,000 × 100% = 20%

If you selected 25% you in fact assumed that the first inflow is coterminous with the initial investment. If you selected 500% you calculated the $732,000 net investment correctly, but your final calculation was 'upside-down'. If you selected 400% you made both of these errors.

103 A, B and F

IRR is based on discounted cash flow principles. It therefore considers all of the cash flows in a project (A), does not include notional accounting costs such as depreciation (B) and it considers the time value of money (F). It is not an absolute measure of return, however, as IRR is expressed as a percentage. It is calculated using linear interpolation, which only provides an estimate of the IRR. It is not useful when liquidity is poor as the timings of cash flows are hidden within the calculation. A project can have a high IRR even if the cash flows are weighted towards the end of the project.

104 B

Tax period	Narrative		Tax saved @ 30%	Timing	DF @ 10%	PV
		$	$			$
y/e 31/12/X2	Cost of asset	90,000				
	Tax allowable depreciation	(22,500)	6,750	1	0.909	6,136
		67,500				
y/e 31/12/X3	Tax allowable depreciation	(16,875)	5,063	2	0.826	4,182
		50,625				
y/e 31/12/X4	Tax allowable depreciation	(12,656)	3,797	3	0.751	2,852
		37,969				
y/e 31/12/X5	Disposal	(25,000)				
	Balancing allowance	12,969	3,891	4	0.683	2,658
		NIL				15,828

105 B

	P	Q	R	S
NPV/$ of capital in restricted period	60/20	40/10	80/30	80/40
	= 3	= 4	= 2.67	= 2

The optimal sequence is QPRS.

106 7,785 units

	Cash flow	10% factor	PV
	$000		$
Time 0 machine	(280)	1	(280,000)
Time 1 – 5 contribution	200	3.791	758,200
Time 1 – 5 fixed costs	(95)	3.791	(360,145)
Positive NPV			118,055

PV of contribution (cash flows affected by change in volume) must fall by $118,055

Sales volume must fall by $118,055/758,200 = 15.57%

Fall in sales volume = 0.1557 × 50,000 = 7,785 units

107 Before, after

The calculation of payback uses all relevant cash flows, so would be calculated before depreciation (not a cash flow) and after taxation.

108 B

As there are different rates of inflation the 'money approach' must be used, i.e. the cash flows must be inflated at their specific rates and discounted at the money cost of capital.

(1 + Money rate) = (1 + Real rate) × (1 + General Inflation rate) = 1.1 × 1.08 = 1.188

Therefore, money rate = 0.188 or 18.8%

109 C

As there is more than one rate of inflation in the question, the money method must be used (inflated cash flows discounted at the money cost of capital)

(1 + Money rate) = (1 + Real rate) × (1 + General Inflation rate)

Therefore, money rate cost of capital = [(1.08 × 1.12) – 1] × 100 = 20.96%

Time	**t0**	**t1**	**t2**
	$	$	$
Outlay	(18,000)		
Labour (8% inflation after year 1)		9,000	9,900
Salvage			5,000
			14,900
20.96% discount factor $(1+r)^{-n}$	1	0.8267	0.6835
Present value	(18,000)	7,440	10,184

NPV = $(376) or $(380) to nearest $10

110 C

	$	**Discount factor**	$
Time 0	(10,000)	1.000	(10,000)
Time 1	(3,000)	0.909	(2,727)
Time 2	(5,000)	0.826	(4,130)
Time 3	(5,000)	0.751	(3,755)
NPV	(20,612)		

Equivalent annual cost = PV of costs/annuity factor for length of replacement cycle

Equivalent annual cost = 20,612/2.487 = $8,288

111 B

	Capital needed at time 0	NPV	NPV/£ needed at time 0	Rank	Invested	NPV
	$	$	$		$	$
Project 1	10,000	30,000	3.0	2	10,000	30,000
Project 2	8,000	25,000	3.125	1	8,000	25,000
Project 3	12,000	30,000	2.5	3	12,000	30,000
Project 4	16,000	36,000	2.25	4 (1/8)	2,000	4,500
					32,000	89,500

112 C

The NPV impact of the initial outflow is unaffected.

The revenue flows will be subject to inflation, but then should be discounted at a money rate that includes this inflation. The net effect is no change in the PV.

The sales proceeds represent a flow of money, not affected by inflation, but this will now be discounted at a higher money rate, lowering the net present value of the project.

113 C and D

The true statements are 'the payback method is based on the project's cash flows' and 'a requirement for early payback can increase a company's liquidity'.

The payback method is based on cash flows whereas the ROCE method is based on accounting profit. ROCE looks at the project's entire life whereas payback may not. Neither method is related to the cost of capital.

114 False, True, False, False

It is sensitivity analysis rather than simulation that can only consider the effect of changing one variable at a time (A). Simulation gives more information about the investment decision but does not point to the correct result or assess the likelihood of a variable changing.

115 A

The tighter the distribution, the lower the standard deviation will be (B). The wider the dispersion, the more risky the situation (C). It is the expected value, not the standard deviation, that is the weighted average of all the possible outcomes (D).

116 D

Under a long-term lease, the lessee is responsible for repairs and maintenance of the leased asset.

117 20%

ROCE = operating profit/(total capital (D + E)) = 2,500/(10,000 + 2,500) × 100 = 20%

118 10%

Initial ROCE = average annual operating profits /initial capital × 100

Operating profits = operating cash flows before taxation – depreciation

Depreciation over project life = $65,000 – $10,000 = $55,000

Depreciation per year = $55,000/4 = $13,750

Average annual profits = $20,000 – $13,750 = $6,250 per year

Initial ROCE = $6,250/$65,000 × 100 = 9.6% or 10% to nearest whole percentage

119 $15,700

Year 1 PV = $10,000 × 1.05 × 0.877 = $9,209

Year 2 PV = $20,000 × 1.05^2 × 0.769 = $16,956

Year 3 PV = $25,000 × 1.05^3 × 0.675 = $19,535

NPV = $9,209 + $16,956 + $19,535 – $30,000 = $15,700

(Note: Other answers which differ due to roundings applied, would also be marked as correct).

120 D

ROCE does take into account all years of operation of an investment project.

Discounted cash flow-based decisions are better than profit based ones. The ROCE calculation is compared to a ROCE-based percentage target that is unrelated to the cost of capital. A decision under ROCE is compared to a target set by management rather than to existing ROCE levels. Otherwise, decisions could be made to reject acceptable projects just because they aren't quite as good as current operations.

121 $82,171

In order to make the decision between different lengths of replacement cycles, an equivalent annual cost (EAC) should be calculated for each cycle. This is calculated as:

present value of the costs of the cycle/annuity factor for the time period of the cycle.

The company's cost of capital should be used to determine the annuity factors.

Years to replacement	Negative NPV	Annuity factor at 11%	Equivalent annual cost
	$		$
2	149,308	1.713	87,162
3	209,142	2.444	85,574
4	254,893	3.102	82,171
5	310,860	3.696	84,107

As the 4 year cycle has the lowest EAC, it represents the optimal replacement cycle.

122 $116,299

The present value of one cycle in $ is:

Outlay	(450,000)
Running costs	(82,280)
Resale	25,800
Total PV	(506,480)

Equivalent annual cost is calculated as:

PV of the costs of the cycle/annuity factor for the length of the cycle

For each cycle of six years, using the six-year 10% annuity factor, this has an equivalent annual cost of $506,480/4.355 = $116,299 (to the nearest dollar).

Some candidates incorrectly just evaluated the present value of one cycle, while some others appeared to simply divide the present value of one cycle by the number of years in the cycle.

BUSINESS FINANCE AND COST OF CAPITAL

123 9.2%

Return per CAPM = Rf + beta (Rm – Rf)

Return = 6% + (0.80 × 4%) = 9.2%

Note: market risk premium = (Rm – Rf). Rm on its own is the return on average market shares.

124 B and E

Bonus issues do not raise any cash. M&M's arguments were: under their no tax theory, the financing decision is irrelevant. Under their 'with tax' theory, financing is relevant and that companies should use as much debt as possible. Their dividend theory concluded that the dividend decision is irrelevant as shareholders would be happy with dividends or capital gains. Therefore, the statement is true only of their with tax theory but not as a whole. Managers/directors decide on dividend amounts. An offer for tender should ensure that all shares on offer are taken up but if the majority tender at a lower price than anticipated, a lower amount of cash will be raised than anticipated.

125 C

The companies are identical except for their gearing and the beta factor of equity shares will increase with the gearing level. The beta of B Co (gearing 80%) is therefore higher than the beta for D Co (gearing 60%), i.e. over 1.22. The beta of C Co (gearing 35%) is higher than the beta for A Co (gearing 30%) and below the beta for D Co. It must therefore be in the range 0.89 to 1.22.

126 Statements 1 and 3 are correct.

Statement 2 is essentially meaningless. Statement 4: gross profit is calculated as gross profit divided by revenue.

127 9.1%

Note that interest, I, is calculated by using the coupon rate (12%) multiplied by the nominal value of the debt ($100). The nominal value will be $100 unless the question states otherwise.

Kd = I(1 – T)/MV = $12 × (1 – 0.3)/$92 = 0.091 or 9.1%

128 C

Ke = 18%

Kp = D_0/P_0 = ($1 × 8%)/$0.92 = 0.087 or 8.7%

Kd = I(1 – T)/MV = ($100 × 12.5%) × (1 – 0.3)/$100 = 0.0875 or 8.75%

Note that for redeemable debt redeemable at nominal value with a market value equal to nominal value, the calculation can be shortened to be the same as for irredeemable debt.

MV equity = $12m/$0.5 × $2.50 = $60.0m (note $0.5 shares so 24m shares are in issue)

MV prefs = $6m × $0.92 = $5.52m

MV debt = $8m (as market value per loan note is same as nominal value at $100)

Total MV = $60.0m + $5.52m + $8m = $73.52m

WACC = 0.18 × $60.0m/$73.52m + 0.087 × $5.52m/$73.52m + 0.0875 × $8m/$73.52m

= 0.1630 or 16.3%. 16% to the nearest whole %

129 True, True, True

All three statements are true. As the cost of equity increases, it pushes the WACC up. A higher WACC leads to a lower market value (as future cash flows would be discounted at a higher rate). Investors facing increased risk on an investment will seek a higher return as compensation. If they do not get the higher return, they would choose to move their investment elsewhere. Debt cost is usually lower then preference share cost as the risk of investing in debt is lower than that of investing in preference shares, so investors do not demand as high a return on debt as for preference shares.

130 27.7%

Using the dividend valuation model, $k_e = D_0(1 + g)/P_0 + g$ (where P_0 is the ex div price)

Ke = $0.256 × 1.16/($2.80 – $0.256) + 0.16

Ke = 0.277 or 27.7%

131 B and D

Operating gearing = fixed costs divided by variable costs, so a decrease in the gearing ratio implies a lower proportion of fixed costs. Therefore, C is wrong.

Consider the following example.

	Higher gearing	Lower gearing
	$m	$m
Sales	100	100
Variable costs	(20)	(30)
Fixed costs	(30)	(20)
Profit	50	50
Operating gearing ratio	3/2	2/3

Suppose sales volume, and hence variable costs, fall by 20%.

The profits will be affected as follows:

	$m	$m
Sales	80	80
Variable costs	(16)	(24)
Fixed costs	(30)	(20)
Profit	34	36

With the lower gearing ratio, profits are less affected by the change in volume (less volatile). D is correct.

A is wrong – profitability is unconnected to gearing. B is correct – profits are less risky (volatile), as the example shows above.

132 B

The traditional view is that, as an organisation introduces debt into its capital structure, the weighted average cost of capital will fall, because initially the benefit of cheap debt finance more than outweighs any increases in the cost of equity required to compensate equity holders for higher financial risk. As gearing continues to increase, equity holders will ask for progressively higher returns and eventually this increase will start to outweigh the benefit of cheap debt finance, and the weighted average cost of capital will rise.

133 A

It increases the number of shares without affecting the value of the company (as there is perfect information, so there should be no misinterpretation by investors as to the fortunes of the company and therefore in theory no change to the share price), so market price per share and earnings per share will fall. The total market value of the shares will be unaffected so the market value gearing would be unaffected.

134 Cost of equity: increases WACC: decreases Total MV: increases

In a perfect capital market, the theories of Modigliani & Miller on gearing apply. In the with tax model, WACC decreases with increased gearing and therefore the market value rises.

135 Financial risk: decreases operating risk: increases

Financial risk is dependent on the debt/equity (gearing) ratio. The lower the value of debt in the ratio, the lower the financial risk. This is because of lower interest and repayment commitments relative to the level of profits.

Operating risk is dependent on the ratio of variable costs to fixed costs. The lower the proportion of variable costs (and the higher the proportion of fixed costs), the higher the operating risk. This is because fixed costs do not fluctuate with sales levels whereas variable costs do. With a high proportion of fixed costs, profits will fluctuate more with changes in sales levels. More fluctuation means more risk.

136 Security X is overpriced Security Y is underpriced

If security Z is correctly priced, its actual return will be the return predicted by CAPM. We can use this to find the value or Rm. For security Z:

13.2 = 6 + 1.2 (Rm – 6)

13.2 – 6 = 1.2 (Rm – 6)

(13.2 – 6)/1.2 = Rm – 6

6 = Rm – 6

6 + 6 = Rm = 12

Security X has a beta value of 1.6 and should provide a return of 6 + 1.6 (12 – 6) = 15.6%

Security Y has a beta value of 0.9 and should provide a return of 6 + 0.9(12 – 6) = 11.4%

Security X does not give a high enough return, so is overpriced. Security Y gives too high a return, so is underpriced.

137 A

Gearing = Debt/equity

The definition of debt for gearing calculations includes preference shares as they are also a form of prior charge capital.

Total debt = Bonds ($4m/$100 × $105) $4.2m + bank loans $6.2m + preference shares ($2m/ × $0.8) $1.6m = $12m

Total equity = $8m/$0.5 × $5 = $80m (note that reserves are not included in market value calculations)

D/E = $12m/$80m = 0.15 or 15%

138 Systematic risk, financial risk

Systematic risk cannot be diversified; it is linked to market factors that influence all shares in a similar way. Gearing up increases financial risk.

139 False, false

Under M&M (implied by the phrase 'perfect capital markets') with no tax, the WACC is unaffected by gearing, but the cost of equity starts to rise immediately gearing is introduced.

140 B and D

High tax rates mean that there is a larger tax shield on interest payments on debt finance, making debt more attractive (B). Intangible assets being a low proportion of assets. Debt providers are more likely to lend if there are tangible assets to secure the debt against. If few of the assets are intangible, then more are tangible and hence finance providers will be more willing to lend. With more potential debt providers, gearing is more likely to be high (D). If the business has low taxable profits then there will not be much of a tax shield to use, so the incentive to use debt is reduced (A). If shares are cheap to issue that makes them relatively more attractive and so gearing is less likely to reach high levels (C).

141 B

Because of the potential for making gains by conversion, investors are willing to accept a lower coupon rate on the debt.

A The equity component is not a risk imposed on holders.

C Additional payments are not required.

D They don't have to rank after ordinary debt and even if they did, this would increase their servicing cost (due to higher risk levels to the investor being compensated for by a higher return demanded by them).

142 D

A M&M applied the assumption (but it is not a conclusion of their theory) that a perfect capital market exists and thus shareholders would be indifferent between receiving dividend income and capital gains (if they require the cash they could sell some shares); it does not apply when there are market imperfections, such as transaction costs on the selling of shares.

B is the Gordon growth model.

C contradicts the dividend valuation model, which is not disputed by M&M.

The correct answer is D.

143 B

If the company were to automate its production line, its level of fixed costs (e.g. maintenance and depreciation) would increase and its variable costs (notably wage) decrease.

Therefore, operating gearing (the measure of the proportion of fixed costs used) would increase.

144 B

CAPM can be used to predict the cost of equity. Using an asset (ungeared) beta will predict the ungeared cost of equity. Using the equity (geared) beta would predict the geared cost of equity.

145 A

Interest cover measures a company's financial risk, gross profit margin measures operating profitability and return on capital employed measures how efficiently the company is using the funds available.

146 Preference shares are a form of <u>equity</u> capital, which carry <u>higher</u> risk from the company point of view than ordinary shares.

Although they share many features in common with loan capital (and are indeed included as debt in calculations such as gearing), preference shares give their holders certain ownership rights in the company, which means that their position is legally very different to that of lenders. Strictly therefore, they are a form of equity capital. Risk wise, from the investor point of view, they are lower risk than ordinary shares and higher risk than debt. From the company point of view, they are higher risk than ordinary shares as they carry a requirement to pay dividends that ordinary shares do not.

147 A

It is the interest yield which is the interest or coupon rate expressed as a percentage of the market price and this is a measure of return on investment for the debt holder (B). It is the total shareholder return ratio which measures the returns to the investor by taking account of dividend income and capital growth (C). It is the dividend per share ratio which helps individual shareholders see how much of the overall dividend payout they are entitled to (D).

148 A and D

The lessor does not retain the risks or rewards of ownership. For long-term leases, there is usually one lease that covers the majority of the useful life of the asset, not many.

149 A

As risk rises, the market value of the security will fall to ensure that investors receive an increased yield.

If the risk levels of the company are rising, investors would demand a higher yield (income/price) to compensate them for the increased risk. As the rate of interest is fixed, the investors' income will not change, so the price must.

Note that this will happen naturally. With increased risk, some investors will start to sell their investment as they are not happy with the change. This will push the market price down, naturally increasing the yield until it reaches a level that investors are satisfied with. The high level of selling of the debt stops and the price stabilises.

150 B

Calculation of TERP = (existing market value + proceeds raised)/new number of shares

Existing number of shares = $5m/$0.5 = 10m shares

Existing market value = 10m × $8 = $80m

New number of shares = 10m/4 × 1 = 2.5m

Proceeds = 2.5m × $6 = $15m

TERP = ($80m + $15m)/(10m + 2.5m) = $7.60

Value of a right per existing share = (TERP – issue price)/number of existing shares needed to obtain a right

In a 1 for 4 issue, 4 existing shares are needed to get the right to purchase one new share

= ($7.60 – $6)/4 = $0.40

151 C

The maturity gap relates to the fact that using its non-current assets an SME may find it easier to secure long-term finance when it may actually need short- or medium-term finance.

152 $9.80

Current share price = $0.5 × 20 = $10 per share

Rights issue price = $10 × 90/100 = $9 per share

Number of shares in issue = $50m/$10 = 5m

Number of shares to be issued = 5m × 1/4 = 1.25m shares

TERP = (5m × $10 + 1.25m × $9)/(5m + 1.25m) = $9.80 per share.

153 Funding gap

The difference between the finance required to operate an SME and the amount obtained is the funding gap. SMEs can find it difficult to obtain enough funding to sustain them because they are small and, for example, may not have good financial track records or experienced managers.

154 A

TSR = (change in share price over the period + dividend for the period)/share price at start of period × 100

TSR = ($3.00 – $2.50 + $0.15)/$2.50 × 100 = 26%

155 B

Dividend to be paid = \$0.80 × 0.55 = \$0.44 per share

Retention ratio = 100% – 55% = 45%

Dividend growth rate (using Gordon's growth approximation on formula sheet):

$g = br_e$ = 45% × 20% = 9% per year

P_0 = ex div price = \$4.60 – \$0.44 = \$4.16

$Ke = D_0 ((1 + g)/P_0) + g$

Ke = ((\$0.44 × 1.09)/\$4.16) + 0.09 = 0.0205 or 20.5%

156 1.4 Times

Contribution = \$180,000 – (\$100,000 × 70%) = \$110,000

Operational gearing = contribution/operating profit = \$110,000/\$80,000 = 1.375 times or 1.4 times to 1 decimal place.

Alternative calculation to give the same answer: % change in EBIT/% change in revenue

Say revenue rises by 10% to \$198,000, what % change is there in EBIT?

70% of cost of sales (\$70,000) will also rise by 10%, while the remainder (\$30,000) will stay the same, giving a new cost of sale of \$30,000 + \$70,000 × 1.1 = \$107,000.

New EBIT = \$198,000 – \$107,000 = \$91,000, a percentage change of (\$91,000 – \$80,000)/ \$80,000 × 100 = 13.75%

Operational gearing is therefore 13.75/10 = 1.375 times

Either method can be used in the exam

157 TERP \$6.60, rights issue price \$5.00

TERP is the market price before the rights issue less the value of a right per existing share = \$7.00 – \$0.40 = \$6.60.

Value of a right = Issue price – TERP

Therefore, the issue price can be calculated from the TERP by subtracting the value of a right.

The value of a right can be calculated by multiplying the value of a right per existing share by the number of shares needed for one right.

Value of a right = 4 × \$0.40 = \$1.60

So the rights issue price is \$6.60 – \$1.60 = \$5.00

158 True, True and True

SMEs are seen as higher risk due to a lack of trading history as well as fewer assets to provide security.

The lack of suitable assets for security will often make it difficult to obtain bank finance unless the founders provide personal guarantees on the debt. These guarantees mean the sacrificing of limited liability as the founders will now be personally liable for the debt.

159 13.4%

$k_e = (D_0(1 + g)/P_0) + g$

We have been given D_0 and g, but must calculate P_0 from the other information given in the question.

Price per share (P_0) = earnings per share × PE ratio

Dividend cover = earnings per share/dividend per share

Therefore, earnings per share = dividend cover × dividend = 4 × $0.1 = $0.4

P_0 = $0.40 × 5 = $2.00

k_e = ($0.10 × (1 + 0.08)/$2.00) + 0.08 = (0.1 × 1.08/2) + 0.08 = 0.134, or 13.4%.

160 389 cents

Dividend yield = Dividend/Price

Rearranging to find price:

Price = Dividend/dividend yield

Price = 35/0.09 = 389 cents

161 A

Value of bank loan redeemed = 50m × $1.50 = $75m

Interest saved at 8% per annum = $75m × 8% = $6m

Post-tax interest saved = $6m × (1 – 20%) = $4.8m

New earnings figure = $55m + $4.8m = $59.8m

New number of shares = 100m + 50m = 150m

New EPS = $59.8m/150m = $0.399

BUSINESS VALUATIONS

162 C

The preferred approach is a good spread of shares, as this minimises the risk in the portfolio and should ensure Mr Mays does achieve something approaching the average return for the market. Strong form efficiency means that Mr Mays cannot do anything to guarantee beating the market – even by insider trading, so options A and D are a waste of time.

163 $92.67

MV redeemable debt = present value of the cash flows of ownership discounted at the investors' rate of return (pre-tax cost of debt).

Discount seven years of 7% interest (annuity) and a redemption value of $105 in seven years, both at a discount rate of 9%.

MV = ($7 × 5.033) + ($105 × 0.547) = $92.67

164 $3.50

Total shareholder return = (change in share price + dividend)/opening share price × 100

19.7 = (current price – $3.10 + $0.21)/$3.10 × 100

Current share price = (19.7/100 × $3.10) – $0.21 + $3.10 = $3.50

165 A

TERP = (existing market value + proceeds of issue)/new number of shares in issue

Note that the calculation can be done either using total market values or the market values of one set of rights, as follows:

TERP = (4 × $4.10 + 1 × $2.50)/(4 +1) = $3.78

166 C

Technical analysis, or chartism, is where investors study past share price movements in order to try and predict future ones.

167 $1.40

The period 20X1 to 20X5 covers four years of growth, and the average growth rate 'g' can be calculated as follows:

$g = (D_0/D_n)^{(1/n)} - 1 = (4,236/2,200)^{(1/4)} - 1 = 0.1778$ (or 17.78%)

$P_0 = D_0(1 + g)/(k_e - g)$

Therefore, P_0 = ($4,236,000 × 1.1778)/(0.25 – 0.1778) = $69,101,950

Price per share (50 million shares) = $1.38 or $1.40 to the nearest ten cents.

168 A

$P_0 = D_0(1 + g)/(k_e - g)$

$g = br_e = 0.7 \times 0.15 = 0.105$

P_0 = ($50m × 1.105)/(0.25 – 0.105) = $381m rounded

169 B

Value = earnings × PE ratio

Use predicted earnings value, so for the combined entity, include the $100k annual savings

Maximum value to pay = difference between value of combined entity and current value of purchasing company alone.

	$000
Value of Alpha and Beta combined (210 + 900 + 100) × 18	21,780
Value of Beta on its own 900 × 21	(18,900)
Maximum value of Alpha	2,880

170 B and D

A higher P/E ratio valuation may be justified when the target company has higher growth prospects, not when the bid company does (A). A higher valuation could also be justified when the target is in an industry/country where the normal P/E ratio is higher than in the industry/country of the bidder (D). Better-quality assets might also be a reason for offering a price that values the target on a higher P/E (B). Higher gearing ratios are more likely to reduce the P/E ratio than increase it (C).

171 Weak form efficient

For the investor to make gains consistently from his/her policy, he/she must believe that he/she is 'one step ahead' of the market, i.e. that published information has not already been incorporated into the market price. Thus, the market can be weak-form efficient at best.

172 $1,247,000

$P_0 = D_0(1 + g)/(k_e - g)$

$g = br_e = 0.4 \times 15\% = 6\%$

P_0 = (\$200,000 × 1.06)/(0.23 – 0.06) = \$1,247,000 to the nearest \$000

173 Statement 1: false   Statement 2: true

Efficient market hypothesis is concerned as to whether share prices are fair, i.e. whether information (for instance about a new positive NPV project) has been incorporated into the price. In a strong form efficient market, the share price would instantly update when a new positive NPV project came to light. There is no contradiction here, so statement 1 is false.

If there were information content in dividends, share prices would react to the information when a dividend is announced. In a strong form market, investors would already know the reasons behind any change in dividends and the share price would already have moved, so there would not be any new information content in them. Thus, statement 2 is true.

174 B

New P/E ratio = New price/New EPS

Price per share after the merger = $2.50 + $.50 = $3.00

To calculate new EPS we need new earnings and new number of shares:

Combined earnings after the merger (including synergies) = $(120m + 35m + 4m)

= $159m

Number of shares offered = 90m/3 × 1 = 30m

Number of shares in issue in Peter Co after the merger = 400m + 30m = 430m

New EPS = $159m/$430m = $0.370

New P/E ratio = Price/EPS = $3.00/$0.370

= 8.11

175 $3.44

$g = (D_0/D_n)^{(1/n)} - 1 = (36.0/31.1)^{(1/3)} - 1 = 0.050$ (or 5.0%)

$P_0 = D_0(1 + g)/(k_e - g)$

$P_0 = (36.0 \times 1.05)/(0.16 - 0.05) = 344$ cents = $3.44

176 B

When the company is being bought for the earnings/cash flow that all of its assets can produce in the future, a price/earnings ratio method or a discounted cash flow technique would be useful (A). Asset-based measures using net realisable values help to identify a minimum, not a maximum, price in a takeover (C). When the company has a highly skilled workforce, this would not be reflected in the value of the assets within the statement of financial position (D). The correct answer is B – asset valuation models are useful in the situation that a company is going to be purchased to be broken up and its assets sold off.

177 A

Answer B = Value per share

Answer C = Earnings yield

Answer D = Price earnings ratio

178 $4.20

$P_0 = D_1/(k_e - g)$

$g = (D_0/D_n)^{(1/n)} - 1 = (33.6/32.0)^{(1/1)} - 1 = 0.050$ (or 5.0%)

MV = 33.6/(0.13 – 0.05) = 420 cents or $4.20

179 D

Expected share price in three years' time = $3.50 × $(1.04)^3$ = $3.94

Conversion value = $3.94 × 30 = $118.20

Compared with redemption at nominal value of $100, conversion will be preferred.

The current market value will be the present value of future interest payments, plus the present value of the conversion value, discounted at the pre-tax cost of debt of 5% per year. Note that the pre-tax cost of debt can also be referred to as the return to the investor.

Annual interest = coupon rate × nominal value per loan note = 6% × $100 = $6

Market value of each convertible loan note = ($6 × 3yr 5% AF) + ($118.20 × 3yr 5% DF)

= ($6 × 2.723) + ($118.20 × 0.864)

= $118.46

180 $14

They should not accept less than the net realisable value of total assets less total liabilities:

(30m + 4m + 18m – 2m – 12m – 10m)/2m = $14 per share.

Note total shares in issue with $0.50 nominal value of shares = $1m/$0.5 = 2m

181 D

Discount the after tax cash flows into perpetuity.

Theoretical value = after tax cash flows × 1/r where r is the WACC

Value = $2m × 1/0.08 = $25m

182 $83

Expected share price in five years' time = $3.60 × 1.05^5 = $4.59

Conversion value = $4.59 × 25 = $114.75

This is higher than the cash redemption value of $100 so should be used in the MV calculation.

The current market value will be the present value of future interest payments, plus the present value of the conversion value, discounted at the pre-tax cost of debt of 5% per year. Note that the pre-tax cost of debt can also be referred to as the return to the investor.

Annual interest = coupon rate × nominal value per loan note = 3% × $100 = $3

Market value of each convertible loan note = ($3 × 5yr 10% AF) + ($118.20 × 5yr 10% DF)

= ($3 × 3.791) + ($114.75 × 0.621) = $82.63 ($83 to the nearest $)

183 False, False, True, False

It is correct that the price/earnings ratio is the reciprocal of the earnings yield. The other statements are incorrect. Earnings valuations and dividend valuations are on different bases and would not be expected to give similar valuations. Part of the skill of valuation is noting the various different values that can be calculated and working out an appropriate one. Market capitalisation is the number of shares multiplied by the price. Business values are often higher than this as buyers may be willing to pay a premium to gain control of a company. Increased risk reduces business value, so the PE ratio should be reduced to account for greater risk.

184 D

It is correct that research has shown that, over time, share prices appear to follow a random walk. Because it is true for weak form efficiency, it is also true for semi-strong and strong-form as they both incorporate weak form efficiency.

Larger companies do not necessarily provide larger returns. All levels of market efficiency assume that investors make rational decisions. It is when they don't make decisions on a rational basis that the market will appear to be inefficient. Allocative efficiency is an economic term that means the economy is allocating goods and services efficiently.

185 A and D

Herding is where investors buy or sell shares in a company or sector just because many other investors have already done so. Noise traders are those who do not base their decisions on fundamental analysis of company performance and prospects.

Fishing is a distractor and simulation is a term relating to investment appraisal. A stock market bubble is the result of herding behaviour rather than a term to explain why irrational decisions were made.

186 D

The market paradox occurs because in order for markets to be efficient, investors have to believe that they are inefficient. For instance, a profit seeking investor would not feel that it is worth buying shares that are fairly priced in an efficient market as they would not believe that there is an opportunity to make a gain on those shares.

187 A

The value of next year's dividend has been given (D_1 = \$0.32), so the share price calculation is:

Share price = $D_1/(ke - g)$ = 0.32/(0.12 – 0.02) = \$3.20

Seema's shareholding is 800,000 × 20% = 160,000 shares

The value of this shareholding is 160,000 × \$3.20 = \$512,000

The formula on the formula sheet uses $D_0(1 + g)$ but remember that this is just a way of calculating the dividend cash flow at time period 1 (next year), D_1, so if D_1 has been given it is simpler to use that. Plus, in this case, the growth between D_0 and D_1 (\$0.32/\$.30 = 1.067, so growth was 6.7%) wasn't the same as the growth after that, so applying a 2% growth figure to D_0 would have been an incorrect approach.

Incorrect answers did not take the given figure for D_1 and either used the dividend just paid with 2% growth to get an answer of \$489,600 or incorrectly added growth of 2% to the given dividend figure of \$0.32 to get an answer of \$522,240.

188 A and C

The correct answers are A and C.

Statements A and C are correct about weak-form efficient markets. Statement B is not true, this would only be true about a strong-form efficient market. Statement D is not true about any form of efficient market.

189 A

A 5% irredeemable debenture pays interest (I) of (nominal value × coupon rate) \$100 × 5% = \$5 annually.

Ex-interest market value = I/k_d = \$5/0.1 = \$50.

Therefore the cum interest market value is (ex-interest value add back interest just paid): \$50 + \$5 = \$55.

Choosing \$50 is incorrect as the market price is cum interest so interest about to be paid needs to be added.

If you are wondering why $k_d(1-t)$ wasn't used, for debt market value calculations the calculation is from the lender's point of view, not the company's. Therefore, the company's tax saving on interest is not relevant for the calculation.

190 Semi-strong form efficient market \$6.20, strong form efficient market \$6.00

In a semi-strong form efficient market, the markets value shares based on information relevant to past movements and also published information.

The share price will react to the NPV of Product B today as news is released. The increase will be \$160m/800m shares = \$0.20 per share, bringing the share price up to \$6.20.

In a strong form efficient market, the share price reflects historic information, published information and insider information. The share price of \$6.00 will already reflect the NPVs of both new products as the decision to launch them was taken two days ago.

191 \$7.08

The floor value is the present value of the redemption option of the loan note, i.e. the value of the loan note today without taking into account the conversion option. In order to make a decision on whether to convert the loan note to shares (which can be done at any time over the next five years), investors would compare this value to the current value of the shares that they would receive upon conversion.

Converting today means receiving 15 shares. Dividing the floor value by the number of shares an investor receives upon conversion gives a value per share of (\$106.20/ 15 shares) \$7.08.

If the investors convert at a price of \$7.08, they will receive shares worth \$106.20, the same as the floor value. At any share price above \$7.08, the value of the shares is worth more than the floor value and so the investors would choose to convert (ignoring transaction fees, etc.).

Therefore, \$7.08 represents the minimum price at which investors would convert.

Commonly seen errors included just giving the floor value and not the value per share as stated in the question and also dividing the redemption/nominal value by 15 shares to get \$6.67.

192 C

Under strong form efficient markets, the share price will reflect all information regardless of whether it is in the public domain or not. A significant number of candidates selected semi-strong form efficiency suggesting a lack of understanding of the EMH. In a semi-strong form efficient market, the share price would quickly react to the information being made public.

193 C

Security price movements should be unpredictable in an efficient market.

Many people assume this unpredictability does not apply to semi-strong form efficient markets, possibly based on the misunderstanding that only strong form efficient markets are efficient. It is worth emphasising that all forms of efficiency under the efficient market hypothesis, even weak form and semi-strong form efficiency, exhibit this trait.

The semi-strong version of the efficient market hypothesis incorporates publicly available information into the security price, but not private information.

For this reason, security prices should move when a takeover is announced in a semi-strong efficient market as this means previously private information now becomes public.

Insider dealing undermines investor confidence in a semi-strong efficient market because there is the potential to make abnormal profits using information which is not yet in the public domain. To avoid a loss of confidence in a semi-strong efficient market, there would therefore need to be a ban on insider dealing.

194 $9.00

In order to determine the value of an ordinary share in Alfreda Co using a PE ratio, we need to use the following calculation:

Price per share = earnings per share × PE ratio

The earnings per share (EPS) is calculated as total earnings divided by the number of shares in issue. Earnings represents the profit available to ordinary shareholders (whether it is paid out as an ordinary dividend or not). We therefore use the $90m figure:

EPS = $90m/200m = $0.45 per share

We're told to use Otis's PE ratio but are not given it directly.

PE ratio = price per share/earnings per share

Otis's EPS is given as $0.25

To calculate its share price, we can use the market capitalisation figure.

Market capitalisation = price per share × number of shares in issue

Therefore:

Price per share = market capitalisation/number of shares in issue

For Otis, this calculates as $2,750m/550m = $5.00 per share

Otis's PE ratio is therefore $5.00/$0.25 = 20

Alfreda's price per share can therefore be calculated as:

$0.45 × 20 = $9.00 per share

RISK MANAGEMENT

195 B

Matching refers to the balancing of receipts and payments in the same currency.

196 A

With a money market hedge, one currency will be borrowed and the other deposited.

When the peso receipt comes in in six months' time, it can be used to pay off a peso borrowing. This will eliminate the need to make a foreign exchange in six months. The other currency, $, will be deposited, so we need peso borrowing rates and $ deposit rates for six months. As the rates given are annual rates, we need to pro-rate them.

6-month peso borrowing rate = 8% × 6/12 = 4%

6-month dollar deposit rate = 3% × 6/12 = 1.5%

Present value today of peso borrowing of 500,000 in six months = 500,000/1.04 = 480,769

Take today the borrowed pesos and exchange for $ (note that a foreign exchange is still made, but it is done today, so removes the risk of the exchange rate changing over time)

$ received from exchange = 480,769/15.00 = $32,051

Put the $ on deposit for 6 months. Final value = $32,051 × 1.015 = $32,532, or $32,500 to the nearest $100.

197 Would not provide cover, Would provide cover, Would provide cover, Would provide cover

Buying Euros in 3 months would not hedge at all – the full risk would still be exposed.

Leading with the payment by paying in full now removed the need to exchange in the future, so removes the exposure to changing exchange rates. Note though that paying early comes at a cost for working capital funding.

Buying Euros today to meet the payment obligation in three months' time matches assets (Euro deposit) and liabilities (Euro supplier payable) and provides cover against the exposure. It is a money market hedge and may require the business to borrow enough home currency to buy the Euros.

A forward exchange contract is a popular method of hedging against exposure.

198 Statement 1: false Statement 2: false

Lagging does not guarantee a lowering of risk, so is not technically a hedging technique. If the exchange rate moves in the opposite direction to what is expected, then the business will suffer as a result.

Matching receipts and payments is a method of reducing the risk of transaction exposure, not translation exposure.

199 UK exporter: gain Swedish importer: no effect

The Swedish importer is unaffected as they are invoiced in local currency; the UK exporter will gain as more pounds will be received for the kroner.

200 2.0383 $/£

The company has to change £ to $ to buy the machine, and will be offered the lower rate for this conversion, 2.0383. One way to determine this is that the bank will buy the counter currency at the high rate (buy high) and sell it at the low rate (sell low). The counter currency is the one that doesn't have a value of 1. In this case £ is the base and $ is counter. The company will need to buy $ from the bank to make the $ payment, so the bank is selling the counter currency and the low rate applies.

201 1.4379 €/£

Applying interest rate parity:

Invest £1,000 at 5.75% for three months (0.0575/4) = £1,014.375

Convert £1,000 to € at 1.4415 = €1,441.5

Invest that at 4.75% for three months (0.0475/4) = €1,458.62

Implied forward rate is therefore 1,458.62/1,014.375 = 1.4379

Or using the formula from the sheet:

$F_0 = S_0 \times (1 + i_c)/(1 + i_b)$

Counter currency is Euros and base is sterling

$i_c = 4.75\% \times 3/12 = 1.1875\%$

$i_b = 5.75\% \times 3/12 = 1.4375\%$

$F_0 = 1.4415 \times 1.011875/1.014375 = 1.4379$

202 The missing word is basis

When there is a basis, there will not be a perfect hedge. This is known as basis risk.

203 B

Once purchased, the close out date is already set for currency futures. Different close out dates can be chosen at the point of purchase.

Forward contracts are binding and will not be allowed to lapse by the bank.

Options are paid for when they are taken on. They may never be exercised if the underlying currency market moves favourably for the option holder.

204 Exercise, let it lapse

1. Call options give the right to purchase the currency of the option at a specific rate. The investor can buy £500,000 for US$950,000 using the option compared to US$975,000 on the spot market, so the option is cheaper.
2. Put options give the right to sell the currency of the option at a specific rate. The investor can sell the £400,000 and receive S$1,160,000 using the option compared to S$1,180,000 on the spot market. Using the option gives a worse deal.

Therefore, the call option should be exercised but the put option should not be exercised (allowed to lapse).

205 Eady Co: loss Canadian supplier: no effect

The Canadian supplier is unaffected as it invoices in its local currency, the Canadian dollar. It will receive the same number of Canadian $ regardless of any movements of the C$ against the £. Eady Co will have to pay more £ to purchase the C$ payable, so will suffer a loss on the weakening of sterling.

206 True and True

Overseas customers will find the home country's goods cheaper, as they will need to use less of their own currency to pay for the home country's currency when purchasing the goods, thus boosting exports. On the other hand, imported raw materials will become more expensive (need to use more of the home currency to pay for the foreign currency that will be used to pay the overseas supplier), resulting in inflationary pressure. There are two types of inflation, demand-pull and cost-push. Demand-pull inflation rises when demand for locally produced goods is high. Cost-push inflation happens when the domestic producer's costs go up and they have to increase prices to remain profitable. If the country's currency falls in value, this is great for exports, but it makes imports more expensive. Any business that uses imported materials in its production will see its costs go up. This can lead to cost-push inflation.

207 A

A contract that gives one party the right to sell an asset (such as currency or shares) at a certain price and the other party an obligation to buy the asset at that price, on or before a specific date in the future, is a put option. A contract that gives one party the right to buy an asset at a certain price and the other party an obligation to sell the asset at that price, on or before a specific date in the future, is a call option.

208 A Both statements are true

The FRA locks the company into the specific interest rate, regardless of which way underlying interest rates move. The IRG is an option on the FRA, which means that it can be allowed to lapse, giving the user more flexibility. A premium is, however, paid up front to get this flexibility.

209 B

If you sell a futures contract, you have a contract to borrow money (not lend). What you are selling is the contract to make interest payments.

DB – for deposits, buy futures contracts

BS – for borrowings, sell futures contracts

On close out of the futures contracts, the opposite transaction will be done.

210 C

Flat yield theory does not influence the yield curve.

Liquidity preference theory helps to explain an upward sloping curve (long-term investors are rewarded for their extra risk levels by receiving a higher yield). Expectations theory suggests, for example, that an upward sloping curve indicates that interest rates will rise in the future. Market segmentation theory explains why there may be different shapes to the curve at the long-term and short-term ends.

211 B

The relationship between time to maturity and the return to bond investors, shown as the form of a yield (return in relation to the price paid).

212 B

An option gives the flexibility to protect against unfavourable movements, but take advantage of favourable ones.

As the UK company will be selling the Euros they receive from the customer, they need a put option (right to sell) on Euros rather than a call option (right to buy).

213 B

The normal yield curve slopes upward to reflect increasing compensation to investors for being unable to use their cash now (B).

Raising interest rates is a contractionary monetary policy that would stifle spending (A).

It is the risk to the investor, not the company, that determines yields (C).

Expectations theory relates to expectations of future interest rates, not inflation rates.

214 D

Inflation rates are not relevant to Interest Rate Parity theory (they are relevant to Purchasing Power Parity Theory).

215 C

Basis risk is the possibility that movements in the currency futures price and the spot exchange rate will be different. It is one of the reasons for an imperfect currency futures hedge.

216 1.62

Six-month country Y $ interest rate = 1% × 6/12 = 0.5%

Six-month country X peso interest rate = 3% × 6/12 = 1.5%

Forward rate = spot rate × (1 + counter currency country interest rate)/(1 + base currency country interest rate).

Because the rate is quoted in pesos per $, pesos is the counter currency and $ is the base currency. Remember to put the interest rates in as decimals in the formula.

Forward rate = 1.60 × 1.015/1.005 = 1.62 pesos per $

217 Incorrect, Correct, Incorrect, Incorrect

It is correct that the cost of an interest rate floor is higher than the cost of an interest rate collar. The other statements are incorrect.

A floor is a minimum rate so is useful for hedging against falls in rates for a deposit. The premium on an option is payable when the option is purchased. The option may be allowed to lapse (i.e. never exercised). The standardised nature of futures contracts means that over- or under-hedging is very likely (an imperfect hedge). They are still effective as hedges despite this.

218 4-9 FRA with a rate fixed at 4.0%

The start date of the FRA should be in 4 months' time when the borrowing will be required and it should end in 9 months when the borrowing will finish. As it is a borrowing, the larger of the spread of rates will be offered by the bank as this would provide more interest income to the bank than using the lower rate and the bank always offers the rate that works to its benefit.

219 5,181

The forward rates provided have the counter currency as Japanese yen and the base currency (always the currency stated as a value of 1) of New Zealand dollars. When choosing a rate, it can be useful to work out what the bank is doing with the counter currency, as with this currency it will buy high and sell low.

Here, Plum Co will need to purchase the counter currency, Yen, in order to make the payment in yen. This means the bank is selling the counter currency and will offer the low rate of the spread.

Yen 400,000/77.2 = 5181 New Zealand dollars to the nearest dollar.

220 1.4718

Future Spot Rate = Current Spot Rate × (1 + inflation rate in counter currency)/(1 + inflation rate in base currency)

The $ is the base currency for the given future spot rate. Note the base currency has a value of 1 and the other currency is the counter currency.

Therefore, an unknown rate × 1.02/1.035 = 1.4505

Rearrange the formula so that Current Spot Rate = Future Spot Rate/(1 + inflation rate in counter currency/1 + inflation rate in base currency)

Therefore 1.4505/(1.02/1.035) = 1.4718 euro per $1

If you got the inflation rates the wrong way round you would have instead calculated 1.4505/(1.035/1.02) = 1.4295 euro per $1

221 A and B

Smoothing is holding a balanced mix of both fixed and floating rate debt. This will reduce the effects of an interest rate change but not eliminate it completely, so interest payments will still increase following a rise in rates, therefore statements A and B are correct.

Full benefit will not be obtained from a fall in rates due to the fixed element of the debt portfolio. Financing fixed cash flow investments with fixed rate debt is a matching strategy, not smoothing.

222 $73,500

The period covered by the FRA is seven months (4-11 represents month 4 to month 11) and it has an interest rate spread of 2.85% – 2.35%. The two rates represent annual borrowing and deposit rates, with the borrowing always being the higher of the two. The rates will be annual unless specified otherwise in the question.

As this company has a loan, their borrowing rate will be fixed by the FRA at 2.85%.

As their actual rate on the loan ended up being 3.75%, the FRA will pay the difference to the company, bringing their overall borrowing rate back down to the FRA rate of 2.85%.

Difference in interest rates = 3.75% – 2.85% = 0.9%

The amount received from the financial institution = $14m × 0.9% × 7/12 = $73,500.

223 C and F

The correct answers are C and F.

Exchange tradable options and futures contracts are the instruments which have standard contract sizes. All of the other instruments can be tailored to the exact requirements of the hedge.

224 B

The difference between the amounts of interest-sensitive assets and liabilities is a description of gap exposure. A significant number of students choose other options to this question, suggesting that this topic is not well understood by many students.

225 B

An over-the-counter option is an agreement with a financial institution and an immediate premium is payable on taking out the option. However, it cannot be traded (over-the-counter means it has been created specifically for this purpose) and it is only exercised if actual interest rates are less favourable.

226 B and D

An interest rate floor is used to protect against a fall in interest rates (think of it as 'you can't go lower than the floor), whereas a cap is used to limit the maximum interest rate. A collar is a combination of a cap and a floor and could be used to protect both against an increase and a decrease in interest rates. A number of candidates selected money market hedge. Although this is used for hedging foreign exchange risk, because interest rates are used in the calculation this may have prompted some candidates to select this option.

227 A $25,000

The correct FRA of the two available is 3 v 7, which covers a loan that starts in 3 months' time and ends in 7 months' time.

As the FRA is being taken on in relation to a borrowing, it is the higher rate that is fixed, 5.0%.

As the actual borrowing ends up being at 5.3%, the FRA will reimburse (5.3% – 5.0%) 0.3% to Kaya Co.

The amount reimbursed is calculated as 0.3% × $25m × 4/12 = $25,000

Remember, unless told otherwise, the rates are annual rates, so you need to pro rate them for the period of the loan – hence the multiplication by 4/12 in the above calculation.

228 $516,129

As a forward contract is being used, it is the forward rate rather than the spot rate that is relevant.

Since Shadow Co is buying pounds, the correct forward rate is 0.775.

You could work this out using the rule that the bank buys the counter currency at the high rate and sells it at the low rate (the bank buys high and sells low). The counter currency is the currency that does not have a value of 1 in the exchange rate. In this case, it is £s.

Shadow Co is buying £s, so the bank is selling them – hence (sells low), the low forward rate of 0.775 is used.

The amount payable is therefore £400,000/0.775 = $516,129.

If you're unsure as to whether to multiply or divide by the exchange rate, remember that the currency with the smaller number in the exchange rate should also have the smaller monetary number. In this case, £s have a value of 0.775 in the exchange rate and $s have a value of 1. Therefore, the $ number should be larger than the £ number. Multiplying by the rate would have produced a smaller $ number and would be incorrect.

Section 5

ANSWERS TO OBJECTIVE TEST CASE STUDY QUESTIONS – SECTION B

FINANCIAL MANAGEMENT FUNCTION AND ENVIRONMENT

229 Y CO

(a) **B and D**

A is false – MM suggested that the pattern of dividends was irrelevant.

B is true – the fear that many shareholders will view the cut similarly is the clientele effect.

C is false – residual theory suggests undertaking all positive NPV investments before paying a dividend.

D is true – the cut in dividend may signal to shareholders that the company is now higher risk.

(b) **B**

PPPT suggests that exchange rates will move to compensate for differences in inflation rates.

(c) **B and D**

A is false – profits have a poor correlation with shareholder value, so it is possible to boost short-term profit at the expense of shareholder wealth.

B is true. A fiduciary duty means that the agents (the directors) must act in the best interests of the principals (the shareholders), both legally and ethically.

C is false – the sackings may generate bad publicity that erodes investor confidence and hence reduces the share price.

D is true.

(d) **B**

Statement (i) is true – restricting the money supply (for instance by increasing the requirement for banks to hold cash reserves leaving less money that those banks are able to lend out to customers) directly impacts demand for goods – especially those that would be bought on credit. It has less impact on costs, for example, oil prices or wages paid.

Statement (ii) is true – restricting the money supply will reduce the ability of banks to lend. They will in turn be more discerning in who they lend to. This often leads to smaller businesses without good track records struggling to obtain funds.

Statement (iii) is false – restricting the money supply is part of monetary policy.

(e) C

A is true – this is known as economic inefficiency.

B is true – the lack of competition means monopolies can make excessive profits without having to spend on new products or processes.

C is false – monopolies are more likely to engage in price discrimination to boost profits.

D is true – monopolies may charge high prices to deter entrants.

230 ARKWRIGHT CO

(a) 8.8%

$g = (D_0/D_n)^{1/n} - 1$

$g = (\$0.21/\$0.15)^{1/4} - 1$

$g = 0.0878$ or 8.8%

Note that there are 5 dividends but only 4 periods of growth between them, hence $n = 4$

(b) B and D

Monetary policy aims to control the economy by using interest rates and amending the size of the money supply.

Fiscal policy aims to manage the economy using taxation and government spending.

If inflation is high due to rising aggregate demand then increasing interest rates rather than cutting them is a way of trying to supress and reduce demand (as saving becomes more attractive and borrowing to spend less attractive).

Increased government borrowing leads to increased government spending, meaning less need for business investment. It also raises interest rates, making it harder for businesses to borrow and invest.

(c) A

If the budget deficit is increasing then government spending exceeds government taxation income and if this is the case then government borrowing will also be rising. If government spending is rising more than taxation income then the deficit will be growing.

(d) B and F

EPS uses earnings after taxation and so would fall. ROCE uses profits before interest and taxation so would not initially be affected.

(e) B

Both statements are true. Externalities do not directly affect the producer or consumer of the product but affect other members of society.

Because it doesn't affect them directly, producers and consumers often ignore externalities and end up producing/buying more of products with external costs and fewer of those with external benefits – a misallocation of resources.

WORKING CAPITAL MANAGEMENT

231 GREEN CO

(a) Is an assumption, Is not an assumption

Demand has to be constant so that average inventory is half of the order quantity. As long as the lead-time is constant and known, this is sufficient for the EOQ formula to hold; it does not have to be zero.

(b) 40 units

C_o = \$10; D = 4,000; C_h = \$2 + 10% of \$480 = \$50

EOQ = $\sqrt{}$(2 × C_o × D ÷ C_h) = $\sqrt{}$(2 × 10 × 4,000 ÷ 50) = 40 units

The alternative answers come from either ignoring the cost of capital tied up in inventory or including the non-relevant fixed salary of the chief buyer (or both).

If the examiner gives you a C_h figure, you can use it directly. Otherwise, look for items like storage/insurance costs for inventory plus the cost of capital and purchase price so that you can calculate the opportunity holding cost of inventory (e.g. above 10% × \$480 represents the opportunity cost of cash being tied up in inventory instead of being available for use elsewhere in the business).

(c) 77 units

The company must be sure that there is sufficient inventory on hand when it places an order to last the weeks' lead-time. It must therefore place an order when there is one weeks' worth of demand in inventory:

i.e. re-order level = 1/52 × 4,000 = **77 units** remaining in inventory.

(d) B

A JIT model operates with very low levels of inventory. It is therefore likely that moving to a JIT system from an EOQ one will reduce the inventory levels and therefore the total annual inventory holding costs. With such low inventory levels, replenishment of the inventory will need to be made more frequently. Therefore it is likely that total annual ordering costs will rise.

Periodic review means ordering inventory at a fixed and regular time interval. Inventory levels are reviewed at a fixed time. The inventory in hand is then made up to a predetermined level.

Under the EOQ model, holding costs and ordering costs are balanced off, with the EOQ being at the point where these are equal to each other.

Statements 1 and 3 are correct.

(e) D

One of the earliest American firms to adopt JIT was Hewlett Packard who put forward all of these, based on a study of four of their divisions.

232 HALL CO

(a) **Would influence, Would influence, Would influence, Would not influence**

Supplier's terms help determine credit policy in respect of accounts payable, rather than accounts receivable.

(b) **$14,400**

Cash sales don't generate a receivables balance, so need only the business sales.

Sales $1,600,000; business sales = 60% of $1.6m = $960,000

Receivables = (0.4 × 1/12 + 0.4 × 2/12 + 0.2 × 3/12) × $960,000 = $144,000

Interest costs = 10% of $144,000 = $14,400

Incorrect answers may come from taking costs of sales into account and reducing the time by which payment has been brought forward by a month.

(c) **A**

Effective annual cost = $(1 + (\text{discount}/\text{amount left to pay}))^{(12/\text{no of months saved})} - 1$

2 month to 1 month (1 month saved) = $(1 + 1.5/98.5)^{12/1} - 1 = 0.1989$ or 19.89%

3 month to 1 month (2 months saved) = $(1 + 1.5/98.5)^{12/2} - 1 = 0.0949$ or 9.49%

Alternative answers come from confusing current receivables collection periods and reduction of receivables collection periods and reducing the time by which payment has been brought forward by a month.

Tutorial note

The IRR of a project that involves bringing forward the date of receipt of cash from a customer can be seen by looking at the comparative cash flows.

Time	*0*	*month 1*	*month 2*
No discount	–	–	*100*
With discount	–	*98.5*	–
Subtracting	–	*(98.5)*	*100*

An extra $1.50 is being made on an 'investment' of $98.50 by a customer, a return over the month of 1.523 per month, or 19.89 per year.

(d) **D**

Under debt factoring the customer will be aware that a factor is being used as the payment details on the invoice will be for the factor. Under invoice discounting this is not the case and the customer will be unaware that invoice discounting is being used.

Invoice discounters lend money using the business's receivables assets as security. Debt factors effectively purchase the receivables assets from the business.

(e) **B**

The list (excluding B) has appeared in a model answer from the ACCA of roles of a credit control department. The second option would be part of the role of a purchase ledger department.

233 JEEPS CO

(a) **A**

To calculate the benefit of paying less money, we can use the formula $[1 + (\text{discount}/\text{amount left to pay})]^{(360/\text{days earlier payment is made})} - 1$

For the invoices currently paid at 60 days, payment will be made 45 days earlier and the annual saving is $[1 + (2/98)]^{(360/45)} - 1 = 0.175$ or 17.5%

For the invoices currently paid at 90 days, payment will be made 75 days earlier and the annual saving is $[1 + (2/98)]^{(360/75)} - 1 = 0.102$ or 10.2%

These figures need to be compared to the cost of capital, which is 12%.

The benefit of the cash saved on the 60 day payment is 17.5%, but the cost (of the increased funding needed due to the lower payables balance) is 12%. This means the settlement discount should be accepted.

The benefit of the cash saved on the 90 day payment is only 10.2%, which is lower than the cost of extra working capital funding needed at 12%, so this discount would not be worthwhile.

> ***Tutorial note***
>
> *Marginally different annual returns are reached (17.8% and 10.2%) if the periods of the 'investment' are taken as 1½ months and 2½ months, but the conclusion is the same.*

(b) **67 days**

Total payables = \$2m × 12 × 30/360 + \$3m × 12 × 60/360 + \$4m × 12 × 90/360 = \$20m

Total credit purchases = (\$2m + \$3m + \$4m) × 12 = \$108m

Accounts payable payment period = \$20m ÷ \$108m × 360 = 67 days

> ***Tutorial note***
>
> *30 days per month = 360 days per year for the calculation.*
>
> *A weighted average of payables would also give the correct figure of 67.*

(c) **B**

Overtrading is stimulated by a rapid increase in revenue. With higher sales levels, current asset balances for inventory and receivables, as well as the payables level, should rise in proportion to the rise in sales.

Rises in working capital need to be funded. If such funding isn't available, the company may not be able to cope with the rapid growth. Collection of debts may become slower, leading to a rise in the value of the receivables collection period. Cash may not be available to pay suppliers, leading to a rise in the payables payment period.

Extra funding needs to be injected to support the business while it is growing. Increasing shareholder funds suggests that the business is aware of an increasing need for extra capital as it expands and that shareholders understand that need. Therefore, increasing the funds available to the business is a means of addressing overtrading rather than a feature of it.

(d) **$6,300**

We're given an annual rate for the cost of capital but need to adjust it to a monthly rate for the calculation:

Monthly rate = $(1.12^{(1/12)} - 1) \times 100 = 0.95\%$

PV = future cash flow × $(1 + r)^{-n}$

PV of instalments = $75 + 45 \times 1.0095^{-1} + 45 \times 1.0095^{-2} + 45 \times 1.0095^{-3} + 45 \times 1.0095^{-4} + 45 \times 1.0095^{-5}$ = $293,727

Paying by instalments will save Jeeps Co $6,273 compared to paying $300,000 immediately (or $6,300 to the nearest $00).

(e) **Aggressive, Aggressive**

Aggressive policies for working capital investment involve keeping the levels of current assets (inventory and receivables) low and of payables high. This is a risky strategy but reduces the cost of funding working capital. Conservative policies keep the level of current assets high and of payables low. This is safer, but more expensive.

Delaying payment to creditors will keep the payables balance high.

234 KING CO

(a) C

Baumol tranche size = $\sqrt{(2 \times \$500 \times \$1,000,000 \div 0.05)}$ = $141,421

Alternative answers arise from not entering the interest rate as a decimal or using total demand for cash rather than annual demand.

(b) D

Miller-Orr spread = $3 \times (\frac{3}{4} \times \$7,000^2 \times \$500 \div (0.05/365))^{1/3}$ = $153,569

Alternative answers come from using standard deviation instead of variance or not calculating a daily interest rate (entered into the formula as a decimal not a percentage) from the annual one given.

(c) **$211,200**

Month	**3**	**4**	**5**	**6**	**7**
Sales volume (000s)	10	11	13	16	20
Sales revenue ($000)	240	264	312	384	480
Cash sales (20%)	48.0	52.8	62.4	76.8	96
Receivables:					
1-month (25% of 80%)	–	48.0	52.8	62.4	76.8
2-month (50% of 80%)	–	–	96.0	105.6	124.8
3-month (25% of 80%)	–	–	–	48.0	52.8
			211.2		

The alternative answers come from not spotting that credit sales are only 80% of total sales and from getting the months muddled.

Tutorial note

The calculations for months other than Month 5 are not essential but tend to reduce the chance of making mistakes (although, without the need for calculations of payments, Months 6 and 7 could be ignored).

(d) **Both statements are true**

(e) **C**

Divisional responsibility for cash will be reduced as the responsibility will be held centrally.

235 GRUMPY CO

(a) **B**

Receivables collection period = trade receivables/credit sales × 365 = $\frac{85,000}{480,000} \times 365$

= 65 days

(b) **52 days**

Payables payment period = trade payables/credit purchases × 365 = $\frac{30,000}{212,000} \times 365$

= 52 days

(c) **B**

Inventory holding period = closing inventory/cost of sales × 365

$= \frac{52,000}{226,000} \times 365 = 84$ days

The cost of sales of £226,000 is equal to opening inventory + purchases – closing inventory (45,000 + 233,000 – 52,000)

(d) **112 days**

The start of the cycle is the point at which the supplier is paid. This is on 25/02/15.

The end point of the cycle is the date on which Grumpy receives the payment from the debtor. The goods were delivered 21 days after the order on 07/02/15. They were sold 62 days later on 10/04/15. The debtor then took 68 days to pay (the offered credit is irrelevant) and so Grumpy was paid on 17/06/15.

The number of days between 25/2/15 and 17/6/15 is the operating cycle for cycle X and this is 112 days.

Alternatively, from the delivery (and invoice) date from the supplier on 07/02/15, the payables payment period (until 25/02/15) comes to 18 days. Add together the inventory holding period of 62 days and the receivables collection period of 68 days and deduct the payables payment period of 18 days to get to the 112 days of the cycle.

(e) True, True

A period of strong growth when a business has a long operating cycle is a classic example of over trading.

New businesses tend to struggle to get credit from suppliers and often have to give longer credit to customers for fear of breaking a new and fragile relationship with them.

236 AMAX CO

(a) B

Compare total annual inventory costs before and after the bulk purchase discount is accepted.

Total annual inventory costs = purchase costs + ordering costs + holding costs

Purchase costs = D × P

Ordering costs = Co × D/Q

Holding costs = Ch × Q/2

Where D = annual demand, P = purchase price, Co = cost per order, Q = order quantity and Ch = annual holding cost per unit per year.

Before the discount is taken:

Purchase costs = 240,000 × $25 = $6,000,000

Ordering costs = $250 × 240,000/20,000 = $3,000

Holding costs = $1.00 × 20,000/2 = $10,000

Total annual inventory costs = $6,013,000

After the discount is taken:

Purchase costs = 240,000 × $25 × 99.5% = $5,970,000

Ordering costs = $250 × 240,000/60,000 = $1,000

Holding costs = $1.00 × 60,000/2 = $30,000

Total annual inventory costs = $6,001,000

Therefore, accepting the discount leads to a benefit of ($6,013,000 – $6,001,000) $12,000

(b) A

Current annual purchases from Colix:

Accounts payables payment period in days = payables/credit purchases × 360

Credit purchases = payables/payables payment period × 360 = $3,200,000/72 × 360 = $16,000,000

Cash saved by paying 1% less = $16,000,000 × 1% = $160,000

Current finance saving from having a payables balance = payables balance × finance cost % = $3,200,000 × 6% = $192,000

New payables balance if the discount is accepted: $3,200,000/72 × 30 = $1,333,333

New finance saving: $1,333,333 × 6% = $80,000

Saving lost = $192,000 – $80,000 = $112,000

Net position = $160,000 – $112,000 = $48,000 saving overall.

(c) D

It is correct that discounting bills of exchange (issuing a bill at a value lower than its maturity value) can reduce foreign accounts receivable (FAR) default risk since it reduces the level of investment in FAR.

A is incorrect because companies expecting to receive foreign currency from FAR will be concerned about the risk of the foreign currency depreciating, rather than appreciating, against the domestic currency. If the foreign currency appreciates, it can be exchanged for more of the home currency and the company will be better off, not worse.

B is incorrect as the company is exposed to non-payment. If payment was received before shipping, this would be much safer.

C is incorrect. Credit worthiness will be assessed as part of obtaining the insurance and the insurance may not cover the entire debt, so the foreign customer should still be assessed to reduce the risk of default. Also, if customers default, future insurance premiums will be higher. Assessing creditworthiness and only taking on creditworthy customers would reduce the likelihood of this happening.

(d) C

It is correct that local autonomy is decreased by centralised treasury management. This also means that local management will be less incentivised rather than more incentivised to maximise profitability as they are able to exert less control over it.

In relation to option B, centralised treasury management would be less responsive, rather than more responsive, to the requirements of local business units, as they are juggling work for all units at the same time.

For option D, a centralised treasury department would minimise the number of hedging transactions and therefore reduce the costs of hedging foreign currency risk. They can do this by netting off currency and borrowing/deposit requirements and only hedging the net exposure rather than every single transaction.

(e) C

Fluctuating current assets are effectively short-term assets and should be matched with short-term finance. This matches the term of the assets to the term of the finance and is an efficient method of funding them.

An aggressive strategy aims to maximise profitability despite the risk of doing so. In relation to working capital funding, this would relate to using a high proportion of cheap but risky short-term finance and a low proportion of safer but more expensive long-term finance.

Short-term finance is generally cheaper than long-term, because there is less risk for the lender and therefore they can't demand a high return. Note that this applies to secured lending and so doesn't apply to overdrafts, which are unsecured and therefore more expensive.

Moderate working capital funding strategies use the matching principle. As some current assets are essentially permanently in place (buffer inventory, minimum receivables from customers paying on time) they should be financed with long-term funding.

INVESTMENT APPRAISAL

237 BELL CO

(a) **A**

(1 + nominal (money) rate) = (1 + real rate) × (1 + general inflation rate)

Nominal cost of capital = (1.05 × 1.02) – 1 = 7.1%

(b) **99**

Actual cash flow in 4 years = $120,000 × 1.04^3 = $134,984

Present value discounted at 8% = $134,984 × 1.08^{-4} = $99,217

Answer to the nearest thousand dollars is **$99,000**

(c) **D**

Time	**0**	**1**	**2**	**3**
	$000	$000	$000	$000
Inflow (in money terms)	–	2,040	3,121	2,122
Outflow (in money terms)	(1,000)	(1,854)	(2,652)	(1,639)
Net cash flow	(1,000)	186	469	483
Present value at 9%	(1,000)	171	395	373
NPV = $(61,000)				

Answer A has discounted current cash flows at the rates of inflation rather than at the money cost of capital, answer B has ignored inflation and answer C has only used one year of inflation for the cash flows at times 2 and 3.

Tutorial note

This final mistake is easy to make; anyone who thought C was correct needs to check how the money cash flows in the model answer were calculated (the figures have been rounded to the nearest $'000 in the workings).

(d) **B**

A is incorrect. There is no decision rule with simulations. B is a clear advantage that simulations have over sensitivity analysis. C is incorrect. The input variables and distributions are estimates. D has some validity potentially, but is not necessarily the case.

(e) The **answer is yes** and the **reason is that it will happen if the rate of inflation exceeds the money cost of capital.**

This was a situation that was highlighted by Brian Carsberg and Tony Hope in the 1970s (a time of high inflation) in their book Business Investment Decisions under Inflation, ICAEW, 1976. With the current state of low interest rates, the situation may be just as relevant today.

Reason A is not correct, the only negative discount rate that makes calculating an NPV tricky is –100%. Tutorial note: You may wish to use a spreadsheet to calculate the NPV of a simple project for a range of discount rates from –200% to + 200%.

Reason B is not correct since there have been many instances of negative interest rates. The European Central Bank recently introduced negative rates, which have also been seen in Sweden, Denmark and Switzerland.

Reason C is not correct since deflation (negative inflation) is likely to increase the chance of having a positive real discount rate (unless your money cost of capital is even more negative).

238 CARE CO

(a) $228,000

Equivalent annual cost = PV of the cash flows of the cycle/annuity factor for that cycle length

Discount machine 2's cash flows to find their present value, which will be a cost:

Net present cost ($) = (540,000) + (47,000) × 2.487 + 120,000 × 0.751 = (566,769)

Equivalent annual cost = $566,769 ÷ 2.487 = $227,893, or $228,000 to the nearest $000

(b) Both statements are correct

The EAC method assumes that the operating efficiency of the machines will be similar. The method also assumes that the assets will be replaced in perpetuity, or at least into the foreseeable future.

(c) C

Take care with the calculation of probabilities. Joint probabilities are where 2 things both happen, and their individual probabilities are multiplied together to determine their overall probability. If either one result or another can happen to satisfy the outcome, their probabilities are added together.

Care Co can expect to receive the full $120,000 if neither negative aspect happens (probability 0.6 × 0.7)

They can expect to receive $108,000 if either one of the negative aspects happens (probability 0.4 × 0.7 for only the new supplier entering the market and 0.6 × 0.3 for only the strength of the dollar)

They can expect to receive only $96,000 if both happen (probability 0.4 × 0.3)

Scrap value	Probability		Expected value
$120,000	0.6 × 0.7	= 0.42	50,400
$108,000	(0.4 × 0.7) + (0.6 × 0.3)	= 0.46	49,680
$96,000	0.4 × 0.3	= 0.12	11,520
		1.00	$111,600

Answers B and D ignore joint probabilities; whereas answers A and B misinterpret the effects of a strong dollar (a strong dollar would make an overseas sale less attractive).

(d) **Only statement 2 is true**

Simulation will not eliminate the effects of risk. It will merely help quantify the effects by producing a range of possible NPVs and an idea of the probability distribution of those NPVs.

(e) **B**

Using the 'lowest common multiple' approach (12 years) is an alternative to simple replacement decisions.

239 EASTER CO

(a) **False, False, True, False**

Hard rationing is the limit on the amount of finance imposed by the lending institutions, so come from external factors. Soft rationing is from internal factors, for instance the decision to save some cash for a later project or the unwillingness to tie up all available cash for many years.

(b) **A and E**

Project	**NPV**	**Investment**	**NPV/$**	**Rank**
	$000	$000	$	
A	4,900	3,200	1.53	2nd
B	7,400	9,320	0.80	5th
C	5,900	7,300	0.81	4th
D	7,500	5,200	1.44	3rd
E	9,000	5,600	1.61	1st

Total investment required is $30.62m, total available is $10m.

Possible combinations (assuming that will give a higher NPV than any single project):

Project A and D NPV ($000) = 4,900 + 7,500 = 12,400

Projects A and E NPV ($000) = 4,900 + 9,000 = 13,900

These are higher than the NPVs of any single project.

The calculation of profitability index (PI) as NPV per $ of investment and the ranking of projects is not needed for this part of the question, but has been included as a working for part (d).

(c) **A**

Based on the workings of the previous question, now the combination A and E is not possible (since they are mutually exclusive). This leaves the highest NPV as combination A and D.

(d) **B**

Using the previous NPV/$ calculations and rankings, the combination accepted must be A plus E plus a portion of D.

Tutorial note

To reach the correct answer to this question, it doesn't matter what proportion of D is required, the answer to the correct option of the four is Option B. The next calculation is therefore unnecessary.

Projects A and E require a total investment of $8.8m, leaving $1.2m to invest in part of Project D. Since Project D requires a total investment of $5.2m, the proportion of that project undertaken can be:

1.2m ÷ 5.2m = 3/13 (as in Option B) or 23.1%

(e) **A and E**

The NPV at a discount rate of zero (the sum of the undiscounted cash flows) is negative at $(30,000), which may cause confusion as the board members may feel that it could therefore never earn a positive NPV.

Knowing that the sign of the cash flows changes twice (an outflow followed by an inflow and then another outflow) means that the project can have up to 2 IRRs, which could also be a source of confusion.

The NPV at an infinitely high discount rate (equal to the initial investment amount as any later cash flows would be discounted to zero) is $(4,000,000).

If the NPV is negative at 0% and at an infinite percent and there are up to 2 IRRs, it suggests an n shaped curve that crosses the $0 NPV line in up to 2 places. There should therefore be a positive NPV at some point (see diagram).

As IRRs can be calculated for the project, it does not have 'no real IRRs'.

The shape of the curve suggests a range of positive IRRs where the curve is above the $0 NPV and a range of negative ones elsewhere. There is not just one positive and one negative IRR.

Graph of NPV (in $00,000) against discount rate for the project.

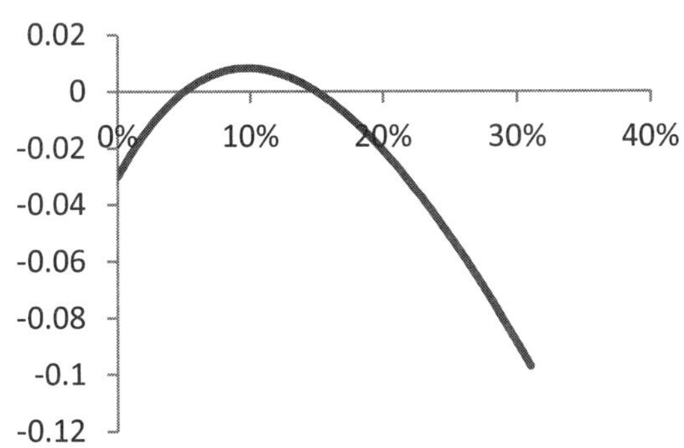

240 ACE CO

(a) B

NPV of project. Note that allocated overheads are not a relevant cash flow and, without them included, the tax cash flow changes to $6,250.

Time	Description	CF	DF @ 12%	PV $
0	Loose tools	(6,000)	1	(6,000)
1–4	Contribution	25,000	3.037	75,925
1–4	Allocated overhead	0		0
2–5	Tax on contribution	(6,250)	2.712	(16,950)
	NPV			52,975

(b) C

Statement 1 is true. Statement 2 is false. The pattern of cash flows can affect this decision, for example, for projects where positive cash flows arise first with negative cash flows thereafter then the statement would be false. Ultimately, the NPV at the cost of capital is the main calculation to determine acceptability.

(c) C

The reported profits are not affected by tax-allowable depreciation. The current NPV is positive and would be made more positive by the extra tax savings so the decision would not alter.

(d) **2.9 months**

The payback period is

In the first year the project spends 6,000 but receives 25,000. The tax flow does not arise until the following year. So, the payback is (6,000/25,000) × 12 months = 2.9 months.

(e) **True, True, False**

One of payback's problems is the lack of a clear decision criterion.

241 FENCE CO

(a) **2.75 years**

Cumulative cash flows:

t0 (3,900)

t1 (3,900) + 1,200 = (2,700)

t2 (2,700) + 1,500 = (1,200)

t3 (1,200) + 1,600 = 400

Payback period = 2 years + (1,200/1,600) = 2.75 years.

(b) 26.0%

Average annual operating profit = (Total operating cash flows – total depreciation)/ life of project.

Note: capital investment and scrap value are not operating cash flows. Total depreciation = difference between capital investment and scrap value.

= (5,880 – 3,800)/4 = $520,000 per year

Average investment = average of capital investment and scrap values.

Average investment = (3,900 + 100)/2 = $2,000,000

ROCE = 520/2,000 × 100 = 26%

(c) C and D

Risk can be taken into account by shortening the required payback period, meaning that only those cash flows closer to the present (and thus less risky) are considered.

Payback period does ignore the timing of cash flows within the payback period. It just considers the cumulative total of the cash flows to date.

ROCE does not incorporate the time value of money and cannot be directly compared to the cost of equity. It needs to be compared to a specific ROCE target.

(d) D

All the statements are correct. Managerial reward schemes should encourage the achievement of shareholder objectives to address the principal – agent problem. The use of ROCE means that profitability instead of shareholder wealth would be the main decision used to evaluate projects – dysfunctional because it does not necessarily align with improving shareholder wealth. For these reasons, the agency problem exists at Fence Co.

(e) C

Introducing a share option scheme would help bring directors' objectives naturally in line with shareholders' objectives as directors will become potential shareholders. Linking financial rewards to a target return on capital employed will encourage short-term profitability and discourage capital investment are correct. Capital projects often return low profits in their early years. Executive directors' pay in a listed company should be subject to the recommendations of a remuneration committee made up wholly of independent non-executive directors.

242 LINK CO

(a) 13.2%

This is a calculation of the sensitivity to the sales volume, calculated as (NPV/PV of cash flows affected by the changing variable) and calculated as a percentage.

When sales volumes change, all variable cash flows will change proportionally, so the cash flows affected are the contribution cash flows, made up of both revenue and variable costs.

$511/$3,880 × 100 = 13.2%

(b) **A**

Sensitivity Analysis does not assess the risk of a project (probability analysis does).

A critical factor may be identified, such as the price of a particular component, but the managers may have no control over that price. Sensitivity analysis is only capable of looking at changes in one variable at a time, so necessarily ignores that a change in one variable may be linked to changes in others.

(c) **C**

Annual operating cash flow = $729,000

Annual depreciation = $1,800,000/4 = $450,000

Annual profit = operating cash flows – depreciation = $729,000 – $450,000 = $279,000

Average investment = $1,800,000/2 = $900,000

ROCE = $279,000/$900,000 × 100 = 31%

(d) **C**

A new issue of loan notes takes place in the primary market.

Long-term debt in Euros would be via the Eurobond capital markets. The interest rate paid on the new issue of debt will be influenced by market rates and the risk level the investors perceive that the company has. They may consider the company's WACC in assessing risk, but this will not be the only factor. Debt can be issued without security, although at a higher rate than secured debt due to the extra risks involved for the lender.

(e) **Correct, Correct, Correct**

All three statements are correct.

243 GAIMETT CO

(a) **D**

As the projects are divisible, the profitability index (NPV/$ invested) should be calculated to rank the projects and the cash allocated in order of the ranking.

Project	NPV	Investment value	Profitability index	Ranking
	$000	$000		
A	125	375	0.33	2
B	240	800	0.3	3
C	80	400	0.2	5
D	40	50	0.8	1
E	150	600	0.25	4

Of the $1.5 million, cash can be allocated to projects D, A and B in full, with $275,000 left for the fourth ranked project, E.

(275/600) 45.8% of project E can be done with this remaining cash.

(b) C

The projects are now indivisible so cannot be done in part. The optimum combination can be found by looking at all possible combinations and choosing the one with the highest NPV. For example:

B, C and D would generate $360,000

C, D and E would generate $270,000

B, D and E would generate $430,000

B, C, D and E is not a possible combination as it would use too much investment cash.

(c) C and D

Soft capital rationing comes from internal decisions, such as managers believing that better quality projects will become available or because they wish to hold onto some cash to provide against unexpected expenditure (the precautionary motive). Answers A, B and E relate to external factors and therefore relate to hard capital rationing.

(d) A and D

The cash is only available for investment over a 3-month period and will be needed at that point to invest in the new project. This means that long-term investments are unsuitable, and high risk investments, where some or all of the cash may be lost, should be avoided. Investments where Gaimett Co may struggle to return the cash should also be avoided.

Certificates of deposit and instant access bank accounts would both be suitable under these circumstances. Listed company shares would be too risky, as the share prices could fall, and the entire cash may not be returned. Listed company debt would also suffer from this risk. Unlisted company shares may be difficult to sell, meaning that cash isn't returned back in time. Their value could also fall.

(e) C

Tax allowable depreciation is not a cash flow and should not be included. All the others do involve payments or receipts of cash, so would be included. Note that any tax savings in relation to the tax allowable depreciation would affect the amount paid for tax and therefore would be included.

BUSINESS FINANCE AND COST OF CAPITAL

244 BRASH CO

(a) **True, False**

Leasing companies sometimes pass the obligation for maintenance back to the lessee, as everything is negotiable.

(b) **A and D**

Both calculations will discount the relevant cash flows at the post-tax cost of borrowing, which accounts for the cost of any interest payments. This means that to include the interest payments themselves would be double counting, so they would not be included. The saving on maintenance, residual value and tax – allowable depreciation all apply to one option and not the other and so would need to be included to make a comparison between the two options. The cash benefits arising from use of the machinery should be the same under either option so do not need to be considered.

(c) **B**

In lease versus buy calculations, the discount rate to use is the post-tax borrowing rate. The borrowing rate is given at 8% and the tax rate is 25%, so the post-tax rate is 8 × (1–0.25) = 6%.

Maintenance is payable at the end of each year, so the first payment will be at t1 and will last 5 years until t6. Tax is a year in arrears so will occur from t2-t7 in respect of the tax savings on the maintenance expenses. As they are tax savings, they will act as a cash inflow.

Years 1 – 5 maintenance annuity of $20,000 and years 2 – 6 tax savings delayed annuity of 25% of the maintenance costs ($5000), all discounted at 6%. Remember the treatment of delayed annuities. The annuity factor discounts the cash flows back by one time period from their start. Applying the factor to an annuity starting at t2 means that a t1 value is calculated. This then needs to be discounted by one more year to get a present, or t0, value.

Annuity factor 5 years at 6% = 4.212

One year discount factor at 6% = 0.943

Maintenance: $(20,000) × 4.212 = $(84,240)

Tax savings: $5,000 × 4.212 × 0.943 = $19,860

Net PV = $(64,380)

(d) **$145,000**

5 lease payments made at start of the accounting year from time period 0 to time period 4. First tax computation at end of the accounting year, at time period 1. First tax saving is then 1 year in arrears at time period 2. Tax savings are therefore over 5 years from time period 2 to time period 6.

Years 2 – 6 tax relief of $146,000 × 0.25 = $36,500 discounted at 6% post-tax borrowing rate. Delayed annuity starting at t2 so needs to be further discounted for one year after the annuity factor is applied.

$36,500 × 4.212 × 0.943 = $144,975

(e) True, True

If the PV of leasing is cheaper than the PV of purchasing then a project NPV will increase through the use of a lease as opposed to purchasing an asset, so could potentially rise from negative to positive. The existence of a lease will represent extra risk for shareholders that may be perceived by them, due to the legal commitments for cash payments that come with the lease.

245 KELVIN CO

(a) $19.60

The TERP value is calculated as:

$$\text{TERP} = \frac{\text{MV of existing shares} + \text{proceeds from issue}}{\text{Number of shares after issue}}$$

$$\text{TERP} = \frac{(4\text{m} \times \$20) + (1\text{m} \times 20 \times 0.9)}{5\text{m}}$$

TERP = $19.60 per share

(b) C

Whilst the TERP would fall, it could not do so to the detriment of existing shareholders. In the formula above, the total on the top line would remain the same whilst the number of shares on the bottom line would increase.

(c) True, True

Both the statements are true. The discount makes the rights offer appear more attractive and therefore does encourage shareholders to take up their rights, but the theory indicates it should make no difference to the wealth levels of the accepting shareholder.

(d) C

As long as the shareholder takes some form of action they will be better off than doing nothing. The second worst action (by the way) is D as the shareholder will lose out on 50% of the offer.

(e) A

Dilution occurs if a shareholders % ownership reduces. This will not happen if a shareholder takes up 100% of the offer.

246 DOMINANCE CO

(a) **D**

All the other options will involve at least the risk of new shareholders diluting ownership for the existing ones.

(b) **D**

The tax shield is the amount of tax saved due to the payment of interest on debt. It occurs because debt interest is a tax deductible expense. The higher the value of interest paid, the greater the tax shield (on the presumption that it hasn't been exhausted by profits being run down to nil).

Option A has no new tax shield at all as preference dividends do not attract it. Option B does contain a tax shield but presumably less than C and D given the lower debt value and interest rate. Option C has \$0.6m of interest paid annually (\$12m × 5%, remember interest is calculated on nominal value, not market value). Option D has \$0.63m interest paid annually (total nominal value = 120,000 × \$100 = \$12m. This pays interest at 5.25%). As option D pays more interest, it generates a higher tax shield than option C. Always assume unless told otherwise that the individual nominal value of a loan note is \$100.

(c) **14.4%**

The cost of equity formula is:

$Ke = \frac{D_1}{P0} + g$ (where P0 is the ex div price of the shares and D1 = next year's dividend, also calculated as D0(1 + g))

$$Ke = \frac{16 \times 1.10}{420 - 16} + 0.10$$

Ke = 14.4%

Note as the next dividend is due any day, it is a D0 figure rather than a D1 figure, even though it has not been paid yet.

The growth figure should be the anticipated growth of dividends in the future, so the extra 2% on top of the old growth figure should be included, giving growth for the calculation of 10%.

As P0 needs to be an ex-div figure, the imminent dividend is deducted from the cum div price for the calculation.

(d) **3.75%**

The cost of debt formula for irredeemable debt is:

$$Kd = \frac{\text{Interest } (1 - t)}{P0}$$

The interest is the coupon rate applied to the nominal value: 4% × \$100 = \$4

$$Kd = \frac{4(1 - 0.25)}{80}$$

Kd = 3.75%

(e) **D**

The tax shield is relevant but let's consider the numbers.

Equity shareholders demand 14.4%.

Debt holders demand 5% (Note, the return to debt investors is calculated without the tax deduction: $4/$80 × 100 = 5%).

Cost of debt to the company 3.75%.

The tax shield itself only reduces the cost to the company by 1.25% compared to if it wasn't available and the company had to incur the full 5% demanded by debt investors. It is not therefore the main reason why the cost of equity is so much higher. Even without the tax shield the equity cost would still be 9.4% higher than the debt cost.

The main driver for risk premium is systematic risk. All the specific (unsystematic) risk will be ignored by the well-diversified shareholder. As the business is quoted it is reasonable to assume that its investors are well-diversified.

247 EMPIRE CO

(a) **C**

Dividend irrelevancy theory states that shareholders wish to increase their wealth but are indifferent as to whether it comes from dividends received or through a rise in the share price. Companies should therefore focus on project value rather than the pattern of dividend payments.

(b) **B**

The signalling effect is where changes in dividend patterns can affect the investors' view of the business.

(c) **A**

Dividend dependency suggests that investors have invested because of the current pattern of dividends and a change in that pattern will upset that and negate their reasons for investing. Also known as the clientele effect.

(d) **D**

Company liquidity issues mean that the company should only pay out what it can afford or offer a non-cash alternative instead.

(e) **False, True**

A scrip issue gives more shares to shareholders but since the overall market value is not affected then the share price falls. The shareholder does not gain except for an increased marketability.

248 BANK

(a) C and E

A bank is rather unusual in that many of the variables that would normally be counted as systematic risks for other businesses are in fact specific (unsystematic) risks for the bank. Interest rates and defaults fall into this category. Equally, the bank will compete for loans in the market and so that too is a specific risk.

(b) C

The rate of return on government securities is an appropriate figure to use as a risk free rate as government securities should be amongst the lowest risk of all. The calculation is from the investor point of view, so the rate should not be adjusted for tax savings by the company.

(c) "In the CAPM formula R = Rf + βj(Rm – Rf) where βj represents the project beta, R represents **the required return on the new project** and the market risk premium is represented by **(Rm – Rf)**."

The CAPM gives you the required return of equity shareholders for the level of risk indicated by the value of the beta used, therefore if the beta is that of the project then the R value is the return required for the project. (Note that if the beta used were the value for the company **as a whole**, the calculation would give the return required from the company by equity investors, which is equal to the cost of equity capital).

The market risk premium is represented by Rm – Rf. Rm on its own is the market return. The premium represents the extra return demanded by equity investors above the value they would demand from a risk free investment.

(d) 16.75%

We must use the project beta to get the return required on the project. If we were to use the bank's beta, we would calculate the cost of equity for the bank.

$R = Rf + \beta j(Rm - Rf)$

$R = 5.2 + 1.52(12.8 - 5.2)$

$R = 16.75\%$

(e) D

The investment has the same level of systematic risk as the market. Beta values larger than one are for investments with higher risk than the market and those lower than one are for investments that are safer than market investments.

249 FREEDLING CO

(a) False, False

Having fixed costs in a cost structure is risky since they have to be paid and are often unavoidable in the short run if the business starts to turn downwards. This has a magnifying effect on the businesses profit for a given volume change. More fixed costs means more volatility in profits = higher risk.

Variable costs do not add this extra volatility.

(b) D

Statement 1 is untrue. Debt is riskier for the company but safer for the investor and therefore the investors do not demand as high a return as they would for equity. Statement 2 is true. Increasing the proportion of debt increases the variability of returns (risk) to equity shareholders and they demand a higher return to compensate for the increased risk.

The determination of how an increased proportion of debt in the capital structure affects the WACC and the business value is the subject of the capital structure theories (traditional, M&M without tax, M&M with tax) included in the FM syllabus.

(c) Does not hold true, Holds true, Holds true

Under M&M no tax the WACC would generally not change. M&M argued that the level of gearing was not relevant to a company WACC. With corporation tax introduced into their model a tax benefit tended to pull down the WACC as gearing increased.

Under the traditional theory of gearing modest amounts of debt often went unnoticed by shareholders and this lack of response (in the form of increased demands for higher return) meant the WACC fell.

(d) D

It is a common error to think that M&M claimed 'it does not matter how a business raises its finance'. Their theory only looks at a high level comparison between equity and debt. It does not then look at, for example, rights issues versus new issues of shares or redeemable versus irredeemable debt. The second statement is true.

(e) True, True, True

All the statements are true. Even debt holders will become concerned about very high levels of debt as the company's ability to pay interest/redemption may become compromised.

Tax exhaustion is where the benefits of getting tax relief on interest paid end because the tax bill has been brought to zero already. Without the tax relief, debt will inherently become more expensive.

Banks will consider risk levels as well as the interest they can earn and will not generally lend to high risk businesses.

250 TULIP CO

(a) **10.7%**

k_e (aka $E(r_i)$) = $R_f + \beta_i(E(r_m) - R_f)$

$k_e = 2.5 + (1.05 \times 7.8) = 10.7\%$

Note that the 'premium' is represented by $E(r_m) - Rf$. $E(r_m)$ itself would be expressed as the return, not the premium.

(b) **D**

Cost of debt can be calculated as the IRR of the cash flows of owning the debt. Usually, the interest value would need to be a post-tax value, but as no tax is mentioned in the question, no tax adjustment is needed.

Year	$	5% DF	PV	6% DF	PV
0	(100.00)	1.000	(100.00)	1.000	(100.00)
1–5	3.00	4.329	12.99	4.212	12.64
5	115.00	0.784	90.16	0.747	85.91
			3.15		(1.45)

$IRR = L + [N_L/(N_L - N_H)] \times (H - L)$

$Kd = 5 + [3.15/(3.15 + 1.45)] \times (6 - 5) = 5.7\%$

(c) **A**

The capital asset pricing model assumes that all shareholders of a company have the same required rate of return. Answers B and D relate to the dividend growth model rather than the CAPM. Answer C is not an assumption made.

(d) **C and E**

Retained earnings are a source of equity finance. Cutting a dividend is a means of using equity finance, by using the cash that would have been paid out as dividends to instead fund projects. Equity finance reserves represent retained profits rather than cash. Cash may not be available even if reserves are large, for example if the cash has already been spent on projects. Bonus issues are free issues of shares, so cannot be used to raise finance for the company as no cash is received. Preference shares are not generally recognised as equity finance as they have more in common with debt finance.

(e) **B**

Murabaha is similar to trade credit and therefore would not meet Tulip Co's needs as it would be appropriate for short-term funding rather than long-term capital funding. It is correct to state that Mudaraba involves an investing partner and a managing partner.

251 NOLCILN CO

(a) 2.4 times

Variable costs are 60% of revenue, so contribution is 40% of revenue.

Contribution = 0.40 × $9,540,000 = $3,816,000.

Operational gearing = Contribution/operating profit

$3,816,000/$1,590,000 = 2.4 times

The most common error here is to take the 60% variable costs figure and use this as the contribution percentage. This gave an answer of 3.6.

(b) 6.4 times

Interest cover is operating profit/interest.

Interest = 0.08 × $3,125,000 = $250,000

$1,590,000/$250,000 = 6.4 times.

The interest cover calculation is not provided in the exam, so the formula should be learned.

(c) C and D

Traditional capital structure theory states that there will be a point at which the weighted average cost of capital is minimised and also that the cost of equity will be higher when there is a high proportion of debt capital.

Option B relates to Modigliani and Miller's (M&M's) model with no tax instead of the traditional theory. Option A relates to the M&M no tax theory.

(d) C

Modigliani and Miller's with-tax theory stated that the optimal capital structure is made up almost entirely of debt. Under this model companies should have high financial gearing.

Option A states the opposite conclusion to the theory. Option B relates to the Modigliani and Miller no-tax theory rather than the with-tax one. None of the models state that the cost of equity remains constant with increased gearing – it always rises with gearing due to the increased return demanded by equity shareholders to compensate them for the increased financial risk they face from higher gearing levels.

(e) B and D

Debt-holders may impose restrictive covenants in loan agreements and when a company's gearing creates a high risk of bankruptcy the weighted average cost of capital will be higher. This is because higher returns will be required as compensation for the higher risk of bankruptcy.

Tax exhaustion occurs when there is a high proportion of debt capital rather than equity capital. Agency costs, tax exhaustion and bankruptcy risk discourage very high gearing levels.

BUSINESS VALUATIONS

252 KEVIN DUTTON

(a) C

MV = PV of future receipts discounted at Kevin's required return of 30%

MV = (Interest of \$5 × 5yr annuity factor @ 30%) + (redemption of \$100 × 5yr DF @ 30%)

MV = (\$5 × 2.436) + (\$100 × 0.269) = 39.08

Thus, total MV = \$390,800 or \$391,000 to the nearest \$1,000.

(b) **8.9%**

As there is no interest on the bonds, the return to the investor comes only from the difference between the purchase price (40% discount to nominal value = \$60) and the redemption value of \$100, which is therefore \$40. However, we're asked for an annual growth rate. The initial value of \$60 will effectively be compounded over six years to reach the final value of \$100. We can show this as:

$F = P(1 + r)^n$

$\$100 = \$60 \times (1 + r)^6$

r represents the annual growth rate of the bond value and is the figure we are looking for. Rearranging this equation to find r, we get:

$(\$100/\$60)^{(1/6)} - 1 = r$

Note that this is the same type of calculation as we use to find the annual growth rate for dividends $[(D_0/D_n)^{1/n} - 1]$. It can be used to find an average annual growth rate between any two figures over a period of time.

1 + r = 1.089, therefore r = 0.089 or 8.9%

(c) C

The issue value (current price) can be calculated as the present value of the future cash flows of ownership discounted at the investor's rate of return, in this case 10%.

As the bonds pay no interest, the only cash flow of ownership once the bond is purchased is the redemption value of \$100 in six years' time. Discounting this will give us the current purchase price that would give the investor a return of 10%.

\$100 × 0.564 = \$56.40

This represents a discount to nominal value of (\$100 – \$56.40) \$43.60, or 43.6%. To the nearest whole %, this is 44%.

(d) **False, True, False**

The first statement is false, otherwise no companies would be able to issue deep discounted bonds in the first place. (Note: it is illegal for companies to issue **shares** at a discount.)

The second statement is true – the nature of forestry is that an initial investment is required (planting saplings), followed by no income until the trees are ready to be harvested. The repayment pattern with deep discounted bonds matches this.

The third statement is false – Investor return is tied to risk levels. Investors' required returns depend on the risk levels associated with owning the bond (which stem from such things as operational and financial gearing, along with the competence of the company's managers), not the pattern of cash flows the investor receives. Coupon rates for deep discounted bonds are lower than for conventional bonds, but the investor return includes both interest and the capital gain between the purchase and redemption values, so the coupon rate alone does not reflect the overall return.

(e) D and E

A: False: MV = PV of future receipts discounted at the investors' required return. A change in interest rates will affect investors' required returns and hence the bond price.

B: False: MV = PV of future receipts discounted at investors' required return. A change in inflation rates will affect investors' required returns in money terms and hence the bond price.

C: False: the statement is the wrong way round – changes in the required return affect the bond value.

D: True. There is an inverse relationship between interest rates and bond prices. As interest rates rise, bonds paying out the same coupon rate as before become less attractive and their price will fall.

E: Without any market imperfections, the theoretical price should be the market price, but as soon as the assumptions made regarding the perfect market do not hold true, this may not be the case. For example, herding behaviour may push a price above or below its theoretical value.

253 LOKI

(a) C

The most appropriate price for the seller to consider for the sale of the business as a going concern (A) would be the break-up value rather than the replacement value. The seller would prefer a higher value, but if other methods of valuation give a lower value than the break-up value, the seller would instead choose to cease to trade and sell the assets off individually.

The maximum amount that a purchaser should pay is more likely to correlate to replacement cost than break-up value (B), given that if the purchaser decides to set up their own business rather than purchase the existing one, they will need to purchase the assets from scratch at full cost. However, even then, the purchaser cannot just buy the assets and expect to have a working business, so should expect to spend more than the replacement cost. The replacement cost is essentially a starting point for the purchaser.

Book value (C) is an accounting value that does not necessarily correspond to real value. It is based on historic cost, which may have changed significantly, and depreciation policy, which is subjective.

Asset based measures ignore intangible non-statement of financial position assets (D), such as internally generated goodwill from having a skilled workforce and loyal customer base.

(b) 0.89

Step 1: 'degear' Q's equity beta to give an asset beta

$$ß_a = ß_e \left[\frac{V_E}{V_E + V_D[1-t]}\right] = 1.2 \left[\frac{2}{2 + 1[1-0.3]}\right] = 0.8888... = 0.89$$

This can then be taken as Loki's asset beta as the two companies have similar business activities.

Given Loki is all equity financed, then this is also Loki's equity beta – no 'regearing' is required.

(c) A

Fair MV = PV of future dividends discounted at the K_e of 14%

Fair MV = \$0.14m/(0.14 – 0.04) = \$1.4m or \$0.70 per share

Note: the dividend of \$0.14m is already a t=1 figure so does not need to be multiplied by a factor of 1.04 or (1 + g) as it would if it were a D0 figure.

However, the issue price will be at a 15% discount, giving \$0.70 × 0.85 = \$0.595 = \$0.60.

(d) \$96.53

Consider a bond with a nominal value of \$100

MV = PV of future receipts discounted at investor's required return of 6%

MV = (Interest of \$5 × 4yr annuity factor) + (redemption of \$100 × 4yr discount factor)

MV = (\$5 × 3.465) + (\$100 × 0.792) = \$96.53

(e) B and C

A is false – the secured bonds will have the lowest risk.

B is true – the option to convert acts as a sweetener, allowing Loki to pay lower dividends.

C is true – the venture capital company is likely to have well diversified shareholders.

D is false – the family are unlikely to want to lose control of their company.

254 DAVINA MCNABB

(a) C

Company A is in a very capital intensive business and it is likely that the value of the housing stock is a very close estimate of the value of the company, particularly given recent losses.

Recent and even future losses make it difficult to use earnings (option A) and/or dividend (option B) approaches.

Given it is unquoted, there is no share price to use to estimate market capitalisation (option D).

(b) $125.0 m

MV = next year's earnings/(earnings yield – g)

MV = $12.5m/(0.12 – 0.02) = $12.5m/0.10 = $125.0m

(c) B

MV = PV of future dividends discounted at the K_e of 14%

Can't use the dividend growth formula of $D_0(1 + g)/(ke – g)$ as this relies on having only one growth rate. Here dividends are not growing at all during time periods 1, 2 and 3, but will then grow at 3% into perpetuity from time period 4 onwards.

We still aim to find the present value of the dividends. Discount the time period 1–3 dividends as a three year annuity at 14% and the dividends from time period 4 onwards as a delayed, growing perpetuity.

T1–3 dividends PV = $5m × 2.322 = $11.61m

T4 onwards dividends = Discounting the t4 cash flow ($5m + 3% growth) onwards using the growing perpetuity factor (1/(ke – g)) will give a t3 value as using the factor discounts the cash flows back to one time period before they start. The value will then need to be discounted for a further 3 years, using the 3 year discount factor at 14%:

($5m × 1.03) × (1/(0.14 – 0.03) × 0.675 = $31.60m

MV = $11.61m + $31.60 = $43.21m

(d) B

A: Strong form implies all shares are fairly priced, even taking into account secret information.

B: In a semi strong market, secret information would enable an investor to outperform the market by identifying undervalued companies, so option B is true.

C: A semi-strong market will incorporate all publicly available information in the share price, so Davina will not unearth anything useful looking at such information.

D: Weak form efficiency is sufficient to imply that there are no trends in share prices and hence Davina will not find any useful by her 'chartism'.

(e) True, False, False

Statement (i) is true. The shareholders of M Inc. are likely to be well diversified (even M Inc itself is likely to be well diversified) so will not be interested in attempts to reduce unsystematic risk further.

Statement (ii) is false – Davina should be looking at risk **and** return and try to develop a portfolio where the anticipated return exceeds the CAPM required return. Taking on extra risk by investing in companies with higher beta factors is not avoided, but needs to be compensated for by appropriately higher returns than for lower risk companies.

Statement (iii) is false – only unsystematic risk can be diversified away, by definition.

255 PIKE

(a) B

Minimum value to the seller is given by net realisable value (NRV). It represents what the seller could get if a buyer for the business could not be found. Asset-based valuations are calculated by taking the value of assets and deducting the value of the liabilities, so the bank loan should be deducted:

$13.7m – $2.5m = $11.2m

(b) $50m

MV = P/E × future sustainable earnings

To get an estimate of future earnings we need firstly to inflate the historic figure by 3% and then, secondly, include a salary deduction for Freda's replacement. Note that this will need to be a post-tax figure to adjust for the effect of the tax savings from the extra expense.

Use Trout and Co's P/E ratio of 7 due to its similarities to Minnow Co.

Sustainable earnings = ($7,000,000 × 1.03) – ($100,000 × 0.70) = $7,140,000

MV = 7 × $7,140,000 = 49,980,000, or $50m

(c) A

The cash flows are a growing perpetuity, so we should discount the time period 1 cash flow using the growing perpetuity formula: 1/(r – g).

PV of future CFs discounted at the WACC = $6m × 1/(0.12 – 0.04) = $75m

However, this gives the value of equity + debt, so the value of the debt must be deducted as we are just asked to calculate the MV of equity.

MV equity = $75m – $2.5m = $72.5m

(d) A and B

A is true. The decision by owner/managers how to take funds out of a company is usually made to reduce tax.

B is true. In a small, owner managed service business the goodwill may be tied up with the owner/manager rather than the company.

C is false – in a strong form market the share price will react before information is made public.

D is false – given Pike is listed and a conglomerate, then it is reasonable to assume that its shareholders are well diversified and, hence, only concerned about **systematic** risk. They will already have diversified away unsystematic risk via their personal investment portfolios.

(e) B

Statement (i) is true. Minnow operates in a service industry that is not capital intensive.

Statement (ii) is true – DCF approaches are generally seen as superior.

Statement (iii) is false for two reasons – firstly historic dividends have been artificially high, a trend unlikely to continue and, secondly, DVM is less useful for valuing a majority stake such as Pike wishes to purchase.

256 PREY CO

(a) $185,000

Value calculated as total assets less total liabilities, adjusting the asset values as per notes 1 and 2:

400 – 100 + 25 + 40 – 140 – 40 = 185

Alternatively, the same value can be reached by starting with shareholders' funds and making the adjustments:

(100 + 170) + (25 – 100) + (40 – 50) = 185

(b) C

Value calculated as total assets less total liabilities, adjusting the asset values as per notes 1 and 2:

400 – 100 + 500 + 50 – 140 – 40 = 670

Alternatively, the same value can be reached by starting with shareholders' funds and making the adjustments:

(100 + 170) + (500 – 100) = $670,000

(c) False, True, False

Statement (i) is false. Despite operating in a capital intensive industry, without an estimate of the value of Prey Ltd.'s brand name, the asset valuation is likely to be far too low.

Statement (ii) is true – Prey Ltd.'s value stems from the quality of its products and its reputation.

Statement (iii) is false – if the statement has said 'net realisable value' rather than 'net book value', then it would have been true.

(d) B

The P/E ratio of the quoted company will be based on historic eps, but value should be based on future earnings potential, so the forecast earnings for 20X6 should be used.

MV = 10 × $156,000 = $1,560,000

There are 200,000 shares, giving a share price of ($1,560,000/200,000) $7.80.

(e) 9.5%

The growth rate used in the DVM should be future growth. The best indicator of future growth can be calculated using years 20X4 to 20X6 (the years before 20X4 are prior to the large boost in sales and profits and so are not representative of the company's current level of performance and potential).

$g = (D_0/D_n)^{(1/n)} - 1$ where D_0 is the most recent dividend of 78 and D_n is the oldest dividend under consideration, 65

$g = (78/65)^{(1/2)} - 1 = 0.0954...$ or 9.5% as a percentage to 1 decimal place

257 RING CO

(a) $9.45

Dividend growth model from formula sheet: $P_0 = D_0(1 + g)/(r_e - g)$

As a value for growth is not given, it needs to be calculated. We can use the historic dividend information to calculate past growth and make the assumption that future growth will be at the same level.

$g = (D_0/D_n)^{(1/n)} - 1$ where D_0 is the most recent dividend of $0.45 and D_n is the oldest dividend under consideration, $0.37. There are 4 growth periods between these dividends, so n = 4

$g = (\$0.45/\$0.37)^{(1/4)} - 1 = 0.05$ (5.0%)

Incorporating this value of g into the dividend growth model, with 10% (0.1) as the equity cost, r_e:

Share price = ($0.450 × 1.05)/(0.1 – 0.05) = $9.45

(b) B

MV of loan note is the value that would bring the purchase of loan note and the receipt of interest and the redemption value to an NPV of $0 when discounted at the investors' discount rate (the pre-tax cost of the note) of 4%. In other words, the MV of the loan note will be equal to the PV of the interest receipts and redemption value.

PV of interest receipts (7 year annuity of interest of $6 discounted at 4%) = $6 × 6.002) = $36.012

PV of redemption value ($100 in 7 years discounted at 4%) = $100 × 0.760 = $76.00

Total PV = current market value = $36.01 + $76.0 = $112.01

(c) C and D

Total assets should be added together, with total liabilities deducted. This is represented by either:

Non-current assets plus current assets less total liabilities or

Net current assets (current assets – current liabilities) plus non-current assets less long-term liabilities.

(d) C

The dividend valuation model makes the unreasonable assumption that average dividend growth is constant is correct. Even if companies strive to pay out a consistently growing dividend, periods of lower profits or economic downturns will compromise their ability to do this over time.

The earnings yield method = earnings × 1/yield

The P/E ratio method = earnings × P/E ratio

The equity market value would not include any debt value.

(e) Correct, Incorrect, Correct

Insider information cannot be used to make abnormal gains in a strong form efficient capital market as the share price would react as soon as the information came to light, even before release to the public.

In a weak form efficient market, share prices react more slowly than in a semi-strong form efficient one, but 'the day after' is too specific.

In a semi-strong form efficient market, share prices do react quickly and accurately to newly-released information about a company.

258 CORAL CO

(a) 221.52

Market value = number of shares in issue × ex div price per share.

Number of shares in issue = \$7.8m/\$0.25 = 31.2m shares.

Equity market value = \$7.10 × 31.2m = \$221.52m.

(b) C

Market value = PV of cash flows of ownership (interest and redemption value) discounted at the investors' required rate of return (also known as the before-tax cost of debt)

For convertible debt, the redemption value is calculated as the higher of the cash redemption amount or the predicted value of shares the debt can be converted into.

Predicted share price in six years: \$7.10 × 1.08^6 = \$11.267

Conversion value – predicted value of 10 shares = \$112.67

As this is higher than the redemption cash value of \$100, use \$112.67 in the MV calculation.

PV of six year annuity of interest discounted at 5%: \$7 × 5.076 = \$35.53

PV of \$112.67 in six years discounted at 5%: \$112.67 × 0.746 = \$84.05

Market value = \$35.53 + \$84.05 = \$119.58.

(c) B

If the capital market is semi-strong form efficient, newly-released insider information will quickly and accurately be reflected in share prices.

The other statements are true. Capital market supply and demand for shares are what determine the share price. This can be due to news received about a company or to other factors, such as rumours of herding behaviour.

When analysing past movements in a share price, there will be no obvious pattern and future movements cannot therefore be predicted.

(d) Is an assumption, Is an assumption, Is an assumption

All three are assumptions made by the dividend growth model. Note that if the growth rate is larger than the cost of equity, the share price would calculate as negative.

(e) B

A valuation for corporate taxation purposes is not necessary.

259 BLUEBELL CO

(a) C

The net realisable value can be calculated by taking the value of tangible assets (adjusted for any named adjustments), making sure that the intangible goodwill is not included. Then deduct the value of the liabilities.

Net realisable value = 1,350 – (768 – 600) – (192 × 0.1) – 30 – 105 – 662 = $365.8m

(b) $1,875 million

Value = earnings × 1/earnings yield

Earnings yield = 1/PE ratio = 1/12.5 = 0.08 (8%)

Value = 150 × 1/0.08 = $1,875 million

Note that the P/E method of valuation and the earnings ratio method are based on the same principles. In fact, the same value would be found by multiplying earnings by the P/E ratio. The earnings yield method has the advantage of being able to include growth in earnings (where it exists) by changing the multiplier to 1/(earnings yield – growth).

(c) A

Asset-based valuations are useful in asset- stripping acquisitions. Intangible assets aren't included in the valuation, although in real life, some attempt to do this may be made. Asset based valuations don't take into account future incomes or cash flows. Deprival value is the lower of replacement cost and recoverable value, so cannot be said to be replacement cost alone.

(d) C

Market imperfections mean that share prices will not react as they would be expected to if the market were efficient. If the market were efficient, investors would react rationally to news, whether expected or not. Overreaction to unexpected news is therefore an example of a market imperfection. So is the low volume of trading of small company shares. With low trading levels, the market will struggle to come to an efficient equilibrium price for the shares.

(e) B and E

A control premium would be paid on shares when buying a controlling stake. An unlisted company like Dandelion Co would be more difficult to value as there is no market price to use as a guide. Scrip dividends increase the liquidity of shares, as there will be more shares in issue, each with a lower value than prior to the issue. The lower the value, the more tradeable they are. Dandelion Co is unlikely to have a lower cost of equity and higher share value than similar listed companies, as the purchase of shares in an unlisted company is a higher risk investment for equity shareholders (as the shares are less tradeable than those in a listed company), leading to a higher return demanded and therefore a higher cost of equity. In a semi-strong form efficient market, insider trading opportunities occur between the time that new information about the business happens and the time that the news is released to the public.

260 GWW CO

(a) $160 million

Value of ordinary shares in statement of financial position = $20.0 million

Nominal (par) value of ordinary shares = $0.50

Number of ordinary shares of company = $20.0m/$0.5 = 40m shares

Ordinary share price = $4.00 per share

Market capitalisation = share price × number of shares in issue = $4.00 × 40m – $160 million

(b) $61.7 million

Current net asset value (NAV) = $91.0m + $8.3m – $7.1m – $25.0m = $67.2 million

Decrease in value of non-current assets on liquidation = $86.0m – $91.0m = $5m

Increase in value of inventory on liquidation = $4.2m – $3.8m = $0.4m

Decrease in value of trade receivables = $4.2m × 0.2 = $0.9m

NAV (liquidation basis) = $67.2m – $5m + $0.4m – $0.9m = $61.7m

(c) C

Valuation = earnings (post-tax profits) × P/E ratio

Historic earnings of GWW Co = $10.1 million

Average price/earnings ratio of GWW Co business sector = 17 times

Valuation = $10.1 million × 17 = $171.7 million

(d) $235 million

Historic dividend growth rate = $(D_0/D_n)^{(1/n)} - 1$

Growth = $(\$6.0\text{m}/\$5.0\text{m})^{(1/3)} - 1 = 0.0627$ (6.27%)

An assumption is then made that future dividend growth is similar to historic dividend growth.

Value using the dividend growth model = $D_0 (1 + g)/(r_e + g)$ (from formulae sheet)

Value = $6.0m × 1.0627/(0.09 – 0.0627) = $233.56 million, or $235 million to the nearest $5 million.

NB: Calculations using a more rounded growth rate of 6.3% would give $236.22 million, which is still $235 million to the nearest $5 million.

(e) B

Gordon's growth approximation estimates the dividend growth rate using $g = br_e$, where b is the retention rate of dividends and r_e is the return on equity capital.

Using the most recent figures, b = ($10.1m – $6.0m)/$10.1m = 0.4059 or 40.59%

r_e = $10.1m/$67.2m = 0.1503 or 15.03%

growth = 0.4059 × 0.1503 = 0.061 or 6.1%

261 DAZVIN CO

(a) **A**

$P_0 = D/k_p$

k_p = cost of preference shares, given at 8%, or 0.08

D = preference share dividend = nominal value × dividend percentage = \$0.50 × 6% = \$0.03 per share

P_0 = \$0.03/0.08 = \$0.375 per share

Number of shares in issue = \$10.0m/\$0.50 = 20m shares

Total MV = 20m × \$0.375 = \$7.5m

(b) **\$40.8M**

Value = earnings × PE ratio

Earnings (profits after tax and preference share dividends) = \$4.0m – (20m × \$0.5 × 6%) = \$3.4m

PE ratio is given as 12

Value = \$3.4m × 12 = \$40.8m

(c) **C**

Market value = the present value of the interest received and the redemption value, discounted at the investors' required return rate.

The investors' required return is also known as the pre-tax cost of capital (or investor yield) and is given in the question as 6%.

Interest per annum = nominal value × coupon rate = \$100 × 7.5% = \$7.50

Redemption value = higher of redemption amount and the value of shares that the debt could be converted into.

Redemption amount = \$100

Conversion value of 40 shares, given that the shares are currently priced at \$2.00 and are anticipated to grow in value at 6% per year in each of the six years until conversion:

\$2.00 × 1.06^6 × 40 = \$113.48

Assume the investors would choose conversion, so use the value of the shares in the market value calculation rather than the redemption amount.

PV of \$7.50 interest for 6 years and \$113.48 in six years' time, discounted at 6% =

\$7.50 × 4.917 + \$113.48 × 0.705 = \$116.88

Total market value = total nominal value/\$100 × market value per loan note = \$18.0m/\$100 × 116.88 = \$21.04m

(d) **B**

It is correct to state that shares are likely to be mispriced where information asymmetry exists between managers and investors. This means that managers know something about the business that would affect its share price. However, market prices are based on the pattern of buying and selling by investors. If the investors don't know this information, it can't be used in their buying and selling decisions and the share price won't reflect it.

In relation to statement A, consider a business that provides consultancy services. The value of this company comes mainly from having experts who provide the services rather than from tangible assets. A valuation based only on tangible assets would significantly undervalue the company.

Similarly, if that business were taken over and those consultants left the business, its value would not be maintained after the takeover. Hence, statement C is not correct.

Unreleased information may well affect the value of the company, but this does not mean that published information has no value. In semi-strong form efficient markets, for instance, the share price is based on publicly available information.

(e) C

The first statement is correct, as the momentum effect can arise when investors believe that recent share price increases will continue, leading to irrational investment decisions by uninformed investors (noise trading) chasing the trend. This behaviour is not rational as past performance does not guarantee future performance.

The second statement is true, as informed investors can make speculative purchases during a stock market bubble with the intention of selling when the price has increased in the future, in the belief that they can realise their gain before the bubble bursts, effectively taking advantage of the uninformed investors.

262 LIGHT CO

(a) **$18.9m**

For irredeemable loan notes, $P_0 = I/r$, where r represents the investors' required rate of return.

I represents the annual interest paid on the loan notes. Interest is paid in relation to nominal value (given as $100 per loan note) and is paid at the coupon rate, given as 6%. Therefore, I = $100 × 6% = $6.

The investors' required rate of return is also known as the before tax cost of debt, which is given as 7%.

Each 6% loan note is therefore worth: $6/0.07 = $85.71

To calculate the total market value, we need to know how many loan notes are in issue. This can be calculated by taking the total nominal value of loan notes in issue and dividing by the nominal value per loan note: $22m/$100 = 220,000 loan notes.

Total market value = 220,000 × $85.71 = $18,856,200, or $18.9m.

A number of candidates gave an answer of $85.7, which suggests they did not read the question carefully and missed the requirement for the total value and possibly also missed the m indicating that the answer is in millions.

(b) B

For convertible loan notes, the market value per loan note can be found by discounting the future interest and redemption/conversion values at the investors' required rate of return.

Interest of ($100 × 8%) $8 will be received for each of the next seven years.

At the end of the 7 years, the loan notes will either be redeemed at nominal value ($100 each) or converted into 15 ordinary shares. The redemption and potential conversion values need to be compared and the higher value chosen for the market value calculation.

15 ordinary shares would be currently worth $6.75 × 15 = $101.25

Given that the shares are expected to grow in value by 5% per year and there are 7 years until conversion, this value would be expected to grow to:

$101.25 × 1.05^7 = $142.47

As this is higher than the redemption value of $100, we will use the $142.47 in the market value calculation.

Present value of the 7 year annuity of interest of $8, discounted at 9% (before-tax cost of debt) = $8 × 5.033 = $40.264

Present value of the conversion amount of $142.47 = $142.47 × 0.547 = $77.93109

Total market value = $40.264 + $77.93109 = $118.20

A number of candidates incorrectly used the floor value rather than the conversion value to get their market value or used eight years of growth in their conversion value to get options A or D respectively.

(c) **C**

The tax rate is not applied when valuing preference shares, so A is incorrect.

Preference shares are not a tax-efficient way of raising finance (the dividends paid in relation to them are not tax-deductible), so B is incorrect.

Redeemable preference shares are classed as debt in the statement of financial position, so D is incorrect.

Leaving the correct option as preference shares can be difficult to value when they pay a variable rate of dividend. Although this makes them no more difficult than many ordinary shares, it makes them more difficult than when they pay a fixed dividend.

(d) **A**

Market expectations of good future prospects mean that the share price of a company can rise even when it has cut its dividend.

Option B is incorrect as a share buyback will decrease the number of issued shares and therefore reduce marketability.

Option C is incorrect as investors may not necessarily react rationally and can overreact to either good or bad news.

Option D is incorrect as random walk theory suggests that share price movements cannot be forecast.

(e) **D**

The momentum effect does suggest that investors may buy shares in the belief that a recent rise in share prices will continue into the future.

Share price anomalies do in fact undermine the perfect capital market theory, stock market bubbles are the result of irrational investor behaviour and noise traders make uninformed, rather than informed, investment decisions.

263 FUCHSIA CO

(a) C

Total value of shares = PE ratio × total earnings

Earnings is the value of profit available to the ordinary shareholders, so it is post-interest, post-tax and post-preference share dividends (where they are present).

From the figures in the question, the earnings figure is $198m.

The industry PE ratio of 11 is appropriate to use.

Total value of shares = 11 × $198m = $2,178m.

(b) A

Using the dividend valuation model formula available on the formulae sheet:

$P_0 = D_0(1+g)/(r_e-g)$

D_0 represents the current dividend. Use the dividend total from the statement of profit or loss.

r_e represents the cost of equity, given in the question as 10%.

g represents the annual growth rate of the dividends, given in the question as 5%.

P_0 = ($110m × 1.05)/(0.1 – 0.05) = $2,310m

(c) C

The value of a loan note is equal to the present value of the future interest and redemption payments, discounted at the investors' required rate of return.

Interest (annuity) paid per year for five years = coupon rate × nominal value per loan note = 8% × $100 = $8

Redemption payment (individual amount) in five years, at a 4% premium to nominal value = $100 × 1.04 = $104

Investors' required return is also known as the before-tax cost of debt, which is given as 7%.

Annuity factor at 7% for five years (from the annuity table available in the exam) = 4.1

Discount factor at 7% for five years (from the present value table available in the exam) = 0.713

PV of five-year interest annuity at 7% = $8 × 4.1 = $32.80

PV of redemption amount in five years' time at 7% = $104 × 0.713 = $74.15

Total PV of one loan note = $32.80 + $74.15 = $106.95

Number of loan notes in issue = total nominal value/nominal value per loan note = $300m/$100 = 3m

Value of all loan notes = $106.95 × 3m = $320.9m

Common errors include: using a before-tax cost of debt of 8% instead of 7% or ignoring the 4% redemption premium to get options A or B respectively.

(d) **B**

It is correct to state that in a weak form efficient capital market, technical analysis cannot produce abnormal returns. However, it is not correct to state that share prices take several days to respond to new information if a capital market is weak form efficient, since weak form efficiency does not say anything about the speed of response to new information.

(e) **A**

It is correct that noise traders generally over-react to good news and bad news. However, noise traders make investment decisions on an uninformed basis, i.e. without using fundamental data.

RISK MANAGEMENT

264 MALLETT CO

(a) **1,174,000 AUD**

Mallett Co will receive 850,000USD in 3 months' time.

The company will) borrow the appropriate amount in US dollars now; (2) convert the US dollars to Australian dollars immediately; (3) invest the Australian dollars in an Australian dollar bank account knowing that it will grow over the next three months; (4) use the client's cash (US dollars) to pay off the US dollar borrowing (which will have grown with interest) and close the account; (5) take the Australian dollars out of its account, it will have increased by interest but will be a known amount that can be calculated now.

The amount to borrow now, as in (1), is 850,000 USD ÷ 1.00825 = 843,045 USD.

This will be converted now, as in (2), to 843,045 ÷ 0.7233 AUD = 1,165,554 AUD.

Placed on deposit, as in (3), it grows to 1,165,554 × 1.00725 AUD = 1,174,004 AUD.

(The client's receipt will pay off the US dollar loan which has increased with interest.)

The alternative answers come from ignoring the need to allow for 3-month's interest on the Australian dollar account and from using annual rates instead of quarterly rates.

(b) **A**

The expectation theory suggests that you would earn the same amount by investing in a one-year bond which is then rolled into a second one-year bond as you would by buying a two-year bond today.

(c) **0.7240 US dollars to the Australian dollar**

The ACCA formula sheet tells you that interest rate parity says that: $F_0 = S_0 \times \frac{(1+i_c)}{(1+i_b)}$

The base currency is the currency denoted with a 1 in the exchange rate and the counter currency is the other currency. Here the Australian dollar is the base currency and the US dollar is the counter currency, hence:

$$F_0 = S_0 \times \frac{(1+\text{US rate})}{(+\text{Australian rate})}$$

As we are calculating a 3 month rate but have been given interest rates as annual rates, we need to pro-rate them to 3 month rates:

US dollar interest rate for 3 months = 3.3% × 3/12 = 0.825% (0.00825 as a decimal)

Australian dollar interest rate for 3 months = 2.9% × 3/12 = 0.725% (0.00725 as a decimal)

Three-month forward rate = 0.7233 × 1.00825/1.00725 = 0.7240 USD to the AUD

(d) **D**

Translation losses can, for example, result from restating the book-value of an overseas branch's assets at the exchange rate at the balance sheet date.

(e) **D**

The option provides you with the right, but not the obligation to exchange currencies.

Therefore, the option provides a benefit when there is no guarantee that the contract will be entered into, as in this example for a tender.

Options are expensive, with an upfront premium paid whether they are exercised or not, so are unlikely to be the cheapest means of entering into a hedge.

Risk can be defined as the variability of potential returns. A method such as a forward contract guarantees the cash to be paid/received up front so would be classed as less risky than an option.

There is no guarantee that readers of the published accounts would look more favourably upon the use of an option than other methods of hedging.

265 NOON CO

(a) **B**

Noon needs to pay 3 million Flyland Francs in three months. The correct forward rate must be determined to calculate the cash flow.

A spread of 6.321–6.362 FF to 1 CC is given. Flyland Francs are the counter currency and Centreland Colons are the base currency. One method of determining which rate from the spread to use is to look at what the bank would be doing with the counter currency and use 'buy high, sell low.

In this case, Noon Co will need to purchase Flyland Francs from the bank in order to pass them onto its supplier as payment. The bank is therefore selling the Francs and will use the low rate of 6.321.

Using this 3-month forward rate, these will cost 3m ÷ 6.321 = 474,608 CC.

Alternative answers are arrived at by using the spot rate or using the rate for selling Flyland Francs rather than buying them.

(b) **C**

Interest rate parity uses the current spot rate combined with the home and foreign currency interest rates to predict the forward rate.

(c) D

Noon needs to pay 3m Flyland Francs in three months.

The company will (1) borrow the appropriate amount in Centreland Colons now; (2) convert the Colons into Flyland Francs immediately; (3) invest the Francs in a Flyland Franc bank account knowing that it will grow to 3 m Francs in three months' time; (4) pay the 3m Francs to the Flyland supplier and close the account; (5) repay the amount borrowed in (1) in Colons which will have increased by interest but will be a known amount that can be calculated now.

The amount to invest in step (3) in Francs at a rate of 13.5% per year or 3.375% over 3 months = 3m Francs ÷ 1.03375 = 2,902,056.

The amount to convert to Francs now in step (2) = 2,902,056 ÷ 6.170 = 470,349 Colons.

The amount that will have to be paid in three months' time to pay off this borrowing in Colons = 470,349 × 1.02025 = 479,874 Colons.

The alternative answers come from using annual rates rather than 3-monthly ones and forgetting that we compare two payments made in three months' time, i.e. forgetting to increase the borrowing in Colons by 3 months' interest.

(d) True, True, True, True

All four statements are true.

(e) 14%

This requires working backwards through the purchasing power parity formula.

Purchasing power parity formula: $S_1 = S_0 \times \frac{1+h_c}{1+h_b}$

We are not given the 3 month spot rate (S_1), but we do have the 3 month forward rate. We can assume (due to four way equivalence) that the spot rate in 3 months' time should be approximately equal to today's 3-month forward rate

= Spot rate in 3 months (S_1) × (1 + counter currency inflation rate)/(1 + base currency inflation rate)

The counter currency is Flyland Francs and the base currency is Centreland Colons.

The annual inflation rates given will need to be pro-rated to 3 month rates:

Centreland 3 month inflation = 3.8% × 3/12 = 0.95% (0.0095 as a decimal)

Using lower of the two exchange rates (as recommended):

6.321 = 6.170 × (1 + 3 month Flyland Franc inflation rate) ÷ (1 + 0.0095)

1 + [annual overseas rate ÷ 4] = (6.321 ÷ 6.170) ×1.0095 = 1.0342

Quarterly Flyland Franc inflation rate = 0.0342 or 3.42%

Annual Flyland Franc rate = 3.42% × 4 = 13.682%, or 14%

Alternative answers come from getting the original purchasing power parity formula the wrong way up or from not spotting that you need to use quarterly inflation rates (since you have been given a three-month forward exchange rate).

Tutorial note

You get a similar result (13.684%) if you use the higher exchange rate, i.e. no difference when working to the nearest percentage point. Many pieces of information about money markets seem to take annual rates and divide them, by 4 to find quarterly rates or take quarterly rates and quadruple them when one would expect to use fourth roots of indexes or raise them to the power four. It only makes a small difference in this case. An annual inflation rate of 14.3% would be found by raising an index number based on a quarterly rate to the power 4, a perfectly understandable calculation in view of the way inflation operates. It was the reason for asking for an answer to the nearest percent.

266 PZK CO

(a) A

The foreign exchange risk exposure relates to the value of the receipt for an individual transaction.

(b) $3,521

As Euros is the counter currency and the bank will be buying Euros from PZK, the high rate of the exchange rate spreads should be used.

The current dollar value of the future euro receipt = €1,200,000/4.2080 = $285,171.

If a forward contract is taken out, PZK Co can lock into the six-month forward exchange rate of 4.2606 euros per dollar.

Future dollar value using the forward contract = €1,200,000/4.2606 = $281,650.

Loss using the forward contract = $285,171 – $281,650 = $3,521.

(c) D

The implied interest rate in the foreign country can be calculated using interest rate parity.

From the formulae sheet, $F_0 = S_0 \times (1 + i_c)/(1 + i_b)$

Hence $4.3132 = 4.2080 \times (1 + i_c)/1.04$

Rearranging, $(1 + i_c) = 4.3132 \times 1.04/4.2080 = 1.066$

The implied annual interest rate in the foreign country is 6.6%.

(d) C

The forward rates indicate that the dollar will buy more euros in the future, i.e. that the dollar is strengthening while the Euro weakens.

Given the receipt is in euros, then PZK can expect the $ equivalent value of the receipt to fall as the dollar strengthens.

Thus, PZK should consider 'leading' and trying to get the receipt sooner.

(e) False, True, True

Statement (i) is false – PZK may still be exposed to transaction risk on purchases.

Statement (ii) is true – One of the simplest ways for PZK Co to avoiding exchange rate risk is to invoice in its home currency, which passes the exchange rate risk on to the foreign customer, who must effectively find the dollars with which to make the payment.

Statement (iii) is also true – This strategy may not be commercially viable, however, since the company's foreign customers will not want to take on the exchange rate risk. They may instead transfer their business to those competitors of PZK Co who invoice in the foreign currency and who therefore shoulder the exchange rate risk.

267 H CO

(a) B and D

A is false – the factory doesn't exist yet so would not be good security on the loan.

B is true – MM with tax concluded that companies should gear up as much as possible.

C is false – some forms of equity, such as cutting a dividend, have very low issue costs.

D is true – the cost of debt will (normally) be lower than the cost of equity, due mainly to lower investor risk and tax relief on interest.

(b) C

Market segmentation theory helps explain any 'wiggle' on the yield curve rather than why it might be normal instead of inverted.

(c) $10,000 payment

The interest payable on the actual loan will be linked to the spot rate of 7.6%.

However, the FRA effectively locks into a reference rate of 7.8% (borrowing so use higher rate).

Thus, H company will have to make a payment to the FRA provider for the difference of 0.2%, bringing the total paid via the loan and the FRA to the pre-agreed rate of 7.8%.

The borrowing is only for 6 months so any value will be pro-rated to this from the annual amount.

This equates to 0.2% × $10m × 6/12 = $10,000.

(d) A, B and C

A is correct – rounding the number of contracts may result in a mismatch.

B is correct – the futures price and the underlying price may be different on any date other than the contract date, leading to basis risk.

C is correct – the basis may not move as expected. Basis risk is the risk that contracts whose values should, in theory, offset each other do not do so. Futures prices are only guaranteed to align with the price of the underlying interest rate on their close out date, so there is basis risk up until this point.

D is false – unpredictability is why we hedge in the first place!

(e) C

Statements (i) and (iii) are true – the hedge is constructed by borrowing at the market rate and then the FRA/futures position will generate a gain or loss that can be offset against the loss or gain on the associated real world borrowing.

Statement (ii) is false – FRAs are OTC instruments arranged with a bank.

268 F CO

(a) A and D

The main reason for an inverted curve is when interest rates are high but expected to fall. A recession often leads to a fall in interest rates as a means of stimulating the economy.

Rising inflation can lead to a rise in interest rates. When interest rates rise, a conventional, upward sloping yield curve is more likely, all other things being equal.

(b) $1,250 payment

The interest receivable on the actual deposit will be linked to the spot rate of 5.5%.

However, the FRA effectively locks into a reference rate of 5% (depositing so use the lower of the two quoted rates).

Thus, F company will have to make a payment of 0.5% to bring down their overall value received to the pre-agreed rate.

The deposit is only for 3 months so any value will be pro-rated to this from the annual amount.

This equates to 0.5% × $1m × 3/12 = $1,250.

(c) A

Interest rate options are the right to buy or sell interest rate futures. The option will only be exercised in order to make a profit on the futures, which will help to mitigate any losses on a loan or deposit due to a rise in interest rates.

A key feature of an option is that it gives the right but not the obligation in relation to something. There is never an obligation to go through with a position, so answer B is not true.

Interest rate options are separate contracts to the loan or deposit being made. Therefore, statement C is not true.

A right but not the obligation to enter into a forward rate agreement is known as an interest rate guarantee, not an interest rate option, so statement D is not true.

(d) C

An interest rate guarantee allows the company a period of time during which it has the option to buy an FRA at a set price (A). An interest rate future locks the company into an effective interest rate (B). An interest rate swap **does not** involve the exchange of the principal, only the exchange of a floating stream of interest payments for a fixed stream of interest payments and vice versa (D).

(e) True, False, False

Statement (i) is true – lenders set rates primarily based on risk assessments.

Statement (ii) is false – under swaps there is no exchange of principals.

Statement (iii) is false – F would only be liable for the loan it borrowed.

269 HERD CO

(a) €1.566 per $1

The ACCA formula sheet tells you that interest rate parity says that: $F_0 = S_0 \times \frac{(1+i_c)}{(1+i_b)}$

Six-month forward rate – use 6 monthly simple interest rates in the calculation.

The counter currency is Euros and the base currency (with a value of 1 in the exchange rate) is $.

Base currency 6 month interest rate = 2% × 6/12 = 1% (0.01 as a decimal)

Counter currency 6 month interest rate = 5% × 6/12 = 2.5% (0.025 as a decimal)

Forward rate = 1.543 × (1.025/1.01) = €1.566 per $1

Note: the same answer is found if, instead of multiplying each rate by 6/12, (1+rate) is taken to the power of 6/12 (or 0.5):

$1.543 \times 1.05^{0.5}/1.02^{0.5}$ = €1.566 per $1

(b) A

The euro receipt is subject to transaction risk – the risk of the cash value changing between the contract date and the date of the cash movement due to movements in exchange rates.

(c) D and E

A forward rate agreement is used for hedging against interest rate risk rather than foreign exchange risk. A currency swap is not a suitable method for hedging a one-off transaction.

(d) B

Under both purchasing power parity and interest rate parity, the country with the higher rate will see a depreciation of its currency.

In statement 1, the dollar has the higher rate, so it will depreciate and this does not support the director's belief. In statement 2, the Euro has the higher rate, so will depreciate. Statement 2 does support the director's belief.

(e) A and C

In exchange for a premium, Herd Co could hedge its interest rate risk by buying interest rate options is correct.

Floors guarantee a minimum rate – good for deposits but not borrowing.

With a borrowing requirement, futures contracts must be sold initially and bought back on close out.

Matching would only be potentially viable with a floating rate on an asset, not on another liability (which would double the exposure to rising interest rates).

270 PARK CO

(a) $202,000

Borrow dinars for the dinar receipt to pay off in six months, swap today the borrowed dinars for $ and then put the $ on deposit for six months.

Dinar value to borrow at 4% per six months = 12m/1.04 = 11,538,462 dinars.

Sell dinars for $ at spot rate (counter currency is dinars, bank buys high), $ received = 11,538,462/57.52 = $200,599.

Dollar maturity value after six months at 0.5% = $200,599 × 1.005 = $201,602, or $202,000 to the nearest $000.

(b) Effective, Effective, Effective

All three hedges will allow Park Co to hedge its foreign currency risk.

Leading should work because, based on the given forward rates between € and $, the $ is due to depreciate and so making payments while the $ is more valuable will mean that fewer $ are needed to buy the € needed.

Forward exchange contracts and tailor made currency options would both provide perfect hedges for the transactions.

(c) B

Only the dinar-denominated overdraft will be effective, by matching assets (receivables in dinars) and liabilities (overdraft in dinars).

The company already has liabilities in Euros so would want a Euro asset to offset the risk. The long-term euro-denominated loan is a liability that will increase payments to be made in euros and hence increase foreign currency risk in relation to Euro payments.

(d) Incorrect, Incorrect

Purchasing power parity predicts the future spot rate, not the forward exchange rate.

The international Fisher effect does not predict real interest rates. It equates the difference in interest rates between two countries to the difference in current and future spot rates for the exchange rate between the countries' currencies.

(e) A

An upward sloping yield curve shows long-term yields as higher than short-term ones. This can stem from either relatively higher long-term than short-term interest rates or relatively lower long-term than short-term bond prices.

If default risk increases with duration, compensation for default risk increases with time and hence the long-term bonds must offer higher yields than short-term ones and the yield curve will slope upwards.

Liquidity preference theory states that investors would have to be persuaded (in the form of a higher yield) to invest for longer time periods, not that short-term rates contain a premium.

In this scenario, short-term rates would be high (if banks are reluctant to lend, only high rates would persuade them) and long-term ones lower.

If short-term rates are high, this would increase short-term yields relative to long-term ones.

271 PEONY CO

(a) C

A kink in the normal yield curve can be due to differing yields in different market segments.

(b) **Payment is made from peony co to the bank of $450,000**

As the forward rate agreement is used for a borrowing, the higher rate of 7.1% is guaranteed under the FRA. As the actual borrowing rate is lower (6.5%), the company will have to pay the difference (0.6%)to the bank via the FRA to bring the total borrowing under both contracts to the pre-agreed rate of 7.1%.

As the borrowing is for 9 months, the calculation must be pro-rated from the annual rates to this time period.

Company pays bank 100m × 0.6% × 9/12 = $450,000 paid

(c) **$112.9 million**

200m pesos received in six months and 380m pesos received in 12 months, so 2 different forward rate calculations needed.

The ACCA formula sheet tells you that interest rate parity says that: $F_0 = S_0 \times \frac{(1+i_c)}{(1+i_b)}$

The counter currency is pesos and the base currency is $

Peso 12 month interest rate = 10% (0.1 as a decimal)

$ 12 month interest rate = 6.5% (0.065 as a decimal)

12-month forward rate = 5 × 1.1/1.065 = 5.1643 pesos per $1

The 6 month forward rate calculation will use 6 month interest rates:

Peso rate = 10.0% × 6/12 = 5% (0.05 as a decimal)

$ rate = 6.5% × 6/12 = 3.25% (0.0325 as a decimal)

6-month forward rate = 5 × 1.05/1.0325 = 5.0848 pesos per $1

Income = (200m/5.0848) + (380m/5.1643) = $112.9 m

(d) C

Both statements are true.

(e) **B**

A borrower can hedge interest rate risk by selling interest rate futures now and buying them back in the future. Interest rate options do not have to be exercised at all, but can be abandoned. Only the interest, not the principal, is exchanged using an interest rate swap. To set up an interest rate collar for borrowing, Peony would have to buy a cap and sell a floor.

272 MARIGOLD CO

(a) B

Translation risk is the gain/loss arising from the retranslation of a foreign subsidiary's results.

Transaction risk is the risk of a currency value changing between the transaction and settlement dates due to a movement in exchange rates. Economic risk is the risk of a variation in the value of the business due to unexpected changes in exchange rates. Political risk is the risk of the business being affected by political decisions and is unrelated to exchange rates.

(b) $269,663

The appropriate forward rate is 1.1125 MS per $1. MS is the counter currency. Marigold will be receiving the counter currency and selling it to the bank. The bank buys the counter currency high (and sells it low), so the higher of the two forward rates is used.

MS 300,000/1.1125 = $269,663

(c) Borrow MS297,030, Deposit $264,027

Marigold has a future receivables asset in MS. To set up the money market hedge, it should create an opposing liability in MS. Therefore, the company will borrow MS and deposit $ for the hedge.

MS borrowing rate pro-rated for three months = 4% × 3/12 = 1%

Amount to borrow today to have MS300,000 in 3 months = MS300,000/1.01 = MS297,030

This will be exchanged today for $, which will be put on deposit. As the bank will be buying the counter currency MS today, the high spot rate will be used.

Amount of $ received and put on deposit = MS297,030/MS1.1250 = $264,027

Note, the question did not ask for the maturity amount of the deposit, only amount to deposit.

(d) A and C

Payment of the option premium upfront will make the option the more expensive means of hedging.

A strengthening of the $ will result in a worse spot rate than the exercise price, forcing exercise of the option. This, along with the premium cost will mean that Marigold Co will be worse off than if they had used the other instruments which offer better rates than even the exercise price. Note that the forward rate of MS1.1125 per $ is a better rate for a receipt than the option exercise price of MS1.125 per $.

Standard contract sizes only apply to tradable options, not over-the-counter options which will be tailored to the needs of the customer. There is no obligation to exercise an option.

(e) B

A money market hedge will bring the cash translation forward and will therefore provide $ today which could be spent rather than deposited.

The forward contract will not do this, as it will be settled at the set future date.

Both methods are tailor made to the transaction needs. Neither allow the company to benefit from favourable movements in exchange rates (options do this). Neither are tradeable products.

273 WREN CO

(a) A

Interest rate futures can be closed out at any time. They have an expiry date, which is the ideal close out date (as the futures price and the spot interest rate will be the same on that date), but can be closed out before that date if preferred. This would lead to an imperfect hedge, but this can still be beneficial to the user.

Forward rate agreements are not long-term instruments, so option B is incorrect.

Even if interest rate options are allowed to lapse and so the user does not have to take the option interest rate, they will still have had to pay a premium upfront to get the right to let the option lapse. There is therefore still a cost – usually an expensive one.

In relation to interest rate caps and floors, the cap and the floor both make use of interest rate options. Buying an interest rate option generates a cap and selling the option generates a floor. Purchasing two options would generate two caps rather than a collar (one cap and one floor), so option D is incorrect.

(b) The FEC costs $28,608 less than the lead payment

Forward exchange contract (FEC) cost = D3m/1.94 = $1,546,392

Lead payment cost today = D3m/2 = $1,500,000

However, comparing these two costs directly would not give a like for like comparison. The FEC payment will be made in six months' time, but the lead payment would be made today. To address this you should assume that in order to make the lead payment, the $1.5m will be borrowed for six months. The borrowing rate given for $ is 10% per year, which can be prorated to 5% over six months.

Compounding the $1.5m at 5% gives a maturity value of $1.5m × 1.05 = $1,575,000. This amount will need to be paid off by the company in six months and can be directly compared to the FEC payment in six months' time.

The cost of leading is therefore ($1,575,000 – $1,546,392) $28,608 more expensive than the FEC.

(c) B

As the borrowing will be made in 3 months' time and will last for 6 months (meaning it ends in 9 months' time), the 3 v 9 FRA at 10.0 – 8.0 will be used.

As the company is borrowing, the higher of the 2 rates will be offered by the FRA provider, 10%.

The given rates are annual rates and the borrowing is only for 6 months, so the interest that the company will pay will be prorated to six months:

$500,000 × 10% × 6/12 = $25,000 interest paid

Note that when using the FRA, technically the company will pay interest at the borrowing rate of 10.5% ($26,250) and the FRA will reimburse 0.5% ($1,250) to the company in order to fix the effective rate at 10%.

(d) C

It is correct that forward exchange rates reflect interest rate parity. Note that this can be seen in the formula for interest rate parity:

$F_0 = S_0 \times (1 + i_c)/(1 + i_b)$

F_0 represents the forward rate, which is determined by the relative interest rates in the two countries.

The formula can also be used to illustrate that the country with the higher interest rate will see a depreciation, not an appreciation, of its exchange rate. In the scenario, dollar rates are higher than dinar rates and the forward rate of 1.94 dinars to the dollar represents a dollar depreciation from the spot rate of 2.00.

Option B is a statement about purchasing power parity rather than the international Fisher effect, which equates the difference in interest rates to the difference in current and future spot rates. Similarly, option D reflects interest rate parity rather than purchasing power parity.

(e) B

Organisations which only operate in domestic markets are still subject to economic risk as long-term currency movements can make foreign exporters more competitive in the domestic market. In other words, exchange rate movements can encourage our domestic customers to import rather than buy from us, making us less competitive, so statement 1 is not correct.

Unanticipated changes in exchange rates are a cause of exchange rate risk, so statement 2 is correct.

274 TAMUNAC CO

(a) **C and D**

A normal yield curve is upward sloping, so that the yield is higher on instruments with long-term maturities.

An inverted yield curve is downward sloping, so that the yield is lower on instruments with long-term maturities. Answer A is therefore incorrect.

With an inverted yield curve, interest rates are expected to fall in the future, which makes it more attractive to borrow long-term (e.g. issue Eurobonds). It also means that Tamunac Co is exposed to falling rather than rising interest rates, so answer B is incorrect.

In these circumstances, longer-term borrowing in the foreign currency with a variable rate is recommended due to potentially lower interest rates in future (borrowing at fixed rates would mean no opportunity to take advantage of falling rates). Therefore, answers C and D are correct.

Note: Eurobonds are simply bonds denominated in a foreign currency.

(b) D

Basis risk arises when a hedge does not exactly offset the cash effect of a change in the price of the underlying asset. This may occur if the funds needed at maturity are not entirely hedged.

(c) **A**

When using an FRA for borrowing, it is the higher of the two rates that is applicable. For this 4.00-3.60 FRA, the applicable interest rate is therefore 4.00% per year.

To calculate the transfer in relation to the FRA, we must compare the FRA rate to the interest rate achieved on the borrowing (remember, the FRA and the borrowing are two completely separate transactions). We're told that this was 3.2%.

The FRA guarantees interest paid at a rate of 4%. As the rate achieved on the borrowing is lower than this, Tamunac must transfer the difference via the FRA.

4% – 3.2% = 0.8% transferred.

To calculate the monetary amount transferred, we must apply this rate to the borrowing amount and pro rate it for the length of the borrowing period.

We're not given the time period directly, but the fact that a 3-6 FRA is used means that the borrowing must start in 3 months' time and end in 6 months, meaning a 3-month borrowing period.

0.8% × €10m × 3/12 = €20,000 paid.

(d) **D**

For a foreign currency receivable, a money market hedge is set up by borrowing the present value of the foreign currency today, converting it into the home currency today (at the spot rate) and depositing the purchased home currency until maturity, which is the same date that the foreign currency is received.

As the hedge is being set up for a 3-month time period, with a foreign currency of € and a home currency of $, to perform the calculations, we will need a € borrowing interest rate for 3 months and a $ deposit one for 3 months:

€ 3-month borrowing interest rate = 6% × 3/12 = 1.5% (0.015 as a decimal)

$ 3-month deposit interest rate = 2% × 3/12 = 0.5% (0.005 as a decimal)

PV of foreign currency to be received = future amount/(1+interest rate)

= €1,500,000/1.015 = €1,477,833

Using the € to purchase $ at the spot rate:

€1,477,833/1.16 = $1,273,994

Maturity value of these $s deposited for 3 months = deposited amount × (1+interest rate) = $1,273,994 × 1.005 = $1,280,364

(e) **B and C**

An over-the-counter interest rate option is agreed with a financial institution for a non-refundable premium which is payable in advance.

The option is only exercised if it is favourable. Over-the-counter options cannot be traded on a financial exchange.

Section 6

ANSWERS TO CONSTRUCTED RESPONSE (LONG) PRACTICE QUESTIONS – SECTION C

WORKING CAPITAL MANAGEMENT

275 KXP CO (DEC 12 – MODIFIED)

Key answer tips

Part (a) draws heavily upon knowledge of financial ratios and how various figures in the financial statements relate to each other.

Part (b) is a fairly common requirement but does require students to work methodically through the information and lay out their working clearly in order for their thought process to be followed.

It is important to make sure the requirement in part (c) is read carefully to ensure students do not go off on a tangent. The words "working capital" and "policy" must not be ignored and discussion should not focus on investment and financing in detail.

The highlighted words are key phrases that markers are looking for.

(a) Calculation of net cost/benefit

Current receivables = $2,466,000

Receivables paying within 30 days = 15m × 0.5 × 30/365 = $616,438

Receivables paying within 45 days = 15m × 0.3 × 45/365 = $554,795

Receivables paying within 60 days = 15m × 0.2 × 60/365 = $493,151

Receivables after changes introduced = $616,438 + $554,795 + $493,151 = $1,664,384

Reduction in receivables = $2,466,000 – $1,664,384 = $801,616

Reduction in financing cost = $801,616 × 0.06 = $48,097

Cost of discount = $15m × 0.5 × 0.01 = $75,000

Net cost of proposed changes in receivables policy = $75,000 – $48,097 = $26,903

Alternative approach to calculation of net cost/benefit

Current receivables collection period = (2,466/15,000) × 365 = 60 days

Revised receivables collection period = (30 × 0.5) + (45 × 0.3) + (60 × 0.2) = 40.5 days

Decrease in receivables collection period = 60 – 40.5 = 19.5 days

Decrease in receivables = $15m × 19.5/365 = $801,370

(The slight difference compared to the earlier answer is due to rounding)

Decrease in financing cost = $801,370 × 0.06 = $48,082

Net cost of proposed changes in receivables policy = $75,000 – $48,082 = $26,918

Comment

The proposed changes in trade receivables policy are not financially acceptable. However, if the trade terms offered are comparable with those of its competitors, KXP Co needs to investigate the reasons for the (on average) late payment of current customers. This analysis also assumes constant sales and no bad debts, which is unlikely to be the case in reality.

(b) Cost of current inventory policy

Cost of materials = $540,000 per year

Annual ordering cost = number of orders × cost per order = 12 × $150 = $1,800 per year

Annual holding cost = average inventory (Q/2) × cost to hold one unit for one year = (15,000/2) × $0.24 = $1,800 per year

Tutorial note

When the ordering and holding cost totals for the year are the same, it means the business is currently using the economic order quantity (which calculates as √(2 × (15,000 × 12) × $150/$0.24) = 15,000 units

Total cost of current inventory policy = purchase cost + ordering cost + holding cost = $540,000 + $1,800 + $1,800 = $543,600 per year

Cost of inventory policy after bulk purchase discount

Cost of materials after bulk purchase discount = $540,000 × 98% = $529,200 per year

Annual demand = 12 × 15,000 = 180,000 units per year

KXP Co will need to increase its order size to 30,000 units to gain the bulk discount

Revised number of orders = 180,000/30,000 = 6 orders per year

Revised ordering cost = 6 × $150 = $900 per year

Revised holding cost = (30000/2) × $0.24 = $3,600 per year

Revised total cost of inventory policy = $529,200 + $900 + $3,600 = $533,700 per year

Evaluation of offer of bulk purchase discount

Net benefit of taking bulk purchase discount = $543,600 – $533,700 = $9,900 per year

The bulk purchase discount looks to be financially acceptable. However, this evaluation is based on a number of unrealistic assumptions. For example, the ordering cost and the holding cost are assumed to be constant, which is unlikely to be true in reality. Annual demand is assumed to be constant, whereas in practice seasonal and other changes in demand are likely.

(c) Working capital investment policy is concerned with the level of investment in current assets, with one company being compared with another. Working capital financing policy is concerned with the relative proportions of short-term and long-term finance used by a company. While working capital investment policy is therefore assessed on an inter-company comparative basis, assessment of working capital financing policy involves analysis of financial information for one company alone.

Working capital financing policy uses an analysis of current assets into permanent current assets and fluctuating current assets. Working capital investment policy does not require this analysis. Permanent current assets represent the core level of investment in current assets that supports a given level of business activity.

Fluctuating current assets represent the changes in the level of current assets that arise through, for example, the unpredictability of business operations, such as the level of trade receivables increasing due to some customers paying late or the level of inventory increasing due to demand being less than predicted.

Working capital financing policy relies on the matching principle, which is not used by working capital investment policy. The matching principle holds that long-term assets should be financed from a long-term source of finance. Non-current assets and permanent current assets should therefore be financed from a long-term source, such as equity finance or loan note finance, while fluctuating current assets should be financed from a short-term source, such as an overdraft or a short-term bank loan.

Both working capital investment policy and working capital financing policy use the terms conservative, moderate and aggressive. In investment policy, the terms are used to indicate the comparative level of investment in current assets on an inter-company basis.

One company has a more aggressive approach compared to another company if it has a lower level of investment in current assets, and *vice versa* for a conservative approach to working capital investment policy.

In working capital financing policy, the terms are used to indicate the way in which fluctuating current assets and permanent current assets are matched to short-term and long-term finance sources.

An aggressive financing policy means that fluctuating current assets and a portion of permanent current assets are financed from a short-term finance source. A conservative financing policy means that permanent current assets and a portion of fluctuating current assets are financed from a long-term source.

An aggressive financing policy will be more profitable than a conservative financing policy because short-term finance is cheaper than long-term finance, as indicated for debt finance by the normal yield curve (term structure of interest rates).

However, an aggressive financing policy will be riskier than a conservative financing policy because short-term finance is riskier than long-term finance. For example, an overdraft is repayable on demand, while a short-term loan may be renewed on less favourable terms than an existing loan.

Provided interest payments are made, however, long-term debt will not lead to any pressure on a company and equity finance is permanent capital.

Overall, therefore, it can be said that while working capital investment policy and working capital financing policy use similar terminology, the two policies are very different in terms of their meaning and application. It is even possible, for example, for a company to have a conservative working capital investment policy while following an aggressive working capital financing policy.

ACCA marking scheme

			Marks
(a)	Revised trade receivables		1
	Reduction in trade receivables		1
	Reduction in financing cost		1
	Cost of early settlement discount		1
	Net cost of change in receivables policy		1
	Comment on findings		1
		Maximum	**6**
(b)	Current annual ordering cost		0.5
	Current holding cost		0.5
	Total cost of current inventory policy		1
	Revised cost of materials		0.5
	Revised number of orders		0.5
	Revised ordering cost		0.5
	Revised holding cost		0.5
	Net benefit of bulk purchase discount		1
	Comment on assumptions		1
		Maximum	**6**
(c)	Working capital investment policy		3–4
	Working capital financing policy		5–6
		Maximum	**8**
Total			**20**

Extracts from examiner's comments

Part (a) common errors:

Weaker answers showed a lack of understanding of how the receivables collection period links credit sales for a period with the trade receivables balance at the end of the period. Some answers, for example, tried to calculate the revised trade receivables balance by applying a changed receivables collection period to current receivables, instead of applying them to credit sales.

Part (b) common errors:

Perhaps because information on holding cost and order cost was provided in the question, many candidates calculated the economic order quantity (EOQ). The question made no reference to the EOQ and an EOQ calculation was not necessary. In fact, what was needed was a comparison between the current ordering policy and the ordering policy employing the bulk discount. Candidates who wasted time calculating the EOQ found that the company was already using an EOQ approach to ordering inventory.

Some answers did not gain full credit because they did not comment on the assumptions made by their calculations. Credit was also lost by candidates who could not calculate order cost, or holding cost, or both.

Part (c) common errors:

Many answers struggled to gain good marks with this question, and yet the topics of working capital investment policy (the level of investment in current assets) and working capital financing policy (the balance between short-term and long-term funds in financing current assets) have been examined a number of times in recent years.

Many answers seemed to be unaware that it is possible for an aggressive working capital investment policy to occur in a given company at the same time as a conservative working capital financing policy, and vice versa. These answers assumed that a company was either aggressive in both kinds of policy, or not, for example.

276 HGR CO (JUNE 09 – MODIFIED)

Key answer tips

The generic requirement of part (a), to "discuss the working capital financing strategy of HGR" can result in a lack of direction and focus in your answer. This sort of question highlights the importance of good exam preparation that includes practising as many past exam questions as possible as requirements such as this are not unusual.

Part (b) may overwhelm some students as the initial perception is that many calculations need to be made. However, this is not the case. Part (i) (for 2 marks) involves simply plugging in the numbers provided before doing a quick calculation of overdraft interest. In part (ii), (for 5 marks) you need to evaluate the impact of the finance director's proposals surrounding both accounts receivable and inventory management. Both calculations involve a manipulation of the standard working capital cycle formulae that students should be familiar, although this might not be obvious to some students. The model answer shows the most efficient way of laying out the answer. Of the 9 marks available for part (b), up to 3 are available for commenting on the forecast position and making suitable recommendations. This could easily be overlooked if you're not careful.

Finally, part (c) gives a good opportunity to pick up some easier marks. This part of the question should be attempted first. The highlighted words are key phrases that markers are looking for.

(a) When considering the financing of working capital, it is useful to divide current assets into fluctuating current assets and permanent current assets. Fluctuating current assets represent changes in the level of current assets due to the unpredictability of business activity. Permanent current assets represent the core level of investment in current assets needed to support a given level of revenue or business activity. As revenue or level of business activity increases, the level of permanent current assets will also increase. This relationship can be measured by the ratio of revenue to net current assets.

The financing choice as far as working capital is concerned is between short-term and long-term finance. Short-term finance is more flexible than long-term finance: an overdraft, for example, is used by a business organisation as the need arises and variable interest is charged on the outstanding balance. Short-term finance is also more risky than long-term finance: an overdraft facility may be withdrawn, or a short-term loan may be renewed on less favourable terms. In terms of cost, the term structure of interest rates suggests that short-term debt finance has a lower cost than long-term debt finance.

The matching principle suggests that long-term finance should be used for long-term investment. Applying this principle to working capital financing, long-term finance should be matched with permanent current assets and non-current assets. A financing policy with this objective is called a 'matching policy'. HGR Co is not using this financing policy, since of the $16,935,000 of current assets, $14,000,000 or 83% is financed from short-term sources (overdraft and trade payables) and only $2,935,000 or 17% is financed from a long-term source, in this case equity finance (shareholders' funds) or traded bonds.

The financing policy or approach taken by HGR Co towards the financing of working capital, where short-term finance is preferred, is called an aggressive policy. Reliance on short-term finance makes this riskier than a matching approach, but also more profitable due to the lower cost of short-term finance. Following an aggressive approach to financing can lead to overtrading (undercapitalisation) and the possibility of liquidity problems.

(b) Bank balance in three months' time if no action is taken:

Month	**1**	**2**	**3**
	$000	$000	$000
Receipts	4,220	4,350	3,808
Payments	(3,950)	(4,100)	(3,750)
Interest on bonds		(200)	
Overdraft interest	(19)	(18)	(18)
Capital investment			(2,000)
Net cash flow	251	32	(1,960)
Opening balance	(3,800)	(3,549)	(3,517)
Closing balance	(3,549)	(3,517)	(5,477)

Bank balance in three months' time if the finance director's proposals are implemented:

Month	**1**	**2**	**3**
	$000	$000	$000
Receipts	4,220	4,350	3,808
Payments	(3,950)	(4,100)	(3,750)
Interest on bonds		(200)	
Overdraft interest	(19)	(15)	(13)
Capital investment			(2,000)
Accounts receivable	270	270	270
Inventory	204	204	204
Net cash flow	725	509	(1,481)
Opening balance	(3,800)	(3,075)	(2,566)
Closing balance	(3,075)	(2,566)	(4,047)

Workings:

Reduction in accounts receivable collection period

Current accounts receivable collection period = (8,775/49,275) × 365 = 65 days

Reduction in days over six months = 65 – 53 = 12 days

Monthly reduction = 12/6 = 2 days

Each receivables collection day is equivalent to $8,775,000/65 = $135,000 (Alternatively, each receivables collection day is equivalent to $49,275,000/365 = $135,000)

Monthly reduction in accounts receivable = 2 × $135,000 = $270,000

Reduction in inventory holding period

Current inventory holding period = (8,160/37,230) × 365 = 80 days

Each inventory holding day is equivalent to $8,160,000/80 = $102,000 (Alternatively, each inventory holding day = $37,230,000/365 = $102,000)

Monthly reduction in inventory = $102,000 × 2 = $204,000

Overdraft interest calculations

Monthly overdraft interest rate = $(1.0617)^{1/12}$ = 1.005 or 0.5%

If no action is taken:

Period 1 interest = $3,800,000 × 0.005 = $19,000

Period 2 interest = $3,549,000 × 0.005 = $17,745 or $18,000

Period 3 interest = $3,517,000 × 0.005 = $17,585 or $18,000

If action is taken:

Period 1 interest = $3,800,000 × 0.005 = $19,000

Period 2 interest = $3,075,000 × 0.005 = $15,375 or $15,000

Period 3 interest = $2,566,000 × 0.005 = $12,830 or $13,000

Discussion

If no action is taken, the cash flow forecast shows that HGR Co will exceed its overdraft limit of $4 million by $1.48 million in three months' time. If the finance director's proposals are implemented, there is a positive effect on the bank balance, but the overdraft limit is still exceeded in three months' time, although only by $47,000 rather than by $1.47 million.

In each of the three months following that, the continuing reduction in accounts receivable collection days will improve the bank balance by $270,000 per month. Without further information on operating receipts and payments, it cannot be forecast whether the bank balance will return to less than the limit, or even continue to improve.

The main reason for the problem with the bank balance is the $2 million capital expenditure. Purchase of non-current assets should not be financed by an overdraft, but a long-term source of finance such as equity or bonds. If the capital expenditure were removed from the area of working capital management, the overdraft balance at the end of three months would be $3.48 million if no action were taken and $2.05 million if the finance director's proposals were implemented. Given that HGR Co has almost $50 million of non-current assets that could possibly be used as security, raising long-term debt through either a bank loan or a bond issue appears to be sensible. Assuming a bond interest rate of 10% per year, current long-term debt in the form of traded bonds is approximately ($200m × 2)/0.1 = $4m, which is much less than the amount of noncurrent assets.

A suitable course of action for HGR Co to follow would therefore be, firstly, to implement the finance director's proposals and, secondly, to finance the capital expenditure from a long-term source. Consideration could also be given to using some long-term debt finance to reduce the overdraft and to reduce the level of accounts payable, currently standing at 100 days.

(c) When credit is granted to foreign customers, two problems may become especially significant. First, the longer distances over which trade takes place and the more complex nature of trade transactions and their elements means foreign accounts receivable need more investment than their domestic counterparts. Longer transaction times increase accounts receivable balances and hence the level of financing and financing costs. Second, the risk of bad debts is higher with foreign accounts receivable than with their domestic counterparts. In order to manage and reduce credit risks, therefore, exporters seek to reduce the risk of bad debts and to reduce the level of investment in foreign accounts receivable.

Many foreign transactions are on 'open account', which is an agreement to settle the amount outstanding on a predetermined date. Open account reflects a good business relationship between importer and exporter. It also carries the highest risk of non-payment.

One way to reduce investment in foreign accounts receivable is to agree early payment with an importer, for example by payment in advance, payment on shipment, or cash on delivery. These terms of trade are unlikely to be competitive, however, and it is more likely that an exporter will seek to receive cash in advance of payment being made by the customer.

One way to accelerate cash receipts is to use bill finance. Bills of exchange with a signed agreement to pay the exporter on an agreed future date, supported by a documentary letter of credit, can be discounted by a bank to give immediate funds. This discounting is without recourse if bills of exchange have been countersigned by the importer's bank.

Documentary letters of credit are a payment guarantee backed by one or more banks. They carry almost no risk, provided the exporter complies with the terms and conditions contained in the letter of credit. The exporter must present the documents stated in the letter, such as bills of lading, shipping documents, bills of exchange, and so on, when seeking payment. As each supporting document relates to a key aspect of the overall transaction, letters of credit give security to the importer as well as the exporter.

Companies can also manage and reduce risk by gathering appropriate information with which to assess the creditworthiness of new customers, such as bank references and credit reports.

Insurance can also be used to cover some of the risks associated with giving credit to foreign customers. This would avoid the cost of seeking to recover cash due from foreign accounts receivable through a foreign legal system, where the exporter could be at a disadvantage due to a lack of local or specialist knowledge.

Export factoring can also be considered, where the exporter pays for the specialist expertise of the factor as a way of reducing investment in foreign accounts receivable and reducing the incidence of bad debts.

ACCA marking scheme

			Marks
(a)	Analysis of current assets	1 – 2	
	Short-term and long-term finance	2 – 3	
	Matching principle	1 – 2	
	Financing approach used by company	1 – 2	
		Maximum	**6**
(b)	Bank balance if no action is taken	2	
	Bank balance if action is taken	5	
	Working capital management implications	1 – 2	
	Advice on course of action	1 – 2	
		Maximum	**9**
(c)	Relevant discussion		**5**
Total			**20**

Extracts from examiner's comments

Part (a) common errors:

Some candidates ignored the word 'financing' and discussed working capital strategy in general.

Not using the statement of financial position information given to realise that the company was financing 83% of its current assets from short-term sources and that this is an aggressive rather than a conservative financing strategy.

Part (b) common errors:

Failing to recognise that the opening balance was the overdraft and therefore having no opening balance: calculating annual interest rather than monthly interest; and including cash flows other than those given in the question (for example from the credit sales and cost of sales figures given in the question).

Part (c) common errors:

Some answers were one-sided, concentrating on exchange rate risk rather than on credit risk. Since the question referred to foreign customers, it was inappropriate to limit answers to a discussion of domestic receivables management.

277 FLIT CO (DEC 14 – MODIFIED)

Key answer tips

Part (a) is relatively simple but needs a methodical approach and should not be rushed. Part (b) is a simple calculation. Parts (c) and (e) are stand-alone knowledge regurgitation questions. Part (d) is the most complex, requiring an understanding that if early settlement speeds up payment from customers, the receivables balance and therefore the cost of financing receivables will be affected along with an understanding of all the other elements that will be affected such as bad debts, more profit from extra sales, etc. The highlighted words are key phrases that markers are looking for.

(a) Cash balances at the end of each month:

	December	**January**	**February**	**March**	**April**
Sales (units)	1,200	1,250	1,300	1,400	1,500
Selling price ($/unit)	800	800	840	840	
Sales ($000)	960	1,000	1,092	1,176	
Month received	January	February	March	April	

	December	**January**	**February**	**March**
Production (units)	1,250	1,300	1,400	1,500
Raw materials (units)	2,500	2,600	2,800	3,000
Raw materials ($000)	500	520	560	600
Month payable	January	February	March	April

	December	**January**	**February**	**March**
Production (units)	1,250	1,300	1,400	1,500
Variable costs ($000)	125	130	140	150
Month payable	December	January	February	March

Monthly cash balances:

	January	**February**	**March**
	$000	$000	$000
Receivables	960	1,000	1,092
Loan			300
Income:	960	1,000	1,392
Raw materials	500	520	560
Variable costs	130	140	150
Machine			400
Expenditure:	630	660	1,110
Opening balance	40	370	710
Net cash flow	330	340	282
Closing balance	370	710	992

(b) Calculation of current ratio

Inventory at the end of the three-month period:

This will be the finished goods for April sales of 1,500 units, which can be assumed to be valued at the cost of production of $400 per unit for materials and $100 per unit for variable overheads and wages. The value of the inventory is therefore 1,500 × 500 = $750,000.

Trade receivables at the end of the three-month period:

These will be March sales of 1,400 × 800 × 1.05 = $1,176,000.

Cash balance at the end of the three-month period:

This was forecast to be $992,000.

Trade payables at the end of the three-month period:

This will be the cash owed for March raw materials of $600,000.

Forecast current ratio

Assuming that current liabilities consist of trade payables alone:

Current ratio = ($750,000 + $1,176,000 + $992,000)/$600,000 = 4.9 times

(c) If Flit Co generates a short-term cash surplus, the cash may be needed again in the near future. In order to increase profitability, the short-term cash surplus could be invested, for example, in a bank deposit. However, the investment selected would normally not be expected to carry any risk of capital loss. Shares traded on a large stock market carry a significant risk of capital loss, and hence are rarely suitable for investing short-term cash surpluses.

(d) Current credit sales income = $30,000,000 × 0.8 = $24,000,000

Credit sales income after introducing discount = $24,000,000 × 1.2 = $28,800,000
Increase in income by introducing discount = $24,000,000 × 0.2 = $4,800,000
Increase in operating profit = $4,800,000 × 0.1 = $480,000

Current level of bad debts = $24,000,000 × 0.005 = $120,000 per year
Revised level of bad debts = $28,800,000 × 0.00375 = $108,000 per year
This would be a benefit of $120,000 – $108,000 = $12,000 per year

	$000
Trade receivables taking discount = $28,800,000 × 0.75 × 30/360 =	1,800
Trade receivables not taking discount = $28,800,000 × 0.25 × 51/360 =	1,020
Revised level of trade receivables	2,820
Current trade receivables = $24,000,000 × 51/360 =	3,400
Reduction in trade receivables	580

	$	$
Benefits		
Reduction in financing costs = 580,000 × 0.04 =	23,200	
Increase in net profit =	480,000	
Reduction in bad debts =	12,000	
		515,200
Costs		
Increase in administration costs	35,000	
Cost of discount = $28,800,000 × 0.005 × 0.75 =	108,000	
		143,000
Net benefit of proposed early settlement discount =		372,200

(e) A company could reduce the risk associated with foreign accounts receivable, such as export credit risk, by reducing the level of investment in them, for example, by using bills of exchange.

If payment by the foreign customer is linked to bills of exchange, these can either be discounted or negotiated by a company with its bank. Discounting means that the trade bills (term bills) are sold to the bank at a discount to their face value. The company gets cash when the bills are discounted, thereby decreasing the outstanding level of trade receivables. Negotiation means that the bank makes an advance of cash to the company, with the debt being settled when the bills of exchange (sight bills) are paid.

Advances against collection means that the bank handling the collection of payment on behalf of the selling company could be prepared to make a cash advance of up to 90% of the face value of the payment instrument, for example, bills of exchange. Again, this would reduce the level of investment in foreign accounts receivable.

The risk of non-payment by foreign accounts receivable can be reduced by raising an international letter of credit (documentary credit) linked to the contract for the sale of goods. This could be confirmed (guaranteed) by a bank in the foreign customer's country.

The exporting company could also arrange for export credit insurance (export credit cover) against the risk of non-payment, which could occur for reasons outside the control of the foreign customer.

The risk of foreign accounts receivable becoming bad debts can be reduced by performing the same creditworthiness assessment processes on foreign credit customers as those used with domestic credit customers, such as seeking credit references and bank references.

Examiner's note: Only TWO methods were required to be discussed.

ACCA marking scheme

			Marks
(a)	Monthly receivables		1
	Loan		0.5
	Raw materials		1
	Variable costs		1
	Machine		0.5
	Closing balances		1
		Maximum	**5**
(b)	Closing finished goods inventory		0.5
	Closing trade receivables		0.5
	Closing trade payables		0.5
	Current ratio		0.5
		Maximum	**2**
(c)	Temporary nature of short-term cash surplus		1
	Investment should have no risk of capital loss		1
	Shares are not suitable for investment		1
		Maximum	**3**
(d)	Increase in net profit		1
	Benefit of reduction in bad debts		1
	Reduction in trade receivables		1
	Reduction in financing costs		1
	Cost of discount		1
	Evaluation of early settlement discount		1
			6
(e)	First method of reducing risk		2
	Second method of reducing risk		2
			4
Total			**20**

Extracts from examiner's comments

Part (a) common errors:

Some answers made timing errors, while others overlooked that each unit produced required two units (not one unit) of raw material.

Some answers lost marks because they wrongly believed that net cash flow was the same as cash balance, or because they located the January opening cash balance in December.

Part (b) common errors:

Many answers, without explanation, omitted one or more of the elements present in the current ratio calculation. While the question stated that no raw materials inventory was held, finished goods inventory had to be calculated, as production of finished goods took place one month before sales.

Another reason why most answers did not gain full marks was including elements that were not current assets or current liabilities, such as a newly purchased machine or a new long-term loan.

Some answers did not explain the figures that were being used to calculate the current ratio, giving markers no guidance as to the working capital elements that the candidate believed were being used.

Part (c) common errors:

The key learning point here is that a short-term cash surplus must be invested with no risk of capital loss, as the cash will be needed again. Shares on a stock market, even a large stock market, can fall in value very quickly and so are not a suitable way of investing a short-term cash surplus. Satisfactory answers recognised this key point, in some cases suggesting appropriate ways of investing the short-term cash surplus.

Part (d) common errors:

Answers to this question demonstrated the importance of reading the question carefully, for example:

- candidates were told to assume that there were 360 days in each year, yet some answers used 365 days
- credit sales were stated to be 80% of total income of $30 million, yet some answers used $30 million as credit sales
- income from credit sales was stated to increase by 20% as a result of offering the early settlement discount, yet some answers did not increase credit sales income.

Answers to this question also demonstrated the importance of labelling all calculations or workings, as some answers offered a sea of calculations with no indication of what each calculation related to. It is up to candidates to communicate clearly what they are doing in their answers, as markers cannot be expected to guess what unlabelled calculations are trying to achieve.

Part (e) common errors:

Answers that discussed more than two ways (specifically requested in the question) wasted valuable time, as marks would only be awarded to the first two ways discussed in an answer.

278 OSCAR CO (SEP/DEC 2018)

Key answer tips

For part (a), remember that a reduction in the receivables' collection period means less financing is needed for receivables and financing costs will fall. This is often the most complex part of calculations on this topic. Don't forget to include the easier costs and benefits in your totals. For part (b) you are only asked for benefits, so disadvantages of factoring will not score marks. For part (c) make sure that your answer focuses on working capital investment policy rather than working capital financing policy. Make sure you're able to distinguish between these two topics in the exam. DO not present more than three factors as any extra will not be marked.

The highlighted words are key phrases that markers are looking for.

(a)

Option 1

	$	
Current trade receivables	5,370,000	
Revised trade receivables (28,000,000 × 30/365)	2,301,370	
Reduction in receivables	3,068,630	
	$	$
Reduction in financing cost (3,068,630 × 0.07)	214,804	
Reduction in admin costs	30,000	
Benefits		244,804
Factor's fee (28,000,000 × 0.005)		(140,000)
Net benefit		104,804

Option 2

	$	$
Reduction in financing cost (3,068,630 × 0.07)	214,804	
Reduction in admin costs	30,000	
Bad debts saved (28,000,000 × 0.02)	560,000	
Benefits		804,804
Increase in finance cost (2,301,370 × 0.8 × 0.02)	36,822	
Factor's fee (28,000,000 × 0.015)	420,000	
Costs		(456,822)
Net benefit		347,982

Both options are financially acceptable to Oscar Co, with Option 2 offering the greatest benefit and therefore it should be accepted.

(b) Oscar Co may benefit from the services offered by the factoring company for a number of different reasons, as follows:

Economies of specialisation

Factors specialise in trade receivables management and therefore can offer 'economies of specialisation'. They are experts at getting customers to pay promptly and may be able to achieve payment periods and bad debt levels which clients could not achieve themselves. The factor may be able to persuade the large multinational companies which Oscar Co supplies to pay on time.

Scale economies

In addition, because of the scale of their operations, factors are often able to do this more cheaply than clients such as Oscar Co could do on their own. Factor fees, even after allowing for the factor's profit margin, can be less than the clients' own receivables administration cost.

Free up management time

Factoring can free up management time and allow them to focus on more important tasks. This could be a major benefit for Oscar Co, where directors are currently spending a large amount of time attempting to persuade customers to pay on time.

Bad debts insurance

The insurance against bad debts shields clients from non-payment by customers; although this comes at a cost, it can be particularly attractive to small companies who may not be able to stand the financial shock of a large bad debt. This could well be the case for Oscar Co. As a small company which supplies much larger car manufacturing companies, it is particularly exposed to default by customers. On the other hand, it could be argued that large multinational companies are financially secure and default is unlikely, rendering bad debt insurance unnecessary.

Accelerate cash inflow

Factor finance can be useful to companies who have exhausted other sources of finance. This could be useful to Oscar Co if it cannot negotiate an increase in its overdraft limit.

Finance through growth

Although factor finance is generally more expensive than a bank overdraft, the funding level is linked to the company's volume of sales. This can help to finance expansion and protects the company against overtrading. In a rapid growth company such as Oscar Co, this could be a major advantage of factor finance.

(c) A company's working capital investment is equal to the sum of its inventories and its accounts receivable, less its accounts payable.

The following factors will determine the level of a company's investment in working capital:

The nature of the industry and the length of the working capital cycle

Some businesses have long production processes which inevitably lead to long working capital cycles and large investments in working capital. Housebuilding, for example, requires the building company to acquire land, gain government permission to build, build houses and when complete, sell them to customers. This process can often take more than a year and require large investment in work-in-progress and therefore in working capital.

Other industries, such as supermarkets, buy goods on long credit terms, have rapid inventory turnover and sell to customers for cash. They often receive payment from customers before they need to pay suppliers and therefore have little (or negative) investment in working capital.

Working capital investment policy

Some companies take a conservative approach to working capital investment, offering long periods of credit to customers (to promote sales), carrying high levels of inventory (to protect against stock-outs), and paying suppliers promptly (to maintain good relationships). This approach offers many benefits, but it necessitates a large investment in working capital.

Others take a more aggressive approach offering minimal credit, carrying low levels of inventory and delaying payments to suppliers. This will result in a low level of working capital investment.

Efficiency of management and terms of trade

If management of the components of working capital is neglected, then investment in working capital can increase. For example, a failure to apply credit control procedures such as warning letters or stop lists can result in high levels of accounts receivable. Failure to control inventory by using the EOQ model, or JIT inventory management principles, can lead to high levels of inventory.

ACCA marking scheme

		Marks
(a)	Revised trade receivables	1
	Finance cost reduction	1
	Admin savings	1
	Factor fee Option 1	1
	Bad debt saving	1
	Finance cost increase	1
	Factor fee Option 2	1
	Comment	1
		8
(b)	Benefits	3
	Oscar Co link	3
		6
(c)	First factor	2
	Second factor	2
	Third factor	2
		6
Total		**20**

Extracts from examiner's comments

Part (a) common errors:

The most frequently occurring error in the calculations for option 2 was a failure to recognise that the factor's advance would bring about an increase in the cost of the financing of the revised trade receivables. In other words, 80% of the trade receivables would be financed at 9%, rather than at 7%.

Some candidates did not make a comment on their findings, which should simply be about which option to choose and why, thereby failing to gain a relatively straightforward mark.

Part (b) common errors:

Errors included answers that were too brief, that ignored the requirement to discuss items other than those already calculated, or that made no link to Oscar Co's circumstances.

Part (c) common errors:

If six marks are offered for discussing three factors, then assuming that two marks are offered for each factor is reasonable. That said, it is worth reiterating, a 'bullet point' or short phrase is rarely, if ever, going to be sufficient to attract the two marks available for each factor.

Common errors in candidates' responses included:

- Discussing (or simply listing) elements of working capital, without relating answers to the question requirement
- Discussing working capital financing policy, when the requirement said working capital investment policy
- Interpreting 'factors determining the level of working capital investment' as 'accounting ratios', such as current ratio or quick ratio
- Stating a factor, but then with no accompanying discussion e.g. the 'nature of the industry', but without explaining why the industry affected working capital or giving examples.

279 DUSTY CO (SEP/DEC 2019)

Key answer tips

Part (a) is mostly calculation based and covers inventory and settlement discount calculations. Note that the settlement discount relates to a supplier, not customers. For the inventory calculations, it would be very easy to miss that reducing the average inventory level (through use of the EOQ) will lead to a reduction in inventory financing costs and increasing inventory (in order to obtain the bulk purchase discount by making larger orders) will increase the financing costs, so these calculations should be included when looking at the financial effect of making changes. Many students would have focused only on holding and ordering costs. The trigger for you to look at financing costs is that the question states that the given holding cost of $0.21 excludes financing costs. The financing cost of inventory is the average inventory value multiplied by the interest rate of inventory financing, here the 3% overdraft cost.

Part (b) is a straightforward discussion question, but on a topic area that students may not have focused on in revision. The study text goes into detail here regarding the permanent versus fluctuating aspect of working capital and the different types of finance available (short-term and long-term). A discussion on how working capital funding strategy focuses on these issues and can be aggressive, matching or conservative in nature is what the examiner is looking for here.

The highlighted words are key phrases that markers are looking for.

(a) (i) Annual holding and ordering costs of the current inventory management system

Each current order is 1,500,000/12 = 125,000 units per order

Average inventory = 125,000/2 = 62,500 units

Current holding cost = 62,500 × 0.21 = $13,125 per year

Current ordering cost = 12 × 252 = $3,024 per year

Current total inventory management cost = $13,125 + $3,024 = $16,149 per year

Example answer in a spreadsheet:

	A	B	C	D	E	F	G	H	I
1	ai								
2	Dusty Co's current inventory management system costs:								
3	Annual holding cost = Holding cost per unit per year × average inventory in units = Ch × Q/2								
4	Ordering cost = Cost per order × number of orders in a year = Co × D/Q								
5									Formulae used:
6	Holding cost		Ch	0.21					
7			Q	125,000					
8									
9			Annual holding cost			13,125			=D6*D7/2
10	Ordering cost		Co	252					
11			D	1,500,000					
12			Annual ordering cost			3,024			=D10*D11/D7
13									
14	**Total inventory management costs per year**						**16,149**		=F9+F12

(ii) Financial effect of adopting EOQ model

EOQ = (2 × 252 × 1,500,000/0.21)0.5 = 60,000 units/order

Number of orders = 1,500,000/60,000 = 25 orders per year

Average inventory = 60,000/2 = 30,000 units

Holding cost = 30,000 × 0.21 = $6,300 per year

Ordering cost = 25 × 252 = $6,300 per year

EOQ total inventory management cost = $6,300 + $6,300 = $12,600 per year

Reduction in total inventory management cost = $16,149 – $12,600 = $3,549 per year

Reduction in average inventory = (62,500 – 30,000) × 14 = $455,000

The overdraft will decrease by the same amount.

Finance cost saving = 455,000 × 0.03 = $13,650 per year

Overall saving = $3,549 + $13,650 = $17,199

(iii) Financial effect of accepting the bulk order discount

Number of orders = 1,500,000/250,000 = 6 orders per year

Average inventory = 250,000/2 = 125,000 units

Holding cost = 125,000 × 0.21 = $26,250 per year

Ordering cost = 6 × 252 = $1,512 per year

Total inventory management cost = $26,250 + $1,512 = $27,762 per year

Increase in total inventory management cost = $27,762 – $16,149 = $11,613 per year

Increase in value of average inventory = (125,000 × 13.93) – (62,500 × 14) = $866,250

The overdraft will increase by the same amount.

Finance cost increase = 866,250 × 0.03 = $25,988 per year

Bulk order discount = 1,500,000 × 14 × 0.005 = $105,000 per year

Overall saving = $105,000 – $11,613 – $25,988 = $67,399

Example answer in a spreadsheet (aii and aiii):

	A	B	C	D	E	F	G	H	I
16	aii		EOQ			60,000			=SQRT(2*D10*D11/D6)
17	Holding cost		Ch	0.21					
18			Q	60,000					=F16
19									
20			Annual holding cost			6,300			=D17*D18/2
21	Ordering cost		Co	252					
22			D	1,500,000					
23			Annual ordering cost			6,300			=D21*D22/D18
24									
25	Total inventory management costs per year						12,600		=F20+F23
26									
27	Reduction in total annual inventory management costs						3,549		=G14-G25
28									
29	As the order quantity is falling, so will the average inventory level and the cost of financing that level								
30	Value of inventory held = average units × purchase price per unit								
31			purchase price per unit		14				
32									
33			current inventory value			875,000			=D7/2*E31
34			inventory value under EOQ			420,000			=D18/2*E31
35			Reduction in inventory value			455,000			=F33-F34
36									
37			Finance cost saving at 3% per year				13,650		=F35*3%
38									
39	**Overall saving under EOQ**						**17,199**		=G27+G37
40									
41	aiii	New Q value				250,000			
42		Current purchase cost				21,000,000			=D11*E31
43		Purchase cost with 0.5% discount				20,895,000			=F42*99.5%
44		Purchase cost saving					105,000		=F42-F43
45									
46		New average inventory				125,000			=F41/2
47		New average inventory value				1,741,250			=F46*E31*99.5%
48		Increase in average inventory value				866,250			=F47-F33
49		Increase in finance cost					- 25,988		=-F48*3%
50									
51		New holding cost				26,250			=D17*F41/2
52		New ordering cost				1,512			=D21*D22/F41
53		Total				27,762			=F51+F52
54		Increase in inventory management costs					- 11,613		=G14-F53
55									
56		**Overall saving**					**67,400**		=G44+G49+G54

(iv) The bulk order discount saves $67,399 compared to the current position, while the EOQ approach saves $17,199. The bulk order discount is recommended as it leads to the greater cost saving.

Tutorial note

It would also have been acceptable to revise the holding costs in (ii) and (iii) to reflect the finance cost of holding inventory (e.g. $0.63 in (ii)) and this approach could be awarded full credit if correct.

(b) Key factors in determining working capital funding strategies

Permanent and fluctuating current assets

One key factor when discussing working capital funding strategies is to distinguish between permanent and fluctuating current assets. Permanent current assets represent the core level of current assets needed to support normal levels of business activity, for example, the level of trade receivables associated with the normal level of credit sales and existing terms of trade. Business activity will be subject to unexpected variations, however, such as some customers being late in settling their accounts, leading to unexpected variations in current assets. These can be termed fluctuating current assets.

Relative cost and risk of short-term and long-term finance

A second key factor is the relative cost of short-term and long-term finance. The normal yield curve suggests that long-term debt finance is more expensive than short-term debt finance, for example, because of investor liquidity preference or default risk. Provided the terms of loan agreements are adhered to and interest is paid when due, however, long-term debt finance is a secure form of finance and hence low risk.

While short-term debt finance is lower cost than long-term debt finance, it is higher risk. For example, an overdraft is technically repayable on demand, while a short-term loan is subject to the risk that it may be renewed on less favourable terms than those currently enjoyed.

Matching principle

A third key factor is the matching principle, which states that the maturity of assets should be reflected in the maturity of the finance used to support them. Short-term finance should be used for fluctuating current assets, while long-term finance should be used for permanent current assets and non-current assets.

Relative costs and benefits of different funding policies

A fourth key factor is the relative costs and benefits of different funding policies.

A matching funding policy would use long-term finance for permanent current assets and non-current assets, and short-term finance for fluctuating current assets. A conservative funding policy would use long-term finance for permanent current assets, non-current assets and some of the fluctuating current assets, with short-term finance being used for the remaining fluctuating current assets. An aggressive funding policy would use long-term finance for the non-current assets and part of the permanent current assets, and short-term finance for fluctuating current assets and the balance of the permanent current assets.

A conservative funding policy, using relatively more long-term finance, would be lower in risk but lower in profitability. An aggressive funding policy, using relatively more short-term finance, would be higher in risk but higher in profitability. A matching funding policy would balance risk and profitability, avoiding the extremes of a conservative or an aggressive funding policy.

Other key factors

Other key factors in working capital funding strategies include managerial attitudes to risk, previous funding decisions and organisation size. Managerial attitudes to risk can lead to a company preferring one working capital funding policy over another, for example, a risk-averse managerial team might prefer a conservative working capital funding policy. Previous funding decisions dictate the current short-term/long-term financing mix of a company. Organisational size can be an important factor in relation to, for example, access to different forms of finance in support of a favoured working capital funding policy.

ACCA marking scheme

			Marks
(a)	(i)	Holding cost current	0.5
		Ordering cost current	0.5
			1
	(ii)	EOQ comp	1
		Holding cost EOQ	0.5
		Ordering cost EOQ	0.5
		Finance costs	1
		EOQ saving overall	1
			4
	(iii)	Holding cost bulk order discount	0.5
		Ordering cost bulk order discount	0.5
		Finance cost	1
		Bulk order discount value	1
		Bulk order discount saving overall	1
			4
	(iv)	Advice	**1**
(b)	Current asset types		2
	Finance cost/risk		2
	Matching principle		2
	Funding policies		2
	Other points		2
			10
Total			**20**

Extracts from examiner's comments

Part (a) common errors:

The most common error here was not 'halving' Dusty's current order size of 125,000 units in order to obtain the average inventory level required, 62,500 units, for the holding cost calculation.

In part (ii), the Economic Order Quantity (EOQ) calculation was usually performed well, but candidates making use of spreadsheet functionality, as they should, must be careful to formulate their cells correctly, especially in respect of computing a square root by raising the figure to 0.5. For example, the correct formulation is:

=(2*252*1500000/0.21)^0.5

By contrast if the brackets are not included, then it is the final variable only, 0.21 in this case, which is raised to the power of 0.5, yielding an incorrectly computed EOQ.

The most common omission in candidates' responses to this question was the lack of recognition that a change in average inventory levels, and hence average inventory values, would change the cost of financing working capital. This is the reason for the inclusion of the cost of the overdraft facility of 3% per year.

280 PUMICE CO (MAR/JUL 2020)

Key answer tips

For part (a) (i), it is important to realise that the working capital holding/collection/payment period calculations can be rearranged so that if you know the number of days and the relevant profit and loss figure, you can calculate the statement of financial position figure, which will allow you to produce the forecast SFP. Use the SFP given in the question to provide a template for your answer and work through methodically. In part (ii), you will need to calculate the specific ratios both before and after the expansion and make comparisons.

For part (b), you need to understand the distinction between working capital investment policy (decisions regarding the level of working capital held) and working capital funding policy (decisions as to whether to fund net working capital with short- or long-term finance). If you do not understand the difference, you will struggle to write a coherent answer and pick up good marks. Part of the confusion lies in both policies having both aggressive and conservative approaches. Keep the discussion about each policy separate in your answer to make it easier for the marker to award marks.

The highlighted words are key phrases that markers are looking for.

(a) (i)

	$000
Assets	
Non-current assets	60,018
Current assets	
Inventories	4,394
Trade receivables	15,979
Cash and cash equivalents	700
	21,073
Total assets	**81,091**
Equity and liabilities	$000
Equity	6,000
Reserves	40,818
Total equity	46,818
Non-current liabilities	26,000
Current liabilities	
Trade payables	5,273
Overdraft	3,000
	8,273
Total equity and liabilities	**81,091**

Workings

Non-current assets = $54,070,000 × 1.11 = $60,017,700

Revenue = $80,768,000 × 1.187 = $95,871,616

Cost of sales = $95,871,616 × 0.33 = $31,637,633

Inventory = cost of sales × inventory holding period/360 = $31,637,633 × 50/360 = $4,394,116

Trade receivables = revenue × receivables collection period/360 = $95,871,616 × 60/360 = $15,978,603

Reserves = Old reserves + forecast profit after tax = $34,000,000 + $6,818,000 = $40,818,000

Non-current liabilities = Old liabilities + value of new debt raised = $18,000,000 + $8,000,000 = $26,000,000

Trade payables = cost of sales × payables payment period/360 = $31,637,633 × 60/360 = $5,272,939

Example answer in a spreadsheet:

	A	B	C	D	E	F	G
1	a i		**Current**		**Forecast**		
2			$000		$000		
3		**Assets**					
4		**Non-current assets**	54,070		60,017.70		=C4*1.11
5		**Current assets**					
6		Inventories	4,000		4,394.12		=E26*50/360
7		Trade receivables	12,320		15,978.60		=E25*60/360
8		Cash and cash equivalents	800		700.00		Taken from question scenario
9			17,120		21,072.72		
10		**Total assets**	**71,190**		**81,090.42**		
11							
12		**Equity and liabilities**					
13		Equity	6,000		6,000.00		No change
14		Reserves	34,000		40,818.00		=C14+E27
15		Total equity	40,000		46,818.00		
16		Non-current liabilities	18,000		26,000.00		=C16+8000
17		**Current liabilities**					
18		Trade payables	9,690		5,272.94		=E26*60/360
19		Overdraft	3,500		3,000.00		Taken from question scenario
20			13,190		8,272.94		
21		**Total equity and liabilities**	**71,190**		**81,090.94**		
22							
23							
24		**Profit statement figures:**					
25		Revenue			95,871.62		=80768*1.187
26		Cost of sales			31,637.63		=E25*33%
27		Profit after tax			6,818.00		Given in question
28							
29		NB: don't worry about the rounding difference in the total values for the SFP					

(ii)

Trade payables payment period (payables/cost of sales × 360):

Currently this is (9,690/27,700) × 360 = 126 days

The company is targeting 60 days, a reduction of (126 – 60) = 66 days

This looks to be ambitious.

Current ratio (current assets/current liabilities):

Currently this is 17,120/13,190 = 1.30 times

After the expansion this becomes 21,073/8,273 = 2.55 times

This suggests the company is looking to increase solvency.

Revenue/net working capital:

Net working capital currently = 4,000 + 12,320 – 9,690 = $6,630,000

Revised net working capital = 4,394 + 15,979 – 5,273 = $15,100,000

Revenue/NWC currently = 80,768/6,630 = 12.18 times

Revised revenue/NWC = 95,872/15,100 = 6.35 times

There would be a substantial increase in the capital supporting revenue.

(b) (i)

Changes in working capital investment policy:

Working capital investment policy considers the level of current assets used to support revenue generation in relation to different companies.

A company adopts an aggressive working capital investment policy relative to another company if it uses a lower level of current assets to support a similar level of revenue generation. Conversely, the second company adopts a conservative working capital investment policy relative to the first company.

While there are no companies here with which to compare Pumice Co's working capital investment policy, the effect of implementing the proposed changes in working capital can be measured by the revenue/current assets ratio. This shows that no significant change has occurred as a result of implementing the proposed changes in working capital, as it has only changed from 4.72 times to 4.55 times.

Revenue/current assets appears a less sensitive measure of working capital investment policy than revenue/net working capital, which has changed from 12.18 times to 6.35 times as a result of the decreased reliance on short-term working capital funding implicit in the proposed changes in working capital.

Tutorial note

The change in working capital from $6.63m to $15.1m is significant, more than doubling over the year, but the change in current assets from $16.32m to $20.373, an increase of 24.8%, is more in line with the increase in revenue of 18.7%. The difference between the two measures of the change is due to the large reduction in payables. Current assets exist to support sales, while the payables balance acts as a source of finance, reducing the need to fund the current assets from other sources such as an overdraft. Hence, the policy regarding the time taken to pay suppliers and hence the level of the payables balance can be considered as a financing policy decision rather than an investment policy decision. This means that the more appropriate measure of the change in the working capital investment policy is to look at changes in revenue/current assets rather than revenue/net working capital.

Workings:

Revenue/current assets now = 80,768/17,120 = 4.72 times

Revised revenue/current assets = 95,872/21,073 = 4.55 times

Net working capital currently = 4,000 + 12,320 – 9,690 = $6,630,000

Revised net working capital = 4,394 + 15,979 – 5,273 = $15,100,000

Revenue/NWC currently = 80,768/6,630 = 12.18 times

Revised revenue/NWC = 95,872/15,100 = 6.35 times

(ii)

Changes in working capital funding policy:

Working capital funding policy can be characterised as conservative, matching or aggressive, depending on the extent to which fluctuating current assets and permanent current assets are financed from short-term or long-term sources.

A conservative funding policy will use long-term funds to finance permanent current assets and a proportion of fluctuating current assets. This is a lower-risk policy as long-term funds are less risky than short-term funds from a company perspective, but as long-term funds are more expensive than short-term funds, this policy also decreases profitability.

An aggressive funding policy will use short-term funds to finance fluctuating current assets and a proportion of permanent current assets. This is a higher-risk policy as short-term funds are more risky than long-term funds from a company perspective, but as short-term funds are cheaper than long-term funds, this policy also increases profitability.

A matching funding policy would apply the matching principle in using short-term funds to finance fluctuating current assets and using long-term funds to finance permanent current assets.

While there is insufficient information to determine the relative levels of permanent and fluctuating current assets, implementing the proposed changes in working capital shows a substantial movement to using long-term funds rather than short-term funds. Before the expansion, 77% of current assets are financed from short-term funds (trade payables plus overdraft). After the expansion, only 39% of current assets would be financed for short-term funds and 61% would be financed from long-term funds. This change is also apparent from the increase in the current ratio from 1.30 times to 2.55 times.

The proposed changes in working capital therefore suggest a movement by Pumice Co from an aggressive working capital funding policy to a conservative working capital funding policy.

This view is also evidenced by the $4,917,000 decrease in short-term funds relative to the $3,953,000 increase in current assets and the $14,818,000 increase in long-term funds: the company's current reliance on short-term funds has been reversed.

Workings:

Current assets financed by short-term funds:

Before expansion = 100 × (13,190/17,120) = 77%

After expansion = 100 × (8,273/21,073) = 39%

Decrease in short-term funds = 13,190 – 8,273 = $4,917,000

Increase in current assets = 21,073 – 17,120 = $3,953,000

Increase in long-term funds = (46,818 + 26,000) – (40,000 + 18,000) = $14,818,000

ACCA marking scheme			
			Marks
(a)	(i)	Non-current assets	0.5
		Revenue	0.5
		Cost of sales	0.5
		Inventory	1
		Trade receivables	1
		Trade payables	1
		Reserves	0.5
		Non-current liabilities	0.5
		Overdraft/cash	0.5
			6
	(ii)	Trade payables payment period	1
		Current ratio	1
		Revenue/net working capital	1
		Changes	1
			4
(b)	(i)	Aggressive investment policy	1
		Conservative investment policy	1
		Revenue/net current assets	1
		Changes discussion	2
			5
	(ii)	Conservative financing policy	1
		Aggressive financing policy	1
		Matching financing policy	1
		Changes discussion	2
			5
Total			**20**

Extracts from examiner's comments

Part (a) (i) common errors:

Some candidates incorrectly used current SFP values in their forecast SFP, such as inventory or trade receivables. A number of candidates were not aware that forecast profits after tax would increase forecast reserves, while some candidates classed an issue of loan notes as an increase in equity. Occasionally, ignoring the information provided in the question, candidates used 365 days when 360 days was specified.

Part (a) (ii) common errors:

Some candidates wasted valuable exam time by calculating working capital ratios not listed by the finance director, such as inventory turnover period and trade receivables collection period, for which no credit could be given. Most candidates made a good attempt at calculating the trade payables payment period and the current ratio, although some candidates only gave values for before, or only for after, when both values were required.

The ratio that tended to cause candidates difficulty was the revenue/net working capital ratio, even though net working capital was defined in the question. Where a definition is provided in an exam question, candidates must use it.

A point that must be strongly emphasised is that the verb used in the requirement here was 'calculate'. Some candidates discussed their calculated ratios, often at length, and markers could give no credit to these discussions as the requirement, clearly stated, was 'calculate'. To gain marks, candidates must meet the question requirement.

Part (b) (i) common errors:

One reason for the lower marks here was that many candidates struggled to differentiate between working capital investment policy (about the level of investment in current assets) and working capital funding policy (about how working capital is funded), to the extent that some candidates discussed working capital funding policy here, instead of working capital investment policy. Candidates must learn to differentiate between these two policy areas, even though the terms aggressive, conservative and moderate are used in both.

Part (b) (ii) common errors:

Discussions of working capital funding policy tended to be more technical than required, given that the requirement was to consider the proposed changes in working capital attendant on the proposed expansion of business.

281 KANDY CO (SEP/DEC 2021)

Key answer tips

When the order size changes, the ordering and holding costs will change. In this question, the purchase price changes too and so you must evaluate the overall change on all three costs. It's best to do this on a consistent basis, so compare total annual costs (of purchasing, ordering and holding) before and after the change.

For receivables calculations, keep in mind what the changes represent overall. Collecting cash earlier means that the receivables balance will fall. This leads to a saving in financing costs. However, you need to balance this fall in costs against the cash lost from offering the discount.

When customers pay in different time periods, break them down and do separate receivables calculations (receivables = credit sales × receivables collection days/360) for each time period, to avoid confusion. Then add the results up to determine the total receivables balance and then you can multiply it by the financing rate to determine the financing cost.

For part (iii), as only 2 marks are available here and you have two separate calculations to comment on, simply state whether each is acceptable and why to pick up the marks.

For part (b), you should define what is meant by the profitability objective and the liquidity objective and you must also include how these can conflict with each other. It is a discussion question, so there must be a discussion aspect to your answer even with only a few marks available. The examiner is not looking for bullet point answers here.

In part (c), a simple explanation of what the cash operating cycle is will only pick up half the available marks. To discuss its relationship with the level of investment, think about how changes in the levels of each aspect of working capital would affect the cycle and what it would mean for the business.

The highlighted words are key phrases that markers are looking for.

(a) (i)

Current policy:

Annual ordering cost = D/Q × C_o = 18,000/1,000 × \$75 = \$1,350 per year

Buffer inventory = 18,000 × 2/360 = 100 units

Average inventory holding = Q/2 + buffer = (1,000/2) + 100 = 600 units

Annual holding cost = average inventory × C_h = 600 × \$30 × 0.09 = \$1,620 per year

Purchase cost per year = 18,000 × \$30 = \$540,000

Total cost per year = \$1,350 + \$1,620 + \$540,000 = \$542,970

With bulk purchase discount:

Purchase price = \$30 × (1 – 0.015) = \$29.55 per unit

Order cost = \$75 + \$25 = \$100 per order

Annual ordering cost = 18,000/1,500 × \$100 = \$1,200 per year

Average inventory holding = (1,500/2) + 100 = 850 units

Annual holding cost = 850 × \$29.55 × 0.10 = \$2,512 per year

Purchase cost per year = 18,000 × \$29.55 = \$531,900

Total cost per year = \$1,200 + \$2,512 + \$531,900 = \$535,612

Example answer in a spreadsheet:

	A	B	C	D	E	F	G	H	I	J	K
1	a i										
2	Current inventory costs										
3		Purchase	D*P		P	30	D	18000		540000	=F3*H3
4		Ordering	D/Q × Co		Q	1000	Co	75		1350	=H3/F4*H4
5		Holding	(Q/2 + buffer) × Ch		Ch	2.7	Buffer	100		1620	=(F4/2+H5)*F5
6									Total:	542970	=SUM(J3:J5)
7											
8	Accepting bulk purchase offer - new inventory costs										
9		Purchase	D*P		P	29.55	D	18000		531900	=F9*H9
10		Ordering	D/Q × Co		Q	1500	Co	100		1200	=H9/F10*H10
11		Holding	(Q/2 + buffer) × Ch		Ch	2.955	Buffer	100		2511.75	=(F10/2+H11)*F11
12									Total:	535611.75	=SUM(J9:J11)
13											
14	Accepting the bulk purchase offer would reduce Kandy Co's inventory costs by									7358.25	=J6-J12

(ii)

Current situation:

30-day receivables = $45m × 0.6 × 30/360 = $2,250,000

40-day receivables = $45m × 0.4 × 40/360 = $2,000,000

Total receivables = $4,250,000

Current finance cost = $4,250,000 × 0.07 = $297,500

After introduction of discount:

10-day trade receivables = $45m × 0.5 × 10/360 = $625,000

30-day trade receivables = $45m × 0.2 × 30/360 = $750,000

40-day trade receivables = $45m × 0.3 × 40/360 = $1,500,000

Total receivables = $2,875,000

Finance cost = $2,875,000 × 0.07 = $201,250 per year

Discount cost = $45m × 0.005 × 0.5 = $112,500 per year

Total cost = $201,250 + $112,500 = $313,750 per year

Example answer in a spreadsheet:

	A	B	C	D	E	F	G	H	I	J
18	a ii									
19	Current position		Receivables:		Pay in 30 days		2250000	=45000000*60%*30/360		
20					Pay in 40 days		2000000	=45000000*40%*40/360		
21					Total		4250000	=G19+G20		
22										
23		Annual financing costs at 7%					297500	=G21*7%		
24										
25	With early settlement discount									
26			Receivables:		Pay in 10 days		625000	=45000000*50%*10/360		
27					Pay in 30 days		750000	=45000000*20%*30/360		
28					Pay in 40 days		1500000	=45000000*30%*40/360		
29					Total		2875000	=SUM(G26:G28)		
30										
31		Annual financing costs at 7%					201250	=G29*7%		
32										
33	Reduction in financing costs						96250	=G23-G31		
34	Loss of cash due to discount						-112500	=-45000000*50%*0.5%		
35										
36	Net cost of early settlement discount						-16250	=G33+G34		

(iii)

Comment on financial acceptability

The bulk purchase discount is financially acceptable as it will reduce gimble stocking costs by $7,358 per year ($542,970 – $535,612).

The early settlement discount is not financially acceptable as it will increase costs by $16,250 ($313,750 – $297,500) per year.

(b) The two main objectives of working capital management are to ensure profitability (generating return for investors) while at the same time ensuring liquidity (meeting its obligations when they fall due). In other words, it is about getting the right balance between current assets and current liabilities.

Having high levels of current assets can help in meeting short-term liabilities, particularly if there is a high cash balance. Good liquidity is important as it is cash which settles the liabilities, not profit. Profitable companies can still fail due to poor liquidity in the short term.

However, the problem with high levels of current assets is that they are not profitable. Cash, for example, does not generate a high return, if indeed any return at all. Holding inventory is similarly not generating any return for the company, only the sale of inventory generates the profitability. Carrying lower levels of current assets with more cash invested in long-term, non-current assets could generate higher returns for the company but would impact its ability to settle its liabilities. Consequently, there is a conflict, or trade off, between profitability and liquidity.

The bulk purchase discount Kandy Co is being offered is a good example of this conflict. By accepting the discount and buying in larger quantities, the cost is reduced (as demonstrated in a(i)), increasing profitability. But this will mean less cash in the bank due to higher levels of inventory holding. This lower level of cash will affect Kandy Co's ability to pay its current liabilities, thus liquidity will be affected.

This conflict between the two objectives is inevitable and there is no correct answer as to the level of current assets and liabilities to hold. It is for every business to determine itself.

(c) The cash operating cycle refers to the average length of time it takes for a business to generate cash having paid for an item of inventory. In other words, having paid for the inventory, the cash operating cycle is the length of time it remains in inventory before being sold and then how long until the customer pays for it and cash is returned to the bank account.

It is calculated by adding the average inventory holding period and the average trade receivables collection period and then subtracting the average trade payables payment period.

The cash operating cycle is effectively measuring the business' liquidity in terms of cash generation – a long cash operating cycle would indicate potential liquidity problems as the business is without cash for a long time.

The relationship of the cash operating cycle with the investment in working capital is that higher levels of investment will generally increase the cash operating cycle. High inventory levels will usually mean longer inventory holding periods, increasing the cash operating cycle. High trade receivables are usually due to longer collection periods for collecting in debt, again increasing the cycle. Finally, paying suppliers very quickly will increase the investment in working capital due to low levels of trade payables, but this will again increase the cash cycle.

ACCA marking scheme

			Marks
(a)	(i)	Order cost (current)	0.5
		Average inventory (current)	1
		Holding cost (current)	0.5
		Purchase cost (current)	0.5
		New purchase price/order	0.5
		New ordering cost/order	0.5
		Order cost (new)	0.5
		Average inventory (new)	1
		Holding cost (new)	0.5
		Purchase cost (new)	0.5
			6
	(ii)	Purchase cost (new)	1
		Finance cost (current)	0.5
		Trade receivables (new)	1
		Finance cost (new)	0.5
		Discount cost	1
			4
	(iii)	Bulk comment	1
		Settlement comment	1
			2
(b)	Liquidity		1
	Profitability		1
	Conflict between them		2
			4
(c)	Explanation of cycle		2
	Link to investment		2
			4
Total			**20**

Extracts from examiner's comments

Part (a)(i) common errors:

Two separate calculations are required: the current and revised situations for the bulk purchase discount. The information in the question provides the re-order levels, and therefore, there is no justification for using economic order quantity, and candidates using this method would not have gained any credit for it.

Two complexities need to be dealt with in this question: First, we have to deal with buffer due to the uncertainty in demand. Second, holding cost per unit is based on 9% of the purchase price, which will also affect the bulk purchase discount values.

Part (a)(ii) common errors:

We need to consider two issues here: First, early settlement calculation will suggest that the trade receivables amount be reduced. Secondly, there will be a cost to Kandy Co for the amount of discount made available. Failure to address both issues would lose marks.

Candidates are advised to practise using the spreadsheet tool to answer questions before attempting the financial management exam.

Part (a)(iii) common errors:

It is important to be able to explain and discuss an understanding of what the calculations show. For two marks candidates cannot just say accept or reject but must justify the bulk purchase and early settlement discount based on their calculations. For example, 'the early settlement discount option has a net cost so it should be rejected.'

Part (b) common errors:

It is important to show an understanding of the two objectives, liquidity and profitability, and explain both using financial management terms. The requirement is to "discuss". Therefore, candidates should refrain from using bullet point or list type answers.

Most candidates managed to comment on the trade-off between profitability and liquidity. However, the discussion on the differences was more limited, with some candidates commenting on poor returns of liquid assets.

Part (c) common errors:

As this was a discussion, it is not sufficient to merely write the equation for the cash operating cycle.

282 PURDY CO (SEP/DEC 2022)

Key answer tips

Total annual costs in relation to inventory are made up of purchasing, ordering and holding costs. Changing the supplier directly affects the price and therefore the annual purchasing cost. It also affects the order quantity, which means the number of orders made each year will change (which changes the total annual ordering costs) and the amount of inventory that has to be held will change (affecting the annual holding costs).

Don't forget that the safety (buffer) inventory also contributes to the holding cost.

This question tests your understanding of inventory in two ways – in part (i), you're asked about the effect on inventory costs. In part (ii), you're asked about the effect on inventory value. It's not directly stated in the question, but remember that inventory, as a current asset, needs to be funded. This company uses an overdraft, so an increase in inventory will need an increase in the overdraft level, something the company is actively looking to avoid!

The topics in parts (b) and (c) are regularly tested. These are areas where rote learning can be of benefit.

For part (b), you should define what is meant by the profitability objective and the liquidity objective and you must also include how these can conflict with each other. It is a discussion question, so there must be a discussion aspect to your answer even with only a few marks available. The examiner is not looking for bullet point answers here. Give examples of the types of conflict that exist for each aspect of working capital to flesh out your answer.

In part (c), a simple explanation of what the cash operating cycle is will only pick up two out of the five available marks. To discuss its relationship with the level of investment, think about how changes in the levels of each aspect of working capital would affect the cycle and what it would mean for the business.

The highlighted words are key phrases that markers are looking for.

(a) (i)

	Current supplier	**New supplier**
Annual demand (litres)	5,000,000	5,000,000
Purchase cost per unit ($)	3.00	2.25
Ordering cost per order	400	400
Holding cost per unit per year ($)	2.5	2.5
Order size (litres) (working 1)	40,000	1,000,000
Safety inventory (litres) (working 2)	68,493	205,479
Holding cost per year ($) (working 3)	50,000	1,250,000
Ordering cost per year ($) (working 4)	50,000	2,000
Purchase cost per year ($) (working 5)	15,000,000	11,250,000
Safety inventory holding cost ($) (working 6)	171,233	513,699
Total procurement cost per year ($)	15,271,233	13,015,699

Switching to the new supplier will reduce procurement costs by $2,255,534 ($15,271,233 – $13,015,699) which is equal to 15% of current procurement cost.

(ii)

Average inventory (litres) (working 7)	88,493	705,479
Average inventory value (working 8)	265,479	1,587,329

Switching supplier would increase average inventory and require an investment in inventory of $1,321,850 ($1,587,329 – $265,479).

(iii) Recommendation

Although switching suppliers would reduce cost, it is not recommended because of the large investment in working capital it would require and the increase in overdraft which this would entail.

Workings

Working 1 – order size

EOQ for current supplier = √((2×Co×D)/Ch) = √((2 × $400 × 5,000,000)/$2.50) = 40,000 litres

Note: you could use $((2 \times Co \times D)/Ch)^{0.5}$ if you prefer. Taking something to the power of 0.5 is the same as taking its square root.

Working 2 – safety inventory

5,000,000/365 days × 5 days = 68,493 litres

5,000,000/365 days × 15 days = 205,479 litres

Working 3 – holding cost per year (Q/2 × Ch)

40,000 litres/2 × $2.5 = $50,000

1,000,000 litres/2 × $2.5 = $1,250,000

Working 4 – ordering cost per year (D/Q × Co)

5,000,000 litres/40,000 litres × $400 = $50,000

5,000,000 litres/1,000,000 litres × $400 = $2,000

Working 5 – purchase cost per year (D × P)

5,000,000 litres × $3.00 = $15,000,000

5,000,000 litres × $2.25 = $11,250,000

Working 6 – safety inventory holding cost per year

68,493 litres × $2.50 = $171,233

205,479 litres × $2.50 = $513,698

Working 7 – average inventory in litres (Q/2 + buffer)

40,000 litres/2 + 68,493 litres = 88,493 litres

1,000,000 litres/2 + 205,479 litres = 705,479 litres

Working 8 – average inventory value

88,493 litres × $3.00 = $265,479

705,479 litres × $2.25 = $1,587,328

(b) Working capital management involves the management of a company's current assets and current liabilities, principally inventory, accounts receivable, cash and accounts payable. When managing working capital, a company faces twin objectives. One objective is to earn profits in order to provide satisfactory returns for its investors and contribute towards the maximisation of shareholder wealth.

Another is to generate enough cash to allow the business to meet its financial commitments, such as wages, salaries, accounts payable, interest and tax.

These two objectives can often conflict. For example, to increase profitability, a firm may increase its inventory levels in order to be able to offer customers prompt delivery. In theory, this will be attractive to customers and sales and profits should increase. However, by increasing inventory levels the company ties up more cash in inventory, thus decreasing its ability to meet its short-term commitments.

On the other hand, a company which pressurises customers for payment by aggressive management of accounts receivable may find that its cash resources increase as customers pay more promptly, but at the same time its sales and profits may fall as customers turn to other suppliers who offer more generous credit terms.

Cash management involves a similar trade off. Cash is often regarded as 'an idle asset' as it earns no return. Companies often invest their cash resources to earn some return and increase profitability. By doing so, they usually have to tie up the cash for a fixed amount of time (otherwise the interest earned would be very small), and hence damage their liquidity.

Finally, companies which take long periods of credit from suppliers may find their liquidity improves but this can be to the detriment of profits as settlement discounts may be lost and supplier relationships damaged.

When managing working capital, firms need to be aware of the conflict between the twin objectives. A sensible approach is to see the need for sufficient liquidity as a constraint on working capital management and then to seek to maximise profits subject to this constraint.

(c) The cash operating cycle (sometimes known as the working capital cycle) measures the interval between the company paying out cash at the start of its production process (in manufacturing, this is normally paying suppliers for raw materials) and receiving cash from customers when products are sold and paid for.

The cash operating cycle for a company can be calculated by adding inventory days (for raw materials, work in progress and finished goods) to accounts receivable days and then deducting accounts payable days.

The length of a company's cash operating cycle has two major drivers. First the type of industry a company operates in. House construction companies often have very long cash operating cycles. Their business involves buying land, gaining permission to build, building houses and infrastructure, selling and then collecting cash from sales. This whole process often takes more than a year.

Large supermarket chains on the other hand often have very short cash operating cycles. Their buying power allows them to enjoy long credit periods from suppliers, whilst inventory holding periods and accounts receivables are very short. Often, they have negative cash operating cycles.

The efficiency of a company's working capital management will also affect the length of the cycle. A company which has poor control of inventory and accounts receivable, yet which pays its suppliers promptly will find that it has a longer cash operating cycle than competitors who manage their working capital well.

The longer a company's cash operating cycle, the greater its investment in net working capital will be. If inventory is held for a large amount of days, physical inventory, and the amount of money invested in it will be high.

Similarly, the longer it takes accounts receivable to be settled, the more money the company will have invested.

Finally, a short accounts payable period will mean that the company takes little credit from suppliers and hence fails to reduce its net working capital investment.

ACCA marking scheme			
			Marks
(a)	(i)	Current EOQ calculation	1
		Current safety inventory	1
		Current total Co/year	0.5
		Current total Ch/year	1
		Current purchase cost	0.5
		New safety inventory	1
		New total Co/year	0.5
		New total Ch/year	1
		New purchase cost	0.5
			7
	(ii)	Average inventories	2
	(iii)	Overall recommendation	1
(b)	Discussion on conflict		3
	Further illustration		2
			5
(c)	Explanation of cycle		2
	Link to investment in working capital		3
			5
Total			**20**

Extracts from examiner's comments

Part (a) (i) common errors:

A difficulty faced in EOQ calculations is that the input values in the calculation for EOQ can vary slightly from scenario to scenario. In general, you need to take care of which figures to enter into the formula. The common issues to remember here are: First, including costs that are affected by order quantity and holding costs. Second – ensure you deal with consistent units, for example, annual demand in units (5,000,000 litres), cost of holding a unit for a year in $ ($2.50) and ordering cost of a single order in $ ($400). Please note that in your practice questions, scenarios may have given the demand per week or per month, and this should be converted to an annual demand.

The most common mistake in calculating the EOQ was to include the annual demand as 5,000. This may have been down to needing to read the scenario more carefully or understand the requirements of the model. In both scenarios, many candidates did not use average inventory for calculating holding costs.

In calculating the total annual order cost if Purdy Co were to use the potential supplier, the most common mistake was missing the calculation of the new safety buffer holding cost, unit prices/costs were mixed up and using the EOQ again.

Part (a) (ii) common errors:

Very few extra calculations were attempted. This suggested that many candidates were not aware of how to manage the calculation. Average inventory quantities are calculated as (Q/2 + safety inventory):

Many ignored (a)(ii) and only a minority of candidates completed it successfully for this part of the working capital management scenario.

Part (b) common errors:

Answers tended to be relatively brief. Some candidates showed that they had learned the explanations of liquidity and profitability but could not discuss the conflict between the two working capital objectives.

Whilst there were some good illustrations of the conflict, some answers drifted into a discussion about the financing of working capital.

Part (c) common errors:

Candidates need to recognise that discussion-type questions require more than brief points, which are not in full sentences.

283 GUILLERMO CO (SEP/DEC 2024)

Key answer tips

As Guillermo Co is a manufacturing company, it has more than one type of inventory: raw materials, work in progress and finished goods. Separate inventory holding period calculations therefore need to be made for inclusion in the cash operating cycle calculation in part (a).

For part (b), there are 6 marks available to discuss three things. You should therefore aim to write a couple of sentences about each way of reducing the cycle. Remember that to reduce the length of the cycle, inventory and payables levels would need to reduce, but the level of payables would need to increase.

In part (c), the target cash balance requested in the question is the return point that is calculated by the Miller-Orr model. In this model, whenever the cash balance reaches its maximum or minimum point, cash is transferred such that the balance returns to this target.

Part (d) requests straightforward knowledge. A couple of sentences about each of the three motives would be enough to pick up the available marks. Therefore, stating what the motive is and then giving an example of a practical reason for that motive would be sufficient.

The highlighted words are key phrases that markers are looking for.

(a) Cost of sales = $6,000,000 × (1 – 0.6) = $2,400,000

Credit sales = $6,000,000 × 0.75 = $4,500,000

Credit purchases = $2,160,000 × 0.9 = $1,944,000

Inventory holding period:

Raw materials = $120,000/$2,160,000 × 360 = 20 days

Work in progress = $20,000/$2,400,000 × 360 = 3 days

Finished goods = $80,000/$2,400,000 × 360 = 12 days

Receivables collection = $850,000/$4,500,000 × 360 = 68 days

Payables payment = $162,000/$1,944,000 × 360 = 30 days

Cash operating cycle = 20 + 3 + 12 + 68 – 30 = 73 days

(b) Improve credit control/receivables collection

At 68 days, the average receivables collection period is over twice the standard terms of 30 days. This would suggest very poor credit control, particularly in relation to chasing up overdue debt. It would appear that the finance department is not taking ownership/responsibility for this and leaving it to the account managers who are probably (and perhaps understandably) more interested in increasing sales rather than chasing up old ones. Credit control should be brought within the finance department's responsibilities and overdue accounts suspended until up to date.

Improve process efficiency

On average, the product is taking three days to manufacture according to the work in progress calculation which would suggest the production process is running at only 67% efficiency (the product should take two days to manufacture). The production process should be looked at to determine if there is a bottleneck in the process which needs addressing or other efficiency improvements which could be made. This would have other knock-on benefits such as being able to reduce the level of finished goods held as demand could be more readily met from production.

Raw material inventory holding

Raw material holding is 20 days which given the three-day production period (see above) would suggest that Guillermo Co's holding of raw may be considered high. If so, then raw material holding should be reduced, perhaps even considering if just-in-time purchasing of raw material should be adopted.

Trade payables payment

Average credit terms with its trade suppliers is 35 days and yet Guillermo Co is paying its suppliers after 30 days on average. Paying earlier than term is detrimental to its cash cycle and even though it likes to maintain a good supplier relationship, this could still be achieved by paying on 35 days and consequently improving the cash cycle by five days.

Note: Only three ways were required.

(c) Daily variance = $\$15{,}000^2$ = $225,000,000 per day

Daily interest rate = 9%/360 = 0.025% per day (0.00025 as a decimal figure)

Transaction cost = $55 per transaction

Spread = $3 \times [(0.75 \times \$55 \times \$225{,}000{,}000)/0.00025]^{1/3} = \$100{,}079$

Target cash balance (return point) = $40,000 + 1/3 × $100,079 = $73,360

(d) Holding cash in a bank account does not usually generate high returns and too high a cash balance is therefore undesirable but there are three key motives/reasons for holding cash.

Transactions motive

Cash should be kept in order to meet day-to-day expenses. Suppliers, for example, will require payment in cash in accordance with the agreed terms, and failure to do so could result in trade accounts being withdrawn, causing business disruption. Inability to be able to pay employees' wages and salaries would also result in severe disruption for the business due to industrial action such as a walkout of the employees.

Precautionary motive

Unexpected costs could occur which require cash outlay. For example, an unexpected fine or claim against the business. Inability to settle such items would negatively impact the business in many ways, including reputational damage or even forced closure in extreme circumstances.

Investment/speculative motive

Unexpected opportunities can arise which, while requiring cash outlay, could bring financial return. Holding an amount of cash for such events could enable a business to take advantage of such opportunities, such as acquiring an undervalued company.

ACCA marking scheme		
		Marks
(a)	Cost of sales	0.5
	Credit sales	0.5
	Credit purchases	0.5
	Raw materials holding	0.5
	Work in progress holding	0.5
	Finished goods holding	0.5
	Receivables collection	0.5
	Payables payment	0.5
	Cash cycle	1
		5
(b)	Suggestion 1	2
	Suggestion 2	2
	Suggestion 3	2
		6
(c)	Daily variance	0.5
	Daily interest rate	0.5
	Spread	1
	Target cash balance	1
		3
(d)	Transaction motive	2
	Precautionary motive	2
	Investment/speculative motive	2
		6
Total		**20**

Extracts from examiner's comments

Part (a) common errors:

– calculating raw material days based on cost of sales instead of raw material purchases.

– failing to recognise that each inventory element requires an individual calculation.

– using total revenue rather than credit sales to determine receivables collection days.

It is essential to recognise that since purchases are provided, utilising the cost of sales as a proxy for the payables period is not necessary. Including all calculations will assist candidates in identifying any errors. Additionally, each inventory element should have its own distinct calculation and clarity in all workings is crucial.

Part (b) common errors:

Not providing enough depth to pick up the two marks available for each way.

For instance, a statement such as 'Guillermo Co's average receivables collection period of 68days is much higher than the standard terms of 30 days' is correct but without enough depth for the 2 marks. The best answers considered the current problems and discussed how to reduce the cash operating cycle. For instance, using the information in the question that there is no credit control function would have led to a recommendation to use one, instead of relying on the customer account managers to perform the task.

Part (c) common errors:

Candidates needed to recognise that the given standard deviation needed to be converted into a variance and that it was given as a daily figure, while the interest rate was an annual one. These figures need to be in the same units, so both could be presented as annual or both as daily.

Part (d) common errors:

Many candidates gained 3 marks from this part by briefly explaining the three motives for holding cash. Candidates need to provide more depth to obtain higher marks, i.e. providing an example or discussing the downside for not holding cash.

INVESTMENT APPRAISAL

284 DUO CO (DEC 07 – MODIFIED) *Walk in the footsteps of a top tutor*

Key answer tips

Given the generic nature of part (b) and the significant number of marks available, it would be sensible to tackle this part of the requirement first. You can then follow on with the calculations in part (a).

The key learning point from this question is the importance of being efficient when reading the scenario to cut down on the amount of time wasted trying to locate information. By forming an expectation of what you'll be given and considering the significance of information that you read, you can easily complete the question in the time allocated. The highlighted words are key phrases that markers are looking for.

(a) Net present value evaluation of investment

Tutor's top tips

An NPV calculation in part (a) followed by an IRR calculation in part (b) is a fairly common exam question. Clearly, it is more logical to tackle part (a) first. One important aspect to note from the requirement is to work to the nearest $1,000. This can help to save a significant amount of time when performing the calculations and noting your workings.

Knowing that you must calculate an NPV, you should carefully read the scenario, looking for details on:

– *Relevant cash flows*
– *Tax payments (1 year time lag or not)*
– *Capital expenditure and scrap values*
– *Timescales and length of the project*
– *Working capital*
– *Inflation*
– *Discount rate.*

Whenever you read any details, make a note in the margin on what that section provides you information on. This will help prevent you having to re-read the scenario several times to find the bit of information you require.

From reading this scenario, you should have noted that:

– *Relevant cash flows will be the incremental contribution and fixed costs only*
– *Incremental contribution will be calculated based on the excess of demand over current production capacity (one million kilograms)*
– *The maximum output of the new machine is 600,000 kg meaning that even with the new machine, Duo will be unable to produce more that 1.6 million kg*

- *The tax rate is 30% and there is a one year time lag*
- *The cost of the machine is $800,000 and it will be scrapped in four years' time for $30,000*
- *The length of the project is four years*
- *You are not given any information on working capital requirements or inflation. These can therefore be ignored*
- *You have not been told what discount rate to use. Instead, you've been given information on the cost of equity and the cost of debt, together with the capital structure (ratio of equity to debt) in the company.*

Having gleaned this information, you should start by setting up your proforma NPV calculation based on 5 periods (4 years of the project + 1 year time lag for tax). Next, you should enter in any easy numbers that require little or no calculation. This would include the asset purchase and scrap and the incremental fixed costs.

Now you can move on to calculating some of the more complex numbers. All of these calculations should be performed using workings that should be clearly cross-referenced to your main NPV calculation. You should end up with workings for contribution (make sure you clearly show how many extra units will be sold), the tax effect of tax allowable depreciation and the weighted average cost of capital/discount factors. As you complete each working, transfer the numbers into your main calculation and add anything extra that you can now complete (for example, once you have calculated contribution, you can enter the tax charge at 30%). When all of your workings are complete, discount the cash flow in each year and work out the net present value. Don't forget that the requirement is to calculate and advise. There will always be marks available for reaching a conclusion and stating whether the project should be accepted or not. Note the examiner's comment (below) about explaining your decision.

After-tax weighted average cost of capital = $(11 \times 0.8) + (8.6 \times (1 - 0.3) \times 0.2) = 10\%$

Year	**1**	**2**	**3**	**4**	**5**
	$000	$000	$000	$000	$000
Contribution	440	550	660	660	
Fixed costs	(240)	(260)	(280)	(300)	
Taxable cash flow	200	290	380	360	
Taxation		(60)	(87)	(114)	(108)
CA tax benefits		60	45	34	92
Scrap value				30	
After-tax cash flows	200	290	338	310	(16)
Discount at 10%	0.909	0.826	0.751	0.683	0.621
Present values	182	240	254	212	(10)

	$000
Present value of benefits	878
Initial investment	800
Net present value	78

The net present value is positive and so the investment is financially acceptable. However, demand becomes greater than production capacity in the fourth year of operation and so further investment in new machinery may be needed after three years. The new machine will itself need replacing after four years if production capacity is to be maintained at an increased level. It may be necessary to include these expansion and replacement considerations for a more complete appraisal of the proposed investment.

A more complete appraisal of the investment could address issues such as the assumption of constant selling price and variable cost per kilogram and the absence of any consideration of inflation, the linear increase in fixed costs of production over time and the linear increase in demand over time. If these issues are not addressed, the appraisal of investing in the new machine is likely to possess a significant degree of uncertainty.

Workings

Annual contribution

Year	**1**	**2**	**3**	**4**
Excess demand (kg/yr)	400,000	500,000	600,000	700,000
New machine output (kg/yr)	400,000	500,000	600,000	600,000
Contribution ($/kg)	1.1	1.1	1.1	1.1
Contribution ($/yr)	440,000	550,000	660,000	660,000

Tax allowable depreciation tax benefits

Year	**TA depreciation** ($)		**Tax benefit** ($)	
1	200,000	(800,000 × 0.25)	60,000	(0.3 × 200,000)
2	150,000	(600,000 × 0.25)	45,000	(0.3 × 150,000)
3	112,500	(450,000 × 0.25)	33,750	(0.3 × 112,500)
	462,500			
	30,000	(scrap value)		
	492,500			
4	307,500	(by difference)	92,250	(0.3 × 307,500)
	800,000			

Tutor's top tips

A careful read of the requirement shows that part (b) is essentially three requirements rolled into one:

(i) Explain the difference between risk and uncertainty

(ii) Describe how sensitivity analysis can be used to incorporate risk into investment appraisal

(iii) Describe how probability analysis can be used to incorporate risk into investment appraisal.

Given the verbs being used (both 'explain' and 'describe' imply much more that merely 'stating') we can expect between 2 and 3 marks for each section, with 2 or 3 relevant comments picking up those marks.

Don't forget, there are often marks available for defining terms. So in part (i), a definition should be given of both risk and uncertainty before the differences between the two are explained. Similarly, in parts (ii) and (iii), you could define both sensitivity analysis and probability analysis before describing how they incorporate risk into the appraisal process.

Finally, you could touch on the common problems with the two techniques although be careful not to spend too much time on this as it wasn't specifically mentioned in the requirement. Now you can move on to the numerical aspects of the question.

(b) Risk refers to the situation where probabilities can be assigned to a range of expected outcomes arising from an investment project and the likelihood of each outcome occurring can therefore be quantified. Uncertainty refers to the situation where probabilities cannot be assigned to expected outcomes. Investment project risk therefore increases with increasing variability of returns, while uncertainty increases with increasing project life. The two terms are often used interchangeably in financial management, but the distinction between them is a useful one.

Sensitivity analysis assesses how the net present value of an investment project is affected by changes in project variables. Considering each project variable in turn, the change in the variable required to make the net present value zero is determined, or alternatively the change in net present value arising from a fixed change in the given project variable. In this way, the key or critical project variables are determined. However, sensitivity analysis does not assess the probability of changes in project variables and so is often dismissed as a way of incorporating risk into the investment appraisal process.

Probability analysis refers to the assessment of the separate probabilities of a number of specified outcomes of an investment project. For example, a range of expected market conditions could be formulated and the probability of each market condition arising in each of several future years could be assessed. The net present values arising from combinations of future economic conditions could then be assessed and linked to the joint probabilities of those combinations. The expected net present value (ENPV) could be calculated, together with the probability of the worst-case scenario and the probability of a negative net present value. In this way, the downside risk of the investment could be determined and incorporated into the investment decision.

ACCA marking scheme

		Marks
(a)	After-tax weighted average cost of capital	2
	Annual contribution	2
	Fixed costs	1
	Taxation	1
	TAX depreciation tax benefits	3
	Scrap value	1
	Discount factors	1
	Net present value	1
	Comment	1–2
		13
(b)	Risk and uncertainty	2–3
	Discussion of sensitivity analysis	2–3
	Discussion of probability analysis	2–3
		7
Total		**20**

Extracts from examiner's comments

Part (a) common errors:

Failure to calculate correctly the weighted average cost of capital of the investing company (for example using the before-tax rather than the after-tax cost of debt in the calculation).

Failure to use incremental demand as the production volume of the new machine.

Failure to recognise the cap on production in Year 4 compared to demand.

Failure to lag tax liability by one year.

Including scrap value or tax benefits of tax allowable depreciation with taxable income.

Incorrect calculation of balancing allowance.

Treating initial investment as a Year 1 rather than a Year 0 cash flow.

Using annuity factors rather than discount factors in calculating NPV.

A number of candidates lost straightforward marks by failing to comment on the calculated NPV, or by simply saying 'accept' without referring to the NPV decision rule. The reason for accepting an investment project must be clearly explained.

Part (b) common errors:

Many candidates were not able to explain the difference between risk and uncertainty in investment appraisal, offering answers that were founded on interpretations of the words 'risk' and 'uncertainty', or which discussed the various kinds of risk to be found in financial management.

285 OKM CO (JUNE 10 – MODIFIED)

Key answer tips

The style of this question is not something we've seen regularly from the examiner. Based on the core topic of investment appraisal, students should easily be able to spot the mistakes in the appraisal presented and, having done that, should not encountered many problems preparing a revised calculation. The highlighted words are key phrases that markers are looking for.

(a) Errors in the original investment appraisal

Inflation was incorrectly applied to selling prices and variable costs in calculating contribution, since only one year's inflation was allowed for in each year of operation.

The fixed costs were correctly inflated, but included $200,000 per year before inflation that was not a relevant cost. Only relevant costs should be included in investment appraisal.

Straight-line accounting depreciation had been used in the calculation, but this depreciation method is not acceptable to the tax authorities. The approved method using 25% reducing balance tax allowable depreciation should be used.

Interest payments have been included in the investment appraisal, but these are allowed for by the discount rate used in calculating the net present value.

The interest rate on the debt finance has been used as the discount rate, when the nominal weighted average cost of capital should have been used to discount the calculated nominal after-tax cash flows.

(b) Nominal weighted average cost of capital = 1.07 × 1.047 = 1.12, i.e. 12% per year

Year	**1**	**2**	**3**	**4**	**5**
	$000	$000	$000	$000	$000
Contribution	1,330	2,264	3,010	1,600	
Fixed costs	(318)	(337)	(357)	(379)	
Taxable cash flow	1,012	1,927	2,653	1,221	
Taxation		(304)	(578)	(796)	(366)
CA tax benefits		150	112	84	178
After-tax cash flow	1,012	1,773	2,187	509	(188)
Scrap value				250	
After-tax cash flows	1,012	1,773	2,187	759	(188)
Discount at 12%	0.893	0.797	0.712	0.635	0.567
Present values	904	1,413	1,557	482	(107)

	$000
Present value of future cash flows	4,249
Initial investment	2,000
Net present value	2,249

The net present value is positive and so the investment is financially acceptable.

Alternative NPV calculation using taxable profit calculation

Year	**1**	**2**	**3**	**4**	**5**
	$000	$000	$000	$000	$000
Contribution	1,330	2,264	3,010	1,600	
Fixed costs	(318)	(337)	(357)	(379)	
Taxable cash flow	1,012	1,927	2,653	1,221	
TA depreciation	(500)	(375)	(281)	(594)	
Taxable profit	512	1,552	2,372	627	
Taxation	(154)	(466)	(712)	(188)	
Profit for the year	512	1,398	1,906	(85)	(188)
TA depreciation	500	375	281	594	
After-tax cash flow	1,012	1,773	2,187	509	(188)
Scrap value				250	
After-tax cash flows	1,012	1,773	2,187	759	(188)
Discount at 12%	0.893	0.797	0.712	0.635	0.567
Present values	904	1,413	1,557	482	(107)

	$000
Present value of future cash flows	4,249
Initial investment	2,000
Net present value	2,249

Workings

Annual contribution

Year	**1**	**2**	**3**	**4**
Sales volume (units/yr)	250,000	400,000	500,000	250,000
Selling price ($/unit)	12.60	13.23	13.89	14.59
Variable cost ($/unit)	7.28	7.57	7.87	8.19
Contribution ($/unit)	5.32	5.66	6.02	6.40
Contribution ($/yr)	1,330,000	2,264,000	3,010,000	1,600,000

Tax allowable depreciation tax benefits

Year	**TA depreciation**	**Tax benefit**
	($)	($)
1	500,000	150,000
2	375,000	112,500
3	281,250	84,375
4	593,750	178,125
Scrap value	250,000	
	2,000,000	

(c) (i) **Multiple internal rates of return**

An investment project may have multiple internal rates of return if it has unconventional cash flows, that is, cash flows that change sign over the life of the project. A mining operation, for example, may have initial investment (cash outflow) followed by many years of successful operation (cash inflow) before decommissioning and environmental repair (cash outflow). This technical difficulty makes it difficult to use the internal rate of return (IRR) investment appraisal method to offer investment advice.

One solution is to use the net present value (NPV) investment appraisal method instead of IRR, since the non-conventional cash flows are easily accommodated by NPV. This is one area where NPV is considered to be superior to IRR.

(ii) **Projects with significantly different business risk to current operations**

Where a proposed investment project has business risk that is significantly different from current operations, it is no longer appropriate to use the weighted average cost of capital (WACC) as the discount rate in calculating the net present value of the project. WACC can only be used as a discount rate where business risk and financial risk are not significantly affected by undertaking an investment project.

Where business risk changes significantly, the capital asset pricing model should be used to calculate a project-specific discount rate that takes account of the systematic risk of a proposed investment project.

ACCA marking scheme

				Marks
(a)	Identification of errors in the evaluation			
			Maximum	**5**
(b)	Nominal weighted average cost of capital			1
	Inflated selling prices			1
	Inflated variable costs			1
	Inflated contribution			1
	Inflated fixed costs			1
	TA depreciation and/or related tax benefits			3
	Scrap value			1
	Discount factors			1
	Net present value			1
	Comment			1–2
			Maximum	**10**
(c)	(i)	Discussion of projects with several IRR		2
	(ii)	Discussion of projects with different business risk		3
			Maximum	**5**
Total				**20**

Extracts from examiner's comments

Part (b) common errors:

Not applying inflation cumulatively for every relevant year.

Not excluding the development costs, which were non-relevant as they had already been incurred.

Not stripping out depreciation, which is not a cash flow.

Including interest payments, which are already taken into account through the discount rate used.

286 HRAXIN CO (JUN 15 – MODIFIED)

Key answer tips

Part (a) is a fairly standard NPV calculation, albeit with the inclusion of probabilities. Do be conscious that it asks for **expected** NPV, meaning that an expected value calculation is likely to be part of your answer. Also note that tax allowable depreciation is given on a straight line basis. As this is not very common in exam style questions, it is often missed, with students producing a reducing balance calculation in error. Part (b) requires an understanding not just of sensitivity analysis but how it is different to probability analysis and is the trickiest section of the question. Only a couple of marks are available for describing what sensitivity analysis is. Don't go into too much detail on part (c). Think about the main things you would need to know in order to do the calculations. The highlighted words are key phrases that markers are looking for.

(a) Calculation of expected net present value

	1	2	3	4
	$000	$000	$000	$000
Revenue	4,524	7,843	13,048	10,179
Variable cost	(2,385)	(4,200)	(7,080)	(5,730)
Contribution	2,139	3,643	5,968	4,449
Overhead	(440)	(484)	(532)	(586)
Cash flow before tax	1,699	3,159	5,436	3,863
Tax	(510)	(948)	(1,631)	(1,159)
Depreciation benefits	338	338	338	338
Cash flow after tax	1,527	2,549	4,143	3,042
Scrap value				500
Project cash flow	1,527	2,549	4,143	3,542
Discount at 11%	0.901	0.812	0.731	0.659
Present values	1,376	2,070	3,029	2,334

	$000
PV of future cash flows	8,809
Initial investment	(5,000)
Expected net present value (ENPV)	3,809

The investment project has a positive ENPV of $3,809,000. This is a mean or average NPV that will result from the project being repeated many times. However, as the project is not being repeated, the NPVs associated with each future economic state must be calculated as it is one of these NPVs that is expected to occur. The decision by management on the financial acceptability of the project will be based on these NPVs and the risk associated with each one.

Workings

Mean or average selling price = ($25 × 0.35) + ($30 × 0.5) + ($35 × 0.15) = $29 per unit

Year	**1**	**2**	**3**	**4**
Inflated selling price ($ per unit)	30.16	31.37	32.62	33.93
Sales volume (units/year)	150,000	250,000	400,000	300,000
Sales revenue ($000/year)	4,524	7,843	13,048	10,179

Year	**1**	**2**	**3**	**4**
Inflated overhead ($000/year)	440	484	532	586

Total tax-allowable depreciation = $5,000,000 – $500,000 = $4,500,000

Annual tax-allowable depreciation = $4,500,000/4 = $1,125,000 per year

Annual cash flow from tax-allowable depreciation = $1,125,000 × 0.3 = $337,500 per year.

(b) Sensitivity analysis assesses the extent to which the net present value (NPV) of an investment project responds to changes in project variables. Two methods are commonly used: one method determines the percentage change in a project variable which results in a negative NPV, while the other method determines the percentage change in NPV which results from a fixed percentage change (for example, 5%) in each project variable in turn. Whichever method is used, the key or critical project variables are identified as those to which the NPV is most sensitive, for example, those where the smallest percentage change results in a negative NPV. Sensitivity analysis is therefore concerned with calculating relative changes in project variables.

When discussing risk in the context of investment appraisal, it is important to note that, unlike uncertainty, risk can be quantified and measured. The probabilities of the occurrence of particular future outcomes can be assessed, for example, and used to evaluate the volatility of future cash flows, for example, by calculating their standard deviation. The probabilities of the future economic states in the assessment of the investment project of Hraxin Co are an example of probability analysis and these probabilities can lead to an assessment of project risk.

Sensitivity analysis is usually studied in investment appraisal in relation to understanding how risk can be incorporated in the investment appraisal process. While sensitivity analysis can indicate the critical variables of an investment project, however, sensitivity analysis does not give any indication of the probability of a change in any critical variable. Selling price may be a critical variable, for example, but sensitivity analysis is not able to say whether a change in selling price is likely to occur. In the appraisal of the investment project of Hraxin Co, the probabilities of different selling prices arising with related economic states have come from probability analysis, not from sensitivity analysis.

Sensitivity analysis will not therefore directly assist Hraxin Co in assessing the risk of the investment project. However, it does provide useful information which helps management to gain a deeper understanding of the investment project and which focuses management attention on aspects of the investment project where problems may arise.

(c) When considering whether to lease or buy an asset, because the cash flows of leasing and buying generally last over the life of the project, discounted cash flow techniques should be used. This will mean that the time value of money is taken into account, the cash flows are all expressed in present value terms and the two options will be directly comparable.

The cash flows related to leasing and those to buying should be compared, discounted at the post tax cost of borrowing. This makes the assumption that the asset is either being leased or purchased with the use of financing – hence the discount rate used for both options is the borrowing cost.

The cash flows of the lease that will be relevant are the lease payments themselves and the tax savings that these lease payments will lead to. This is on the assumption that the business is making enough profits overall to benefit from the reduced tax bill seen from offsetting the lease payments against profits.

The cash flows of the purchase option will be those of the purchase itself, any scrap value and the tax savings from any tax allowable depreciation available. Interest cash flows on any borrowing used for the purchase will not be included as these are accounted for within the cost of capital used for discounting.

Cash flows that are common to both options can be ignored as it's the differences between the two options that will determine which is chosen.

Once the two sets of discounted cash flows have been calculated, they are compared and the lowest cost option is chosen.

ACCA marking scheme

			Marks
(a)	Mean selling price per unit		0.5
	Inflated selling price per unit		1
	Inflated revenue		1
	Inflated overhead		1
	Tax liabilities		1
	Timing of tax liabilities		1
	Tax-allowable depreciation benefits		1
	Scrap value		0.5
	Present values of future cash flows		1
	Comment on financial acceptability		1
			9
(b)	Explanation of sensitivity analysis		1–3
	Explanation of risk in investment appraisal		1–2
	Discussion of sensitivity analysis and risk		1–3
		Maximum	**6**

(c)	Discounted cash flows should be used	1
	Post tax cost of borrowing should be used	1
	Lease cash flows	1
	Purchase cash flows	1
	Ignore common cash flows	1
	Interest cash flows on financing are part of cost of capital	1
	Make comparison and choose lowest cost option	1
	Maximum	**5**
Total		**20**

Extracts from examiner's comments

Part (a) common errors:

Calculating multiple NPVs instead of using EVs for selling price and calculating one NPV based on the expected price.

Applying inflation incorrectly.

Incorrectly deferring tax cash flows by 1 year.

Incorrectly using reducing balance depreciation for tax-allowable depreciation calculations.

Treating the tax-allowable depreciation as a cash flow.

Part (b) common errors:

Even though the requirement was for a critical discussion, many answers attempted to calculate sensitivities of project variables. No credit was given for these calculations because they were not required.

287 HEBAC CO (SEP 16)

Key answer tips

Part (a) is a straightforward NV calculation including inflation, tax and working capital. For part (b), note in the question that the project is to be launched in a new market outside its current operations. This is the indicator that the CAPM may be useful here, to deal with the changed risk of this new project in comparison to its current business. If you spot this then the question lends itself nicely to discussion of risk levels and proxy beta factors that may need to be de-geared and re-geared. The highlighted words are key phrases that markers are looking for.

(a)

Year	**1**	**2**	**3**	**4**
	$000	$000	$000	$000
Sales revenue	3,120	15,576	22,275	10,296
Variable cost	(1,890)	(7,936)	(9,378)	(4,376)
Contribution	1,230	7,640	12,897	5,920
Fixed cost	(540)	(583)	(630)	(680)
Taxable cash flow	690	7,057	12,267	5,240
Taxation	(138)	(1,411)	(2,453)	(1,048)
TAD tax benefits	125	94	70	186
After-tax cash flow	677	5,740	9,884	4,378
Scrap value				125
Working capital	(90)	(95)	(102)	1,787
Net cash flows	587	5,645	9,782	6,290
Discount at 12%	0.893	0.797	0.712	0.636
Present values	524	4,499	6,965	4,000

	$000	
PV of future cash flows	15,988	
Initial investment	4,000	(2.5m equipment + 1.5m working capital)
NPV	11,988	

The NPV is strongly positive and so the project is financially acceptable.

Workings

Sales revenue

Year	**1**	**2**	**3**	**4**
Selling price ($/unit)	15	18	22	22
Inflated at 4% per year	15.60	19.47	24.75	25.74
Sales volume (000 units/year)	200	800	900	400
Sales revenue ($000/year)	3,120	15,576	22,275	10,296

Variable cost

Year	**1**	**2**	**3**	**4**
Variable cost ($/unit)	9	9	9	9
Inflated at 5% per year	9.45	9.92	10.42	10.94
Sales volume (000 units/year)	200	800	900	400
Variable cost ($000/year)	1,890	7,936	9,378	4,376

Tax benefits of tax-allowable depreciation

Year	**1**	**2**	**3**	**4**
	$000	$000	$000	$000
Tax-allowable depreciation	625	469	352	929
Tax benefit	125	94	70	186*

*((2,500 – 125) × 0.2) – 125 – 94 – 70 = $186,000

Working capital

Year	**0**	**1**	**2**	**3**	**4**
	$000	$000	$000	$000	$000
Working capital	1,500				
Inflated at 6%	1,500	1,590	1,685	1,787	
Incremental	(1,500)	(90)	(95)	(102)	1,787

Alternative calculation of after-tax cash flow

Year	**1**	**2**	**3**	**4**
	$000	$000	$000	$000
Taxable cash flow	690	7,057	12,267	5,240
Tax-allowable depreciation	(625)	(469)	(352)	(929)
Taxable profit	65	6,588	11,915	4,311
Taxation	(13)	(1,318)	(2,383)	(862)
After-tax profit	52	5,270	9,532	3,449
Add back TAD	625	469	352	929
After-tax cash flow	677	5,739	9,884	4,378

(b) A company can use its weighted average cost of capital (WACC) as the discount rate in appraising an investment project as long as the project's business risk and financial risk are similar to the business and financial risk of existing business operations. Where the business risk of the investment project differs significantly from the business risk of existing business operations, a project-specific discount rate is needed.

The capital asset pricing model (CAPM) can provide a project-specific discount rate. The equity beta of a company whose business operations are similar to those of the investment project (a proxy company) will reflect the systematic business risk of the project. If the proxy company is geared, the proxy equity beta will additionally reflect the systematic financial risk of the proxy company.

The proxy equity beta is ungeared to remove the effect of the proxy company's systematic financial risk to give an asset beta that solely reflects the business risk of the investment project.

This asset beta is re-geared to give an equity beta that reflects the systematic financial risk of the investing company.

The re-geared equity beta can then be inserted into the CAPM formula to provide a project-specific cost of equity. If this cost of capital is used as the discount rate for the investment project, it will indicate the minimum return required to compensate shareholders for the systematic risk of the project. The project-specific cost of equity can also be included in a project-specific WACC. Using the project-specific WACC in appraising an investment project will lead to a better investment decision than using the current WACC as the discount rate, as the current WACC does not reflect the risk of the investment project.

ACCA marking scheme

		Marks
(a)	Inflated selling price per unit	1
	Sales revenue	1
	Inflated variable cost	1
	Inflated fixed costs	1
	Tax liabilities	1
	Tax-allowable depreciation benefits years 1–3	1
	Tax allowable depreciation benefits year 4	1
	Incremental working capital and recovery	2
	Calculation of present values	1
	Correct initial investment	1
	Comment on financial acceptability	1
		12
(b)	Business risk, financial risk and WACC	2
	Using a proxy company	1
	Systematic risk, business risk and financial risk	1
	Ungearing the equity beta	1
	Regearing the asset beta	1
	Project-specific cost of equity and WACC	2
		8
Total		**20**

288 DYSXA CO (DEC 2016)

Key answer tips

Part (a) is a straightforward NPV calculation. Be methodical to avoid making unnecessary areas in a question that should pick you up some good marks. Don't forget to comment on the result.

Make sure in part (b) that you pick up that the projects are divisible rather than indivisible due to the different approaches needed for each type.

For students who have revised the theory, part (c) should also provide some relatively easy marks. Make sure you at least know the difference between the two types.

In part (d), try to focus on risk rather than uncertainty. Probability analysis deals with risk by using probabilities to weight the different outcomes and the CAPM is a really good example of adjusting equity returns (and subsequently the WACC) to compensate for changes in risk.

The highlighted words are key phrases that markers are looking for.

(a) NPV calculation

Year	**1**	**2**	**3**	**4**	**5**
$000	$000	$000	$000	$000	
Sales revenue	2,712	2,797	2,882	2,967	
Variable costs	(995)	(1,054)	(1,114)	(1,182)	
Contribution	**1,717**	**1,743**	**1,768**	**1,785**	
Fixed costs	(110)	(205)	(330)	(330)	
Taxable cash flow	**1,607**	**1,538**	**1,438**	**1,455**	
Taxation at 20%		(321)	(308)	(288)	(291)
TAD tax benefits		160	120	90	270
After-tax cash flows	**1,607**	**1,377**	**1,250**	**1,257**	**(21)**
Discount at 10%	0.909	0.826	0.751	0.683	0.621
Present values	**1,461**	**1,137**	**939**	**859**	**(13)**

	$000
PV of future cash flows	4,383
Initial investment	(3,200)
NPV	**1,183**

Comment

The NPV is positive and so the investment project is financially acceptable.

Workings

Sales revenue

Year	**1**	**2**	**3**	**4**
Selling price ($/unit)	3.10	3.10	3.10	3.10
Inflated at 3% per year	3.19	3.29	3.39	3.49
Sales volume (000 units/year)	850	850	850	850
Sales revenue ($000/year)	**2,712**	**2,797**	**2,882**	**2,967**

Variable cost

Year	**1**	**2**	**3**	**4**
Variable cost ($/unit)	1.10	1.10	1.10	1.10
Inflated at 6% per year	1.17	1.24	1.31	1.39
Sales volume (000 units/year)	850	850	850	850
Variable cost ($000/year)	**995**	**1,054**	**1,114**	**1,182**

Year	**1**	**2**	**3**	**4**
TAD ($000)	800	600	450	1,350
Tax benefits ($000)	160	120	90	270*

*($3,200 × 0.2) – 160 – 120 – 90 = $270,000

Alternative calculation of after-tax cash flow

Year	**1**	**2**	**3**	**4**	**5**
	$000	$000	$000	$000	$000
Taxable cash flow	1,607	1,538	1,438	1,455	
TAD	(800)	(600)	(450)	(1,350)	
Taxable profit	**807**	**938**	**988**	**105**	
Taxation at 20%		(161)	(188)	(198)	(21)
After-tax profit	**807**	**777**	**800**	**(93)**	**(21)**
Add back TAD	800	600	450	1,350	
After-tax cash flows	**1,607**	**1,377**	**1,250**	**1,257**	**(21)**

(b) **Analysis of profitability indexes**

Project	**Initial investment**	**Net present value**	**Profitability index***	**Rank**
A	$3,000,000	$6,000,000	2.0	2nd
B	$2,000,000	$3,200,000	1.6	4th
C	$1,000,000	$1,700,000	1.7	Excluded
D	$1,000,000	$2,100,000	2.1	1st
E	$2,000,000	$3,600,000	1.8	3rd

*NPV divided by initial investment

Optimum investment schedule

Project	**Initial investment**	**Rank**	**Net present value**	
D	$1,000,000	1st	$2,100,000	
A	$3,000,000	2nd	$6,000,000	
E	$2,000,000	3rd	$3,600,000	
B	$1,000,000	4th	$1,600,000	($3.2m × $1m/$2m)
	$7,000,000		**$13,300,000**	

The NPV of the optimum investment schedule for Delta division is $13.3 million.

(c) Capital rationing can be divided into hard capital rationing, which is externally imposed, or soft capital rationing, which is internally imposed.

Soft capital rationing

Investment capital may be limited internally because a company does not want to take on a commitment to increased fixed interest payments, for example, if it expects future profitability to be poor. A company may wish to avoid diluting existing earnings per share or changing existing patterns of ownership and control by issuing new equity. A company may limit investment funds because it wishes to pursue controlled growth rather than rapid growth. Given the uncertainty associated with forecasting future cash flows, a company may limit investment funds in order to create an internal market where investment projects compete for finance, with only the best investment projects being granted approval.

Hard capital rationing

External reasons for capital rationing can be related to risk and to availability of finance. Providers of finance may see a company as too risky to invest in, perhaps because it is highly geared or because it has a poor record or poor prospects in terms of profitability or cash flow. Long-term finance for capital investment may have limited availability because of the poor economic state of the economy, or because there is a banking crisis.

(d) The risk of an investment project could be assessed by using probability analysis or by using the capital asset pricing model (CAPM).

Probability analysis

Project risk can be assessed or quantified by attaching probabilities to expected investment project outcomes. At an overall level, this could be as simple as attaching probabilities to two or more expected scenarios, for example, associated with different economic states. Key project variables might then take different values depending on the economic state.

At the level of individual project variables, probability distributions of values could be found through expert analysis, and the probability distributions and relationships between variables then built into a simulation model. This model could then be used to generate a probability distribution of expected project outcomes in terms of net present values. Project risk could then be measured by the standard deviation of the expected net present value.

CAPM

The CAPM uses a beta that represents the systematic risk of a project and of the company undertaking the project to find a risk-adjusted cost of equity for use in discounting. The systematic business risk of an investment project can be assessed by identifying a proxy company in a similar line of business. The equity beta of the proxy company can then be ungeared to give the asset beta of the company, which reflects systematic business risk alone as the effect of the systematic financial risk of the proxy company is removed by the ungearing process. The asset beta can then be regeared to reflect the systematic financial risk of the investing company, giving an equity beta that reflects the systematic risk of the investment project.

ACCA marking scheme		
		Marks
(a)	Inflated sales revenue	1
	Inflated variable cost	1
	Tax liabilities	1
	Tax-allowable depreciation benefits years 1–3	1
	Tax-allowable depreciation benefits year 4	1
	Timing of tax liabilities and depreciation benefits	1
	Calculation of present values	1
	Comment on financial acceptability	1
		8
(b)	Calculating profitability indexes	1
	Formulating optimum investment schedule	1
	NPV of optimum investment schedule	1
		3
(c)	Soft capital rationing	2
	Hard capital rationing	2
	Additional detail	1
		5
(d)	Risk assessment method 1	2
	Risk assessment method 2	2
		4
Total		**20**

Extracts from examiner's comments

Part (a) common errors:

Not reading the information in the question properly, such as that regarding the timing of the cash flow associated with taxation or when the initial investment is made.

Applying inflation incorrectly.

Candidates need to say more than "accept" or "reject" in order to meet the criteria for a comment about financial acceptability.

Part (b) common errors:

Taking the trial and error approach associated with indivisible projects or calculating the profitability indices for the projects but then not knowing what to do with them.

Providing schedules which included both of the mutually exclusive projects, the latter of which seems to suggest a lack of understanding of the term 'mutually exclusive' (some candidates were even treating such items as complimentary pair and not as substitutes).

Part (c) common errors:

Answers lacking in detail.

Stating that hard rationing is the use of external finance and soft rationing being the use of retained earnings is not correct.

When stating that hard capital rationing is due to banks being unwilling to lend, a discussion should follow incorporating the reasons for this, such as government imposed bank lending restrictions or that the bank views the company as too risky due to its existing level of indebtedness.

Part (d) common errors:

Misinterpreting the requirement and ignoring the risk factor, instead writing in general terms about simply how to assess projects with detailed, irrelevant discussions about ROCE, payback and NPV. IRR also featured often, yet incorrectly, as a method with which risk can be assessed.

The most common error was to discuss sensitivity analysis as a way in which risk can be assessed. This is not the case. Sensitivity analysis is a method of analysing the uncertainty surrounding a project.

289 PELTA CO (SEP/DEC 2017)

Key answer tips

Part (a) (i) is a relatively straightforward net present value calculation, although with an element (the use of the terminal value) that is different to what you will have practised before. Follow the instructions and you should pick up good marks here. For part (a) (ii) discounted payback uses the annual present values that you have already calculated and looks at them cumulatively for 2 marks. In part (b) you should refer back to your calculations in your answer and remember that NPV is always the superior method if it clashes with other methods used. The key to part (c) is restricting your answer to what is specifically asked for – a critique of the directors' views. Answers that don't fit into this remit will not pick up marks.

The highlighted words are key phrases that markers are looking for.

(a) (i)

Year	**1**	**2**	**3**	**4**	**5**
	$000	$000	$000	$000	$000
Sales income	16,224	20,248	24,196	27,655	
Variable costs	(5,356)	(6,752)	(8,313)	(9,694)	
Contribution	10,868	13,495	15,883	17,962	
Fixed costs	(700)	(735)	(779)	(841)	
Cash flow before tax	10,168	12,760	15,104	17,121	
Corporation tax		(3,050)	(3,828)	(4,531)	(5,136)
TAD tax benefits		1,875	1,406	1,055	2,789
After-tax cash flow	10,168	11,585	12,682	13,644	(2,347)
Terminal value				1,250	
Project cash flow	10,168	11,585	12,682	14,894	(2,347)
Discount at 12%	0.893	0.797	0.712	0.636	0.567
Present values	9,080	9,233	9,030	9,473	(1,331)

PV of future cash flows ($000)	35,485
Initial investment ($000)	(25,000)
NPV	10,485

Workings

Year	**1**	**2**	**3**	**4**
Sales volume (units/year)	520,000	624,000	717,000	788,000
Selling price ($/unit)	30.00	30.00	30.00	30.00
Inflated by 4% per year	31.20	32.45	33.75	35.10
Income ($000/year)	16,224	20,248	24,196	27,655

Year	**1**	**2**	**3**	**4**
Sales volume (units/year)	520,000	624,000	717,000	788,000
Variable costs ($/unit)	10.00	10.20	10.61	10.93
Inflated by 3% per year	10.30	10.82	11.59	12.30
Variable costs ($000/year)	5,356	6,752	8,313	9,694

Year	**1**	**2**	**3**	**4**
Fixed costs ($000/year)	700	735	779	841
Year	1	2	3	4
TAD ($000 per year)	6,250	4,688	3,516	9,297
TAD benefits ($000/year)	1,875	1,406	1,055	2,789

(ii)

Year	**1**	**2**	**3**	**4**	**5**
	$000	$000	$000	$000	$000
Present values	9,080	9,233	9,030	9,473	(1,331)
Cumulative NPV	(15,920)	(6,687)	2,343	11,815	10,485
Discounted payback (years)		2.7			

(b) The investment project is financially acceptable under the NPV decision rule because it has a substantial positive NPV.

The discounted payback period of 2.7 years is greater than the maximum target discounted payback period of two years and so from this perspective the investment project is not financially acceptable.

The correct advice is given by the NPV method, however, and so the investment project is financially acceptable.

(c) The views of the directors on investment appraisal can be discussed from several perspectives.

Evaluation period

Sales are expected to continue beyond year 4 and so the view of the directors that all investment projects must be evaluated over four years of operations does not seem sensible. The investment appraisal would be more accurate if the cash flows from further years of operation were considered.

Assumed terminal value

The view of the directors that a terminal value of 5% of the initial investment should be assumed has no factual or analytical basis to it. Terminal values for individual projects could be higher or lower than 5% of the initial investment and in fact may have no relationship to the initial investment at all.

A more accurate approach would be to calculate a year 4 terminal value based on the expected value of future sales.

Discounted payback method

The directors need to explain their view that an investment project's discounted payback must be no greater than two years. Perhaps they think that an earlier payback will indicate an investment project with a lower level of risk. Although the discounted payback method does overcome the failure of simple payback to take account of the time value of money, it still fails to consider cash flows outside the payback period. Theoretically, Pelta Co should rely on the NPV investment appraisal method.

ACCA marking scheme			
			Marks
(a)	(i)	Inflated sales	1
		Inflated VC/unit	1
		Inflated total VC	1
		Tax liabilities	1
		TAD benefits years 1–3	1
		TAD benefits year 4	1
		Timing of tax flows	1
		Terminal value	1
		Calculate PVs	1
			9
	(ii)	Cumulative NPV	1
		Discounted payback	1
			2
(b)	Acceptability – NPV		1
	Acceptability – payback		1
	Correct advice		1
			3
(c)	Evaluation period		2
	terminal value		2
	Discounted payback		2
			6
Total			**20**

Extracts from examiner's comments

Part (a) (i) common errors:

Failure to apply a 'per year inflation rate' correctly. If an inflation rate of 3% per year needs to be applied to a variable cost per unit, then by the end of year 3, the given variable cost per unit needs to be inflated three times i.e. by 1.03^3.

A number of answers to this question used an incorrect discount rate, usually the real discount rate, to discount the nominal values already calculated.

Other errors seen quite often included:

- incorrectly placing initial investment at year 1 rather than year 0
- incorrectly placing the terminal value at year 5 rather than year 4, or not including it altogether
- not placing tax-related cash flows one year in arrears
- omitting the tax-related cash flows in year 5
- not calculating a balancing allowance, or calculating a balancing allowance but not adjusting it for the scrap value of the asset.

Part (a) (ii) common errors:

A recalculation of the present values from (a) (i) by erroneously using the real discount rate or using cash flows before tax.

Part (b) common errors:

Most candidates were able to refer to the decision rules relevant to net present value and discounted payback, but do need to justify financial acceptability comments. Standalone comments such as 'Accept' or alternatively 'Positive NPV' should be explained as should 'more than 2 years' in respect of the discounted payback period.

Weaker responses simply referred to the positive NPV calculated in (a) (i), which is insufficient for a part question worth three marks.

Part (c) common errors:

For a critical discussion, it is rarely sufficient to simply list a few points. A critical discussion should involve looking at a viewpoint or a statement in more than one way, for instance by looking at both its good aspects and those aspects which could be criticised.

Many candidates simply ignored the directors' view on terminal value.

Saying that NPV considered the whole life of an investment project, even though the directors had limited NPV's application to four years.

Saying that payback failed to take account of the time value of money, even though the directors required DPB to be used.

Some answers assumed that the investment project ended after four years, when in fact the directors simply required that only the first four years be evaluated using NPV.

Discussing investment appraisal in general rather than the directors' views specifically.

Discussing only forecasting problems, such as difficulties in forecasting cash flows, inflation rate, changes in the cost of capital etc.

290 COPPER CO (MAR/JUN 2018)

Key answer tips

All elements of part (a) can be addressed using the joint probability table. The key here is to remember that the probability of one thing and another thing happening can be found by multiplying the probabilities of the individual events together, whereas the probability of one thing or another thing happening can be found by adding the probabilities of the individual events together.

The joint probabilities here refer to the probabilities of a particular cash flow occurring in year 1 and then a particular cash flow occurring in year 2.

Once the table has been put together, the questions can then be addressed. For instance the probability of a negative NPV happening is the probabilities of each of the negative outcomes added together as the NPV will be negative if one of these events OR any of the others occurs.

Added complexity came from having to apply discounting to the cash flows before including them in the table.

Part (b)'s marks should have been simpler to achieve, although make sure that only two methods were discussed – discussion of the third one would not pick up marks.

The highlighted words are key phrases that markers are looking for.

(a) (i) ENPV calculation

Year	**PV of Y1 CF**	**prob**	**PV of Y2 CF**	**prob**	**Total PV**	**joint prob**	**PV × JP**	**NPV**
	$000		$000		$000		$000	$000
PV of c/f 1	893	0.1	1,594	0.3	2,487	0.03	74.6	(1,013)
			2,391	0.6	3,284	0.06	197.0	(216)
			3,985	0.1	4,878	0.01	48.8	1,378
PV of c/f 2	1,786	0.5	1,594	0.3	3,380	0.15	507.0	(120)
			2,391	0.6	4,177	0.30	1,253.1	677
			3,985	0.1	5,771	0.05	288.6	2,271
PV of c/f 3	2,679	0.4	1,594	0.3	4,273	0.12	512.8	773
			2,391	0.6	5,070	0.24	1,216.8	1,570
			3,985	0.1	6,664	0.04	266.6	3,164
						Sum of PV	4,365	
						Investment	(3,500)	
						ENPV	865	

Workings

Year	**Yr 1**	**factor**	**PV**	**Yr 2**	**factor**	**PV**
Cash flow 1	1,000	0.893	893	2,000	0.797	1,594
Cash flow 2	2,000	0.893	1,786	3,000	0.797	2,391
Cash flow 3	3,000	0.893	2,679	5,000	0.797	3,985

(ii) Negative NPV probability 24% Sum of joint probabilities with negative NPVs

(iii) Most likely outcome ($000) 677.0 Highest joint probability

(iv) Comment

The mean (expected) NPV is positive and so it might be thought that the proposed investment is financially acceptable. However, the mean (expected) NPV is not a value expected to occur because of undertaking the proposed investment, but a mean value from undertaking it many times. There is no clear decision rule associated with the mean (expected) NPV.

A decision on financial acceptability must also consider the risk (probability) of a negative NPV being generated by the investment. At 24%, this might appear too high a risk to be acceptable. The risk preferences of the directors of Copper Co will inform the decision on financial acceptability; there is no decision rule to be followed here.

(b) Simulation

Simulation is a computer-based method of evaluating an investment project whereby the probability distributions associated with individual project variables and interdependencies between project variables are incorporated.

Random numbers are assigned to a range of different values of a project variable to reflect its probability distribution. Each simulation run randomly selects values of project variables using random numbers and calculates a mean (expected) NPV.

A picture of the probability distribution of the mean (expected) NPV is built up from the results of repeated simulation runs. The project risk can be assessed from the probability distribution as the standard deviation of the expected returns, together with the most likely outcome and the probability of a negative NPV.

Adjusted payback

If risk and uncertainty are considered to be the same, payback can be used to adjust for risk and uncertainty in investment appraisal.

As uncertainty (risk) increases, the payback period can be shortened to increase the emphasis on cash flows that are nearer to the present time and hence less uncertain. Conversely, as uncertainty (risk) decreases, the payback period can be lengthened to decrease the emphasis on cash flows that are nearer to the present time.

Discounted payback adjusts for risk in investment appraisal in that risk is reflected by the discount rate employed. Discounted payback can therefore be seen as an adjusted payback method.

Risk-adjusted discount rates

The risk associated with an investment project can be incorporated into the discount rate as a risk premium over the risk free rate of return.

The risk premium can be determined on a subjective basis, for example, by recognising that launching a new product is intrinsically riskier that replacing an existing machine or a small expansion of existing operations.

The risk premium can be determined theoretically by using the capital asset pricing model in an investment appraisal context. A proxy company equity beta can be ungeared and the resulting asset beta can be regeared to reflect the financial risk of the investing company, giving a project-specific equity beta that can be used to find a project-specific cost of equity or a project-specific discount rate.

(Examiner note: Only two methods were required to be discussed.)

ACCA marking scheme

			Marks
(a)	(i)	Initial PVs	1
		Total PVs	2
		CF1 joint prob	1
		CF2 joint prob	1
		CF3 joint prob	1
		ENPV	2
			8
	(ii)	Negative NPV prob	1
	(iii)	Most likely NPV	1
	(iv)	Comment on ENPV	1
		Comment on risk	1
			4
(b)	First method		4
	Second method		4
			8
Total			**20**

Extracts from examiner's comments

Part (a) (i) common errors:

Not using a joint probability table despite it being stated in the requirement.

Failing to understand how a joint probability is calculated.

Thinking that using probabilities meant that discounting was not needed.

Part (a) (ii) common errors:

Some candidates made the surprising error of calculating the sensitivity of the project ENPV to a change in year one cash flow and called this the probability of a negative NPV.

Some candidates did not understand that a probability is a percentage value and calculated a monetary value, which they called the probability of a negative NPV.

Part (b) common errors:

Discussing a third method when only two were asked for.

291 PINKS CO (MAR/JUN 2019)

Key answer tips

In part (a) (i) the nominal NPV calculation is relatively straightforward. Apply inflation to the cash flows and use the nominal cost of capital. You may come unstuck on part (a) (ii). The real terms appraisal in theory should be done from scratch using uninflated values for all numbers, but for only four marks, an approximation can be found by taking the pre-tax nominal cash flows and deflating them by the general rate of inflation (divide the cash flows by (1 + general inflation rate), before taxing them and discounting the total at the real cost of capital.

Limit your answer to part (b) to only four ways. This part of the syllabus will rarely be tested in section C but the examiner has reserved the right to do so by using the word 'mainly' in his/her description of which syllabus sections are valid for testing in section C. Don't let this put you off. Make sure you revise all areas of the syllabus thoroughly.

The highlighted words are key phrases that markers are looking for.

(a) (i) Nominal terms appraisal of the investment project

Year	**1**	**2**	**3**	**4**
	$000	$000	$000	$000
Sales revenue	39,375	58,765	85,087	32,089
Variable cost	(22,047)	(31,185)	(41,328)	(17,923)
Contribution	17,328	27,580	43,759	14,166
Fixed costs	(3,180)	(3,483)	(3,811)	(3,787)
Cash flows before tax	14,148	24,097	39,948	10,379
Tax at 26%	(3,679)	(6,265)	(10,387)	(2,699)
TAD tax benefits	1,300	975	731	2,194
Cash flows after tax	11,769	18,807	30,292	9,874
Discount at 12%	0.893	0.797	0.712	0.636
Present values	10,510	14,989	21,568	6,280

	$000
Sum of PV of future cash flows	53,347
Initial investment	(20,000)
NPV	33,347

Workings

Year	**1**	**2**	**3**	**4**
Selling price ($/unit)	125	130	140	120
Inflated by 5%/year	131.25	143.33	162.07	145.86
Sales volume (units)	300,000	410,000	525,000	220,000
Sales revenue ($000)	39,375	58,765	85,087	32,089

Year	**1**	**2**	**3**	**4**
Variable costs ($/unit)	71	71	71	71
Inflated by 3.5%/year	73.49	76.06	78.72	81.47
Sales volume (units)	300,000	410,000	525,000	220,000
Variable costs ($000) ($000/year)	22,047	31,185	41,328	17,923

Year	**1**	**2**	**3**	**4**
Fixed costs ($000) ($000/year)	3,000	3,100	3,200	3,000
Inflated by 6%/year	3,180	3,483	3,811	3,787
TAD ($000)	5,000	3,750	2,813	8,437
TAD benefit ($000/year)	1,300	975	731	2,194

Example answer in a spreadsheet:

	A	B	C	D	E	F	G
1	a i	**Nominal (money) method**					
2		Sales units (000s)		300	410	525	220
3			t0	t1	t2	t3	t4
4			$000	$000	$000	$000	$000
5		Sales revenue		39,375	58,763	85,085	32,089
6		Variable cost		- 22,046	- 31,183	- 41,327	- 17,924
7		Fixed costs		- 3,180	- 3,483	- 3,811	- 3,787
8							
9		Operating cash flows		14,150	24,097	39,947	10,378
10		Tax on operating cash flows		- 3,679	- 6,265	- 10,386	- 2,698
11							
12		Investment cashflow	- 20,000				
13		Tax savings on tax allowable depreciation (working 1)		1,300	975	731	2,194
14							
15		Total cash flows	- 20,000	11,771	18,807	30,292	9,873
16							
17		PV years 1 to 4	53,338				
18		**NPV**	**33,338**				
19							
20		**Example formulae used:**					
21		In cell D5:	=125*1.05*D2				
22		In cell E5:	=130*1.05^2*E2				
23		In cell F5:	=140*1.05^3*F2				
24		In cell G5:	=120*1.05^4*G2				
25		In cell C17:	=NPV(12%,D15:G15)				
26		In cell C18:	=C17+C15				
27							
28		**Working 1**	$000	Tax savings on depreciation at 26%			
29		t0 purchase asset	20000		time period		
30		t1 claim 25% reducing balance depreciation	5000	1,300.00	t1		
31		t1 written down value	15000				
32		t2 claim 25% reducing balance depreciation	3750	975.00	t2		
33		t2 written down value	11250				
34		t3 claim 25% reducing balance depreciation	2812.5	731.25	t3		
35		t3 written down value	8437.5				
36		t4 sell asset - proceeds	0				
37		t4 balancing allowance	8437.5	2,193.75	t4		

(ii) Real terms appraisal of the investment project

Year	**1**	**2**	**3**	**4**
	$000	$000	$000	$000
Nominal cash flows before tax	14,148	24,097	39,948	10,379
Real cash flows before tax	13,643	22,408	35,823	8,975
Tax at 26%	(3,547)	(5,826)	(9,314)	(2,334)
TAD tax benefits	1,300	975	731	2,194
Cash flows after tax	11,396	17,557	27,240	8,835
Discount at 8%	0.926	0.857	0.794	0.735
Present values	10,553	15,046	21,629	6,494

	$000
Sum of PV of future cash flows	53,722
Initial investment	(20,000)
NPV	33,722

Note: the real cash flows before tax are found by taking the nominal cash flows and deflating by the **general** rate of inflation, 3.7%:

Year 1 $14,147/1.037 = 13,643$

Year 2 $24,097/1.037^2 = 22,408$

Year 3 $39,948/1.037^3 = 35,823$

Year 4 $10,379/1.037^4 = 8,975$

Comment: The real terms appraisal gives almost the same positive NPV as the nominal terms appraisal, the difference being due to the different discount rate being applied to the same TAD benefits. As the NPV is positive, the investment project is financially acceptable.

Example answer in a spreadsheet:

	A	B	C	D	E	F	G
40	a ii	**Real method**		t1	t2	t3	t4
41				$000	$000	$000	$000
42		Nominal operating cash flows pre-tax (from a i)		14,150	24,097	39,947	10,378
43		(1+general inflation rate)^n		1.03700	1.07537	1.11516	1.15642
44							
45		Real operating cash flows		13,645	22,408	35,822	8,974
46		Tax at 26%		- 3,548	- 5,826	- 9,314	- 2,333
47		Tax allowable depreciation savings (as for a i)		1,300	975	731	2,194
48		Total cash flows		11,397	17,557	27,239	8,834
49							
50		PV years 1 to 4	53,722				
51		Year 0 cash flow	- 20,000				
52		NPV	33,722				
53							
54		**Example formulae used:**					
55		In cell E43:	=1.037^2				
56		In cell F43:	=1.037^3				
57		In cell D45:	=D42/D43				
58		In cell C50:	=NPV(8%,D48:G48)				

(b) The achievement of stakeholder objectives by managers can be encouraged by managerial reward schemes, for example, share option schemes and performance-related pay (PRP), and by regulatory requirements, such as corporate governance codes of best practice and stock exchange listing regulations.

Share option schemes

The agency problem arises due to the separation of ownership and control, and managers pursuing their own objectives, rather than the objectives of shareholders, specifically the objective of maximising shareholder wealth. Managers can be encouraged to achieve stakeholder objectives by bringing their own objectives more in line with the objectives of stakeholders such as shareholders. This increased goal congruence can be achieved by turning the managers into shareholders through share option schemes, although the criteria by which shares are awarded need very careful consideration.

Performance-related pay

Part of the remuneration of managers can be made conditional upon their achieving specified performance targets, so that achieving these performance targets assists in achieving stakeholder objectives. Achieving a specified increase in earnings per share, for example, could be consistent with the objective of maximising shareholder wealth. Achieving a specified improvement in the quality of emissions could be consistent with a government objective of meeting international environmental targets.

However, PRP performance objectives need very careful consideration if they are to be effective in encouraging managers to achieve stakeholder targets. In recent times, long-term incentive plans (LTIPs) have been accepted as more effective than PRP, especially where a company's performance is benchmarked against that of its competitors.

Corporate governance codes of best practice

Codes of best practice have developed over time into recognised methods of encouraging managers to achieve stakeholder objectives, applying best practice to many key areas of corporate governance relating to executive remuneration, risk assessment and risk management, auditing, internal control, executive responsibility and board accountability. Codes of best practice have emphasised and supported the key role played by non-executive directors in supporting independent judgement and in following the spirit of corporate governance regulations.

Stock exchange listing regulations

These regulations seek to ensure a fair and efficient market for trading company securities such as shares and loan notes.

They encourage disclosure of price-sensitive information in supporting pricing efficiency and help to decrease information asymmetry, one of the causes of the agency problem between shareholders and managers. Decreasing information asymmetry encourages managers to achieve stakeholder objectives as the quality and quantity of information available to stakeholders gives them a clearer picture of the extent to which managers are attending to their objectives.

Monitoring

One theoretical way of encouraging managers to achieve stakeholder objectives is to reduce information asymmetry by monitoring the decisions and performance of managers. One form of monitoring is auditing the financial statements of a company to confirm the quality and validity of the information provided to stakeholders.

Note: Only four ways to encourage the achievement of stakeholder objectives were required to be discussed.

ACCA marking scheme

			Marks
(a)	(i)	Sales nominal	1
		VC nominal	1
		FC nominal	1
		Tax liability	1
		TAD	1
		TAD benefits	1
		Tax timing	1
		PVs and nominal NPV	1
			8
	(ii)	Real CF before tax	1
		Tax treatment	1
		PVs and real NPV	1
		Comment	1
			4
(b)	First way		2
	Second way		2
	Third way		2
	Fourth way		2
			8
Total			**20**

Extracts from examiner's comments

Part (a) (i) common errors:

Inflating each year by one year only, when inflation has a compounding effect.

Using an inflation rate of 50% instead of 5% in relation to selling price inflation, and 35% instead of 3.5% for variable cost inflation.

Forecast fixed costs were different in the second and third years to those in the first year, but some candidates incorrectly inflated the first-year value throughout the four-year period.

Some candidates, having applied specific inflation correctly to selling prices, variable costs and fixed costs, then applied the general rate of inflation as well.

Omitting a balancing allowance from the fourth-year calculation of tax-allowable depreciation (TAD).

Incorrectly placing tax cash flows one year in arrears.

Incorrectly used a taxation rate which was different from the 26% figure provided in the question.

Incorrectly locating the initial investment at the end of the first year when, as an initial investment, it should have been located at year 0.

Although the question provided a nominal after-tax cost of capital, some candidates calculated and applied a different figure by putting values into the Fisher equation.

Part (a) (ii) common errors:

Many candidates did not adopt the correct approach of deflating the nominal before-tax cash flows using the general rate of inflation. These cash flows could then be adjusted for taxation and discounted using the real cost of capital.

Many candidates were not aware that the nominal terms approach and the real terms approach should give the same NPV, and discussed, sometimes at length, the reasons for the differences in value between their nominal and real NPVs.

Part (b) common errors:

Since eight marks were offered for discussing four ways of encouraging managers, it seems a reasonable deduction that two marks were offered for each way discussed. Marks would clearly be lost if candidates discussed fewer than four ways.

Some candidates discussed the need to separate the roles of CEO and MD, but did not explain how this separation might encourage managers to achieve stakeholder objectives.

Some candidates suggested that managers should receive a bonus, but did not suggest what that bonus might be for.

Some candidates lost marks by offering answers which were too brief for the marks available.

Candidates lost marks by discussing topics outside the requirement of the question, such as the origins of the agency problem, or the shortcomings of EPS as a managerial performance target, or the need for managers to use DCF investment appraisal techniques.

292 DINK CO (SEP/DEC 2019)

Key answer tips

Taxation is incorporated in this lease versus buy question so you must make sure that you focus on the timings of any tax cash flows and that you use a post-tax cost of borrowing for the discounting. Remember that when tax is paid a year in arrears, it is a year from the end of an accounting period rather than from the start. So when lease payments are made at the start of a year, there is effectively a two year delay until the relevant tax cash flows. This is not an NPV calculation but a calculation of the present value of the costs of leasing or borrowing to purchase. Therefore a cost of capital is not used. Instead the decision is evaluated using a borrowing cost, given as 8.2%, but this must be adjusted for the tax savings which reduce the cost.

For part (b) (i), you can break down your answer into hard versus soft capital rationing, but this alone won't be enough to pick up six marks. Make sure you have some examples of each ready to use for this type of question. For part (b) (ii) the focus is only on external capital rationing, so solutions to soft (internal) capital rationing will not pick up marks here. It is specifically mentioned that the company is small, which links to the syllabus area of financing for SMEs. This should lead to some discussion points.

The highlighted words are key phrases that markers are looking for.

(a) (i)

After-tax cost of borrowing = 8.6 × (1 – 0.3) = 8.6 × 0.7 = 6%

Calculating PV of cost of borrowing to buy:

Year	**0**	**1**	**2**	**3**	**4**	**5**
	$	$	$	$	$	$
Purchase	(750,000)					
Residual value					50,000	
Service costs		(23,000)	(23,000)	(23,000)	(23,000)	
TAD benefit			56,250	42,188	31,641	79,922
Service cost tax benefits			6,900	6,900	6,900	6,900
Net cash flow	(750,000)	(23,000)	40,150	26,088	65,541	86,822
Discount at 6%	1.000	0.943	0.890	0.840	0.792	0.747
	(750,000)	(21,689)	35,734	21,914	51,908	64,856

PV of cost of borrowing to buy is $597,277.

Using the spreadsheet NPV function and spreadsheet-calculated discount factors, PV of cost of borrowing to buy is $597,268.

Working: TAD benefit

Year	**0**	**1**	**2**	**3**	**4**	**5**
	$	$	$	$	$	$
Purchase	750,000					
TAD		187,500	140,625	105,469	266,406*	
30% TAD benefit			56,250	42,188	31,641	79,922

*750,000 – 187,500 – 140,625 – 105,469 – 50,000 = $266,406

(ii) Calculating PV of cost of leasing:

Year	**0**	**1**	**2**	**3**	**4**	**5**
	$	$	$	$	$	$
Lease rentals	(200,000)	(200,000)	(200,000)	(200,000)		
Tax benefits			60,000	60,000	60,000	60,000
Net cash flow	(200,000)	(200,000)	(140,000)	(140,000)	60,000	60,000
Discount at 6%	1.000	0.943	0.890	0.840	0.792	0.747
	(200,000)	(188,600)	(124,600)	(117,600)	47,520	44,820

PV of cost of leasing is $538,460.

Using the spreadsheet NPV function and spreadsheet-calculated discount factors, PV of cost of leasing is $538,464.

(iii) Financial benefit of leasing = $597,277 – $538,460 = $58,817

Using the spreadsheet NPV function and spreadsheet-calculated discount factors, financial benefit of leasing = $597,268 – $538,464 = $58,804.

Leasing the new machine is recommended as the option which is more attractive in financial terms to Dink Co.

(b) (i) **Reasons why investment capital may be rationed**

Theoretically, the objective of maximising shareholder wealth can be achieved in a perfect capital market by investing in all projects with a positive NPV. In practice, companies experience capital rationing and are limited in the amount of investment finance available, so shareholder wealth is not maximised.

Hard capital rationing is due to external factors, while soft capital rationing is due to internal factors or management decisions.

General reasons for hard capital rationing affect many companies, for example, the availability of new finance may be limited because share prices are depressed on the stock market or because of government-imposed restrictions on bank lending.

If a company only requires a small amount of finance, issue costs may be so high that using external sources of finance is not practical.

Reasons for hard capital rationing may be company-specific, for example, a company may not be able to raise new debt finance if banks or investors see the company as being too risky to lend to. The company may have high gearing or low interest cover, or a poor track record, or if recently incorporated, no track record at all. Companies in the service sector may not be able to offer assets as security for new loans.

Reasons for soft capital rationing include managerial aversion to issuing new equity, for example, a company may want to avoid potential dilution of its EPS or avoid the possibility of becoming a takeover target. Managers might alternatively be averse to issuing new debt and taking on a commitment to increased fixed interest payments, for example, if the economic outlook for its markets is poor.

Soft capital rationing might also arise because managers wish to finance new investment from retained earnings, for example, as part of a policy of controlled organisational growth, rather than a sudden increase in size which might result from undertaking all investments with a positive net present value.

One reason for soft capital rationing may be that managers want investment projects to compete for funds, in the belief that this will result in the acceptance of stronger, more robust investment projects.

(ii) Ways in which Dink Co's external capital rationing might be overcome

Dink Co is a small company and the hard capital rationing it is experiencing is a common problem for SMEs, referred to as the funding gap. A first step towards overcoming its capital rationing could be for Dink Co to obtain information about available sources of finance, since SMEs may lack understanding in this area.

One way of overcoming the company's capital rationing might be business angel financing. This informal source of finance is from wealthy individuals or groups of investors who invest directly in the company and who are prepared to take higher risks in the hope of higher returns. Information requirements for this form of finance may be less demanding than those associated with more common sources of finance.

Dink Co could consider crowdfunding, whereby many investors provide finance for a business venture, for example, via an internet-based platform, although this form of finance is usually associated with entrepreneurial ventures.

Dink Co might be entitled to grant aid from a government, national or regional source which could be linked to a specific business area or to economic regeneration in a specified geographical area.

On a more general basis, Dink Co could consider a joint venture as a way of decreasing the need for additional finance, depending on the nature of its business and its business plans, and whether the directors of Dink Co are prepared to sacrifice some control to the joint venture partner.

Rather than conventional sources of finance, Dink Co could evaluate whether Islamic finance, for example, an ijara contract, might be available, again depending on the nature of its business and its business plans.

ACCA marking scheme

			Marks
(a)	(i)	Kd after tax	1
		TAD	1
		TAD benefits	1
		Service tax benefit	1
		Tax timing	1
		PV buying	1
			6
	(ii)	Lease tax benefits	1
		Lease timing	1
		PV leasing	1
			3
	(iii)	Recommendation	**1**
(b)	(i)	Hard reasons	3
		Soft reasons	3
			6
	(ii)	Ways to overcome	**4**
Total			**20**

Extracts from examiner's comments

Part (a) common errors:

Some candidates did not apply the tax rate to the before-tax interest rate on the loan of 8.6%, in order to arrive at an after-tax interest rate of 6%, which is appropriate for the after-tax cash flows present in this question.

It is a fundamental error to include interest payments within the computation of net cash flow, although it is somewhat comforting to report that this error was seen less frequently than when previously tested.

Omission of the service costs of $23,000 or treating them as an inflow.

Omitting or incorrectly treating the tax benefits of the service costs.

Incorrectly applying the corporation tax rate directly to the purchase cost and/or ignoring the need to compute tax-allowable depreciation on a 25% reducing balance basis. Not recognising the need for a balancing allowance in the tax-allowable depreciation computation.

Mistiming of the lease rental payments of $200,000 (treated as year-end cash flows and not, as the question stated, cash flows in advance). Omitting or mistiming the tax relief on the lease payments.

Some candidates did not discount the cash flows at all. Some candidates also erroneously included the same cash flows, such as service costs, in both options.

Some candidates incorrectly chose the highest figure in their recommendation, thereby not recognising that it was a cost figure which they were dealing with.

Part (b) common errors:

Insufficient detail offered in responses, such that few marks out of the six on offer could be gained. Short, undeveloped bullet points do not comprise a discussion.

Answers which simply stated sources of finance which are not relevant in the circumstances of Dink Co, such as a rights' issue, were inappropriate and not awarded any marks.

293 CROCKET CO (SEP/DEC 2020)

Key answer tips

Part (a) combines an NPV calculation and a capital rationing selection. The projects are divisible and two are mutually exclusive – make sure you take these factors into account in your method. With mutually exclusive projects, if in doubt, produce two sets of calculations, one with each project, and pick the combination with the highest NPV. In the NPV calculation, you cannot just ignore inflation and use the real discount rate as there is more than one inflation rate in the scenario. The money method must be used.

Part (b) needs you to explain the equivalent annual cost technique. Make sure you can list out the required steps, including how to make the final decision.

Part (c) will be poorly answered by many students as it requires a knowledge of both the real and money methods of dealing with inflation as well as an understanding of when they can and should be used. Most of the time, it is the money (nominal) approach that should be used. Remember that the real approach can only be used when there is only one rate of inflation (the general rate) that applies to all of the ash flows and to the cost of capital. This will be rare.

The highlighted words are key phrases that markers are looking for.

(a) (i)

Calculate the NPV of project B:

Year	**1**	**2**	**3**	**4**
	$000	$000	$000	$000
Sales (inflated at 4%)	754	827	996	716
Costs (inflated at 5%)	(152)	(185)	(234)	(114)
Net cash flow	602	642	762	602
DCF @ 10%	0.909	0.826	0.751	0.683
Present values	547	530	572	411
Total PV	2,061			
Less: initial outlay	(1,500)			
NPV	**561**			

(ii)

Firstly, calculate the profitability index for each project and rank.

Project	Outlay	NPV	(NPV/Outlay) =	P. Index	Rank
	$000	$000			
A	1,000	390	390/1000 =	0.390	5
B	1,500	561	561/1500 =	0.374	6
C	750	325	325/750 =	0.433	exclude
D	1,125	590	590/1125 =	0.524	1
E	1,850	840	840/1850 =	0.454	3
F	1,300	635	635/1300 =	0.488	2

Projects C and E are mutually exclusive so cannot be done together. As all projects are divisible, the project with the highest PI will be chosen out of the two, which in this case is E at 0.454, rather than C with 0.433.

Optimal combination:

Rank	Project	%	Capital $000	NPV $000
1	D	100	1,125	590
2	F	100	1,300	635
3	E	100	1,850	840
4	A	72.5	725	283
			5,000	**2,348**

After selection of project E, only $725,000 of capital remains. Consequently, only 72.5% (725/1,000 = 0.725) of project A can be undertaken. This will result in only 72.5% of the NPV (0.725 × $390,000 = $283,000) being earned.

The optimum investment plan is to invest fully in projects D, F and E and only 72.5% in project A. This will yield a maximum net present value of $2,348,000.

(b) Firstly, the cash flows must be determined for each cycle under consideration (3, 4 and 5 years). These cash flows will include the initial outlay of the car fleet, maintenance and running costs and the residual value of the car fleet at the end of the cycle.

These cash flows will then require discounting at a suitable discount rate to determine the present value (PV) for each cycle. All of the PVs will be negative as they represent the cost of running the company car fleet with no relevant income attributable.

Given the continual replacement nature of the decision, a common timescale must then be incorporated. To put it simply, while the PV of the three year cycle will appear the cheapest, it will be incurred more frequently than the four or five year cycles going forward indefinitely.

To allow for the difference in timescales, the PV for each cycle will need converting to an equivalent annual cost (EAC). The EAC will represent the annuity cash flow which when discounted gives the same PV as the actual cash flows themselves. The EAC would be calculated by taking each cycle's PV and dividing by the annuity factor for the cycle length. For example, the three-year PV will need to be divided by a three-year annuity factor.

Once the EAC has been calculated for each cycle, the lowest figure, i.e. cheapest, will indicate the optimum replacement cycle for the fleet. By comparing the EAC for each cycle, a common timescale (one year) will be considered, making the figures comparable.

(c) When appraising an investment, the treatment of inflation needs to be considered as it will affect both cash flows and the required rate of return used as the discount rate. Real-terms and nominal-terms approaches to investment appraisal differ in the way that the effects of inflation are incorporated into the appraisal calculation.

Nominal-terms approach

With the nominal-terms approach (also known as the money method), both the cash flows and the discount rate incorporate the effects of inflation. The cost of capital would also need to include the effects of general inflation on the investors' required rate of return. This means Crocket Co will need to apply the specific rates of inflation to sales, material costs and other cash flows and ensure the cash flows in the appraisal incorporate these. The uncertainty surrounding the rates of inflation that Crocket Co faces with this project will certainly make an appraisal in nominal-terms more difficult to prepare with any accuracy and this should be considered when reviewing the results.

Real-terms approach

A real terms approach would exclude the effects of general inflation. Therefore, nominal cash flows incorporating the effects of specific inflation rates would be deflated by the general rate of inflation to give real-terms cash flows. The discount rate will also exclude the effects of inflation. Consequently, a real discount rate would be used which represents the investors' base level of return for risk before inflation is taken into account.

Tutorial note

Real-terms cash flows are not the same as current cash flows. Current cash flows include no inflation at all. Real terms cash flows are nominal cash flows (which include specific inflation) that have been deflated by the general rate of inflation.

Choice of approach

A real-terms approach would result in a much easier appraisal exercise for Crocket Co as the uncertainty surrounding the estimation of inflation is removed, however, a number of conditions must be met in order for the real-terms approach to be suitable.

Firstly, there must be a single rate of inflation affecting all of the project's cash flows. Given that the estimated increase in material costs is different to the expected rise in sales prices this means that a real-terms approach is already deemed unsuitable. As Crocket Co expects the rate of inflation on sales to be less than the rate of inflation on its costs, particularly materials, then it would be expected that any real-terms NPV is likely to be overstated compared to a nominal-terms NPV as costs will be rising faster than income.

Secondly, the single rate of inflation affecting the cash flows must also be the same as the general rate of inflation suffered by investors. If the inflation rate affecting cash flows is the same as the inflation rate ignored by the real discount rate, this common rate of inflation can be ignored. Given that Crocket Co expects the general rate of inflation to differ from the rates affecting sales and material cost, this also means a real-terms approach ignoring specific inflation is not suitable.

Recommendation

As a result of the above conditions not being met, use of the real-terms approach will not be suitable for Crocket Co to appraise this project. A nominal-terms approach should be used.

ACCA marking scheme

			Marks
(a)	(i)	Inflated sales	1
		Inflated costs	1
		NPV	2
			4
	(ii)	PI calculation	2
		PI ranking	1
		Choose project E over C	1
		Optimal NPV	2
			6
(b)	Determine cash flows		1
	PV for each cycle		1
	Calculate EAC		1
	Decision rule		1
			4
(c)	Specific inflation		1
	Cost of capital		1
	Nominal method		1
	Real method		1
	Other points		1
	Recommendation		1
			6
Total			**20**

Extracts from examiner's comments

Part (a) (i) common errors:

Not applying inflation at all to sales and cost values or using incorrect inflation rates for them

Inflation of sales and costs for one year only, such that the sales revenue figure for year 4 was incorrectly calculated as $612,000 * 1.04 = $636,480.

Inflation and use of the Year 1 figures only such that the sales revenue figure for year 4 was incorrectly calculated as $725,000 * 1.04^4 = $848,147

Using total capital available, $5,000,000, as the initial investment, rather than the specified amount of $1,500,000.

Spreadsheet errors, such as incorrect summation and errors in formulae. One such error is deducting the initial investment figure when it has already been entered as a negative figure, thereby giving an incorrect NPV due to the 'double negative'.

e.g. \$2,061,000 – (\$1,500,000) = \$3,561,000

Failing to use spreadsheet functionality at all, for example entering calculated values in cells rather than in-cell calculations, so that computations could not be checked, and method marks could not be awarded.

Part (a) (ii) common errors:

It is important that the detail of the scenario is read and understood. There was some evidence that this was lacking here. For example, projects C and E were mutually exclusive. This was sometimes ignored, or incorrectly treated as meaning that they must be undertaken together, such that C and E were combined and treated as a one investment package.

Misunderstanding that the detail of the scenario was in respect of divisible projects. Incorrect approaches here included the failure to use the remaining funds in a proportionate way for the next ranked project.

Some candidates incorrectly took an indivisible approach to the projects, for example by calculating NPVs of different combinations of projects, thereby wasting a lot of valuable time.

Other errors encountered included:

- Ranking projects by absolute NPV, rather than by profitability index
- Calculating profitability index as investment/NPV, rather than NPV/Investment, and therefore ranking the projects in completely the reverse order to the correct one.

Part (b) common errors:

Not providing enough detail in the explanation such as describing a range of cash flows without explaining the need to use a present value approach and/or lacking precision.

Some candidates incorrectly believed that EAC is calculated by dividing the NPV of a cycle by the length of the cycle in years.

As with any requirement to 'explain', candidates need to write in enough detail in relation to the marks on offer. For example, one sentence or two short bullet points are highly unlikely to score more than one mark.

Part (c) common errors:

Some candidates incorrectly believed that the real approach ignored inflation.

Weaker responses often lack such structure and terms are sometimes used in a 'scattergun' approach in the hope that something will 'stick' and score a mark or two. Such an approach displays uncertainty surrounding the meaning of the terms.

There was some evidence of confusion between deflation and discounting when discussing real and nominal cash flows.

Examples of concepts that scored no marks included discussing inflation in very general terms such as in relation to macroeconomic policy or discussing probability analysis, sensitivity analysis, and the relative merits of NPV and IRR.

294 CABRERAS CO (MAR/JUN 2021)

Key answer tips

In part (a) remember that when looking at equivalent annual cost calculations, it's the cheapest option that you are looking to recommend. Plus, it isn't enough to just compare NPVs as they are not calculated on a like for like basis. Understanding that a net present cost that lasts for 3 years and then has to be spent again isn't comparable to one that lasts for four years before it has to be spent again will help with your understanding of why and how the EAC is calculated.

This understanding will help you put together your answer for part (b) too. You may not be able to replicate the model answer for this in full, but if you can make four separate points about why NPV alone isn't appropriate and why EAC is more useful, you should pick up the available marks.

Part (c) tests straightforward knowledge, but you may feel that you don't know enough to write six marks' worth of answer. Remember that there are two distinctions with discounted cash flow methods – the use of discounting to take into account the time value of money and the fact that they use cash flows rather than profits. Treat these two elements separately in your answer to pick up maximum marks. Then, as long as the cost of capital is known by the business concerned, the DCF methods provide clear decision rules, while other methods tend to be more subjective in terms of the targets that are set.

The highlighted words are key phrases that markers are looking for.

(a) Optimal replacement interval

	t0	t1	t2	t3	t4
	$000	$000	$000	$000	$000
Three-year interval					
Purchase cost		(800.0)			
Maintenance cost (W1)		(20.0)	(21.0)	(22.1)	
Fuel cost		(28.0)	(33.0)	(38.0)	
Resale value (W2)				270.0	
Net cash flow	0.0	(848.0)	(54.0)	210.0	
Present value factors at 8%	1.000	0.926	0.857	0.794	
Present value	0.0	(785.2)	(46.3)	166.7	
Net present value	(664.8)				
Equivalent annual cost (W3)	(258.0)				

	t0	t1	t2	t3	t4
	$000	$000	$000	$000	$000
Four-year interval					
Purchase cost		(800.0)			
Maintenance cost (W1)		(20.0)	(21.0)	(22.1)	(23.2)
Fuel cost		(28.0)	(33.0)	(38.0)	(43.0)
Safety test (W4)				(64.0)	
Resale value (W5)					202.5
Net cash flow	0.0	(848.0)	(54.0)	(124.1)	136.3
Present value factors at 8%	1.000	0.926	0.857	0.794	0.735
Present value	0.0	(785.2)	(46.3)	(98.5)	100.2
Net present value	(829.8)				
Equivalent annual cost (W6)	(250.5)				

Recommendation:

The four-year replacement interval has the lowest equivalent annual cost and on an expected cost basis, Cabreras Co should replace the Beast every four years.

However, it is a close decision and there is a 20% chance that the cost of the government test will be $120,000 and this would make the four-year interval more expensive than the three-year option (W7). Also, Cabreras Co should consider that it has only looked at three and four-year replacement intervals. Other, potentially cheaper, intervals should be considered.

Workings

(W1) $20,000 × 1.05 = $21,000

$20,000 × 1.05^2 = $22,050

$20,000 × 1.05^3 = $23,153

(W2) $800,000 × 0.6 × 0.75 × 0.75 = $270,000

(W3) NPV/3-year annuity factor at 8% = $664,800/2.577 = $258,000

(W4) $50,000 × 0.8 + $120,000 × 0.2 = $64,000

(W5) $800,000 × 0.6 × 0.75 × 0.75 × 0.75 = $202,500

(W6) NPV/4-year annuity factor at 8% = $829,800/3.312 = $250,500

(W7) Effect of government test costing $120,000

	t0	t1	t2	t3	t4
	$000	$000	$000	$000	$000
Four-year interval					
Purchase cost		(800.0)			
Maintenance cost (W1)		(20.0)	(21.0)	(22.1)	(23.2)
Fuel cost		(28.0)	(33.0)	(38.0)	(43.0)
Safety test				**(120.0)**	
Resale value					202.5
Net cash flow	0.0	(848.0)	(54.0)	(180.1)	136.3
Present value factors at 8%	1.000	0.926	0.857	0.794	0.735
Present value	0.0	(785.2)	(46.3)	(143.0)	100.2
Net present value	(874.3)				
Equivalent annual cost	(264.0)				

Note: (W7) is not required to get the marks available.

(b) Rationale behind equivalent annual cost (EAC) based decisions

In simple situations, choosing between one-off projects of different length lives is quite straight forward; the NPV technique is used to evaluate the costs and benefits of a project over its life and the project with the largest NPV is selected in order to maximise shareholder wealth.

However, when projects with different length lives can be endlessly repeated, and form part of an infinite chain of identical projects, then the situation is more complicated. In this situation, project NPVs cannot be meaningfully compared. Is a chain of three-year projects with an NPV of $20 per project better than a chain of five-year projects with an NPV of $30 per project?

To answer this, the NPV earned by the project needs to be related to the period of time required to earn it.

Deciding the optimal replacement interval for an asset which will be required for the foreseeable future is very similar to the problem of choosing between investment projects of different length lives which form part of an infinite chain of similar projects.

Each possible replacement interval is a project (for example, a three-year replacement interval project, a four-year replacement interval project, etc.). If the asset is going to be required by the business for the foreseeable future, then each replacement interval forms part of an infinite chain of similar replacement intervals.

To choose the optimal replacement interval, the NPV of each possible replacement interval needs to be calculated to take into account the time value of money and the costs and benefits which are spread across the interval.

In order to allow for the different lengths of the replacement intervals, the NPVs are divided by the annuity factor appropriate to their lives (three-year factors for a three-year interval, etc.). The resultant figure is the EAC. The EAC represents the cost payable at the end of each year of the replacement interval which is equivalent to the NPV of the replacement interval.

The calculation above allows for the present value cost of the replacement interval and the length of the interval. If it is assumed that continual replacement of like with like assets continues, EACs for different lengths of replacement interval can be compared meaningfully to find the optimal replacement interval.

(c) Discounted cash flow (DCF) based methods of investment appraisal include NPV, IRR and discounted payback.

They all share the same two advantages.

First, they allow for the time value of money and recognise that a $ received today is worth more than a $ received in one year's time.

The two commonly used non-discounted cash flow methods of investment appraisal, return on capital employed and payback, do not consider the time value of money.

Second, DCF methods are cash flow (rather than accounting profit) based. Cash is the lifeblood of a business and is used to pay the claims of stakeholders. Profit is an accounting concept. The amount of profit earned in a period is sometimes quite a subjective matter and depends upon the accounting policies followed. The amount of cash received in a period is a far more objective measure.

Return on capital employed is based upon accounting profit and ignores cash flow.

Both NPV and IRR have clear cut decision rules which should lead to the maximisation of shareholder wealth. Under NPV, any projects with positive NPVs should be adopted and the size of the NPV is directly related to the increase in shareholder wealth from adopting the project. Under IRR, projects with IRRs bigger than the company's cost of capital should be adopted, and if they are, shareholder wealth will increase.

Return on capital employed and payback have arbitrarily set targets based upon internal corporate targets.

NPV and IRR both consider returns earned throughout a project's life. Payback only considers returns up to the payback point, and as a result ignores later returns.

ACCA marking scheme

		Marks
(a)	Purchase cost	0.5
	3-year maintenance cost	1
	3-year fuel cost	1
	3-year resale value	1
	3-year NPV	1
	3-year EAC	0.5
	4th year maintenance	0.5
	4th year fuel	0.5
	Safety test cost	1
	4-year resale value	0.5
	4-year NPV	1
	4-year EAC	0.5
	Recommendation	2
		11
(b)	Discussion of EAC (up to 2 marks per relevant point)	4
(c)	Discussion of methods (up to 2 marks per relevant point)	5
Total		**20**

Extracts from examiner's comments

Part (a) common errors:

Many candidates combined the calculations for 3-year and 4-year replacements, but this approach is more complicated and tends to lead to more mistakes being made.

Many candidates have learnt how to deal with inflation correctly, but there were some candidates who still need to master this.

Many candidates did not show the detailed working for the inflation, and any errors were difficult to assess.

Another typical error is the mistiming of the cash flows such as the purchase cost (stated as being payable one year after delivery i.e., Year 1), resale value, and the safety test (stated as being at the beginning of the fourth year i.e., Year 3).

A few candidates did not discount cash flows, thereby making any subsequent 'EAC' figure incorrect because an NPV has not been computed.

Candidates should ensure that they put brackets or minus sign for cash outflows as otherwise negative items may be treated as positive when the cash flows are totalled.

A few candidates failed to recognise that the normal assumption for the NPV cash flows is that the asset is disposed of on the last day of the last year of either the 3-year or 4-year replacement intervals.

Since the question was specific for three-year and four-year replacement intervals, some candidates unnecessarily spent time calculating the residual values for 1 and 2-year replacement intervals and included them in their NPV cash flows.

Some candidates included depreciation in the NPV cash flows.

A justification should be provided and answers without justification, for example, "choose 4-year cycle" only will not get the required mark allocated.

Part (b) common errors

Candidates need to discuss that for a continual replacement of an asset, a meaningful comparison using NPV's of different lengths of replacement intervals is not possible.

Time value of money was often mentioned but there was not enough discussion about relevant costs.

Many answers concentrated on the factors to be considered when making replacement decisions such as capital cost of the equipment, operating costs, resale value, taxation and inflation – which did not address the requirement of the reasons why replacement interval decisions should be based on EAC.

Part (c) common errors

Candidates must recognise that for a requirement worth five marks needing them to 'discuss' the answer should yield more than brief points, sometimes comprising sentences of fewer than six words and/or where the technical discussion is unsatisfactory.

It was common to see that the only discussion on offer was about time value of money and many answers scored limited credit as a result.

Often there was a lack of comparison between the discounted cash flow and non-discounted cash flow methods.

295 HAWKER CO (SEP/DEC 2021)

Key answer tips

Part (a) compares a 'borrow to buy' and a lease option for acquiring the use of an asset. The calculations include taxation, so don't forget to include tax savings for any expenses such as the lease payments and the emissions tax. Be very careful with the timings in this type of question. Leases are usually paid in advance and often their first cash flow is at time period zero. But because taxation is calculated at the end of an accounting period and often then paid (and saved) a year in arrears, it may be (as is the case here) that the taxation in relation to the lease payments doesn't start until time period 2. Also remember that this is a finance decision, not an overall project decision, so the calculated values will be net present costs rather than net present benefits and the option with the lowest present cost should be chosen.

Part (b) requires more practical reasons to lease an asset rather than buy it. Note that any more than two reasons will not be marked, so pick your best two and write them in enough detail to pick up two marks each. Making a point and then explaining it should be enough for each reason chosen.

For part (c), note that only advantages are required, not disadvantages. There are six marks available here for discussing three things. Each advantage must be discussed fully to pick up the marks. For example, simply stating that NPV correlates directly with shareholder wealth may pick up one mark, but expanding on that by saying what that means and why IRR doesn't have the same advantage will enable both marks to be picked up. Don't be afraid to give examples to help explain a discussion point. For instance, a small project may only bring a small NPV to the business, but may have a very large IRR. The IRR would suggest that shareholders will become significantly wealthier, but if the project is small, that will not be the case.

The highlighted words are key phrases that markers are looking for.

(a) Option 1 – Borrow and buy

Year	**0**	**1**	**2**	**3**	**4**	**5**
	$	$	$	$	$	$
Purchase price	(34,000)					
Residual value					14,000	
TAD benefits			1,000	1,000	1,000	1,000
Emissions tax		(600)	(600)	(600)	(600)	
Emissions tax benefits			120	120	120	120
Net cash flow	(34,000)	(600)	520	520	14,520	1,120
Discount at 4%	1.000	0.962	0.925	0.889	0.855	0.822
	(34,000)	(577)	481	462	12,412	921

Present value cost of borrowing: $(20,320)

Option 2 – Lease

Year	**0**	**1**	**2**	**3**	**4**	**5**
	$	$	$	$	$	$
Lease payment	(6,000)	(6,000)	(6,000)	(6,000)		
Lease payment tax benefits			1,200	1,200	1,200	1,200
Net cash flow	(6,000)	(6,000)	(4,800)	(4,800)	1,200	1,200
Discount at 4%	1.000	0.962	0.925	0.889	0.855	0.822
	(6,000)	(5,769)	(4,438)	(4,267)	1,026	986

Present value cost of leasing: $(18,462)

Hawker Co should lease the new vehicle because this option has the lower present value cost.

(b) Reasons, other than after-tax cost, for leasing

Leasing can offer more flexibility than borrowing and buying. Lease periods can be for less than an asset's useful life, or break clauses may be offered by the lessor. If technology changes and the asset becomes out of date before the end of its expected life, the lessee does not have to keep on using it.

– Under the 'borrow and buy' option, Hawker Co would carry the risk of the vehicle failing to achieve a disposal value of $14,000. If leased, this risk would be transferred to the lessor.

– The lessee may not have enough cash to pay for the vehicle and might have difficulty obtaining a bank loan. If this is the case, leasing may be the only way of getting use of the asset.

(Note: Only two reasons were required.)

(c) Advantages of NPV over IRR in investment appraisal

In most simple accept or reject decisions, IRR and NPV will select the same project. However, NPV has certain advantages over IRR.

The NPV of a proposed project, if calculated at an appropriate cost of capital, is equal to the increase in shareholder wealth which the project offers. In this way, NPV is directly linked to the assumed objective of the company, the maximisation of shareholder wealth. IRR calculates the rate of return on projects, and although this can show the attractiveness of the project to shareholders, it does not measure the absolute increase in wealth which the project offers.

NPV looks at absolute increases in wealth and thus can be used to compare projects of different sizes. IRR looks at relative rates of return and in doing so ignores the size of the investment projects.

NPV is not subject to the technical difficulties which limit the usefulness of the IRR method.

First, in situations involving multiple reversals in project cash flows, it is possible that the IRR method may produce multiple IRRs (that is, there can be more than one interest rate which would produce an NPV of zero). If decision makers are aware of the existence of multiple IRRs, it is still possible for them to make the correct accept or reject decision using IRR, but if unaware, they could make the wrong decision.

Second, in situations of mutually exclusive projects, it is possible that the IRR method will (incorrectly) rank projects in a different order to the NPV method. This is due to the inbuilt reinvestment assumption of the IRR method. The IRR method assumes that any net cash inflows generated during the life of the project will be reinvested at the project's IRR. NPV, on the other hand, assumes a reinvestment rate equal to the cost of capital. Generally NPV's assumed reinvestment rate is more realistic and hence it ranks projects correctly.

Finally, NPV can be used in situations where the cost of capital changes from year to year. Although IRR can be calculated in these circumstances, it can be difficult to make accept or reject decisions as it is difficult to know which cost of capital to compare it with.

ACCA marking scheme

		Marks
(a)	Disposal value	1
	TAD	1
	TAD benefits	1
	CO_2 tax	1
	CO_2 tax benefits	1
	PV of borrowing	1
	Lease payment	1
	Tax relief thereon	1
	PV of leasing	1
	Decision	1
		10
(b)	1st reason	2
	2nd reason	2
		4
(c)	1st advantage	2
	2nd advantage	2
	3rd advantage	2
		6
Total		**20**

Extracts from examiner's comments

Part (a) common errors:

Some candidates wasted time, but did not lose marks, by including the saved running costs under both options.

Many candidates incorrectly used the after-tax weighted average cost of capital of 8% for one or both options.

Some candidates erroneously included the loan interest payments (and in some cases a loan repayment schedule) in their cash flow forecasts for borrowing to buy

For example, the government CO2 emissions tax, payable under Option 1, was paid by the lessor under Option 2 (leasing), and therefore was not a cost to be included in Hawker's cash flow forecast for Option 2.

Other errors included not treating tax as payable one year in arrears, which, under Option 2, means commencing the tax benefits of leasing in year 2 since the lease payments are made at the start of each year, and, under Option 1, incorrectly placing the residual value in year 5, when the value of $14,000 is clearly stated as being at the end of the 4 year period.

Part (b) common errors:

Some candidates seemed to ignore the requirement for reasons 'other than possible after-tax cost advantages' and instead discussed issues such as tax relief on lease payments, maintenance costs saved (as they would be borne by the lessor) and the lessor paying the CO2 emissions tax. Such reasons attracted no marks.

Stating that leasing is not a form of debt finance, which is incorrect.

When asked to discuss two reasons for 4 marks, it should be clear that each reason is worth 2 marks. For a reason to attract 2 marks, it should be discussed in sufficient detail in that the reason should be developed and/or illustrated (best done by reference to the scenario i.e., the circumstances of Hawker).

Part (c) common errors:

Stating that the NPV of a proposed project is equal to the increase in shareholder wealth offered by the project is a correct statement, but, for two marks, should be supplemented by stating that this is an advantage over IRR because the IRR does not measure the absolute increase in value arising from the proposed project. IRR ignores the size of the project, instead IRR considers relative rates of return.

The requirement asks for advantages of using NPV over IRR and therefore the two methods must be compared when discussing each advantage.

296 MELPLASH CO (MAR/JUN 2022)

Key answer tips

Part (a) is an excellent question to use to practise the various methods of investment appraisal. Remember that ROCE uses profits whereas the other methods use cash flows. More particularly, ROCE uses operating profits divided by capital. Capital cash flows such as the initial investment and redemption amounts are not part of operating cash flows or profits.

ACCA encourage the use of spreadsheet formulae where possible, including the =NPV and =IRR functions. You may find that these can speed up your work in the exam, making it less time pressured.

There are a lot of marks available for the discussion in part (b) here. Make sure you make comments about each individual method, both positive and negative, rather than trying to find 9 marks from an overall viewpoint. Breaking it down this way will enable more marks to be picked up. The question asks for discussion of the techniques and for advice, so make sure that you do come to a conclusion on financial acceptability as there will be at least 1 specific mark for that.

The highlighted words are key phrases that markers are looking for.

(a) (i) Calculation of net present value (NPV)

Year	**0**	**1**	**2**	**3**	**4**
	$m	$m	$m	$m	$m
Revenue		500.00	954.00	898.88	476.40
Variable costs		(350.00)	(667.80)	(629.20)	(333.48)
Contribution		150.00	286.20	269.68	142.92
Fixed costs		(120.00)	(132.00)	(145.20)	(159.72)
Investment	(220.00)				30.00
Net cash flow	(220.00)	30.00	154.20	124.48	13.20
Discount at 14%	1.000	0.877	0.769	0.675	0.592
Present values	(220.00)	26.31	118.58	84.02	7.81

Net present value = $16.72m

Alternatively, once you have calculated the net cash flows, you can use the =NPV function in the exam to calculate the PV of the cash flows from time period 1 onwards. Then deduct the time period 0 cash outflow to determine the NPV.

= NPV(type in the rate as 14% or 0.14,select the cells containing the net cash flows)

Workings:

Calculation of income

Year	**1**	**2**	**3**	**4**
Inflated selling price ($/unit)	20,000	21,200	22,472	23,820
Demand (units/yr)	25,000	45,000	40,000	20,000
Revenue ($m/yr)	500.00	954.00	898.88	476.40

Calculation of variable costs

Year	**1**	**2**	**3**	**4**
Inflated variable cost ($/unit)	14,000	14,840	15,730	16,674
Demand (units/yr)	25,000	45,000	40,000	20,000
Variable cost ($m/yr)	350.00	667.80	629.20	333.48

Example answer in a spreadsheet:

	A	B	C	D	E	F	G	H
1	(a) (i)	sales volume (units)			25000	45000	40000	20000
2								
3				**t0**	**t1**	**t2**	**t3**	**t4**
4				$m	$m	$m	$m	$m
5		Initial investment		-220.00				
6		Residual value						30.00
7		Sales			500.00	954.00	898.88	476.41
8		Variable costs			-350.00	-667.80	-629.22	-333.48
9		Fixed costs			-120.00	-132.00	-145.20	-159.72
10								
11		Total cash flows		-220.00	30.00	154.20	124.46	13.20
12								
13		PV years 1-4 ($m)	236.79					
14		yr 0 cash flow ($m)	- 220.00					
15		**Total NPV ($m)**	**16.79**					
16								
17		**Example formulae used:**						
18								
19		In cell H7	=20000*1.06*1.06*1.06*H1/1000000 OR =20000*1.06^3*H1/1000000					
20		In cell H8	=-14000*1.06*1.06*1.06*H1/1000000					
21		In cell C13	=NPV(14%,E11:H11)					
22		In cell C15	=C13+C14					

Notes:

As shown in cell H7, inflation is cumulative. In this cell, three years' worth of inflation at 6% can be included, by multiplying by 1.06 three times or by showing *1.06^3. The symbol ^ represents the power function in the spreadsheet and is found by using shift and 6.

The NPV function in the spreadsheet can only be used from time period 1 onwards. The time period 0 cash flow has to be included separately.

(ii) Calculation of internal rate of return (IRR)

Year	**0**	**1**	**2**	**3**	**4**
	$m	$m	$m	$m	$m
Net cash flow	(220.00)	30.00	154.20	124.48	13.20
Discount at 20%	1.000	0.833	0.694	0.579	0.482
Present values	(220.00)	24.99	107.01	72.07	6.36

Net present value = $(9.57)m

IRR = L + ((H – L) × (N_L/(N_L – N_H)))

IRR = 14 + ((20 – 14) × (16.72/(16.72 + 9.57))) = 17.82%

Alternatively, you can use the =IRR formula on the spreadsheet available in the exam:

= IRR(select the cells containing the net cash flows)

Example answer in a spreadsheet (follows on from the spreadsheet figures in (a) (i):

	A	B	C	D	E	F	G	H	I
24	(a) (ii)	**IRR**	**17.7%**						
25									
26		Formula used:	=IRR(D11:H11)						

Notes:

The IRR function in the spreadsheet can only be used if the cash flows are shown year by year in time order. They can be in columns (as for this spreadsheet) or rows.

Using the IRR function can be substantially quicker than working through a linear interpolation calculation.

(iii) Calculation of payback period

Year	**0**	**1**	**2**	**3**
	$m	$m	$m	$m
Net cash flow	(220.00)	30.00	154.20	124.48
Cumulative cash flow	(220.00)	(190.00)	(35.80)	88.68

Payback period = 2 + (12 × (35.80/(35.80 + 88.68))) = 2 years 3 months

Or payback period = 2 + (35.80/(35.80 + 88.68)) = 2.3 years

Example answer in a spreadsheet (follows on from the spreadsheet figures in (a) (i) and (ii):

	A	B	C	D	E	F	G	H	I
28	(a) (iii)			**t0**	**t1**	**t2**	**t3**	**t4**	
29		Total cash flows from (i)		-220.00	30.00	154.20	124.46	13.20	
30		cumulative cash flows		-220.00	-190.00	-35.80	88.66	101.87	
31									
32		Payback occurs after:	2 years and						
33			4 months		Months calculation:			3.4516	
34				Formula to calclate the months:				=-F30/G29*12	

(iv) Calculation of return on capital employed (ROCE)

Total cash inflow = \$30.00m + \$154.20m + \$124.48m + \$(13.20 – 30)m = \$291.88m

Total depreciation = \$220m – \$30m = \$190m

Total accounting profit = \$291.88m – \$190m = \$101.88m

Average accounting profit = \$101.88m/4 = \$25.47m

Average investment = (\$220m + \$30m)/2) = \$125m

ROCE = (\$25.47m/\$125m) × 100% = 20.4%

Example answer in a spreadsheet (follows on from the spreadsheet figures in (a) (i) to (iii):

	A	B	C	D	E	F	G	H	I
36	(a) (iv)	Operating cash flows (sales – variable & fixed costs)			30.00	154.20	124.46	- 16.80	
37		Less: depreciation			47.50	47.50	47.50	47.50	
38		Profit			- 17.50	106.70	76.96	- 64.30	101.87
39		average annual profit							25.47
40									
41		average capital	125						
42									
43		**ROCE**	**20.4%**						
44									
45		Example formulae used:							
46		In cell E37 (and F, G and H on the same row)			=(220-30)/4				
47		In cell I39			=I38/4				
48		In cell C41			=(220+30)/2				
49		In cell C43			=I39/C41				
50		The answer in cell C43 is formatted as a percentage							

(b) Net present value (NPV)

NPV uses cash flows rather than subjective profits. It takes into account the time value of money and the whole investment life. It is an absolute measure, enabling better business planning. The cost of capital it uses takes into account the risk of the investment and its financing. However, the results of the NPV calculation will depend on whether the cost of capital has been accurately estimated.

If the options which the board is considering are mutually exclusive, NPV can be used to rank them, as it indicates the effect on shareholder wealth. However, if shareholders have a short time horizon, they may not be prepared to wait for an investment to generate returns over its later life, even if it does have the best NPV.

Internal rate of return (IRR)

IRR takes into account the time value of money, cash flows and the whole life of the investment. However, whilst IRR can be calculated without knowing the company's cost of capital, a benchmark is needed to determine whether the IRR is acceptable or not.

If IRR is being used for comparison, it does not indicate which investment will generate more wealth for shareholders. It may give a different result to NPV because rather than being an indicator of wealth creation, it shows how sensitive the investment is to changes in the cost of capital. In some situations, there is more than one IRR.

Payback

Payback has the advantage of using cash flows. It indicates when the investment will break even and whether this is before projected cash flows become very uncertain. However, payback ignores the cash flows after the payback period, which for years 3–4 here are a significant proportion of total cash flows. It also ignores the total return on the investment. The simple payback figure ignores the time value of money, although a discounted payback figure can be calculated. The payback target is subjective.

Using payback to compare investments may result in choosing shorter-term investments giving immediate returns, rather than investments offering greater returns in the longer term. However, investments with a shorter period for recouping the amount invested may be preferred if Melplash Co has liquidity problems.

Return on capital employed (ROCE)

The ROCE method may reflect the wishes of shareholders that the company generates sufficient profits and does consider the entire life of the investment. However, the choice of an acceptable rate is subjective, here the justification for choosing the 20% figure is unclear. ROCE does not take into account the time value of money. It is possible that an investment which increases company value will be rejected if its ROCE is below the target ROCE. The acceptability of the ROCE may also depend on the assumptions about realisable value at the end of the project.

As ROCE is a percentage measure, it can be used to compare this investment with other options. However, the ROCE does not indicate the absolute change in shareholder wealth generated by different investments.

Advice

The investment is acceptable using three of the four methods, but fails the payback test which the directors have set. However, the directors should choose to go ahead with the investment if they can, on the basis that it has a positive NPV and therefore will increase long-term shareholder wealth. If the directors are concerned about the uncertainties of the income in later years, they should carry out sensitivity analysis.

ACCA marking scheme

			Marks
(a)	(i)	Income	1
		Variable costs	1
		Fixed costs	1
		Initial investment	0.5
		Residual value	0.5
		PVs and NPV	1
			5
	(ii)	IRR setup	1
		IRR calculation	1
			2
	(iii)	Payback	**1**
	(iv)	Average accounting profit	1
		Average investment	1
		ROCE	1
			3
(b)	NPV		2
	IRR		2
	Payback		2
	ROCE		2
	Advice		1
			9
Total			**20**

Extracts from examiner's comments

Part (a) (i) common errors:

The selling price and variable costs per motorcycle, together with the incremental fixed costs, are all stated in year 1 price terms and therefore it is **incorrect** to apply the expected inflation to the year 1 figures. This was the most common error on this question.

Failure to compound the inflation e.g., the year 3 selling price needs to be the year 1 selling price inflated by two years' worth of 6% per year inflation, $20,000 * 1.06^2 = $20,000 * 1.1236 = $22,472. Sometimes errors occur because of careless use of spreadsheet functionality in that the 6% per year inflation figure is applied to the year 1 figure in both year 3 and year 4, instead of applying the inflation figure to the prior year e.g., the year 3 selling price should be 6% higher than the year 2 selling price

Inclusion of the initial investment in year 1

Omission of the residual value

Careless use of the sum formula such that the whole column of figures for a year were added, which caused the contribution to be double counted

Errors of magnitude such as income and variable costs being shown in $ or $000 but fixed costs shown incorrectly as $m.

Part (a) (ii) common errors:

Some candidates (those who used linear interpolation) calculated two new NPVs at nominal discount rates other than 14%. This is unnecessary and wastes valuable time. The NPV at 14% in (a) (i) can be used in conjunction with one other NPV at a different rate.

Whilst this calculation was generally done well, some candidates made careless mistakes such as errors of arithmetic in the IRR formula or calculating incorrectly the 2nd NPV by using present values (PVs) at 14% rather than the net cash flow figures.

IRR can be calculated using spreadsheet functionality. This is the quickest and most efficient way of performing this task. Typing "=IRR" and then selecting the row of net cash flow figures, placed inside brackets, returns the IRR for that series of cash flows.

For those using the =IRR formula, care must be taken to select the correct figures. Some candidates incorrectly used the PVs instead of the net cash flow figures and hence scored zero marks here.

Part (a) (iii) common errors:

Aside from careless arithmetic errors, the most common mistake in this part-question was to use the present value of the cash flows and not the net cash flow figures themselves. Such responses were therefore calculating the discounted payback period, maybe unwittingly, and could not gain the one mark on offer.

Part (a) (iv) common errors:

Understanding the difference between cash flow and accounting profit is fundamental knowledge, which was lacking in many responses which made no attempt to deduct deprecation.

The second most common error was to include the $30m of residual value as part of the project profit.

The calculation of the denominator requires the average investment to be found. This is clearly in the requirement "...based on average investment".

Therefore, the initial investment of $220m and the residual value of $30m need to be averaged.

Part (b) common errors:

Too much focus on a discussion of the results calculated in part (a) rather than the suitability of the techniques.

A scattergun, short bullet point approach trying to cover too much too quickly. This approach rarely scores many, if any, marks and is to be avoided as the part (b) requirement states "Discuss....", meaning that a discussion is required.

The advice was not clear. Instead of being based solely on NPV, some hedging of the advice took place where all four investment techniques were discussed, with no clear conclusion.

297 CLOVER CO (SEP/DEC 2022)

Key answer tips

Part (a). The equivalent annual cost formula is not given to you in the exam, so you must learn it as part of your revision. Use the spreadsheet to lay out the cash flows of each option and calculate their net present costs. You may wish to use the NPV spreadsheet formula, but you don't have to. Once you've calculated the NPC, then use it in the EAC formula. Remember that the results here are costs rather than project values, so the cheaper the better. Note that there are 4 marks available in part ii, so simply stating which is cheaper is not enough. Look for clues in the question to determine what else to discuss. For instance, consider why they have mentioned the different lengths of commitment, or the difference in how the residual values have been determined.

Part (b) is a frequently tested discussion of the theory behind the benefits of discounted cash flow (DCF) methods of investment appraisal. Note that only reasons why DCF methods are superior are asked for, so don't focus on any disadvantages. To earn 6 marks, you should aim to write 3 well-rounded discussion points with the aim of picking up 2 marks for each. It isn't therefore enough to say that DCF methods use the time value of money, whereas non-DCF ones don't. This is a simple statement rather than a well-rounded discussion point. Get the second mark by explaining why this is important. Apply this methodology to each point that you make.

The highlighted words are key phrases that markers are looking for.

Calculations have been done using a spreadsheet, rounding differences may occur in candidates' answers, for example, relating to discount factors.

(a) (i) Equivalent annual cost of Machine 1 (three-year cycle)

Year	**1**	**2**	**3**
Residual value			200,000
Maintenance cost	(52,000)	(56,160)	(60,653)
Operating cost	(300,000)	(330,000)	(363,000)
Net cash flow	(352,000)	(386,160)	(223,653)
13% discount factor	0.885	0.783	0.693
Present values	(311,504)	(302,363)	(154,991)
Sum of PVs	(768,858)		
Initial investment	(2,000,000)		
NPV	(2,768,858)		

EAC = ($2,768,858)/2.361 = ($1,172,748)

Equivalent annual cost of machine 2 (five year cycle)

Year	**1**	**2**	**3**	**4**	**5**
Residual value					150,000
Maintenance cost	(39,000)	(41,340)	(43,820)	(46,450)	(49,237)
Operating cost	(248,000)	(277,760)	(311,091)	(348,422)	(390,233)
Net cash flow	(287,000)	(319,100)	(354,912)	(394,872)	(289,469)
13% discount factor	0.885	0.783	0.693	0.613	0.543
Present values	(253,995)	(249,855)	(245,954)	(242,056)	(157,182)
Sum of PVs	(1,149,042)				
Initial investment	(2,500,000)				
NPV	(3,649,042)				

EAC = ($3,649,042)/3.517 = ($1,037,544)

Example answer in a spreadsheet:

	A	B	C	D	E	F	G	H	I	J	K
1	a i	PV of machine 1 cash flows						Discount	PV		
2			cost	maintenance	operating	residual	Total	13%			
3		t0	- 2,000,000				- 2,000,000	1	- 2,000,000		
4		t1		- 52,000	- 300,000		- 352,000	0.885	- 311,520		
5		t2		- 56,160	- 330,000		- 386,160	0.783	- 302,363		
6		t3		- 60,653	- 363,000	200,000	- 223,653	0.693	- 154,991		
7									- 2,768,875	NPV	
8				annuity factor	EAC						
9		EAC 3 year cycle		2.361	- 1,172,755	=I7/D9					
10											
11											
12		PV of machine 2 cash flows						Discount	PV		
13			cost	maintenance	operating	residual	Total	13%			
14		t0	- 2,500,000				- 2,500,000	1	- 2,500,000		
15		t1		- 39,000	- 248,000		- 287,000	0.885	- 253,995		
16		t2		- 41,340	- 277,760		- 319,100	0.783	- 249,855		
17		t3		- 43,820	- 311,091		- 354,912	0.693	- 245,954		
18		t4		- 46,450	- 348,422		- 394,872	0.613	- 242,056		
19		t5		- 49,237	- 390,233	150,000	- 289,469	0.543	- 157,182		
20									- 3,649,042	NPV	
21				annuity factor	EAC						
22		EAC 5 year cycle		3.517	- 1,037,544	=I20/D22					
23											
24					135,211	=E22-E9					
25											
26	Note:										
27		Inflation of 8% added to machine 1's maintenance costs by multiplying the previous year's figure by 1.08									
28		Inflation of 10% added to machine 1's operating costs by multiplying the previous year's figure by 1.1									
29		Inflation of 6% added to machine 2's maintenance costs by multiplying the previous year's figure by 1.06									
30		Inflation of 12% added to machine 2's operating costs by multiplying the previous year's figure by 1.12									

Note: if you used non-rounded discount/annuity factors or the NPV formula within your spreadsheet answer, your answer will be slightly different due to rounding differences. Either method is acceptable in the exam.

(ii) Financial acceptability

Choosing between the two machines on financial grounds cannot be achieved using NPV, since they have different replacement cycles, reflecting their unequal lives. However, the two investment decisions can be compared using the equivalent annual cost (EAC) method, which indicates that Machine 2 should be chosen as it has a lower EAC than Machine 1. On financial grounds alone, therefore, Machine 2 with its five-year replacement cycle should be recommended.

Uncertainty

The future value of the residual value of Machine 1 is certain insofar as it will be a contractual commitment by the selling company. The future value of the residual value of Machine 2 is an estimate made by Clover Co and is therefore subject to uncertainty. The three-year replacement cycle might therefore be chosen, even though it has a higher EAC, because its residual value is more certain than that of the five-year replacement cycle. However, even if the residual value of Machine 2 were zero, Machine 2 would still have the lower EAC.

Obsolescence

Purchasing Machine 1 and committing to a three-year replacement cycle looks to carry little risk of Clover Co suffering from obsolescence due to technological advances. By contrast, purchasing Machine 2 and committing to a five-year replacement cycle appears to lead to significant obsolescence risk late in the life of the machine. The three-year replacement cycle might therefore be chosen, even though it has a higher EAC, because Clover Co believes it carries significantly less obsolescence risk.

Flexibility

Purchasing Machine 1 may give Clover Co greater flexibility in that its shorter replacement cycle could facilitate a more rapid response to changing technology through investment in other machines than the two under consideration, if such were to become available.

(b) Discounted cash flow (DCF) investment appraisal methods, such as net present value (NPV) and internal rate of return (IRR), are considered superior to non-DCF investment appraisal methods, such as payback and return on capital employed (ROCE), for a variety of reasons, as follows.

Time value of money

DCF investment appraisal methods are seen as superior to non-DCF methods because DCF methods take account of the time value of money by discounting future cash flows to their present values, while non-DCF methods ignore the time value of money. While DCF methods therefore give more weight in an investment appraisal to cash flows in the near future compared to cash flows in the distant future, payback ignores the amount and timing of cash flows within the payback period, while ROCE averages profit over the life of the project.

Cash flow basis

DCF investment appraisal methods are seen as superior to non-DCF methods because DCF methods use cash flows. Cash flows are not distorted by company-specific factors such as depreciation policy and amortisation decisions which can affect profit, for example, the average annual accounting profit used by ROCE. From this point of view, DCF methods can be seen as more objective than non-DCF methods.

Whole project considered

DCF investment appraisal methods consider cash flows over the whole life of an investment project, whereas payback ignores cash flows after the payback period. Investment decisions using payback period may therefore be sub-optimal in relation to the financial management objective of maximising shareholder wealth, because a project with a higher NPV might be rejected in favour of a project with a lower NPV but a shorter payback period.

ACCA marking scheme

			Marks
(a)	(i)	Initial investment	1
		Residual values	1
		Machine 1 maintenance costs	1
		Machine 1 operating costs	1
		Machine 1 PVs	1
		Machine 1 EAC	1
		Machine 2 maintenance costs	1
		Machine 2 operating costs	1
		Machine 2 PVs	1
		Machine 2 EAC	1
			10
	(ii)	Financial decision on EAC	1
		Uncertainty	1
		Obsolescence	1
		Other relevant points	1
			4
(b)	Time value of money		2
	Cash flow basis		2
	Whole project considered		1
	Other relevant points		1
			6
Total			**20**

Extracts from examiner's comments

Part (a) (i) common errors:

The application of the specific cost inflation of 8% per year for machine 1 (6% per year for machine 2) commenced in year 2 e.g. \$52,000 × 1.08 = \$56,160 with a further 8% inflation applied for year 3. An error seen here quite often was the application of two years' inflation in year 2, when only one year's inflation was needed, even when the correct year 1 cost had been entered.

Some candidates incorrectly omitted the maintenance and operating costs for the final year of the machine's life.

A common error in the EAC calculation was to simply divide the NPV by the number of years of the life of the machine. Such a calculation does not result in the EAC of the machine.

Improvements can be made by candidates presenting their work better. Examples of areas for improvement include displaying all the calculations in one column or using a column width which was too small resulting in a line of ######, which meant each column had to be expanded. Ideally, work should be presented as it would be in a professional accounting or finance environment.

Part (a) (ii) common errors

It should have been clear to candidates that a discussion requirement worth 4 marks was asking for more than just "choose machine x because it has a lower cost". Unfortunately, some candidate's responses offered little more than this.

Short bullet points of, for example, three or four words do not constitute a discussion and are usually not creditworthy.

Part (b) common errors:

The main issues with weaker responses were largely based upon not addressing the requirement and candidates just writing 'everything they know' about the four investment appraisal techniques. This often took the form of advantages and disadvantages of each method, and scored few, if any, marks. Other mistakes included the suggestion that IRR was a non-discounted cash flow method, which led to a comparison of IRR and NPV, and also stating that DCF methods gave a clear decision rule whereas ROCE and payback need a target, forgetting, however, that IRR also needs a target.

298 GINI CO (MAR/JUN 2023)

Key answer tips

Part (a). An 'expected' NPV in the FM exam means an NPV that includes an expected value calculation in its workings. The NPV itself is relatively straightforward. With a good level of practise before the exam, most learners should be able to pick up solid marks on this part of the question. The most difficult aspect is making sure to include inflation in the working capital balances before determining the incremental cash flows. Make sure to include a comment on the result to pick up the final mark.

Part (b) (i). The very first piece of information given in the question is that Gini is listed. This means that you can assume that their primary objective is that of shareholder wealth maximisation. Link this to the NPV result and you can pick up both marks available.

Part (b) (ii). Only discuss limitations and only discuss three of them. With 6 marks available, you should aim to write two separate points about each limitation. For instance, you could describe the limitation to pick up the first mark (e.g. EVs hide the variability (risk) of the outcome) and then explain it in relation to the specific project for the second mark (in this case, the fact that the variable cost could range between $40 and $70 could make a big difference to the overall NPV, but this is hidden).

The highlighted words are key phrases that markers are looking for.

(a) Project cash flows

Year	**1**	**2**	**3**	**4**	**5**
	$000	$000	$000	$000	$000
Sales (W1)	1,890	1,985	2,084	2,188	
Variable costs (W1)	(1,112)	(1,146)	(1,180)	(1,216)	
Fixed costs	(309)	(318)	(328)	(338)	
Taxable cash flow	**469**	**521**	**576**	**634**	
Taxation at 20%		(94)	(104)	(115)	(127)
Tax savings from t.a.d. (W2)		75	56	42	102
Residual value				125	
Working capital cash flows (W3)	(3)	(3)	(3)	109	
Net cash flows	**466**	**499**	**525**	**795**	**(25)**
Discount factors (12%)	0.893	0.797	0.712	0.636	0.567
Present values	**416**	**398**	**374**	**506**	**(14)**
Sum of PVs (t1-t4)	1,680				
Initial investment	(1,500)				
Initial working capital	(100)				
NPV	**80**				

The expected NPV is positive and is therefore financially acceptable. It should be noted, however, that this assumes that variable cost per unit is $54 which is not a possible value. There is a 60% chance that the variable cost per unit could be less than $54 which would have a beneficial effect on the NPV obtained but there is a 40% chance that the variable cost per unit could be more than $54 which will reduce the NPV, possibly resulting in a negative NPV.

Workings

(W1) Sales and variable cost

Year	1	2	3	4
Volume (000 units/year)	20	20	20	20
Sales price ($)	90.00	90.00	90.00	90.00
Inflated at 5% per year	94.50	99.23	104.19	109.40
Total sales ($000)	1,890	1,985	2,084	2,188
Expected VC per unit ($)	54.00	54.00	54.00	54.00
Inflated at 3% per year	55.62	57.29	59.01	60.78
Total VC ($000)	1,112	1,146	1,180	1,216

Expected variable cost per unit = ($40 × 0.2) + ($50 × 0.4) + ($60 × 0.2) + ($70 × 0.2) = $54

(W2) Tax savings from tax allowable depreciation (t.a.d.)

Year	1	2	3	4
Cost/WDV b/f	1,500	1,125	844	633
t.a.d. at 25%/balancing allowance	375	281	211	
WDV c/f	1,125	844	633	0
Residual value				125
Balancing allowance				508

(W3) Working capital cash flows

Year	0	1	2	3	4
Working capital balance ($000)	100	100	100	100	0
Inflated at 3%		103	106	109	0
Incremental cash flows	(100)	(3)	(3)	(3)	109

Example answer in a spreadsheet:

	A	B	C	D	E	F	G	H	I
1	(a)			t0	t1	t2	t3	t4	t5
2		Operating cash flows							
3									
4		Sales revenue			1,890,000	1,984,500	2,083,725	2,187,911	
5		Variable costs	W1		-1,112,400	-1,145,772	-1,180,145	-1,215,550	
6		Fixed costs			- 309,000	- 318,270	- 327,818	- 337,653	
7									
8		Total op cash flows			468,600	520,458	575,762	634,709	
9		Tax on op cash flows (1 year in arrears)				- 93,720	- 104,092	- 115,152	- 126,942
10		Tax savings from tad	W2			75,000	56,250	42,188	101,563
11									
12		Purch/residual		-1,500,000				125,000	
13									
14		WC	W3	- 100,000	- 3,000	- 3,090	- 3,183	109,273	
15									
16		total c/f		-1,600,000	465,600	498,648	524,737	796,017	- 25,379
17									
18		NPV 1-5		1,678,213	=NPV(12%,E16:I16)				
19		NPV		78,213	=D18+D16				
20									
21		A positive NPV means the project is financially acceptable and so should be accepted							
22									
23		Example formulae used:							
24		In cell E4:	=20000*90*1.05						
25		In cell F4:	=E4*1.05						
26		In cell E5:	=-20000*D32*1.03						
27		In cell F5:	=E5*1.03						
28		In cell F8:	=-E8*20%						
29									
30	W1	**Variable cost working**		Expected variable cost per unit					
31				54	=40*0.2+50*0.4+60*0.2+70*0.2				
32									
33	W2	**Tax savings due to tax allowable depreciation working**							t5
34				t0	t1	t2	t3	t4	
35		Asset cost/WDV		1,500,000		1,125,000	843,750	632,813	
36		tax allowable depreciation 25%			375,000	281,250	210,938		
37		tax written down value			1,125,000	843,750	632,813		
38		Sale proceeds						125,000	
39		Balancing allowance						507,813	
40									
41		Tax savings at 20% (1 year in arrears)				75,000	56,250	42,188	101,562.50
43		Note: asset purchase at t0, but assume first tax allowable depreciation is given at t1							
44									
45		Example formulae used:							
46		In cell E36:	=D35*25%						
47		In cell E37:	=D35-E36						
48		In cell H39:	=H35-H38						
49		In cell F41:	=E36*20%						
50		In cell I41:	=H39*20%						

	A	B	C	D	E	F	G	H
52	W3	**Working capital working**						
53				t0	t1	t2	t3	t4
54		balance		100,000	103,000	106,090	109,273	-
55		Incremental cash flow		- 100,000	- 3,000	- 3,090	- 3,183	109,273
56								
57		Note: assume the working capital investment is released at the end of the project						
58								
59		Example formulae used:						
60		In cell E54:	=D54*1.03					
61		In cell D55:	=-D54					
62		In cell E55:	=-(E54-D54)					

Alternative method of net cash flow calculation:

Year	**1**	**2**	**3**	**4**	**5**
	$000	$000	$000	$000	$000
Taxable cash flow	469	521	576	634	
t.a.d	(375)	(281)	(211)	(508)	
Taxable profit	94	240	365	126	
Taxation at 20%		(19)	(48)	(73)	(25)
Add back t.a.d.	375	281	211	508	
After-tax cash flow	**469**	**502**	**528**	**561**	**(25)**
Residual value				125	
Working capital cash flows (W3)	(3)	(3)	(3)	109	
Net cash flows	**466**	**499**	**525**	**795**	**(25)**

(b) **(i)** Gini Co is a listed company and will therefore be a for-profit organisation with a primary objective to maximise shareholder wealth. A project's positive NPV represents the amount of value added to the company by undertaking the project. Given the positive NPV of $80,000 for LP500 (subject to the variable cost per unit), accepting the project will add $80,000 to the value of Gini Co and consequently, increase the shareholders' wealth.

Note: Full credit given for any negative NPV recommendation to reject due to the reduction in shareholder wealth.

(ii) **Subjective probabilities**

Probability estimation ideally requires historic data of the event frequency in order to give any reliability to the figures. Even then, past frequency/probability is not necessarily an indication of the future frequency/probability. There is little detail regarding the source of the probabilities used to determine the expected variable cost and if these are little more than an educated guess, this would undermine the credibility of the expected figure calculated.

Variability of the outcome

The variability of the outcomes is being ignored in the decision as the EV of the variable cost of $54 per unit gives no indication of the best and worst case figures ($40 and $70). There is a 40% (20% + 20%) probability that the variable cost could actually be more than $54. If that was to happen, the impact on the NPV could be significant – at a variable cost per unit of $60, there would be an increase in total variable cost of $96,000 per year after tax (20,000 × $6 × 0.8). Even without discounting, this would seem to indicate a negative NPV would result.

Attitude to risk

The previously highlighted problem of outcome variability would also mean that Gini Co's attitude to risk is also being ignored in its decision. If Gini Co has a cautious approach to risk, knowing that there could be a significant chance of negative NPV could result in it rejecting the project. On the other hand, a more adventurous approach to risk could see Gini Co being happier to accept the project, particularly with a 60% chance of variable cost per unit being less the $54 which would then increase the NPV further.

Long-run average

An expected value is essentially a long-run average over a sufficiently high number of repetitions and consequently may not be a possible outcome. Certainly, for the LP500 project, $54 as a unit variable cost is not one of the possible outcomes. There is no detail given as to whether the price volatility will be a regular/repetitive event or if it is one-off event which once resolved in the next year (say) results in the removal of the volatility for the remaining three years of the project.

Note: Only three limitations were asked for.

ACCA marking scheme			*Marks*
(a)	Sales revenue		1
	Expected variable cost per unit		1
	Total variable cost		1
	Fixed costs		0.5
	Tax liability		1
	t.a.d.		1
	t.a.d. benefit		1
	Tax timing		1
	Residual value		0.5
	Working capital (0–3)		1
	Working capital release		1
	PV at 12%		1
	Comment		1
			12
(b)	(i)	State objective	1
		Impact of NPV	1
			2
	(ii)	First limitation	2
		Second limitation	2
		Third limitation	2
			6
Total			**20**

Extracts from examiner's comments

Part (a) common errors:

Not applying inflation from year 1

Not recognising that initial investment and initial working capital amounts are shown as outflows in year 0 and not in year 1.

Candidates must identify whether tax allowances are granted on a reducing balance or a straight-line basis and whether the tax is payable immediately or in arrears.

The working capital should be shown after the tax figures as they do not have any tax impact. Some candidates added it to taxable profit and therefore affected the tax liability figures, for which no mark was awarded.

Some candidates showed the residual value in year 0 or year 5 and as cash outflow, for which no marks were awarded. Some candidates added the residual value to taxable profit, affecting the tax liability figure in year 5, for which no mark was awarded.

When using the =NPV formula, the formula computes the sum of the PVs from year 1 onwards. To execute the computation correctly, the year 0 cash outflows must be added separately. I strongly emphasise that you must show all workings, otherwise marks cannot be awarded if the final figure is incorrect.

It is important to not ignore the element of the requirement to comment on the financial acceptability, which should be based on the calculated figure; for example, the project should be accepted if the NPV is positive, i.e., greater than zero.

Part (b) (i) common errors:

Very few responses emphasised the use of the expected value of the variable cost per unit, and it is possible that the positive net present value may not be achievable.

Part (b) (ii) common errors:

Limitations need to be accurately stated. For example, saying that an expected value does not account for the range of values is incorrect, as all values are considered.

Generic points such as "it's complex" are not creditworthy. Some candidates mistakenly referred to profitability indices.

For both (b) (i) and (ii), the requirement was "discuss," and therefore, short bullet points do not address the requirement.

299 PULOROUGH CO (SEP/DEC 2023)

Key answer tips

The discussion aspects of this question are relatively frequently tested and relate to standard textbook knowledge. The NPV calculation in part (b) is straightforward and leads to more difficult calculations for sensitivity. Remember that when tax is included in an NPV, sensitivity calculations should include the effect on tax.

When you have access to a spreadsheet in the exam, IRR calculations, such as that needed for part (b) (iii) are much more straightforward than using linear interpolation. Make sure you're comfortable with using the =IRR formula.

The highlighted words in the written sections are key phrases that markers are looking for.

(a) Both risk and uncertainty deal with future situations where there are several possible outcomes arising from a decision to invest.

Analysis of risk is possible in situations where probabilities can be assigned to different outcomes and mathematical techniques can be used for analysis. The probability of each outcome is often determined on the basis of past experience, which is the approach Pulorough Co's finance director has taken when calculating the expected values of sales. Risk increases as the variability of returns increases.

Analysis of uncertainty applies to situations where it is not possible to assign probabilities to different outcomes. The position may be new or very different to what has happened before, so past experience cannot be used to determine probabilities. Uncertainty increases over time.

Because economic conditions may change significantly and uncertainty therefore exists, Pulorough Co's finance director may have taken an incorrect approach when calculating the expected values of sales. Past results may not be relevant as a basis for the probabilities of future sales.

(b) **(i)**

	1	**2**	**3**	**4**	**5**
	$000	$000	$000	$000	$000
Contribution	12,000	30,000	28,000	16,000	
Fixed costs	(2,500)	(2,650)	(2,756)	(2,839)	
Before-tax cash flow	9,500	27,350	25,244	13,161	
Tax liability at 25%		(2,375)	(6,838)	(6,311)	(3,290)
After-tax cash flow	9,500	24,975	18,407	6,850	(3,290)
Discount at 11%	0.901	0.812	0.731	0.659	0.593
Present values	8,560	20,280	13,455	4,514	(1,951)

	$000
Sum of present values	44,858
Initial investment	39,000
NPV	**5,858**

NPV is positive, therefore accept the investment.

(ii)

	1	2	3	4	5
	$000	$000	$000	$000	$000
Contribution	12,000	30,000	28,000	16,000	
Tax liability at 25%		(3,000)	(7,500)	(7,000)	(4,000)
Post tax contribution	12,000	27,000	20,500	9,000	(4,000)
Discount at 11%	0.901	0.812	0.731	0.659	0.593
Present values	10,812	21,924	14,986	5,931	(2,372)

	$000
Discounted post-tax contribution	51,281

Sensitivity = ($5,858,000/$51,281,000) × 100% = 11.4%

(iii) By interpolation:

	1	2	3	4	5
	$000	$000	$000	$000	$000
After-tax cash flow	9,500	24,975	18,407	6,850	(3,290)
Discount at 20%	0.833	0.694	0.579	0.482	0.402
Present values	7,914	17,333	10,657	3,302	(1,323)

	$000
Sum of present values	37,883
Initial investment	39,000
NPV	**(1,117)**

IRR = 11 + ((5,858/(5,858 – 1,117)) × (20 – 11)) = 18.6%

Sensitivity = ((18.6 – 11)/11) × 100% = 69.1%

By spreadsheet: (calculating the IRR of the after-tax cash flows T0 – T5 in (b) (i))

IRR = 18.4%

Sensitivity = ((18.4 – 11)/11) × 100% = 67.3%

(c) Description of methods

- Sensitivity analysis involves looking at what level of change in expected outcomes will mean a change in the decision, so that, for example, a decision to proceed with an investment project turns into a decision to reject it, or vice versa.
- Probability analysis involves looking at the likelihood that different outcomes will occur.

Likelihood of outcomes

Sensitivity analysis does not take into account the probabilities of outcomes occurring. Probability analysis shows how likely it is that outcomes will occur which will change the decision, such as the probability that an investment which is expected to have a positive net present value (NPV) will have a negative one.

Decision-making

Sensitivity analysis does not provide a simple indication of whether to undertake a project which is not expected to, but could, have a negative NPV. Sensitivity analysis indicates by how much variables will have to change for a project to have a negative NPV, but that figure does not tell the decision-maker whether the project should go ahead. The decision-maker will need to assess subjectively whether the level of change in a variable needed to change a decision is too small given the level of uncertainty.

Probability analysis can be used to calculate the expected NPV of the project, which can provide the decision-maker with a simple decision rule to go ahead if the expected NPV is positive.

However, if the decision-maker is also concerned about the dispersal of results and the likelihood of a negative NPV, probability analysis does not provide a simple decision rule. Simple probability analysis indicates the probability of making a loss, but the decision-maker will have to decide whether the probability is too large for their risk appetite. More sophisticated risk analysis, using standard deviations, can measure volatility of outcomes, but again the decision-maker has to determine what an unacceptable result would be.

Number of variables

Simple sensitivity analysis involves isolating the impact of each variable on the outcome. Probability analysis, by contrast, can allow for more than one variable changing by combining their probabilities and can also allow for the probabilities of different variables changing being interdependent.

ACCA marking scheme			
			Marks
(a)	Define risk		1
	Define uncertainty		1
	Additional points		1
			3
(b)	(i)	Contribution	1
		Fixed costs	1
		Taxation	1
		Present values	1
		Comment	1
			5
	(ii)	Contribution NPV	1
		Tax effects	1
		Contribution sensitivity	1
			3
	(iii)	2nd NPV calculation	1
		IRR calculation	1
		Discount rate sensitivity	1
			3
(c)	Sensitivity analysis		1
	Probability analysis		1
	Likelihood outcomes		1
	Decision making		1
	Number of variables		1
	Additional points		1
			6
Total			**20**

Extracts from examiner's comments

Part (a) common errors:

Responses here were often too brief with a typical response stating only that risk can be quantified but not uncertainty (or similar wording). This was likely to gain one mark at most.

Part (b) (i) common errors:

Omitting the fixed costs, despite the case stem clearly stating they were incremental and therefore relevant to the project.

Inflating the incremental fixed costs incorrectly at different yearly rates.

Not placing the tax liability in the correct time period, despite the case stem clearly stating that they were payable "one year in arrears".

Omitting the tax liability in year 5.

Not justifying the financial acceptability comment by failing to refer to the decision rule relevant to NPV, or indeed not including a comment at all, despite the requirement clearly asking for one.

Part (b) (ii) common errors:

When asked to perform a sensitivity analysis calculation, the basic structure of the percentage computation is usually reproduced and performed by prepared candidates, but too many candidates fail to take into account the tax effects of a change in a variable such as contribution per unit, or the payment of tax one year in arrears. Moreover, some candidates ignore the need to express the denominator of the sensitivity computation in present value terms.

Part (b) (iii) common errors:

When asked to perform sensitivity analysis on the discount rate, computation of the IRR was usually well executed by candidates but there were issues when using the IRR to calculate discount rate sensitivity. The difference between the calculated IRR figure and the company's discount rate was sometimes shown incorrectly as the discount rate sensitivity itself. Also, there were occasions where the incorrect 'base' was chosen from which to calculate the percentage change. Percentage changes are always computed using the original figure as the base.

Part (c) common errors:

Unfortunately, candidates' responses were often too short, expressing little more than a definition of each type of analysis, to have any chance of getting the marks on offer. Furthermore, responses were too often of variable quality and a number of answers were often disorganised and poorly expressed such as providing a list of brief points, evidencing a lack of planning or maybe a lack of knowledge.

Few candidates could clearly compare and contrast the two methods. Instead, with respect to each method, many appeared to write all that they knew about sensitivity analysis and then all that they knew about probability analysis. Whilst (very) basic definitions were seen frequently, deeper knowledge, such as comparatively explaining the usefulness of each method for decision making, was rare.

300 ELAAN CO (MAR/JUN 2024)

Key answer tips

The NPV calculation in part (a) is relatively complex, with 12 marks allocated to it.

Make sure to pick up the more straightforward marks, such as entering the asset purchase, residual value and inflating the prices and costs each year. Also, make sure you comment on the NPV, even if you feel that it is incorrect.

The examiner likes to ask about the real method of NPV calculation, so make sure to review the model answer for part (b). You can practise the technique by applying it to the numbers from part (a).

For part (c), aim to remember the stages of simulation and be able to briefly expand on each one to gain the marks.

The highlighted words in the written sections are key phrases that markers are looking for.

(a) Hotel net present value (NPV)

	1	2	3	4
	$000	$000	$000	$000
Accommodation revenue	776	987	1,307	1,663
Restaurant revenue (35%)	271	345	458	582
Total revenue	1,047	1,332	1,765	2,245
Variable costs (20%)	(209)	(266)	(353)	(449)
Fixed costs	(433)	(450)	(468)	(487)
Taxable cash flow	405	616	944	1,309
Taxation at 20%	(81)	(123)	(189)	(262)
TAD benefit	75	56	42	107
After-tax cash flow	399	549	797	1,154
Sale value				7,600
Working capital	(14)	(22)	(24)	112
Net cash flow	385	527	773	8,866
DCF (10%)	0.909	0.826	0.751	0.683
Present value (PV)	350	435	581	6,055

	$000
PV of future cash flows at 10%	7,421
Less: Initial investment:	
Property	(5,500)
Fitting out	(1,500)
Initial working capital	(52)
NPV	369

NPV is positive and is therefore financially acceptable.

Nominal cost of capital = 1.048 × 1.05 – 1 = 0.1 (10%)

PV of future cash flows could alternatively be calculated using the =NPV spreadsheet formula.

Workings

Accommodation revenue

	1	2	3	4
Total rooms	50	50	50	50
Occupancy	50%	60%	75%	90%
Total room-nights (365 days)	9,125	10,950	13,688	16,425
Room rate ($)	85.00	90.10	95.51	101.24
Revenue ($000)	776	987	1,307	1,663

TAD benefit (fittings)

	1	2	3	4
	$000	$000	$000	$000
Value b/f	1,500	1,125	844	633
TAD at 25%	375	281	211	
Proceeds				100
Balancing allowance				533
TAD benefit at 20%	75	56	42	107

Working capital

	1	2	3	4
	$000	$000	$000	$000
Total revenue	1,047	1,332	1,765	2,245
Working capital (5%)	52	67	88	112
Cash flow (start of year)	(52)	(14)	(22)	(24)

Alternative calculation of after-tax cash flow

Year	**1**	**2**	**3**	**4**
	$000	$000	$000	$000
Taxable cash flow	405	616	944	1,309
Less: TAD	(375)	(281)	(211)	(533)
Taxable profit	30	335	733	776
Taxation at 20%	(6)	(67)	(147)	(155)
Add back TAD	375	281	211	533
After-tax cash flow	399	549	797	1,154

(b) The NPV calculation in part (a) included the effects of inflation. Under a real-terms approach, the effects of general inflation are excluded which will affect both the cash flows and cost of capital used for the NPV.

Cash flows

Cash flows which already suffer general inflation would be left uninflated at today's prices (current terms). For Elaan Co, no cash flows fall into this category.

Where cash flows suffer specific rates of inflation rather than general rate, the cash flows would firstly need to be inflated at their specific rate (as in part (a)). These nominal cash flows would then be deflated using the general (not specific) rate of inflation to give them in real terms. The real-terms figures would be different to the current price figures due to the difference between the specific and general rates of inflation.

Cost of capital

The real cash flows would need to be discounted using the real cost of capital (4.8%) not the nominal cost of capital (10%) used in (a).

Result

In the absence of tax-allowable depreciation, which suffers no inflation, the NPV obtained under both methods would be the same. In the case of the NPV for Elaan Co, the effects of tax-allowable depreciation would result in a slight difference, but it is likely to be insignificant.

(c) Where there is risk within a proposed project, tools such as simulation analysis can assist. In the case of Elaan Co's hotel project, it appears there are many risks within the forecasting assumptions so simulation analysis would be useful in deciding whether to proceed.

To perform simulation analysis, the following process would need to be followed:

1 Specify the variables

2 Specify the relationship between the variables

3 Simulate the environment

4 Analyse the results

Stages 1 and 2: Elaan Co would need to identify all the major variables and for each variable, the range of possible values and their associated probabilities. Elaan Co would then need to input the constructed mathematical model into a computer to enable the next stage to be performed.

Stage 3: To simulate the environment, the computer would use random number generation to change multiple variables at a time and recalculate the NPV each time. This routine would be repeated many, many times over (possibly millions).

Stage 4: The end result of the simulation would be a mathematical distribution of all envisaged possible NPV outcomes along with a likelihood/probability of occurrence.

Benefits

Basic sensitivity analysis can only assess the impact of one variable changing at a time whereas simulation looks at many variables (possibly all) changing at the same time. Consequently, simulation is considered to be more 'real-world' as it is unlikely a single variable will change in isolation.

Simulation can also help Elaan Co's decision making by showing the full range of envisaged possible outcomes (stage 4). The range of outcomes would be shown in the form of a statistical distribution, enabling further mathematical analysis to be performed, such as determining the probability of a negative NPV.

Given the relatively small NPV for the hotel project, compared with the investment required, a small change in some of the variables could easily result in a negative NPV. Consequently, knowing the probability of a negative NPV could be extremely useful to Elaan Co.

ACCA marking scheme

		Marks
(a)	Total room-nights	1
	Room rate and revenue	1
	Restaurant revenue	0.5
	Variable costs	0.5
	Fixed costs	1
	Tax on cash flow	1
	TAD	1
	TAD benefit	1
	Working capital balance	1
	Working capital cash flow	1
	Nominal cost of capital	1
	NPV	1
	Comment	1
		12
(b)	Real-time approach	**4**
(c)	Simulation analysis	**4**
	Total	**20**

Extracts from examiner's comments

Part (a) common errors:

Many candidates did not calculate total room nights for 365 days, ignoring the percentage of occupancy, 365 days or both, and this affected their answers.

Some candidates did not include restaurant revenue as part of the total income.

Some candidates included working capital and/or the residual value of $7,600 in the taxable cash flow and therefore lost a mark for the tax liability.

There were problems with dealing with residual value and hence the balancing allowance in year 4.

Incremental working capital calculations had problems. These included the following: timing, incorrect signs, and using an incorrect percentage.

Part (b) common errors:

Candidates needed to clearly explain the following to score full marks:

- Difference between general and specific inflation
- Changes will be reflected in the cost of capital and the cash flows
- Effect of taxation.

Part (c) common errors:

It was very rare that all the steps of the simulation process were explained.

Many candidates seemed to lack the knowledge required to make a substantive response to this requirement.

301 GALLE CO (SEP/DEC 2024)

Key answer tips

The NPV calculation in part (a) is relatively straightforward, although you should recognise that the sales volumes for years two to four should be expected values.

With two marks available for the comment, consider what extra to say above the usual financial viability comment. In this case, the use of expected sales volumes means that the calculated NPV is an average figure. There is a 30% chance that the NPV will be lower and a 70% one that it will be higher than the one calculated in part (a) (i).

For part (b), discussion of four techniques for 8 marks means that there are two marks per technique. Aim to write at least two full sentences about each. You can include advantages or disadvantages to fill out your answer.

The highlighted words in the written sections are key phrases that markers are looking for.

(a) (i) Project cash flows

Year	**1**	**2**	**3**	**4**
	$	$	$	$
Revenue	731,500	649,740	678,980	709,580
Variable costs	(463,500)	(405,790)	(417,945)	(430,525)
Fixed costs	(10,000)	(10,000)	(10,000)	(10,000)
Taxable cash flow	258,000	233,950	251,035	269,055
Taxation at 20%	(51,600)	(46,790)	(50,207)	(53,811)
TAD benefit	25,000	18,750	14,063	42,187
After-tax cash flow	231,400	205,910	214,891	257,431
Working capital	(2,400)	(2,472)	(2,546)	87,418
Net cash flow	229,000	203,438	212,345	344,849
Discount factors at 13%	0.885	0.783	0.693	0.613
Present value (PV)	202,665	159,292	147,155	211,392
PV of future cash flows	720,504			
Initial investment	(500,000)			
Working capital	(80,000)			
Expected NPV	**140,504**			

(ii) Expected NPV is positive and is therefore financially acceptable.

However, the expected NPV is based upon an expected volume of 8,500 units for years 2 to 4. There is a 30% probability that the sales volume for these years could be as low as 5,000 units which would reduce the NPV, possibly resulting in a negative NPV.

Workings

(W1) Volume

Volume for year 1 = 10,000

Expected volume for years 2 to 4 = 0.3 × 5,000 + 0.7 × 10,000 = 8,500 per year

(W2) Sales and variable cost

Year	**1**	**2**	**3**	**4**
	$	$	$	$
Selling price ($/unit)	70.00	70.00	70.00	70.00
Inflated at 4.5% ($/unit)	73.15	76.44	79.88	83.48
Volume (units/year)	10,000	8,500	8,500	8,500
Revenue ($)	731,500	649,740	678,980	709,580
Variable cost ($/unit)	45.00	45.00	45.00	45.00
Inflated at 3% ($/unit)	46.35	47.74	49.17	50.65
Volume (units/year)	10,000	8,500	8,500	8,500
Variable cost ($)	463,500	405,790	417,945	430,525

(W3) TAD benefit

Year	**1**	**2**	**3**	**4**
	$	$	$	$
TAD at 25%	125,000	93,750	70,313	210,937
TAD benefit at 20%	25,000	18,750	14,063	42,187

Note: Year 4 TAD = 500,000 – 125,000 – 93,750 – 70,313 = 210,937

(W4) Working capital (WC)

Year	**1**	**2**	**3**	**4**
	$	$	$	$
WC at start of year	80,000	82,400	84,872	87,418
WC at end of year (3%)	82,400	84,872	87,418	0
Cash flow	(2,400)	(2,472)	(2,546)	87,418

Alternative calculation of after-tax cash flow

Year	1	2	3	4
	$	$	$	$
Taxable cash flow	258,000	233,950	251,035	269,055
TAD	(125,000)	(93,750)	(70,313)	(210,937)
Taxable profit	133,000	140,200	180,722	58,118
Taxation at 20%	(26,600)	(28,040)	(36,144)	(11,624)
Add back TAD	125,000	93,750	70,313	210,937
After-tax cash flow	231,400	205,910	214,891	257,431

(b) Expected values (EV) (Probability analysis)

An EV is a long-run, weighted average outcome using the probability of occurrence for each outcome as the weights. An EV simplifies the appraisal by incorporating the variation in outcomes into a single figure. However, an EV does require knowledge of not only the individual outcomes but also their probability of occurrence which can make the use of EV difficult in practice unless past data can be used for prediction purposes. It also only has any meaning for repetitive events.

Sensitivity analysis

This is a form of 'what if?' analysis where the impact on a project's NPV due to a change in a key variable can be quantified. This allows key, sensitive variables to be identified for further investigation and ongoing project monitoring. Unfortunately, it does not give any indication of the likelihood of occurrence of the changes, nor does it allow for more than one variable to be changed at a time so the interdependence between variables is ignored.

Simulation

Simulation is a more sophisticated version of sensitivity analysis whereby it allows for more than one variable to change at a time. The analysis usually has to be performed with computer modelling techniques due to its complexity, but it will give a good indication of potential outcomes. Its main disadvantages are its complexity, it is a much more time-consuming process, and probabilities are still required for the variable changes.

Adjusted payback

Payback measures how long in years until the project has broken even in its cash flows. The longer the payback period, the more the project has a greater reliance on later, more uncertain, cash flows. Project acceptance is usually based on setting a maximum payback limit for projects. By reducing the maximum payback benchmark, the longer payback, more uncertain projects will tend to be rejected. Choice of the maximum payback is subjective, however, and no account is taken of the project's return as cash flows after payback are ignored.

Risk adjusted discount rate

The discount rate in an NPV calculation should be determined by the risk within the project being undertaken. For higher risk projects, the discount rate should be increased to ensure future present values are reduced sufficiently to allow for the increased return required by the finance providers. This increase could be performed arbitrarily by simply adding a return premium to the existing rate or using more sophisticated, complex techniques such as the capital asset pricing model (CAPM).

Note: Only four techniques were required.

ACCA marking scheme

			Marks
(a)	(i)	Expected volume	1
		Sales revenue	1
		Variable cost	1
		Tax liability	1
		Tax timing	1
		TAD calculation	1
		TAD benefit	1
		Working capital investment	0.5
		Working capital increments	1
		Working capital recovery	0.5
		PVs/NPV	1
			10
	(ii)	Comments	**2**
(b)	First technique		2
	Second technique		2
	Third technique		2
	Fourth technique		2
			8
Total			**20**

Extracts from examiner's comments

Part (a) common errors:

– Not recognising that a balancing allowance arises at the end of this four-year project.

– Calculating tax allowable depreciation (TAD), but using it in the computation as the TAD benefit i.e. not applying the tax rate to the TAD.

– Incorrectly deferring tax-related cashflows (as above) when the question is clear that they are paid at the end of the year to which they relate.

– Not adding back TAD, after correctly deducting it to arrive at taxable profit (see alternative calculation of after-tax cash flow in the suggested solution).

Common errors regarding working capital (WC) were mainly concerned with incorrect increments and/or timing and/or direction of cash flow, with some responses simply ignoring WC investment or assuming WC recovery was $80,000.

Some candidates, unfortunately, set out the calculations in a haphazard manner i.e. not in a columnar form, which makes candidate errors more likely and makes it more difficult for a question marker to understand the candidate's logic. Where workings are clearly shown in the spreadsheet (either within a formula or with clear labelling) marks can be awarded on the own figure rule (OFR) when minor errors are made.

Part (b):

Stronger responses to this requirement used the information provided in the scenario to highlight aspects such as:

- The expected sales volume (8,500 units) is dependent upon the accuracy of the probabilities of each volume, as well as the volumes themselves, and these are often not easy to predict, especially for a new battery, and
- Expected values only have reliable meaning for repeated events. The launch of the GPE is highly unlikely to be a repetitive event.

Many candidates made a good attempt at part (b) but too many provided only a brief list of techniques with no discussion or typed "all they knew" about techniques such as NPV, IRR and ROCE, which scored no marks. Time was also wasted on defining risk and uncertainty which was not asked for.

BUSINESS FINANCE AND COST OF CAPITAL

302 ECHO CO (DEC 07 – MODIFIED) *Walk in the footsteps of a top tutor*

Key answer tips

The key learning points from this question are the benefits of answering requirements in an order that best suits you as well as the need to take guidance from the specific words used in both the scenario and the requirement itself. The highlighted words are key phrases that markers are looking for.

Tutor's top tips

Start by reading the requirement. Having a good understanding of what is expected from you will allow you to read the scenario more effectively, processing the information as you go. Scribble you thoughts in the margins on what each piece of information could be used for in relation to the requirements.

The first thing that should strike you is this question has 3, very independent requirements. This means you can pick the order in which to tackle them to suit your strengths. The question is very generic and requires little more than regurgitation of knowledge from the syllabus.

Part (c) has the most guidance on the structure and content of your answer. These therefore represent the easiest marks. The layout of the scenario means you can immediately re-read the information on proposal C and then consider what additional information you will need.

The slightly different requirements in part (a) and part (b) is reflected in the mark allocation. In part (a) the requirement is to 'analyse' and 'discuss' compared to 'evaluate' and 'discuss' in part (b). Part (b) will therefore require some further calculations.

In part (a) you need to link back to the scenario where we're told the aim of proposal A is to make the company more attractive to equity investors. A sensible approach is to consider what makes a share attractive. You should immediately highlight the dividend payment, discussion of which would lead on to Modigliani & Miller's theories on dividend policy and efficient markets hypothesis.

(a) Echo Co paid a total dividend of $2 million or 20c per share according to the statement of profit or loss information. An increase of 20% would make this $2.4 million or 24c per share and would reduce dividend cover from 3 times to 2.5 times. It is debatable whether this increase in the current dividend would make the company more attractive to equity investors, who use a variety of factors to inform their investment decisions, not expected dividends alone. For example, they will consider the business and financial risk associated with a company when deciding on their required rate of return.

It is also unclear what objective the finance director had in mind when suggesting a dividend increase. The primary financial management objective is the maximisation of shareholder wealth and if Echo Co is following this objective, the dividend will already be set at an optimal level. From this perspective, a dividend increase should arise from increased maintainable profitability, not from a desire to 'make the company more attractive'. Increasing the dividend will not generate any additional capital for Echo Co, since existing shares are traded on the secondary market.

Furthermore, Miller and Modigliani have shown that, in a perfect capital market, share prices are independent of the level of dividend paid. The value of the company depends upon its income from operations and not on the amount of this income that is paid out as dividends. Increasing the dividend would not make the company more attractive to equity investors, but would attract equity investors who desired the new level of dividend being offered. Current shareholders who were satisfied by the current dividend policy could transfer their investment to a different company if their utility had been decreased.

The proposal to increase the dividend should therefore be rejected, perhaps in favour of a dividend increase in line with current dividend policy.

Tutor's top tips

In part (b), the scenario directs us towards the differences between short term and long-term interest rates. As in part (c) the impact on gearing and interest cover can be highlighted and the lack of any investment opportunity should by highlighted as a problem.

(b) The proposal to raise \$15 million of additional debt finance does not appear to be a sensible one, given the current financial position of Echo Co. The company is very highly geared if financial gearing measured on a book value basis is considered. The debt/equity ratio of 150% is almost twice the average of companies similar to Echo Co. This negative view of the financial risk of the company is reinforced by the interest coverage ratio, which at only four times is half that of companies similar to Echo Co.

Raising additional debt would only worsen these indicators of financial risk. The debt/equity ratio would rise to 225% on a book value basis and the interest coverage ratio would fall to 2.7 times, suggesting that Echo Co would experience difficulty in making interest payments.

The proposed use to which the newly-raised funds would be put merits further investigation. Additional finance should be raised when it is needed, rather than being held for speculative purposes. Until a suitable investment opportunity comes along, Echo Co will be paying an opportunity cost on the new finance equal to the difference between the interest rate on the new debt (10%) and the interest paid on short-term investments. This opportunity cost would decrease shareholder wealth. Even if an investment opportunity arises, it is very unlikely that the funds needed would be exactly equal to \$15m.

The interest charge in the statement of profit or loss information is \$3m while the interest payable on the 8% loan notes is \$2.4m (30 × 0.08). It is reasonable to assume that \$0.6m of interest is due to an overdraft. Assuming a short-term interest rate lower than the 8% loan note rate – say 6% – implies an overdraft of approximately \$10m (0.6/0.06), which is one-third of the amount of the long-term debt. The debt/equity ratio calculated did not include this significant amount of short-term debt and therefore underestimates the financial risk of Echo Co.

The bond issue would be repayable in eight years' time, which is five years after the redemption date of the current loan note issue. The need to redeem the current \$30m loan note issue cannot be ignored in the financial planning of the company. The proposal to raise £15m of long-term debt finance should arise from a considered strategic review of the long-term and short-term financing needs of Echo Co, which must also consider redemption or refinancing of the current loan note issue and, perhaps, reduction of the sizeable overdraft, which may be close to, or in excess of, its agreed limit.

In light of the concerns and considerations discussed, the proposal to raise additional debt finance cannot be recommended.

Analysis

Current gearing (debt/equity ratio using book values) = 30/20 = 150%

Revised gearing (debt/equity ratio using book values) = (30 + 15)/20 = 225%

Current interest coverage ratio = 12/3 = 4 times

Additional interest following debt issue = 15m × 0.1 = \$1.5m

Revised interest coverage ratio = 12/(3 + 1.5) = 2.7 times

Tutorial note

The industry gearing has been calculated as debt/equity. You must ensure your calculation is consistent with this otherwise an effective comparison could not be made.

Tutor's top tips

To calculate the theoretical ex-rights price (TERP), you will need the current share price, the subscription price and the basis of the issue. All are contained in the paragraph labelled 'Proposal C'. To calculate the amount of finance that would be raised, you also need to know the number of shares to be issued. This can be worked out based on the current number of shares in issue given in the Statement of financial position information. Be careful to read this carefully. There is $5m of share capital but as the nominal value of each share is 50c, this means there are 10m in issue. Both of these are simple calculations and will most likely attract 1 mark each. This therefore leaves 5 marks for your evaluation and discussion of the proposal.

A requirement to 'evaluate' implies some further calculations will be needed, this time relating to gearing and financial risk. Start by reviewing the information given in the scenario and consider what calculations would be both possible and useful. You should identify:

- *Gearing calculations. Whilst you have market values for equity, you only have the book value of debt. To be consistent you should therefore use book values of both to calculate gearing. In order to discuss the proposal, you will need to know the existing gearing and the new gearing under the proposal. Both can be usefully compared to the industry average.*
- *You have also been provided with average data on interest cover. This signals that calculation of current and projected interest cover will be a source of further marks. Some further calculations need to be done by assuming the proceeds from the rights issue are able to earn the same rate of return as existing funds. This will therefore give an estimate of the new level of profitability. These calculations might not seem obvious and are not essential to passing the question.*

When discussing the impact of the proposal on gearing and financial risk it is essential to highlight that there doesn't appear to be a need to raise this finance as there is no plan on how it will be spent.

(c) Analysis

Rights issue price = $2.30 × 80% = $1.84

Theoretical ex rights price = (($2.30 × 4) + ($1.84 × 1))/(4 + 1) = $2.21 per share

Number of shares currently in issue = $5m/$0.5 = 10m shares

Number of new shares issued = 10m/4 × 1 = 2.5 million

Cash raised = $1.84 × 2.5m = $4.6 million

Number of shares in issue after rights issue = 10 + 2.5 = 12.5 million

Current gearing (debt/equity ratio using book values) = 30/20 = 150%

Revised gearing (debt/equity ratio using book values) = 30/24.6 = 122%

Current interest coverage ratio = \$12m/\$3m = 4 times

Current return on equity (ROE) = \$6m/\$20m = 30%

In the absence of any indication as to the return expected on the new funds, we can assume the rate of return will be the same as on existing equity, an assumption consistent with the calculated theoretical ex rights price. After-tax return on the new funds = \$4.6m × 0.3 = \$1.38 million. Current tax rate \$3m/\$9m = 33.33%. Before-tax return on new funds = \$1.38m/(1–33.33%) = \$2.07 million. Revised interest coverage ratio = (\$12m + \$2.07m)/\$3m = 4.7 times

The current debt/equity and interest coverage ratios suggest that there is a need to reduce the financial risk of Echo Co. A rights issue would reduce the debt/equity ratio of the company from 150% to 122% on a book value basis, which is 50% higher than the average debt/equity ratio of similar companies. After the rights issue, financial gearing is still therefore high enough to be a cause for concern.

The interest coverage ratio would increase from 4 times to 4.7 times, again assuming that the new funds will earn the same return as existing equity funds. This is still much lower than the average interest coverage ratio of similar companies, which is 8 times. While 4.7 times is a safer level of interest coverage, it is still somewhat on the low side.

No explanation has been offered for the amount to be raised by the rights issue. Why has the Finance Director proposed that \$4.6m be raised? If the proposal is to reduce financial risk, what level of financial gearing and interest coverage would be seen as safe by shareholders and other stakeholders? What use would be made of the funds raised? If they are used to redeem debt they will not have a great impact on the financial position of the company, in fact it appears likely that the overdraft is twice as big as the amount proposed to be raised by the rights issue. The refinancing need therefore appears to be much greater than \$4.6m. If the funds are to be used for investment purposes, further details of the investment project, its expected return and its level of risk should be considered.

There seems to be no convincing rationale for the proposed rights issue and it cannot therefore be recommended, at least on financial grounds.

ACCA marking scheme		
		Marks
(a)	Discussion of proposal to increase dividend	**5**
(b)	Evaluation of debt finance proposal	3–4
	Discussion of debt finance proposal	4–5
		8
(c)	Theoretical ex rights price per share	1
	Amount of finance raised	1
	Evaluation of rights issue proposal	2–3
	Discussion of rights issue proposal	3–4
		7
Total		**20**

Extracts from examiner's comments

Part (a) common errors:

Many candidates calculated correctly the increased dividend per share and then offered very little by way of discussion in order to gain any further marks.

Part (b) common errors:

The sector average debt/equity ratio (D/E) was provided, but many candidates chose to calculate capital gearing (D/(D + E)) in the mistaken belief that this was the debt to equity ratio. Comparison with the sector average gearing was therefore pointless, since the gearing ratios were on a different basis.

Some candidates also calculated incorrectly the interest coverage, dividing interest into profit before tax or profit after tax, rather than into operating profit (before both interest and tax).

It was surprising to see many candidates attempting to calculate the cost of debt (internal rate of return) of the bond issue. The bonds were to be issued and redeemed at nominal value and so their cost of debt was the same as their interest rate, as these unnecessary calculations confirmed (where they were made correctly).

Part (c) common errors:

Some candidates mistakenly assumed that the proceeds of the right issue would be used to redeem some of the existing debt, but the question did not specify this and in practice this might not be possible.

Very few candidates recognised that, just as with the proposal to make a bond issue, there had been no evaluation of the funding needs of the company. Why raise $4.6m? Why not $10m? What were the rights issue funds going to be used for? A more concrete plan than raising cash to reduce gearing was needed if shareholder wealth was going to be maximised.

303 PAVLON

Key answer tips

This is a difficult question that requires some imaginative thinking in order to tackle efficiently. The idea of calculating the dividend payout ratio for part (a) is one which seems logical when you review the answer but might not necessarily have occurred to you when attempting the question under timed conditions.

Part (b) is a more clear cut application of the dividend valuation model with the change in growth rate being the only complication. Remember that the dividend valuation model formula calculates the present value of a growing dividend perpetuity. The calculations we need to do are still present value ones. The highlighted words are key phrases that markers are looking for.

(a) **(i)** Payout ratio is the proportion of earnings that are paid out as dividends.

Year	Shares in issue	EPS	Dividend per share	Payout ratio	Growth
20X6	21,333,333	8.44¢	3.6¢	42.7%	–
20X7	21,333,333	11.25¢	4.8¢	42.7%	33%
20X8	26,666,667	14.44¢	6.16¢	42.7%	28%
20X9	26,666,667	15.38¢	6.56¢	42.7%	6%
20Y0	26,666,667	16.69¢	7.12¢	42.7%	8.5%
20Y1	40,000,000	13.75¢ (est)	5.5¢ (proposed)	40%	–18% (EPS) –23% (DPS)

Pavlon appears to be adopting a policy of a fixed payout ratio of 42.7% pa over the five year period. In general, such a policy can lead to wide variations in dividends per share. In Pavlon's case over the last five years earnings have been rising, although at fluctuating levels, leading to the dividend also growing but at an inconsistent rate.

If it is believed that share price is affected by dividend policy then these fluctuations in dividends and the decline in growth could depress equity value.

Most listed companies attempt to adopt a stable or rising level of dividend per share even in the face of fluctuating earnings. This approach is taken in order to maintain investor confidence. If Pavlon were to continue with its present policy and earnings were to decline the resultant fall in dividend could have serious repercussions for the share price.

(ii) The proposed final dividend for 20Y1 gives a total for the year of 5.5¢. This is a significant fall in dividend per share and a small decline in the dividend payout ratio. In the absence of market imperfections such as taxation and transaction costs, it could be argued that dividend policy has no impact on shareholder wealth. It is the firm's future earnings stream that is of importance, not the way in which it is split between dividend and retentions.

However, once market imperfections are introduced dividend policy can be shown to have an impact on investor wealth.

Depending on the tax regime they inhabit and their own personal needs, private individuals may pay income tax at a higher rate than capital gains tax due to available CGT annual exemptions. They may therefore prefer retentions to distributions and would not be disappointed with a cut in dividends.

However, they may prefer income to capital gains, meaning that they would not find a dividend cut acceptable. In theory, any income they require could be generated by selling shares to manufacture 'home made' dividends (note however the market imperfection of transaction costs that would be incurred when selling shares).

If the majority of shares are owned by wealthy, private individuals then it may be possible for the company to explain the background of any reduction in dividend payout to gain acceptance from the shareholders and reduce any negative consequences of the cut.

The tax position of institutional shareholders varies and so therefore will their attitude to dividend policy. Most, however, require a steady flow of income to meet their day-to-day obligations (pensions, insurance claims etc.) and may not wish (or be able) to generate homemade dividends.

It could be argued that new investors have bought shares in Pavlon with full knowledge of its dividend policy and should therefore not be surprised if it sticks to a policy of a 40% payout. However, many shareholders might expect it to change its policy now that it has obtained a listing.

A further factor to consider is the informational content of dividends. The proposed dividend cut might be seen as a signal of poor earnings in the future and lead to investors of either group selling shares.

Overall, there is no conclusive evidence on what makes for an optimal dividend policy. Pavlon should however consider the tax position of its investors and the potential reaction of the market to a cut in dividend.

(b) Here, we can't directly use the dividend valuation model formula because it assumes only one rate of growth into perpetuity, whereas this question has growth of 15% for time periods 1 to 3 (20Y2–20Y4) and then growth of 8% after that. Instead, we need to split the calculation into two. We can value separately the first three years of dividends and then the delayed growing perpetuity from time period 4 onwards and add the values together to get an overall price.

If the company's profits and dividends are expected to increase initially by 15% pa then investors will expect this year's dividend (paid at the end of the year at t1) to be 7.12¢ × 1.15 = 8.188¢.

Value of first three years' dividend

Year	**Dividend**		**PV factor 12%**	**Present value**
20Y2 (t1)	7.12 × 1.15	= 8.188	0.893	7.312
20Y3 (t2)	8.188 × 1.15	= 9.416	0.797	7.505
20Y4 (t3)	9.416 × 1.15	= 10.829	0.712	7.710
				22.527

Value of dividends years 4 – ∞ (delayed growing perpetuity)

$$= \frac{d(1+g)}{i-g} = \frac{10.829(1.08)}{0.12-0.08} = 292.383$$

Use of this formula discounts the cash flows back by one time period, so with the t4 dividend on the top of the formula, the value calculated will be at time period 3. To obtain year 0 values we must discount back another three years at 12%.

292.383 × 0.712 = 208.2

Value of share at time 0 = 22.527 + 208.2 = 231¢

Since the current market value of Pavlon's shares is \$78m/40m = \$1.95 the share appears to be undervalued.

304 GTK INC (JUNE 07 – MODIFIED) *Walk in the footsteps of a top tutor*

Key answer tip

Part (a) is a relatively straightforward investment appraisal calculation that shouldn't pose many problems. In part (b) it is essential that you read the requirement carefully. As you have to make a recommendation you must ensure any advantages or disadvantages you note are relevant to the scenario given. The highlighted words are key phrases that markers are looking for.

(a) Expected net present value of Proposed 1

Tutor's top tips

It's worthwhile giving some quick consideration to the best way to layout your answer to this part of the requirement. A columnar format, like that presented here, will often be the most efficient and will reduce the amount of information you need to write more than once. This is particularly important here since your answer to part (i) will naturally lead into your answer to part (ii).

Don't forget the requirement to comment on your findings. In situation involving expected values, your comments should generally focus on the reliability of the probability estimates and the risk involved (look at the variability between the best result and the worst).

	Scenario 1	**Scenario 2**	**Scenario 3**
Number of sunny days	100	125	150
Saving ($/day)	700	700	700
Annual saving ($)	70,000	87,500	105,000
Costs	(24,000)	(24,000)	(24,000)
Net annual savings	46,000	63,500	81,000
Present value of net savings at 10%	460,000	635,000	810,000
Investment	500,000	500,000	500,000
Net present value	(40,000)	135,000	310,000
Probability	30%	60%	10%

Expected net present value = (–40,000 × 0.3) + (135,000 × 0.6) + (310,000 × 0.1) = $100,000

The expected NPV is $100,000 so if the investment is evaluated on this basis, it is financially acceptable. In reaching a decision, however, the company should consider that there is a 30% chance of making a loss. This may be seen as an unacceptably high risk. Furthermore, the number of sunny days each year will not be constant, as assumed here, and may or may not be exactly 100, 125 or 150 days. It is possible the net present values of Scenarios 1 and 3 represent extremes in terms of expectations, and that the net present value of Scenario 2 may be most useful as representing the most likely outcome, even on a joint probability basis. It is also worth noting that inflation has not been taken into account and that the ever-increasing cost of energy may make the proposed investment much more financially attractive if it were factored into the analysis.

Workings

Present values must be calculated with the before-tax cost of capital of 10%, since before-tax cash flows are being evaluated here. The present value of a perpetuity is found by dividing the constant annual cash flow by the cost of capital.

Present value of net savings, Scenario 1 = 46,000/0.10 = $460,000

Present value of net savings, Scenario 2 = 63,500/0.10 = $635,000

Present value of net savings, Scenario 3 = 81,000/0.10 = $810,000

Tutor's top tips

You are asked how equity finance or traded debt might be raised and will therefore need to discuss the different methods of issuing shares (rights issue, and placing being the most suitable here) and different things to consider when issuing debt.

(b) GTK Inc is a company with a small overdraft and no long-term debt. The $1.1 million could be raised as follows:

Equity finance

The equity financing choices available to GTK Inc are a rights issue or a placing.

Rights issue

In this method of raising new equity finance, new shares are offered to existing shareholders pro rata to their existing shareholdings, meeting the requirements of company law in terms of shareholders' pre-emptive rights. Since GTK Inc has several million dollars of shareholders' funds, it may be able to raise $1.1 million through a rights issue, but further investigation will be needed to determine if this is possible. Factors to consider in reaching a decision will include

- the number of shareholders, the type of shareholders (institutional shareholders such as pension or investment funds may be more willing to subscribe than small shareholders)
- whether a recent rights issue has been made
- the recent and expected financial performance of GTK Inc, and
- the effect of a rights issue on the company's cost of capital.

A rights issue would not necessarily disturb the existing balance of ownership and control between shareholders. Approximately half of the finance needed is for a permanent investment and the permanent nature of equity finance would match this.

Placing

This way of raising equity finance involves allocating large amounts of ordinary shares with a small number of institutional investors. Existing shareholders will need to agree to waive their pre-emptive rights for a placing to occur, as it entails issuing new shares to new shareholders. The existing balance of ownership and control will therefore be changed by a placing. Since GTK Inc is a listed company, it is likely that a significant percentage of its issued ordinary share capital will be in public hands and the effect of a placing on this fraction will need to be considered. There may be a change in shareholder expectations after the placing, depending on the extent to which institutional investors are currently represented among existing shareholders, but since the company is listed there is likely to be a significant institutional representation.

Traded debt

A new issue of traded debt could be redeemable or irredeemable, secured or unsecured, fixed rate or floating rate, and may perhaps be convertible. Deep discount bonds and zero coupon bond are also a possibility, but much rarer. The effect of an issue of debt on the company's cost of capital should also be considered.

Security

Bonds may be secured on assets in order to reduce the risk of the bond from an investor point of view. Fixed charge debt is secured on specified non-current assets, such as land or buildings, while floating charge debt is secured on all assets or on a particular class of assets. In the event of default, holders of secured debt can take action to recover their investment, for example by appointing a receiver or by enforcing the sale of particular assets.

Redemption

Irredeemable corporate debt is very rare and a new issue of traded debt by GTK Inc would be redeemable, i.e. repayable on a specified future date. The project life of two of the proposed capital investments suggests that medium-term debt would be appropriate.

Fixed rate and floating rate

Fixed rate debt gives a predictable annual interest payment and, in terms of financial risk, makes the company immune to changes in the general level of interest rates. If interest rates are currently low, GTK Inc could lock into these low rates until its new debt issue needs to be redeemed. Conversely, if interest rates are currently high and expected to fall in the future, GTK Inc could issue floating rate debt rather than fixed rate debt, in the expectation that its interest payments would decrease as interest rates fell.

Cost of capital

GTK Inc has no long-term debt and only a small overdraft. Since debt is cheaper than equity in cost of capital terms, the company could reduce its overall cost of capital by issuing traded debt. A decrease in the overall cost of capital could benefit the shareholders in terms of an increase in the market value of the company, and an increase in the number of financially acceptable investment projects.

305 THP CO (JUNE 08 – MODIFIED) ***Walk in the footsteps of a top tutor***

Key answer tips

The key learning point from this question is the importance of making sure your marker can follow your answer. This will often involve explaining your thought process, including commenting on why the calculation you've performed is the right approach. The highlighted words are key phrases that markers are looking for.

Tutor's top tips

In the 15 minutes reading time you should aim to have skim read the scenario, getting a feeling for the information you've been provided with and paying particular attention to names and dates. You should also have skim read the requirement, underlining the models referred to and noted the calculations that are being asked for. Look for any part of the question that relies purely on knowledge of the syllabus (i.e. no calculations) and flag these as a good place to start. Part (e) of this question falls into this category.

Once you've completed part (e) you should look at the other requirements. Is there a specific order you will need to do them in or can you choose your strongest area to do first. Here we'll need to tackle the requirements in order as you need the output of part (a) to answer part (b).

Tutor's top tips

In part (a) you should follow the order presented in the requirement. It is leading you through the process. All the information is stated in the scenario or can be calculated without many complications. Part (iv) is the area most likely to cause problems (although you might not realise it at the time). The majority of situations the market capitalisation after an issue would be the TERP × new number of shares in issue. However, in this scenario, we've been told of some issue costs which must be deducted. Don't worry if you didn't spot this, it will only have been worth 2 marks (maximum). However, this does show the benefits of querying every piece of information provided by the examiner and asking "why have I been told that?"

(a) Rights issue price

This is at a 20% discount to the current share price = \$4.80 × 0.8 = \$3.84 per share

New shares issued = 3m/3 × 1 = 1m

Cash raised = 1m × \$3.84 = \$3,840,000

Theoretical ex rights price (TERP) = (old market value of shares plus proceeds of issue)/new number of shares in issue

Theoretical ex rights price = [(3m × \$4.80) + \$3.84m]/(3m + 1m) = \$18.24m/4m = \$4.56 per share

Market capitalisation after rights issue = value of shares at the TERP less the price paid to undertake the issue = \$18.24m – \$0.32m = \$17.92m

This is equivalent to a share price of \$17.92m/4m = \$4.48 per share

The issue costs result in a decrease in the market value of the company and therefore a decrease in the wealth of shareholders equivalent to 8c per share.

Tutor's top tips

The key to part (b) is recognising that since CRX is in the same business sector as THP, you can use THP's P/E ratio as a proxy for CRX. Whilst you're not specifically told this, you do have the information to work it out. Make sure your answer explains what you're doing and why this is an acceptable approach.

(b) Price/earnings ratio valuation

Price/earnings ratio of THP Co = 480/64 = 7.5 (given in question)

Earnings per share of CRX Co = 44.8c per share or \$0.448

Using THP Co's P/E ratio to value CRX Co:

Share price of CRX Co = EPS × P/E ratio = (\$0.448 × 7.5) = \$3.36

Market capitalisation of CRX Co = \$3.36 × 1m = \$3,360,000

(Alternatively, earnings of CRX Co = 1m × \$0.448 = \$448,000 × 7.5 = \$3,360,000)

Tutor's top tips

Part (c) starts by asking you to assume a semi-strong form efficient market. Your first thought should be to consider the implications of this, which is that only publicly available information will be reflected in the share price. Again, you should note down your thought process. Next, you will need to identify what will affect the market capitalisation post acquisition. You should conclude this will be the market capitalisation of THP plus the market capitalisation of CRX less the price paid for CRX (since this cash has left the business). All of this information is available, either as a result of your previous calculations or given in the scenario. Only in part (ii) will we need to factor in the additional savings since this information has now been made public.

(c) In a semi-strong form efficient capital market, share prices reflect past and public information. If the expected annual after-tax savings are not announced, this information will not therefore be reflected in the share price of THP Co. In this case, the post acquisition market capitalisation of THP Co will be the market capitalisation after the rights issue, plus the market capitalisation of the acquired company (CRX Co), less the price paid for the shares of CRX Co, since this cash has left the company in exchange for purchased shares. It is assumed that the market capitalisations calculated in earlier parts of this question are fair values, including the value of CRX Co calculated by the price/earnings ratio method.

Price paid for CRX Co = rights issue funds raised less issue costs = \$3.84m – \$0.32m = \$3.52m

Market capitalisation = \$17.92m + \$3.36m – \$3.52m = \$17.76m

This is equivalent to a share price of \$17.76m/4m = \$4.44 per share

The market capitalisation has decreased from the value following the rights issue because THP Co has paid \$3.52m for a company apparently worth \$3.36m. This is a further decrease in the wealth of shareholders, following on from the issue costs of the rights issue.

If the annual after-tax savings are announced, this information will be reflected quickly and accurately in the share price of THP Co since the capital market is semi-strong form efficient. The savings can be valued using the price/earnings ratio method as having a present value of \$720,000 (7.5 × \$96,000). The revised market capitalisation of THP Co is therefore \$18.48m (\$17.76m + \$0.72m), equivalent to a share price of \$4.62 per share (\$18.48m/4m). This makes the acquisition of CRX Co attractive to the shareholders of THP Co, since it offers a higher market capitalisation than the one following the rights issue. Each shareholder of THP Co would experience a capital gain of 14c per share (\$4.62 – \$4.48).

In practice, the capital market is likely to anticipate the annual after-tax savings before they are announced by THP Co.

Tutor's top tips

Part (d) is an opportunity to score an easy 8 marks by discussing the relative things to consider when deciding between debt and equity. Be careful though, the requirement does specify that your points should be relevant to THP. So for example, don't just talk about the impact on gearing, work it out using the information provided. To ensure you don't spend too much time on this part of the question, you should think about the mark allocation. For 8 marks where you are being asked to 'discuss' you should be spend no more than 14 minutes (8 × 1.8 mins per mark) talking about 4 factors THP should consider. Contrast this with a requirement to 'state' or 'list' which is more likely to attract only 1 mark per relevant point.

(d) There are a number of factors that should be considered by THP Co, including the following:

Gearing and financial risk

Equity finance will decrease gearing and financial risk, while debt finance will increase them. Gearing for THP Co is currently 68.5% and this will decrease to 45% if equity finance is used, or rise to 121% if debt finance is used. There may also be some acquired debt finance in the capital structure of CRX Co. THP Co needs to consider what level of financial risk is desirable, from both a corporate and a stakeholder perspective.

Target capital structure

THP Co needs to compare its capital structure after the acquisition with its target capital structure. If its primary financial objective is to maximise the wealth of shareholders, it should seek to minimise its weighted average cost of capital (WACC). In practical terms this can be achieved by having some debt in its capital structure, since debt is relatively cheaper than equity, while avoiding the extremes of too little gearing (WACC can be decreased further) or too much gearing (the company suffers from the costs of financial distress).

Availability of security

Debt will usually need to be secured on assets by either a fixed charge (on specific assets) or a floating charge (on a specified class of assets). The amount of finance needed to buy CRX CO would need to be secured by a fixed charge to specific fixed assets of THP Co. Information on these fixed assets and on the secured status of the existing 8% loan notes has not been provided.

Economic expectations

If THP Co expects buoyant economic conditions and increasing profitability in the future, it will be more prepared to take on fixed interest debt commitments than if it believes difficult trading conditions lie ahead.

Control issues

A rights issue will not dilute existing patterns of ownership and control, unlike an issue of shares to new investors. The choice between offering new shares to existing shareholders and to new shareholders will depend in part on the amount of finance that is needed, with rights issues being used for medium-sized issues and issues to new shareholders being used for large issues. Issuing traded debt also has control implications however, since restrictive or negative covenants are usually written into the bond issue documents.

Workings

Current gearing (debt/equity, book value basis) = 100 × 5,000/7,300 = 68.5%

Gearing if equity finance is used = 100 × 5,000/(7,300 + 3,840) = 45%

Gearing if debt finance is used = 100 × (5,000 + 3,840)/7,300 = 121%

ACCA marking scheme

			Marks
(a)	Rights issue price		1
	Cash raised		1
	Theoretical ex rights price per share		1
	Market capitalisation		2
			5
(b)	Calculation of price/earnings ratio		1
	Price/earnings ratio valuation		2
			3
(c)	Calculations of market capitalisation		2–3
	Comment		3–4
		Maximum	**5**
(d)	Relevant discussion		6–7
	Links to scenario in question		2–3
		Maximum	**7**
Total			**20**

Extracts from examiner's comments

Part (a) common errors:

A significant number of candidates showed that they were unfamiliar with this part of the syllabus and gave answers that gained little credit. Candidates should be aware that rights issues will not be made at a discount to nominal value.

Part (b) common errors:

Answers to this part of question 2 were often incomplete or adopted an incorrect methodology, for example calculating the price/earnings ratio of the target company when the question did not give the information needed for this. The correct approach is to multiply an earnings per share figure (or total earnings) by a suitable price/earnings ratio (in this case that of the acquirer).

Part (c) common errors:

Many candidates did not offer any calculations to support their discussion here, or offered calculations that did not relate to the question asked.

Part (d) common errors:

Weak answers offered a brief list of points with no discussion.

306 GXG CO (JUNE 13 – MODIFIED)

Key answer tips

This is a nice, relatively simple business finance question, although part (a) is more difficult. The key is to realise that the dividend valuation model is just a present value calculation. The formula presented on the formulae sheet can be used when the dividend pattern is of a perpetuity or a growing perpetuity, but when the dividend pattern is more irregular, you must go back to the basics of calculating present values.

Note also that the first two requirements ask the student to comment on their findings.

The highlighted words are key phrases that markers are looking for.

(a) Predicted dividend pattern under proposal 1:

t0 $0

t1 $0

t2 $0

t3 $0.25, growing by 4% in perpetuity.

The pattern is therefore of a delayed growing perpetuity. Using the growing perpetuity factor of (1/(r – g)) will give a value as at time period 2. This will then need to be discounted by 2 more years to give a time period 0 value (present value):

$0.25 × (1/(0.09 – 0.04)) × 0.842 = $4.21 price per share

Where r = 9%, g = 4% and 0.842 is the discount factor at 9% for two years. As the dividend per share has been used in the calculation, it is the price per share that is calculated. Using total dividends would have produced a total share value.

To determine whether this will be acceptable to shareholders, compare it to the share value that would be expected if the company continued to follow its existing dividend policy:

Most recent dividend = $1.6m

Number of shares in issue = $5m/$0.5 = 10m shares

Most recent dividend per share = $1.6m/10m = $0.16 per share

Using the dividend growth model to value the shares:

$P_0 = D_0(1 + g)/(re – g)$

P_0 = ($0.16 × 1.03)/(0.09 – 0.03) = $2.75

The proposal will increase shareholder wealth by $4.21 – $2.75 = $1.46 per share and so is likely to be acceptable to shareholders.

Examiner note:

Calculations on a total basis could also be used to evaluate the effect of the proposal on shareholder wealth.

(b) Earnings per share = earnings (post-tax profits)/number of shares in issue

Current earnings per share = $2,600,000/10,000,000 = $0.26 per share

Increase in before-tax income = 0.18 × $3.2m = $576,000

Revised operating profit = $576,000 + $3,450,000 = $4,026,000

Interest on new debt = $3,200,000 × 0.06 = $192,000

Revised interest = $192,000 + $200,000 = $392,000

Revised profit before income taxes = $4,026,000 – $392,000 = $3,634,000

Revised profit for the year = $3,634,000 × 0.8 = $2,907,200

Revised earnings per share = $2,907,200/10,000,000 = $0.291 per share

Earnings per share would increase by $0.031 or 3.1 cents per share.

Interest cover = operating profit/interest

Current interest cover = $3,450,000/$200,000 = 17 times

Revised interest cover = $4,026,000/$392,000 = 10 times

The increase in earnings per share would be welcomed by shareholders, but further information on the future of the company following the investment in research and development would be needed for a more comprehensive answer. The decrease in interest cover is large but its value is still high, with anticipated profit covering the interest commitment 10 times over. Therefore, the increase in financial risk seen due to the fall is unlikely to upset shareholders.

(c) Traded bonds are debt securities issued onto the capital market in exchange for cash received by the issuing company. The cash raised must be repaid on the redemption date, usually between five and fifteen years after issue. Bonds are usually secured on non-current assets of the issuing company, which reduces the risk to the lender. In the event of default on interest payments by the borrower, the bond holders can appoint a receiver to sell the assets and recover their investment. Interest paid on the bonds is tax-deductible, which reduces the cost of debt to the issuing company. Provided the borrower continues to pay the interest, however, bond finance is a low risk financing choice by the issuer.

There are a number of differences between bond finance and a new equity issue via a placing that will influence the choice between them. Equity finance does not need to be redeemed, since ordinary shares are truly permanent finance. While bond interest is usually fixed, the return to shareholders in the form of dividends depends on the dividend decision made by the directors of a company, and so these returns can increase, decrease or be passed. Furthermore, since dividends are a distribution of after-tax profit, they are not tax-deductible like interest payments, and so equity finance is not tax-efficient like debt finance.

Venture capital is found in specific financing situations, i.e. where risk finance is needed, for example, in a management buyout. Both equity and debt finance can be part of a venture capital financing package, but the return expected on venture capital is very high because of the level of risk faced by the investor.

ACCA marking scheme		
		Marks
(a)	Value of company at end of two years using DGM	2
	Value of company at year zero	1
	Current value of company using Dividend Valuation Model	2
	Acceptability of option 1 to shareholders	1
	Comment on findings	1
	Maximum	**6**
(b)	Revised operating profit	0.5
	Revised interest	0.5
	Revised profit for the year	0.5
	Revised earnings per share	0.5
	Current interest cover	0.5
	Revised interest cover	0.5
	Comment on earnings per share	1
	Comment on findings	1
	Comment on findings	1
	Maximum	**5**
(c)	Discussion of bond finance	3–4
	Discussion of equity finance via placing	3–4
	Discussion of venture capital	3–4
	Comment on findings	1
	Maximum	**9**
Total		**20**

Extracts from examiner's comments

Part (a) common errors.

Candidates struggled to determine an approach to the answer.

Part (b) common errors:

Some answers calculated correctly the interest on the new debt, but ignored interest payable on the current debt when calculating interest cover.

Another error was ignoring the return on the new funds invested, so that both current and revised interest cover were calculated using the same operating profit.

Some answers calculated interest cover using profit before income taxes, or profit for the year (after tax), indicating a lack of understanding of accounting ratios.

Part (c) common errors:

A number of answers showed limited understanding of placing venture capital.

Some answers limited themselves to discussing each source of finance separately, without addressing the requirement to discuss the factors to be considered in choosing between them, and so could not be awarded full marks.

At the other extreme, some answers discussed a number of factors, but related these very loosely, if at all, to the three sources of finance to which the question referred. For example, saying that a company should consider maturity, without indicating how maturity is a feature of the three sources of finance, does not help in choosing between them.

307 CARD CO (DEC 13 – MODIFIED)

Key answer tips

Parts (a) and (c) require the use of models that students should feel comfortable with. Care must be taken to extract the relevant information from the scenario and a clear layout must be used in order for marks to be allocated where due.

Part (d) is standard fare in terms of a discussion about the impact of changing capital structure on the value of the company. Students must be well prepared for this common requirement.

The highlighted words are key phrases that markers are looking for.

(a) Cost of equity of Card Co using DGM

The average dividend growth rate in recent years is 4%:

$g = (D_o/D_n)^{1/n} - 1$ where D_0 is the current dividend, D_n is the dividend from n years ago and n is the number of growth periods between the two dividends.

$(62.0/55.1)^{0.333} - 1 = 1.040 - 1 = 0.04$ or 4% per year

Using the dividend growth model:

$r_e = D_0(1 + g)/P_0 + g$ where r_e is the return to equity shareholders and also the cost of equity

$r_e = [(62 \times 1.04)/716] + 0.04 = 0.09 + 0.04 = 0.13$ or 13%

(b) The dividend growth model calculates the apparent cost of equity in the capital market, provided that the current market price of the share, the current dividend and the future dividend growth rate are known. While the current market price and the current dividend are readily available, it is very difficult to find an accurate value for the future dividend growth rate. A common approach to finding the future dividend growth rate is to calculate the average historic dividend growth rate and then to assume that the future dividend growth rate will be similar. There is no reason why this assumption should be true.

The capital asset pricing model tends to be preferred to the dividend growth model as a way of calculating the cost of equity as it has a sound theoretical basis, relating the cost of equity or required return of well-diversified shareholders to the systematic risk they face through owning the shares of a company. However, finding suitable values for the variables used by the capital asset pricing model (risk-free rate of return, equity beta and equity risk premium) can be difficult.

(c) First, the proxy company equity beta must be ungeared (degeared), using the proxy values for equity (75%) and debt (25%):

Asset beta = [Ve/(Ve + Vd(1–t))] × equity beta

Asset beta = (1.038 × 0.75)/(0.75 + (0.25 × 0.7)) = 0.842

The asset beta must then be regeared to reflect the financial risk of Card Co, using Card Co's values for equity and debt (see below workings):

Equity beta = asset beta/[Ve/(Ve + Vd(1–t))]

Equity beta = 0.842/[57,280/(57,280 + (5,171 × 0.7))] = 0.895

Project-specific cost of equity, using the CAPM = 4 + (0.895 × 5) = 8.5%

Note that the average equity risk premium is given in the question. The word **premium** indicates that this figure represents (Rm – Rf) rather than just Rm for use in the CAPM.

Workings

Market values of equity and debt

	$000
Equity: 8m × 7.16 =	57,280
Loan notes: 5m × 103.42/100 =	5,171
Total value of Card Co	62,451

(d) The value of a company can be expressed as the present value of its future cash flows, discounted at its weighted average cost of capital (WACC). The value of a company can therefore theoretically be maximised by minimising its WACC. If the WACC depends on the capital structure of a company, i.e. on the balance between debt and equity, then the minimum WACC will arise when the capital structure is optimal.

The idea of an optimal capital structure has been debated for many years. The traditional view of capital structure suggests that the WACC decreases as debt is introduced at low levels of gearing, before reaching a minimum and then increasing as the cost of equity responds to a higher degree to increasing financial risk.

Miller and Modigliani originally argued that the WACC is independent of a company's capital structure, depending only on its business risk rather than on its financial risk. This suggestion that it is not possible to minimise the WACC, and hence that it is not possible to maximise the value of a company by selecting a particular capital structure, depends on the assumption of a perfect capital market with no corporate taxation.

However, real world capital markets are not perfect and companies pay taxes on profit. Since interest is a tax-allowable deduction in calculating taxable profit, debt is a tax-efficient source of finance and replacing equity with debt will decrease the WACC of a company. In the real world, therefore, increasing gearing will decrease the WACC of a company and hence increase its value.

At high levels of gearing, the WACC of a company will increase due, for example, to increasing bankruptcy risk. Therefore, it can be argued that use of debt in a company's capital structure can reduce its WACC and increase its value, provided that gearing is kept to an acceptable level.

ACCA marking scheme

			Marks
(a)	Calculation of historic dividend growth rate		1
	Calculation of cost of equity using DGM		2
		Maximum	**3**
(b)	Dividend growth model discussion		2–3
	Capital asset pricing model discussion		2–3
		Maximum	**5**
(c)	Ungearing proxy company equity beta		1
	Regearing asset beta		1
	Project-specific cost of equity using CAPM		2
		Maximum	**4**
(d)	Traditional view of capital structure		1–2
	Miller and Modigliani views of capital structure		3–4
	Market imperfections view of capital structure		2–3
	Other relevant discussion		1–2
		Maximum	**8**
Total			**20**

308 TUFA CO (SEP/DEC 2017)

Key answer tips

In part (a) the only information given about the bank loan is its nominal value and that it has a variable rate, which isn't enough to calculate a cost of debt. Don't let this put you off – if there is not enough information given then put in something appropriate so that you can carry on with the question and gain the remaining marks. Parts (b) and (c) require careful reading of the question to ensure that you are answering specifically what has been asked.

The highlighted words are key phrases that markers are looking for.

(a) Cost of equity

$ke = D_0 (1 + g)/P_0 + g$

D_0 = cum div price – ex div price = \$7.52 – \$7.07 = \$0.45

$g = [D_0/D_n]^{1/n} - 1 = [\$0.45/0.37]^{1/4} - 1 = 0.050$ or 5%

ke = \$0.45 × 1.05/\$7.07 + 0.05 = 0.117 or 11.7%

Cost of preference shares

$kp = D/P_0$

D = nominal value × % rate = \$0.50 × 5% = \$0.025

kp = \$0.025/\$0.31 = 0.0806 or 8.06%

Cost of redeemable debt

Interest rate of loan notes (%)	7
Nominal value of loan notes ($)	100.00
Market price of loan notes ($)	102.34
Time to redemption (years)	4
Redemption premium (%)	5
Tax rate (%)	30

Post-tax interest value = I(1 – t) = $7 × (1 – 0.30) = $4.90

Year	Item	%	5% DF	PV ($)	6% DF	PV ($)
0	MV	(102.34)	1.000	(102.34)	1.000	(102.34)
1–4	Interest	4.90	3.546	17.38	3.465	16.98
4	Redeem	105.00	0.823	86.42	0.792	83.16
			NPV	1.45	NPV	(2.20)

IRR = L + $[N_L/(N_L - N_H)]$ × (H – L)

IRR (%) (5 + (1.45/(1.45 + 2.20))) × (6 – 5) = 5.40

Cost of bank loan (%) = 5.40

Market values and WACC calculation

	Total Nominal Value ($000)	Individual Nominal Value ($)	Number in issue (000)	Indiv. MV (S)	Total MV ($000)	Cost (%)	WACC
Ordinary shares	12,000	0.50	24,000	7.07	169,680	11.7	10.67
Pref shares	5,000	0.50	10,000	0.31	3,100	8.06	0.13
Loan notes	10,000	100.00	100	102.34	10,234	5.40	0.30
Bank loan	3,000				3,000	5.40	0.09
					186,014		11.19

(b) The current WACC of Tufa Co represents the mean return required by the company's investors, given the current levels of business risk and financial risk faced by the company.

The current WACC can be used as the discount rate in appraising an investment project of the company provided that undertaking the investment project does not change the current levels of business risk and financial risk faced by the company.

The current WACC can therefore be used as the discount rate in appraising an investment project of Tufa Co in the same business area as current operations, for example, an expansion of current business, as business risk is likely to be unchanged in these circumstances.

Similarly, the current WACC can be used as the discount rate in appraising an investment project of Tufa Co if the project is financed in a way that mirrors the current capital structure of the company, as financial risk is then likely to be unchanged.

The required return of the company's investors is likely to change if the investment project is large compared to the size of the company, so the WACC is likely to be an appropriate discount rate providing the investment is small in size relative to Tufa Co.

(c) The following advantages of using convertible loan notes as a source of long-term finance could be discussed.

Conversion rather than redemption

If the holders of convertible loan notes judge that conversion into ordinary shares will increase their wealth, conversion of the loan notes will occur on the conversion date and Tufa Co will not need to find the cash needed to redeem the loan notes. This is sometimes referred to as 'self-liquidation'.

Lower interest rate

The option to convert into ordinary shares has value for investors as ordinary shares normally offer a higher return than debt. Investors in convertible loan notes will therefore accept a lower interest rate than on ordinary loan notes, decreasing the finance costs for the issuing company.

Debt capacity

If Tufa Co issued convertible loan notes, its gearing and financial risk will increase and its debt capacity will decrease. When conversion occurs, its gearing and financial risk will decrease and its debt capacity will increase because of the elimination of the loan notes from its capital structure. There will be a further increase in debt capacity due to the issue of new ordinary shares in order to facilitate conversion.

Attractive to investors

Tufa Co may be able to issue convertible loan notes to raise long-term finance even when investors might not be attracted by an issue of ordinary loan notes, because of the attraction of the option to convert into ordinary shares in the future.

Facilitates planning

It has been suggested than an issue of fixed-interest debt such as convertible loan notes can be attractive to a company as the fixed nature of future interest payments facilitates financial planning.

ACCA marking scheme

		Marks
(a)	Dividend for 20X7	1
	Dividend growth rate	1
	Cost of equity	1
	Cost of pref. shares	1
	After-tax interest	1
	kd calculation setup	1
	Calculating kd	1
	Cost of bank loan	0.5
	MV ordinary shares	0.5
	MV pref. shares	0.5
	MV loan notes	0.5
	WACC calculations	2
		11

(b)	Business risk	1
	Financial risk	1
	Size of investment	1
		3
(c)	First advantage	2
	Second advantage	2
	Third advantage	2
		6
Total		**20**

Extracts from examiner's comments

Part (a) common errors:

Some candidates were not able to calculate the current dividend as the difference between the cum div and ex div share prices, nor were they able to recognise that there were four years of dividend growth.

Correct calculations of the cost of capital of preference shares were disappointingly low in number. Too many candidates made errors such as using an 'after tax' preference dividend or appeared to be simply guessing at the combination of figures that needed to be used.

Using an IRR approach to calculate the after tax cost of loan notes was generally done well. Errors in calculation included not using after tax interest in the IRR calculation, not including the redemption value of the loan note at its stated premium and/or using nominal value as the purchase price of loan notes rather than market value.

Omissions of the cost of the bank loan, and indeed its value, due to it 'having a variable rate' were common, but in error. The bank loan was part of the total finance of the company and needed to be included by using an appropriate substitute value for its cost, such as the after-tax cost of debt of the loan notes or the after-tax interest rate of the loan notes.

Some candidates were combining sources of finance and this led to errors. Examples of this were treating preference shares as ordinary shares and treating the bank loan as loan notes.

The question asked for the WACC on a market value basis, hence using book values instead of market values as weightings is simply incorrect.

Part (b) common errors:

Too many responses simply said "the WACC can be used if business risk and financial risk are unchanged" without further development. Whilst correct, the statement needs further discussion.

A common mistake in this question at this diet was to discuss circumstances under which it was **not** appropriate to use the current WACC and how WACC could be amended to address these circumstances. This was not what was asked.

Some answers were not even related to the requirement, discussing instead capital structure theory, or the creditor hierarchy, or pecking order theory, to name just some. There were also a disappointing number of candidates marking no attempt at this part question.

Part (c) common errors:

Firstly, a discussion is asked for. If six marks are offered for discussing three advantages, then assuming that two marks are offered for each advantage is reasonable. A 'bullet point' or short phrase is rarely, if ever, going to be sufficient to attract the two marks available for an advantage.

Secondly, if three advantages are required, then discussing a fourth or even fifth advantage is both poor examination technique and poor time management.

Thirdly, the question was clearly asked from the viewpoint of the user of the finance, which was a company listed on a large stock exchange, and not the providers of the finance.

Weaker responses ignored the possibility of conversion and were related only to the debt or non-equity nature of the loan notes e.g. debt is cheaper than equity or interest on debt is tax deductible. Some answers thought that conversion was a choice exercised by the company, rather than the investor and other answers assumed that conversion was automatic, rather than a wealth-maximising decision made by investors.

309 LAFORGE CO (MAR/JUL 2020)

Key answer tips

The calculation of the TERP in part (a) (i) is fairly straightforward. You will need to use the investment value and the issue price (remember the discount) to calculate the number of shares that will be issued. Be careful with the second requirement, which asks for the value **per existing share**, meaning the initial value is divided by the number of shares needed to earn a right.

For part (b), a good approach given that you will be using a spreadsheet workspace, is to lay out a forecast profit statement, starting with profit from operations, taking into account changes to profit, interest and taxation under each option, so that you can calculate the new earnings figures. Note that a bit of business valuation knowledge is used here for the calculation of the share price (EPS × PE ratio).

Part (c) is a generic knowledge regurgitation requirement that does not need to relate to the scenario. For 5 marks, aim to make 5 solid points. You may not be able to think of 5 ways of issuing shares, but you should be able to pick up a couple of marks on more familiar methods such as rights issues.

In part (d), the first consideration would be whether the dividend cut would provide enough funding. The rest of the answer can then be based around whether there would be any advantages or detrimental effects of cutting the dividend. As you're given information about LaForge's current dividend policy and about its investors, make sure you consider this in your answer.

The highlighted words are key phrases that markers are looking for.

(a) **(i)**

TERP:

Current number of shares = $35m/$0.50 = 70m

Issue price (30% discount) = $2.60 × (1 – 0.3) = $1.82 per share

Number of shares to be issued = $25.48m/$1.82 = 14 million shares

TERP = (70m × $2.60 + $25.48m)/(70m + 14m) = $2.47 per share

Alternatively:

Ratio of issued shares = 14m:70m = 0.2, and therefore a 1 for 5 issue

TERP = ($1.82 + 5 × $2.60)/(1 + 5) = $2.47 per share

(ii)

Value of a right (VOR):

VOR per new share = TERP – issue price = $2.47 – $1.82 = $0.65 per new share

VOR per existing share = $0.65 × 14m/70m = $0.13 per existing share

Alternately using 1 for 5 ratio = VOR/number of shares needed to earn one right = $0.65/5 = $0.13 per existing share

(b) **(i) and (ii)**

	Current	**Rights issue**	**Loan notes**
	$m	$m	$m
Operating profit	25.5	30	30
Interest on loan notes	4.8	4.8	6.3288
Profit before income taxes	20.7	25.2	23.6712
Tax at 20%	4.14	5.04	4.73424
Profit for the year (earnings)	16.56	20.16	18.93696
Number of shares	70m	84m	70m
Earnings per share ($)	0.2366	0.2400	0.2705
PE ratio	11	11	11
Share price ($) (EPS × PE ratio)	2.60	2.64	2.98

(c) **Methods of issuing new equity shares**

Rights issue

A rights issue involves issuing shares to the existing shareholders in proportion to their existing holding. Rights issues are often successful, easier to price and are cheaper to arrange than a public issue but the amount of finance raised is limited as there is a finite amount that shareholders will be willing to invest. A rights issue would be mandatory if shareholders have not elected to waive their pre-emptive rights.

Private placing

A private placing is when a company, usually with the assistance of an intermediary, seeks out new investors on a one-to-one basis. Shares are normally issued to financial institutions when performing a placing rather than to individuals. This can be a useful source of new equity for an unlisted company but control of the company will be diluted as a result. A placing is also cheaper to arrange than a public issue but only useful for relatively small issues.

Public offer

If the company is listed, it may undertake a public offer whereby shares are offered for sale to the public at large. This is an expensive way of issuing shares as there are significant regulatory costs involved and like the placing, control of the existing shareholders will be diluted. A public issue will, however, allow very large amounts of equity finance to be raised, and will also give a wide spread of ownership.

Initial public offering (IPO)

If the company is not listed, it can list through the process of an IPO which will raise equity at the same time. An IPO will be more expensive than a public offer as there are further regulations having to be complied with, increasing costs. Consequently, only a large company wishing to raise a significant amount of finance would consider this option.

(d) The director's suggestion of reducing the forthcoming dividend would raise at most, \$5.6m (70m × \$0.08) so in itself, would not be sufficient but would provide 22% (\$5.6m/\$25.48m) of the total required. This would reduce the amount of new external finance needing to be raised, potentially reducing financing cost, but there are further problems with this suggestion.

Signalling effect

The signalling argument suggests that in the absence of perfect information, for example in a semi-strong form efficient capital market, the dividend announcement will send a message or "signal" to the market. Generally, a reduction in dividend (such as proposed here) could be interpreted as bad news by investors and result in a fall in LaForge Co's share price.

Clientele effect

Different investors have different needs relating to income or capital growth. LaForge Co has consistently paid dividends in the past so switching to a lower/zero pay-out could alienate some shareholders, resulting in large volumes of share sales. Given the different shareholders that LaForge Co has, this could be a real issue for them.

Liquidity preference

Generally, it is thought that shareholders, even those who prefer low pay-outs/high reinvestment, still wish to receive some dividend now as this is a certain return compared with the more risky and uncertain future dividends or capital growth.

Recommendation

Given that LaForge Co is a listed company with different shareholders and has consistently paid dividends in the past, a reduction in dividend could damage shareholder relations and possibly result in reduced shareholder wealth. The reduction in dividend is not recommended.

ACCA marking scheme			
			Marks
(a)	(i)	Existing shares	0.5
		New shares	0.5
		Issue price	1
		TERP	1
			3
	(ii)	Value of rights per new share	0.5
		Value of rights per existing share	0.5
			1
(b)	(i)	New PAT	0.5
		EPS	0.5
		Share price	1
			2
	(ii)	Interest	0.5
		New PAT	1
		EPS	0.5
		Share price	1
			3
(c)	Up to 2 marks per method		**5**
(d)	Signalling effect		2
	Clientele effect		2
	Other		1
	Recommendation		1
			6
Total			**20**

Extracts from examiner's comments

Part (a) (i) common errors:

The only persistent error was errors with the form of the rights issue. Some candidates used a 1 for 1 weighting, which is heavily at odds with the amount of finance required, since a 1 for 1 issue would raise 70m × $1.82 = $127.4m, five times the $25.48m required.

Part (a) (ii) common errors:

The requirement here was for candidates to calculate the value of a right per existing share and many candidates gained good marks here too. There are several ways to arrive at a figure of $0.13 per existing share and all were given credit. Some candidates offered a value of $0.65 but this was the value per new share, rather than the value per existing share.

Part (b) (i) common errors:

Many candidates experienced difficulty calculating the forecast profit for the year (after tax). A common approach was to use the after-tax value of the increased profit from operations as the forecast PAT, but this approach overstated the forecast PAT by ignoring existing finance costs, which were $16.56m/0.8 = $20.7m – $25.50m = $4.8m.

A further problem here was that some answers did not use the increased number of shares following the rights issue when calculating the EPS.

Part (b) (ii) common errors:

While many candidates calculated the finance cost of the proposed issue of loan notes, existing finance costs were again often ignored. Many answers then gained subsequent marks under the own figure rule, which awards marks for correct method even when an earlier error has made the figures incorrect.

Part (c) common errors:

Many answers were very brief for the marks on offer, with some adopting a bullet-point approach, which did not satisfy the question requirement for discussion.

Part (d) common errors:

One problem was the approach adopted by some candidates of discussing, often at length, the views of Miller and Modigliani on dividend policy. Given the listed status of the company in question, such a discussion would only be of marginal interest to the dividend reduction decision.

Few candidates recognised that cutting a dividend of $0.08 × 70m = $5.6m would generate only part of the finance required by the company, although it would reduce the amount of external finance needed to be raised.

As in the previous part-question, many answers were very brief for the marks on offer, and often employed a bullet-point approach, which did not meet the requirement for discussion. Surprisingly, even though it was part of the requirement, few candidates made a recommendation on whether the dividend should be cut.

310 SPINE CO (SEP/DEC 2020)

Key answer tips

Sometimes in questions like this, some representative performance indicators such as gearing and interest cover are given, which help guide the format of your answer. Part (a) of this question is more difficult because it's down to you to work out which calculations will help you with the evaluation.

You should realise that you can prepare forecasts for the changes that will result from either financing option. Debt increases the interest commitment, while the profits are spread over more shares after a rights issue. Always use the current year figures as a starting point and put through known changes.

Calculation of EPS and interest cover will be useful for the evaluation. Here, you also have the ability to calculate the PE ratio from the current figures, which can then be used to value the shares after the financing has taken place.

Part (b) is a straightforward knowledge requirement. Note the requirement to both explain and discuss. You might start with an explanation of each type of risk and then discuss any similarities and differences to pick up the remaining marks.

Part (c) is also a knowledge requirement, although many students will find this tricky. Have a go and then review the model answer with the aim of being able to pick up more marks next time.

The highlighted words are key phrases that markers are looking for.

(a) Increased operating profit = $13.040m × 1.2 = $15,648,000

Financing by debt

Current interest payment = $240,000

Increase in interest = $15m × 0.08 = $1,200,000

Revised interest payment = $1,200,000 + $240,000 = $1,440,000

Revised PBT = new operating profit – new interest = $15,648,000 – $1,440,000 = $14,208,000

Revised PAT = PBT × (1 – tax rate) = $14,208,000 × 0.7 = $9,945,600

Current EPS = $8,960,000/ 12,000,000 = $0.747 per share

Revised EPS = $9,945,600/12,000,000 = $0.829 per share

Current PE ratio = price per share/earnings per share = $6.25/ $0.747 = 8.37 times

Revised share price = PE ratio × new EPS = 8.37 × $0.829 = $6.94 per share

Capital gain = $6.94 – $6.25 = $0.69 per share

Financing by equity

Revised PBT = $15,648,000 – $240,000 = $15,408,000

Revised PAT = PBT × (1 – tax rate) = $15,408,000 × 0.7 = $10,785,600

New shares issued = 12m/4 × 1 = 3m shares

Revised number of shares = 12m + 3m = 15m shares

Revised EPS = $10,785,600/15,000,000 = $0.719

Current PE ratio = price per share/earnings per share = $6.25/ 0.747 = 8.37 times

Revised share price = PE ratio × new EPS = 8.37 × $0.719 = $6.02 per share

TERP = ((4 × $6.25) + $5.00)/ 5 = $6.00 per share

Capital gain = $6.02 – $6.00 = $0.02 per share

Note: as there are no preference dividends, profit after tax = earnings.

Comment on findings

Financing by debt is recommended as this leads to the larger capital gain for the shareholders. This recommendation could have been made on the basis of EPS values alone, as the price/earnings ratio multiplier is the same for both financing choices. However, it is important to compare the share price arising from the equity financing option with the theoretical ex rights share price, rather than with the cum rights share price.

Example answers in a spreadsheet:

	A	B	C	D	E	F	G	H	I
1	a			Current	Debt	Equity			
2								**Example formulae used:**	
3		PBIT		13040	15648	15648		New PBIT with 20% growth	=D3*1.2
4		Int		240	1440	240		Additional debt interest for debt column	=15000*8%
5		PBT		12800	14208	15408			
6		Tax		3840	4262.4	4622.4			
7		Earnings		8960	9945.6	10785.6			
8								Number of new shares for equity column	=12000/4*1
9								Total new shares for equity column EPS calculation	=12000+3000
10		EPS		0.746667	0.8288	0.71904			
11		Int cover		54.33333	10.86667	65.2			
12		PE ratio		8.370536					
13		price		6.25	6.9375	6.01875		Price in equity column	=D12*E7/12000
14									
15		The calcuations for price assume that the PE ratio stays the same after the expansion							

(b) With any investment, there is a risk that the actual outcome may be different from the expected or predicted outcome. This risk can be reduced by holding several different investments, since different investments are affected to differing extents by changes in economic variables such as interest rates and inflation rates. The return from one investment may increase, for example, when the return from a different investment decreases. Holding a range of different investments is known as portfolio diversification.

Experience shows that there is a limit to the reduction in total risk that can be achieved as a result of portfolio diversification. The risk that cannot be removed by portfolio diversification is called systematic risk. It represents risk relating to the financial system as a whole that cannot be avoided by any company in which an investment is made.

The risk that can be removed through portfolio diversification is called unsystematic risk or specific risk, as it relates to specific companies in which investments are made.

Experience has shown that investing in the shares of between 20 and 30 companies is sufficient to eliminate almost all of the unsystematic risk from an investment portfolio.

Systematic risk contains both business risk and financial risk. A company with no debt finance faces business risk alone, while a company with both equity and debt finance faces both business risk and financial risk.

(c) The capital asset pricing model (CAPM) is based on several key assumptions.

Investors hold diversified portfolios

While portfolio theory considers total risk, the CAPM considers only systematic risk, as it makes the assumption that all investors hold diversified portfolios. Investors will therefore only require compensation for the systematic risk in their portfolios.

Single-period transaction horizon

In order to compare the returns on different assets such as shareholdings, the CAPM assumes that all returns are over a standard single-period transaction horizon, usually taken to be one year.

Perfect capital market

The CAPM assumes a perfect capital market, with no taxes, no transaction costs and perfect information freely available to all participants.

Borrowing and lending at the risk-free rate

The CAPM assumes that all investors can borrow and lend at the risk-free rate of return. This represents a minimum rate of return required by all investors and is one of the variables in the CAPM equation.

ACCA marking scheme		
		Marks
(a)	Increased operating profit	0.5
	Debt – increased interest	1
	Debt – increased PBT	0.5
	Debt – increased PAT	0.5
	Debt – revised EPS	1
	Debt – capital gain	1
	Equity – increased PBT	0.5
	Equity – revised EPS	1
	Equity – TERP	1
	Equity – capital gain	1
	Recommendation	1
	Other discussion	1
		10
(b)	Portfolio diversification	2
	Systematic risk	1
	Unsystematic risk	1
	Other discussion	1
		5
(c)	Diverse portfolios	1
	Single-period	1
	Perfect capital market	1
	Risk-free rate	1
	Other discussion	1
		5
Total		**20**

Extracts from examiner's comments

Part (a) common errors:

The requirement asked candidates to 'evaluate' the options and candidates were presented with various pieces of financial information in the scenario. It's therefore difficult to perceive how the question can be answered fully without reference to such information. Some candidates chose to 'discuss' debt and equity in quite a generic way, with little or no reference to the scenario.

Most candidates were able to compute the increased operating profit, although, as with other computations, it is disappointing to see basic errors of arithmetic, for example, errors of magnitude where a 20% rise was processed as 2%.

Under the debt financing option, interest is certain to rise, and the scenario clearly stated that the finance charges (interest) on the new $15,000,000 of loan notes will be at 8%. It is difficult to see why any other interest rates would be used. Once again, errors of arithmetic arose, instead of 8% × $15,000,000 = $1,200,000 being included, there were examples of $120,000 and other errors of magnitude and/or decimal points.

A source of error was adding after-tax additional interest payments to current before-tax interest payments, in calculating revised finance costs. This suggests both carelessness and lack of familiarity with the format of financial statements. Furthermore, some candidates were incorrect to simply apply a 20% increase to the PAT.

Whilst many candidates could calculate the TERP, some incorrectly claimed that the TERP was the share price after investing the rights issue funds, when in fact the TERP is the share price after the cash has been raised but before it has been invested, and/or also incorrectly claimed that shareholders would be unhappy with the rights issue because it would lead to a fall in the share price to the TERP, when in fact, the TERP is a wealth-neutral share price, resulting from shareholders transferring some of their cash wealth into share wealth. The TERP can then be used, as above, to assess any capital gain or loss arising from the investment.

Part (b) common errors:

Answers that attempted to discuss diversification from a corporate perspective often strayed into a discussion of risk hedging that did not address the question requirement and that overemphasised internal risk relative to external risk.

Some answers were too brief for the marks on offer. However, even where answers were more substantial, marks could not be awarded due to candidates wandering off the point, for example by discussing financial risk and business risk, or by discussing the relationship between equity beta and asset beta.

Weaker answers failed to mention portfolio diversification at all and focused instead on describing systematic and unsystematic risk, often very briefly and with little else added to the discussion.

Part (c) common errors

Many answers showed limited understanding of this syllabus area. Too often, responses were irrelevant to the requirement e.g. how to calculate a project-specific discount rate, or written in a general way about CAPM with no attempt to discuss the assumptions made by the CAPM, often taking instead individual aspects of the CAPM and describing them incorrectly as assumptions, e.g. the CAPM assumes that betas can be ungeared and regeared.

311 ZEDDEMORE CO (MAR/JUN 2021)

Key answer tips

Part (a) of this question contains a standard set of calculations, which you should have seen multiple times during your studies. There is a slight tweak in that there are two debt sources that need to be included in the value of V_d, but otherwise this is a set of calculations that you should get to grips with before taking the exam as it does come up regularly.

For the comment, note that the commercial director does not feel that the calculations done in part (i) were necessary. If there had been negligible change in the value of ke, the director may have been correct in this case, but as the equity cost has risen, using a lower k_e could lead to projects being accepted that don't actually generate enough of a return to keep the shareholders happy.

Part (b) is a straightforward knowledge requirement. Note in the model answer how, for each problem, the problem is stated and then expanded on. This is what the examiner expects for 'discuss' type questions – not just a one line answer stating what the problem is.

It is crucial for this syllabus to have an understanding of the risk-return relationship and part (c) tests this. Make sure you can replicate the first paragraph of the answer as this contains the key elements. The question then specifically asks you to relate it to Zeddemore, so you need to look at the data in the question and use it to illustrate the relationship just discussed.

The highlighted words are key phrases that markers are looking for.

(a) (i)

Current k_e:

Using Zeddemore's own equity beta:

$k_e = R_f + \text{beta}(R_m - R_f)$

$k_e = 4\% + 2.3(10\% - 4\%) = 17.8\%$

Project specific k_e:

Need to use the proxy (WCP) to derive a suitable beta as Zeddemore Co's own beta is not suitable for the new venture due to different business risk.

Degear the proxy beta first:

Asset beta = equity beta × $[V_e/(V_e + V_d(1 - t))]$

V_e = 100m × \$2.60 = \$260m

V_d = \$110m/\$100 × \$96 = \$105.6m

Asset beta = 1.25 × [\$260m/(\$260m + \$105.6m × (1 – 0.2))]

Asset beta = 1.25 × \$260m/\$344.48m = 0.94

Now regear using Zeddemore Co's gearing:

V_e = \$40m/\$0.50 × \$1.05 = \$84m

V_d (loan notes) = \$250m/\$100 × \$65 = \$162.5m

V_d (loan) = \$20m

Total V_d = \$162.5m + \$20m = \$182.5m

Equity beta = asset beta × [(V_e + V_d(1 – t))/V_e]

Equity beta = 0.94 × [(\$84m + \$182.5m × (1 – 0.2)/\$84m]

Equity beta = 0.94 × \$230m/\$84m = 2.57

Now use the beta in the CAPM to find k_e:

$k_e = R_f + \text{beta } (R_m - R_f)$

k_e = 4% + 2.57 × (10% – 4%) = 19.42%

(ii)

Comment:

The project-specific cost of equity is higher than the current cost of equity, indicating that a higher return would be needed by shareholders to compensate for the higher risk of the new venture. Appraising the venture using the existing cost of equity, as advised by the commercial director, would therefore result in an over-statement of the venture's net present value, potentially leading to an incorrect decision being made.

(b) Gearing problems

Increased earnings volatility

High gearing increases the volatility of Zeddemore Co's earnings as the interest payable is unaffected by any change in the activity level. If Zeddemore Co experiences a reduction in its activity level, the percentage reduction in earnings will be greater than the percentage reduction in activity level. This increased volatility in earnings represents the financial risk of the company.

Cost of equity finance

Increased volatility of earnings will increase the cost of equity, making equity finance more expensive. The financial risk premium can be seen by comparing the asset beta of 0.94 (ke = 9.64%) with the equity beta of 2.57 (ke = 19.42%).

Debt capacity

The gearing level will affect Zeddemore Co's ability to raise new debt finance and how much debt it can support (debt capacity). Given its high gearing level, Zeddemore Co may find that it cannot raise any more debt finance.

Bankruptcy risk

High gearing leads to a high interest obligation for Zeddemore Co and an increased risk of being unable to pay all of its interest following an unexpected reduction in profits/cash flow. This could result in default by Zeddemore Co on its interest payments and subsequent forced liquidation by its lenders.

Note: Only three problems were required.

(c) Risk-return relationship

The risk-return relationship explains why different sources of finance have different costs. An investor's required rate of return will be determined primarily by the level of risk the investment has. If an investment carries a high level of risk, the investor will require a high rate of return to compensate for that risk. Investing in a low-risk investment will mean a lower level of return will be required.

A rational investor would not invest in a high-risk investment offering a low return as they could obtain the same return from a lower-risk investment. A low-risk investment offering high returns would not exist as it would be undervalued and the high demand for that investment would increase the price and therefore reduce the return.

Zeddemore Co's finance costs

The risk-return relationship will result in Zeddemore Co's shareholders and lenders having different required rates of return.

The equity holders have no guaranteed return as Zeddemore Co is under no obligation to pay a dividend each year and capital growth is also not guaranteed (in fact, the share price has fallen). Also, if the company was liquidated, the equity holders would come last in the order of payment and possibly receive nothing.

By comparison, the lenders (loan note holders and the bank) face lower risk as their interest is a contractual obligation and must be paid. The fall in share price will not directly affect the lenders as they do not participate in any capital growth/decline.

Zeddemore Co's lenders do face the risk of default in the event of Zeddemore Co being unable to pay the interest, but both the loan notes and the bank loan are secured on Zeddemore Co's assets so the risk of any loss on default is reduced, assuming the assets realise sufficient value to repay the debt.

The above effects can be seen in Zeddemore Co's finance costs with their cost of equity being higher than their cost of debt. For example, the current cost of equity is 17.8% which is higher than the cost of the bank loan which is only 7%. The loan notes are also cheaper, costing 10% ($6.50/$65.00). The loan notes are more expensive than the bank loan as they are irredeemable and thus have no guaranteed repayment date, increasing the risk compared with the bank loan which is repayable in the future.

ACCA marking scheme

			Marks
(a)	(i)	Current cost of equity	0.5
		WCP Co equity MV	0.5
		WCP Co debt MV	0.5
		Asset beta	1
		Number of shares	0.5
		Zeddemore Co equity MV	0.5
		Zeddemore Co debt MV	0.5
		Total debt	0.5
		Equity beta	1
		Project cost of equity	0.5
			6
	(ii)	Higher risk/return	1
		Wrong decision	1
			2

(b)	Problem 1	2
	Problem 2	2
	Problem 3	2
		6
(c)	Risk-return principle	2
	Equity v debt	2
	Irredeemable debt	1
	Secured debt	1
		6
Total		**20**

Extracts from examiner's comments

The question, Zeddemore Co, is based on syllabus section E, Business Finance.

Part (a) (i) common errors:

Many candidates have erroneously used book values in degearing or regearing calculations, or ignored taxation. When tax was used, some candidates used an incorrect tax rate, which was not provided in the question.

The difficulty in part (a) (i) was reading through the detail in the scenario to pick out the figures needed in the calculations/equations shown above. The formula seems daunting, but remember it is given in the formula sheet and a little practice at similar examples will get you through. It does require some planning and then the correct use of the spreadsheet to make the calculations easier. You will need to practise these skills before sitting the exam.

Requirement (a) (ii) common errors

Some candidates just agreed/disagreed with the commercial director but needed to go beyond and say why.

Requirement (b) common errors:

Candidates failed to achieve full marks for the following reasons: the discussion was usually sparse; the discussion was on operational gearing and not financial gearing; the discussion was very generic and not related to the question scenario.

In this example, no financial analysis was required to gain full marks, but some candidates only provided financial analysis for this part, thus not obtaining marks as the requirement was to discuss.

Requirement (c) common errors:

A good answer would have begun by discussing the relationship between risk and return. This would be followed by the discussion of equity and debt and highlighting the reasons why equity is higher risk and debt is lower risk. Ideally the discussion would have then expanded on the loan notes and the bank loan and whether they are irredeemable/redeemable; secured/unsecured on Zeddemore Co's assets. Using the figures from part (a) (i), the discussion should have further related to the financing costs with equity (17.8%) and comparing it to the cheaper loan notes (10%) and the bank loan (7%).

Again, the discussion of capital structure theory may gain some marks provided it addresses the requirements of the question.

312 TANZA CO (MAR/JUN 2022)

Key answer tips

Part (a) is a standard cost of capital calculation. If you're able to get good marks on this, you should be able to do so for most similar questions. Note that when calculating an IRR, you would get the same marks for laying out the annual cash flows year by year and then using the spreadsheet formula as you would for using the linear interpolation approach. Use whichever you find quickest and easiest in the exam.

The answer shows the WACC calculated using a table, but you may wish to use the formula as given on the formula sheet. Both methods would pick up the same marks.

To provide a good answer to part (b) (i), you must have studied the syllabus area of capital structure and be able to recognise which capital theories the directors' remarks relate to. Once you recognise that director A's view correlates to the Modigliani and Miller tax inclusive model and that director B's view correlates to the traditional theory, you discuss these theories as part of your answer.

You can also relate the scenario to the theories. If Tanza does indeed have lower gearing than its competitors, it may have room under both theories to add debt and reduce the WACC However, changes may upset shareholders regardless of which theory holds true.

For part (b) (ii), for 4 marks on a discussion of two other factors, you should aim for 2 well-made points for each factor. Think of the more practical aspects of gearing, such as the ease of raising finance or the risk involved for each type of finance.

The highlighted words are key phrases that markers are looking for.

(a) Cost of equity (k_e)

$K_e = D_1/P_0 + g$

Note that $D_0 (1 + g)$ is equivalent to D_1. As D_1 is given in the question as \$0.90, use that, although as $D_0 (1 + g)$ comes to (\$0.85 × 1.06) \$0.901, this would also pick up the marks.

K_e = \$0.90/\$5.55 + 0.06 = 0.222 or 22.2%

Cost of convertible loan notes (k_{conv})

k_{conv} = internal rate of return of cash flows of ownership of the convertible debt

The debtholder has a choice on conversion to either take the redemption amount of \$100 or to convert to 20 ordinary shares.

Predicted value of 20 ordinary shares at conversion, given that the growth rate of the share price has been steady at 6% per annum:

$20 \times \$5.55 \times 1.06^3 = \$132.20$

Therefore we will assume that the debtholder would choose to convert rather than redeem to obtain the higher value.

Post-tax interest value for IRR calculation = \$100 × 6% × (1 – 15%) = \$5.10

Year	Cash flow	\$	DF 10%	PV (\$)	DF 15%	PV (\$)
0	market value	(108.51)	1.000	(108.51)	1.000	(108.51)
1 – 3	interest	5.10	2.487	12.68	2.283	11.64
7	redemption	132.20	0.751	99.28	0.658	86.99
				3.45		(9.88)

IRR = L + ((H – L) × (N_L/(N_L – N_H)))

IRR = 10 + ((15 – 10) × (3.45/(3.45 + 9.88))) = 11.3%

[Note: If the IRR spreadsheet formula is used, the answer is 11.2%. Both methods would pick up full marks]

Cost of bank loan

The bank loan pays 4% interest. The cost to the company is the post-tax interest rate:

4 × (1 – 15%) = 3.4%

Market values:

Equity = \$5.55 × (\$50m/\$0.5) = \$555m

Convertible loan notes = \$150m/\$100 × \$108.51 = \$162.765m

Bank loan = use nominal value = \$120m

WACC calculation:

	MV \$m	Cost	MV × cost
Ordinary shares	555	0.22	123.30
6% convertible loan notes	162.765	0.11	18.26
4% bank loan	120	0.034	4.08
	837.765		145.64

WACC = 145.64/837.765 = 0.174 or 17.4%

Example answer in a spreadsheet:

	A	B	C	D	E	F	G	H	I
1	a		MV $m	Cost	MV*cost				
2		Ordinary shares	555.00	0.222	123.30				
3		6% convertible loan notes	162.77	0.112	18.26				
4		4% bank loan	120.00	0.034	4.08				
5			837.77		145.64				
6									
7			WACC	17.4%	=E5/C5				
8				Format as a percentage					
9									
10		**cost of equity**	P0	5.55					
11			D0	0.85					
12			g	6%					
13									
14			predicted D1 at 6% growth			0.901			
15		this is in line with the indicated dividend so is acceptable to use in the calculations							
16			D1	0.9					
17			ke = D1 / P0 + g		**0.222**	=D16/D10+D12			
18									
19		**MV of equity**	**555**	=50/0.5*5.55					
20									
21		**cost of loan notes**	NV	100					
22			MV	108.51	assume is ex interest value				
23			Interest		6				
24			post-tax interest		5.1	=E23*(1-0.15)			
25									
26			value of redemption per loan note				100		
27			value of 20 shares if grow at 6% for 3 years				132.20	=20*5.55*1.06^3	
28									
29		As the share value is larger than the redemption amount, choose to convert rather than redeem							
30									
31			IRR calculation:		t0	t1	t2	t3	
32				cash flows	-108.51	5.1	5.1	137.3	
33				IRR	**0.112**				
34									
35			Formula in cell H32:		=5.1+132.2				
36			Formula in cell E33:		=IRR(E32:H32)				
37		At time period 3 we include both the final year of interest and the chosen conversion value							
38									
39		**MV of loan notes**	**162.77**	=150/100*108.51					
40									
41		**cost of bank loan**	Tax adjusted cost of 4%			**0.034**	=0.04*(1-0.15)		
42		**MV of bank loan**	Use nominal value in place of market value						

(b) (i) Director A

Director A is suggesting that Modigliani & Miller's (M&M) theory of capital structure is most relevant. M&M suggested that a company's weighted average cost of capital (WACC) is primarily determined by its business activities rather than its capital structure.

They also proposed that the only way a company's capital structure can affect the WACC and therefore the value of the company is by introducing more debt and thereby increasing the tax shield (the present value of the tax savings made because interest is tax-deductible whereas dividends are not).

It is based on this theory that Director A is suggesting a much more aggressive regearing of Tanza Co.

The problems or risks that this would pose:

– Providers of debt finance (e.g. banks) are not likely to tolerate such high levels of capital gearing as it increases the risk of default. If the banks are willing to lend at all, they are likely to require a much higher interest rate to compensate them for higher credit risk.

– It is possible that Tanza Co exhausts its taxable profits with deductions for interest costs.

Director B

Director B appears to be supporting the traditional theory by suggesting that there is an optimum. Because the cost of debt is generally lower than that of equity, by increasing gearing, Tanza Co's WACC would fall. However, as borrowing gets larger, equity investors see their financial risk increasing as more and more debt interest has to be paid before they receive a return on their equity. To compensate for this increased financial risk, the returns demanded by equity holders increase. As gearing continues to increase, the benefit of cheap debt finance is eventually outweighed by the cost of more expensive equity and WACC starts to rise. The optimal gearing level is achieved when WACC has stopped falling but has not yet started rising.

The problem with this is that the optimum level of gearing can only be estimated by trial and error.

(ii) Other factors to consider:

– The finance is needed quickly, this would favour the use of debt which is less time consuming to raise. Because of this and other administrative factors, it is also less expensive to raise.

– The cost of new debt may be lowered if Tanza Co has any non-current assets to offer as security. Using non-current assets as collateral will lower the risk for the lender.

– It is important to consider the clientele effect too. The current shareholder-base seems to be comfortable with a gearing level which is lower than average for the industry. By changing that policy, this may change the investors' perceived risk exposure, leading to the sale of their shares.

ACCA marking scheme

				Marks
(a)	Cost of equity			1
	Future share price			0.5
	Conversion value			0.5
	Conversion decision			1
	Cost of convertible loan notes			3
	Cost of bank loan			1
	Market value of equity			0.5
	Market value of convertible debt			0.5
	WACC			2
				10
(b)	(i)	Director A		3
		Director B		3
				6
	(ii)	Factor 1		2
		Factor 2		2
				4
Total				**20**

Extracts from examiner's comments

Part (a) common errors

Using total dividend in the numerator but individual share price (not total share value) in the denominator or vice versa

Not using the future dividend in the DGM calculation

Subtracting rather than adding the growth rate when calculating the cost of equity.

Not providing a rationale for using either the conversion or redemption value for the redeemable debt.

Laying out cashflows incorrectly for the IRR formula to be used. They must be laid out on a year by year basis and not grouped together for multiple years when there is an annuity.

Calculating the cost of debt from perpetuity instead of using an IRR calculation

Ignoring tax in calculating the cost of convertible debt and cost of bank loans

Using the after-tax interest payment as the cost of debt in the WACC, thereby ignoring the need to calculate the cost of capital of the convertible loan and losing substantial marks

Mixing per loan note interest payments with total market value and redemption value in an interpolation calculation

Arithmetic errors in the linear interpolation of the IRR, using two negative NPVs caused more problems in calculating IRR

Making errors when using the spreadsheet IRR function, e.g. outflows used as inflows.

Some candidates used book values and lost marks, despite the question requiring the use of market values.

Many candidates ignored the bank loan or used the cost of convertible debt for the cost of a bank loan.

There were arithmetic errors in calculating WACC, for example, calculating a WACC higher than the highest cost of capital.

Part (b) (i) common errors:

Candidates need to read the requirements and address them directly. If a critical discussion is asked for, one would then discuss the limitations and/or disadvantages of a theory or concept to achieve full marks. Furthermore, where specific reference to the case scenario is made as in (b) (i) and (ii), then full marks cannot be gained with theory alone – the company circumstances must be used in a relevant and applied way.

Part (b) (ii) common errors:

Two factors were required here for four marks, i.e. a discussion of each factor sufficient to gain two marks. Furthermore, two other factors were required separate to those already discussed.

Given that the question had already focused on the WACC and the relative costs of debt and equity, these did not count as other factors. Instead, candidates could have selected from the following: speed of financial need, availability of finance, security, debt capacity, flexibility, cost of issuing new shares/debt, and effect on existing shareholders. This was unsatisfactorily done, and many did not refer to the scenario set.

313 GRAFFHAM CO (MAR/JUN 2023)

Key answer tips

In part (a), the TERP calculation should be relatively straightforward, although a formula is not provided in the exam, so you do have to learn how to calculate it. The information to help you calculate the EPS isn't given all in one place, so you'll have to hunt around for it. A good way of putting together EPS calculations is to use operating profit as a starting point and then consider what needs to be deducted (interest, taxation) to get to an earnings figure. To calculate the new share price, don't assume that it will be the TERP. The information that the PE ratio will stay the same is crucial here. Remember that you can multiply EPS by the ratio to determine a share price.

In the discussion part, focus on what each named group has stated in the question scenario and consider whether their aim has been achieved, as well as what other aspects would make a difference to them (such as the share price rising from $8.40 to potentially $8.88).

For part (b), it is not enough to know the names of the various different Islamic finance products – you must ensure that you understand some details about them. Aim to be able to write a couple of different points about each, so that you can put them into the context of a particular question scenario.

The highlighted words are key phrases that markers are looking for.

(a) (i)

Rights issue price = \$8.40 × (1 – 0.25) = \$6.30

TERP (\$per share) = ((5 × \$8.40) + (2 × \$6.30))/(5 + 2) = \$7.80

Example answer in a spreadsheet:

	A	B	C	D	E	F	G
1	a i	TERP calc					
2		Number of shares currently in issue				7,500,000	=15000000/2
3		MV of shares before issue				63,000,000	=F2*8.4
4		Number of new shares issued				3,000,000	=F2/5*2
5		Proceeds of issue				18,900,000	=F4*8.4*0.75
6		MV of shares after issue				81,900,000	=F3+F5
7		Total new number of shares				10,500,000	=F2+F4
8		TERP				7.8	=F6/F7

(ii)

	\$000
Operating profit	9,500
Interest expense (\$25m × 8%)	(2,000)
Profit before income taxes	7,500
Taxation at 16%	(1,200)
Profit for the year	6,300

Number of shares = \$15m/\$2 = 7.5 million

Earnings per share = \$6.3m/7.5 million = \$0.84

(iii) Profit on new project = \$20m × 18% = \$3.6m

	\$000
Revised operating profit (\$9.5m + \$3.6m)	13,100
Interest expense (\$25m × 8%)	(2,000)
Revised profit before income taxes	11,100
Taxation at 16%	(1,776)
Revised profit for the year	9,324

Number of shares issued = 7.5 million × 2/5 = 3 million

Revised number of shares = 7.5 million + 3 million = 10.5 million

Revised earnings per share = \$9.324m/10.5 million = \$0.888

Price-earnings ratio before rights issue = \$8.40/\$0.84 = 10

Revised share price = \$0.888 × 10 = \$8.88

Example answer in a spreadsheet:

	A	B	C	D	E	F
11	a ii and a iii		before		after	
12		PBIT	9,500		13,100	=9500+20000*18%
13		Interest	2,000		2,000	=25000*8%
14		PBT	7,500		11,100	
15		Tax at 16%	1,200	=C14*16%	1,776	=E14*16%
16						
17		PAT (earnings)	6,300		9,324	
18						
19		No. of shares	7,500	=F2/1000	10,500	=F7/1000
20						
21		EPS	0.84	=C17/C19	0.888	=E17/E19
22						
23		Share price	8.4			
24		PE ratio	10			
25		New share price			8.88	=C24*E21
26		(assuming same PE ratio)				

(iv) Gearing before rights issue = ($25m × 1.10)/(($25m × 1.10) + (7.5 million × $8.40)) = 30.4%

Gearing after rights issue = ($25m × 1.10)/(($25m × 1.10) + (10.5 million × $8.88)) = 22.8%

Example answer in a spreadsheet:

	A	B	C	D	E	F
28	a iv					
29		Gearing	before		after	
30		MV equity	63,000	=F3/1000	93,240	=E25*F7/1000
31		MV debt	27,500	=25000/100*110	27,500	=C31
32						
33		Gearing	30.4%	=C31/(C31+C30)	22.8%	=E31/(E31+E30)

(v) **Directors**

The current level of gearing exceeds the average industry gearing, which does concern the directors. However, the rights issue's impact would be to take gearing below the industry average. The new gearing would give the directors some scope to obtain loan finance if they invest in future projects.

Small shareholders

Small shareholders do not have to subscribe to the rights issue, they could always sell their rights. This would give them cash if they currently have a cash shortage. Selling their rights would lower their % shareholdings in Graffham Co. However, as their percentage holdings are already small, it would be unlikely to make any difference to the influence they have. They would benefit from a capital gain of $1.08 per share ($8.88 – $7.80).

Large shareholders

The current operating profit margin ((9,500/45,200) × 100%) is 21%, which means the new project would not meet the large shareholders' criterion. However, the new project would earn profits and result in a capital gain, assuming the price-earnings ratio stayed the same. The project should result in a positive long-term increase in shareholder wealth, assuming it has a positive net present value. It should also act as a gateway to investing in further projects with higher profit margins in future.

(b) Mudaraba

A mudaraba contract is a profit-sharing arrangement for a venture between an investor and Graffham Co. The investor would be the sole provider of the capital. Management of the venture would be the sole responsibility of Graffham Co, reflecting Graffham Co's expertise in running profitable ventures. Under the mudaraba contract, profits generated would be shared in a pre-arranged ratio. Only the capital provider would bear any losses, but would only be liable to the extent of capital provided.

Musharaka

Under a musharaka contract Graffham Co, along with another investor or investors, would contribute capital to a joint venture. Net profits would be divided in pre-arranged ratios. Any losses would be borne by the partners in proportion to their net capital contributions. All parties could be involved in management of the venture, though they might choose not to be.

Comments

From Graffham Co's viewpoint, a musharaka contract would still mean that Graffham Co would have to contribute some capital, raising the issue of how this contribution would be financed. A mudaraba contract would have the advantages that the capital provider would contribute all the capital and bear all the losses, but would have no role in management.

Both contracts should provide stability, as both should represent a longer-term investment and relationship with the other investors based on mutual interest and co-operation.

The business operations under both types of contract would have to be run in compliance with Sharia law.

Both arrangements would represent an effective provision of equity finance by external providers which would not give the external providers shareholdings in Graffham Co itself.

However, the larger shareholders might not welcome the new project if the profit sharing ratio which Graffham Co negotiated, combined with the operating profit margin, did not appear to be adequate for the managerial resources committed. If a musharaka contract is used, the overall profit obtained must be sufficient to compensate for the financial resources invested as well.

ACCA marking scheme

			Marks
(a)	(i)	Rights issue price	1
		TERP	1
			2
	(ii)	Finance cost	0.5
		Tax	0.5
		Number of shares	0.5
		EPS	0.5
			2
	(iii)	Additional profit from new contract	0.5
		Revised tax	0.5
		Revised number of shares	0.5
		Revised EPS	0.5
		Revised share price	1
			3
	(iv)	Current gearing	1
		Revised gearing	1
			2
	(v)	Directors	1
		Small shareholders	1
		Large shareholders	1
		Other points	2
			5
(b)	Description of mudaraba		2
	Description of musharaka		2
	Discussion of criteria affecting decision		2
			6
Total			**20**

Extracts from examiner's comments

Part (a) (i) common errors:

Calculating the rights issue price at 25% i.e. $8.40 × 25% = $2.10

Inverting the '2 for 5' into an effective '5 for 2'

Incorrectly using arithmetic functions when entering a long set of numbers in a single cell, as an incorrect approach will give an incorrect answer.

For example, (2 × 0.75 × 8.4 + 5 × 8.4)/5 + 2 = 12.92 (incorrect)

Instead of

((2 × 0.75 × 8.40) + (5 × 8.40)/(5 + 2) = 7.80 (correct)

Part (a) (ii) common errors

Unfortunately, some candidates moved straight from operating profit to profit for the year (after tax) without deducting finance costs, whilst others used operating profit for the EPS without deducting finance costs or tax. Where this occurred, it showed a disappointing lack of knowledge as to the exact nature of earnings.

Part (a) (iii) common errors:

Several candidates incorrectly used only the profit on the new project to calculate the revised EPS instead of adding that profit to current profit levels.

Many responses lacked the final step i.e., the need to calculate the share price using the formula including the price-earnings (PE) ratio, namely:

Market price = PE × EPS.

The lack of the calculation of the new share price hindered some candidates when it came to calculate the market value of equity for the gearing ratio in part (a) (iv).

Other candidates incorrectly thought that the revised share price was the same as the TERP.

Part (a) (iv) common errors:

The formula for calculating the gearing ratio is given in the case scenario

"The current industry average gearing figure at market values, measured as ((Non-current liabilities/(Non-current liabilities + Equity)) × 100%) is 25%".

Using Debt/Equity instead of Debt/(Debt + Equity) was simply incorrect.

Additionally, the requirement is clear, "using market values". Hence, calculations that used book values scored no marks.

Two further errors were seen often in this part-question in relation to the value of equity:

- Including retained earnings in the market value of equity
- Using the incorrect market value per share such as the pre-investment $8.40 or the TERP of $7.80.

Part (a) (v) common errors:

The views of the directors and large shareholders seemed to have been understood better than the views of the small shareholders, but too many responses repeated only the content in the scenario and hence scored few, if any, marks.

Part (b) common errors:

The inability to demonstrate knowledge about the specific Islamic financing methods was a weakness of some responses and therefore meant that such responses could gain few, if any, marks.

Another weakness was to waste time discussing the nature of Islamic finance such as prohibited forms of trade (in a general sense and not applied to Graffham Co) and that interest (riba) is forbidden under Sharia law. Whilst such points may be technically correct, they do not directly address the requirement under consideration.

314 MARBLE CO (SEP/DEC 2023)

Key answer tips

Part (a) is a standard cost of capital calculation. If you're able to get good marks on this, you should be able to do so for most similar questions. Note that when calculating an IRR, you would get the same marks for laying out the annual cash flows year by year and then using the spreadsheet formula as you would for using the linear interpolation approach. Use whichever you find quickest and easiest in the exam.

The answer shows the WACC calculated using a table, but you may wish to use the formula as given on the formula sheet. Both methods would pick up the same marks.

Part (b) is a difficult discussion question, but learning the advantages and limitations of both the DGM and CAPM will greatly help here.

The creditor hierarchy in part (c) is a favourite topic for the exam. Make sure that you're happy with the concept of risk versus return – investors taking on higher risk will require a higher return in order for them to invest. Providing a higher return costs the company more.

The highlighted words are key phrases that markers are looking for.

(a) Cost of equity

Dividend growth rate = ((0.84/0.69)0.25 – 1) × 100 = 5.0%

Ex dividend share price = 11.93 – 0.84 = $11.09 per share

Ke = [((0.84 × 1.05)/11.09) + 0.05] × 100 = 13.0%

Cost of preference shares

Kp = 100 × (0.25 × 1.00)/2.27 = 11.0%

Cost of convertible loan notes

After-tax interest payment = 6.5 × (1 – 0.26) = $4.81 per loan note

Conversion value = 11.09 × 1.065 × 8 = 14.84 × 8 = $118.73 per loan note

The conversion value of $118.73 per loan note is greater than the redemption value of $100.00 per loan note and, as shareholders are assumed to choose the option that maximises their wealth, conversion is expected to occur.

Linear interpolation can be used to find the after-tax cost of the convertible debt.

Year	**CF**	$	**6% DF**	**PV $**	**7% DF**	**PV $**
0	MV	(107.11)	1.000	(107.11)	1.000	(107.11)
1–5	After-tax interest	4.81	4.212	20.26	4.100	19.72
5	CV	118.73	0.747	88.69	0.713	84.65
				1.84		(2.74)

After-tax Kd = 6 + [(1.84 × 1)/(1.84 + 2.74)] = 6 + 0.4 = 6.4%

Note: Using the spreadsheet function, IRR = 6.4% also.

Market values

		$m
Ordinary shares	226m × 11.09 =	2,506.34
Preference shares	20m × 2.27 =	45.40
Loan notes	94m × 107.11/100 =	100.68
		2,652.42

WACC calculation

WACC = [(2,506.34 × 13.0) + (45.40 × 11.0) + (100.68 × 6.4)]/2,652.42 = 12.7%

Example answer in a spreadsheet:

	A	B	C	D	E	F
1						
2		Cost	MV ($m)	cost × MV		Formulae used:
3	Ordinary shares	0.1300	2,506.34	325.75		
4	Preference shares	0.1101	45.40	5.00		
5	Convertible loan notes	0.0640	100.68	6.44		
6			2,652.42	337.19		
7						
8		**WACC**	**12.7%**			=D6/C6
9						
10	**MV ordinary shares**	ex div price (cum div price – D0)		11.09		=11.93-0.84
11		no. of shares		226	m	
12		total MV (ex div price × no. of shares)		2506.34		=D11*D10
13						
14	**Cost ordinary shares**	Dividend valuation model	Do	0.84		
15			g	0.0504		=D18
16			P0	11.09		=D10
17						
18	growth of ordinary dividenc	=(D0/Dn)^(1/n)–1		0.0504		=(0.84/0.69)^(1/4)-1
19						
20	ke	=D0×(1+g)/P0+g		0.1300		=D14*(1+D15)/D16+D1
21						
22	**MV preference shares**	ex div price		2.27		
23		no. of shares		20	m	
24		total MV (ex div price × no. of shares)		45.4		=D23*D22
25						
26	**Cost preference shares**		D0	0.25		=1*25%
27			P0	2.27		=D22
28						
29	kp		=D0/P0	0.1101		=D26/D27
30						
31	**MV loan notes**	Total nominal value (NV)		94	$m	
32		NV per note		100		
33		MV per note ex interest		107.11		
34						
35	Total MV	=total NV/NV per loan note×MV per loan note		100.68		=D31/D32*D33
36						
37	**Cost of loan notes**					
38	Conversion v redemption					
39		Redemption value		100		
40		Conversion value (including 6% growth for 5 years)		118.73		=11.09*8*1.06^5
41		Choose to convert as it has the higher value				
42						
43	IRR	t0	-107.11			
44		t1	4.81			=6.5*(1-26%)
45		t2	4.81			
46		t3	4.81			
47		t4	4.81			
48		t5	123.54			=6.5*(1-26%)+D40
49						
50		IRR of loan note cash flows	6.4%			=IRR(C43:C48)

(b) Risk

One of the commonly suggested weaknesses of the dividend growth model (DGM) in calculating the cost of equity is that the model does not consider risk, but this is only true in explicit terms. The model considers risk implicitly because the risk faced by a company is reflected in its share price: for example, an increase in risk will lead to a decrease in the share price and hence an increase in the cost of equity calculated by the DGM.

In calculating the cost of equity, therefore, a clear advantage of the capital asset pricing model (CAPM) over the DGM is that the CAPM explicitly considers risk, specifically systematic risk since the model assumes that all investors hold diversified portfolios. The CAPM therefore calculates what the cost of equity should be for the systematic risk faced by ordinary shareholders.

Dividend growth rate

Another important weakness of the DGM is that the dividend growth rate is assumed to be constant, when experience shows that, historically, it changes frequently. In the case of Marble Co, for example, the dividend growth rate in successive years has been 5.8%, 6.8%, 2.6% and 5.0%, the arithmetic mean is 5.05% and the geometric mean is 5.0%. Which historical dividend growth rate best represents the future dividend growth rate?

DGM weaknesses

Further suggested weaknesses of the DGM are that the model ignores taxation and issue costs, but the model can be modified to consider both factors. Another criticism is that the model implies that a company has no value if it does not pay dividends, but the model can be applied at that future point from which dividends are paid, with the calculated future share price being discounted back to the present day to give a current share price.

CAPM weaknesses

An important weakness of the CAPM is that it can be difficult to firmly establish values for the model's key variables: the equity risk premium, the risk-free rate of return and the equity beta. The equity risk premium is found from statistical analysis of historical data over long periods of time and different studies can provide different values. Determining the risk-free rate of return is hampered by the fact that a risk-free asset does not exist; a substitute such as the yield on short-dated government debt is used instead. The equity beta is derived from statistical analysis of historic data and therefore cannot be assumed to predict future values with any certainty. While beta values are assumed to be constant, experience shows that they change on a regular basis.

In a perfect world with perfect data, both the DGM and the CPM should give the same value for the cost of equity.

(c) The creditor hierarchy gives the order of preference for the settlement of financial claims when a company is liquidated. In relation to sources of finance, the higher the position in the creditor hierarchy, the greater the chance of receiving a full settlement of financial liability.

At the top of the creditor hierarchy in relation to sources of finance is secured debt, such as loan notes or bank loans with a fixed charge over the non-current assets of the company being liquidated. The providers of this kind of finance face the lowest relative risk of non-settlement of their financial claims and so require the lowest relative return on the finance they have provided. Theoretically, therefore, the before-tax cost of secured debt should be the lowest before-tax cost of capital of a company.

Ranking below secured debt in the creditor hierarchy is unsecured debt, such as unsecured loan notes or bank loans which do not have a charge over any non-current assets of the company being liquidated. The providers of this kind of finance face a higher risk of non-settlement of their financial claims than secured debt and so require a higher rate of return on finance provided. Theoretically, therefore, the before-tax cost of capital of unsecured debt is higher than the before-tax cost of capital of secured debt.

Ranking below unsecured debt in the creditor hierarchy are preference shares, which commonly pay a fixed percentage of their nominal value as a dividend. The preference dividend must be paid in full before any ordinary dividends are paid and, in liquidation, preference share capital must be repaid before payment is made to ordinary shareholders. Preference shareholders therefore face a higher risk of non-settlement of their financial claims than secured or unsecured debt and the cost of capital of preference shares is therefore theoretically higher than the before-tax cost of debt.

At the bottom of the creditor hierarchy, ranking below secured and unsecured debt and preference shares, are ordinary shares. Only when all the other financial claims have been met can any payment be made to ordinary shareholders, who therefore carry the highest relative risk of non-payment. Ordinary shareholders therefore require the highest level of return of any provider of finance to a company and theoretically, therefore, the cost of equity is higher than either the cost of preference shares or the before-tax cost of debt.

The costs of capital for Marble Co illustrate this hierarchy, as the cost of equity is 13.0%, the cost of preference shares is 11.0% and the before-tax cost of secured debt is 7.8%.

ACCA marking scheme

		Marks
(a)	Dividend growth calculation	1
	Cost of equity	1
	Cost of preference shares	1
	Convertible value	1
	Convert decision	1
	After-tax interest	1
	IRR set up	1
	Cost of debt	1
	Market value of equity	0.5
	Market value of preference shares	0.5
	Market value of debt	0.5
	WACC calculation	1.5
		11
(b)	Risk	1
	Dividend growth rate	1
	DGM discussion	1
	CAPM discussion	1
		4
(c)	Explain hierarchy	1
	Cost of secured debt	1
	Cost of unsecured debt	1
	Cost of preference shares	1
	Cost of equity	1
		5
Total		**20**

Extracts from examiner's comments

Part (a) common errors

In the calculation using the dividend growth model to determine the cost of equity, some candidates did not use the ex dividend share price of $11.09 and come candidates ignored the growth rate.

In the cost of convertible debt calculation:

– Not justifying a comparison between the conversion and redemption values.

– Not calculating after-tax values of interest.

– Not knowing which values to enter for year 0 and for year 5.

Some candidates used book values instead of market values for the WACC weighting values.

Part (b) common errors:

Too often, responses were irrelevant to the requirement. e.g. how to calculate a project-specific discount rate or written in a general way about CAPM with no attempt to discuss the relative merit of CAPM over DGM or vice versa, often taking instead individual aspects of the CAPM/DGM.

Candidates writing all they know about a topic rather than addressing question requirements.

Part (c) common errors:

Candidates were aware of the different sources of finance; however, they scored low marks as the creditor hierarchy was shown as a list and then lacked significant relevant knowledge to show adequate discussion of the relationship between the creditor hierarchy and the relative costs.

315 GAMGEE CO (MAR/JUN 2024)

Key answer tips

In part (a), you're asked to calculate both interest cover and earnings per share (EPS) but are not given a formula to use. These are formulae that you must learn as part of your studies. Because the gearing calculation can take more than one form, the examiner is likely to give the required form to you, as in this question.

Remember that issuing debt immediately leads to an increase in interest costs. Issuing shares means that profits are spread over a higher number of shares, diluting the EPS. When considering which source of finance to recommend, think from the investors' point of view – do they want to see rises or falls in the ratios? Will they be concerned about big changes to them?

Part (b) is a discussion question on a specific aspect of capital structure. Rote learning will be beneficial for this type of question.

There's no easy way to remember the specifics of Islamic finance to guarantee good marks in questions such as part (c). You may be asked about the principles that cover it, such as that interest is forbidden and that investments must comply with Sharia law, but there are also questions like this, where specific knowledge of forms of Islamic funding are required. If remembering this knowledge doesn't come easily, go back over it the day before the exam if possible.

The highlighted words are key phrases that markers are looking for.

(a) (i) Loan notes

Interest cover:

Operating profit = $177m + $64.8m = $241.8m

Finance charges = $450m × 6% + $360m × 5% = $45m

Interest cover = $241.8m/$45m = 5.4 times

Earnings per share (EPS):

Earnings = ($241.8m – $45m) × (1 – 0.2) = $157.4m

EPS = $157.4m/800m = $0.20

Gearing:

Share price = 8 × $0.20 = $1.60

Equity market value (MV) = $1.60 × 800m = $1,280m

Debt MV = $450m + $360m = $810m

Gearing = $810/($810 + $1,280m) = 38.8%

(ii) Rights issue

Interest cover:

Interest cover = $241.8m/($450m × 6%) = 9.0 times

EPS:

Earnings = ($241.8m – 6% × $450m) × (1 – 0.2) = $171.8m

Current share price = 8 × $0.15 = $1.20

Rights issue price = $1.20 × 0.75 = $0.90

Number of shares issued = $360m/$0.90 = 400m

EPS = $171.8m/(800m + 400m) = $0.14

Gearing:

New share price = 8 × $0.14 = $1.12

Equity MV = $1.12 × 1,200m = $1,344m

Debt MV = $450m

Gearing = $450m/($450m + $1,344m) = 25.1%

(iii) Comment

As expected, the loan note option increases Gamgee Co's financial risk with total gearing increasing to 38.8% (currently 32.3%) and interest cover reducing to 5.4 times (currently 6.5 times). Arguably, this increase in financial risk may be considered significant and moving to a level which the shareholders may consider undesirable. Industry averages would be useful here but given Gamgee Co's diverse operational base, it may be problematic to find a sensible comparative.

On the positive side, EPS increases under the loan note option giving a greater increase in shareholder wealth than the rights issue where the EPS falls. Therefore, providing shareholders are happy with the level of financial risk, the loan notes issue is recommended.

Tutorial note

Shareholder wealth can be shown to increase as follows (this is not required to gain full marks):

Current shareholder wealth (SW) = 8 × \$0.15 × 800m = \$960m

SW after loan note issue = \$1,280m

Increase = \$1,280m – \$960m = \$320m

SW after rights issue = \$1,344m

Increase = \$1,344m – \$960m – \$360m = \$24m

(b) Problems of high financial gearing

Bankruptcy risk

Unlike equity, debt imposes payment obligations on the company. High levels of debt (high financial gearing) will mean high levels of interest and capital repayment. Even in times of financial difficulty, these obligations must still be met, increasing the risk of default and being forced into liquidation.

Agency costs/restrictive conditions

Lenders are likely to impose more restrictive conditions (covenants) in loan agreements with highly geared companies, in order to protect their investment in what could be seen as higher risk lending. Examples of such covenants include restrictions on dividend payments and restricting the raising of further debt.

Debt capacity

The amount of debt a company can raise will depend upon its debt capacity which is driven mainly by its level of tangible assets which can be pledged as collateral. High levels of debt, if achieved, will probably mean that there are few, if any, unpledged assets remaining to use as collateral, restricting the ability to raise more debt finance.

Increase in financing costs

Shareholders will view dividend pay-out in a highly geared company as risky as profits could be consumed by high levels of interest. Under the risk return trade-off, this will mean that shareholders in a highly geared company will require a higher rate of return, increasing the cost of equity. Debt holders too could increase their required rate of return, increasing the cost of debt.

Tax exhaustion

High levels of debt could mean that interest charges exceed taxable profits resulting in a deferral or even potential loss of tax relief, a key benefit with debt finance.

(c) Suitable sources of Islamic finance

Murabaha (trade credit)

Under a Murabaha, the Islamic Finance Institution (IFI) would purchase the assets for the project and then sell them to Gamgee Co who would pay the IFI in fixed instalments. A 10-year term (same as the proposed loan notes) should be possible and the IFI would not have any involvement in the running of Gamgee Co.

Ijara (lease)

Any assets required for the project would be purchased by the IFI and Gamgee Co would be given the right to use the assets in return for payments to the IFI, like a conventional lease. Just like a Murabaha, payments would be fixed with no management involvement but unlike the Murabaha, legal title to the assets would not transfer to Gamgee Co until the end of the Ijara period.

Sukuk (bonds)

Under a Sukuk arrangement, Sukuk bonds would be linked to the underlying assets with the Sukuk holders effectively the owners or partial owners in the assets, receiving a fixed income.

Note: Only two types were asked for. Mudaraba and Musharaka types would not be suitable as they are similar to traditional equity with profit sharing (both) and management involvement under the Musharaka.

ACCA marking scheme				
				Marks
(a)	(i)	New operating profit		0.5
		Loan notes	– Share price	0.5
			– interest	0.5
			– interest cover	0.5
			– PAT	0.5
			– EPS	0.5
			– MV equity	0.5
			– Gearing ratio	0.5
				4
	(ii)	Rights issue	– Interest cover	0.5
			– PAT	0.5
			– Issue price	0.5
			– Number shares	0.5
			– EPS	0.5
			– New share prices	0.5
			– MV equity	0.5
			– Gearing ratio	0.5
				4
	(iii)	Comments		2
		Recommendations		1
				3
(b)	Problems of high gearing			5
(c)	Islamic finance 1			2
	Islamic finance 2			2
				4
Total				**20**

Extracts from examiner's comments

Part (a) (i) common errors

Some candidates did not calculate PAT, and therefore could not score the marks for EPS. The calculation of EPS using operating profit is technically incorrect.

Some candidates did not realise that the EPS figure was required in the calculation of the market value of equity, and incorrectly assumed that the market price per share would be unchanged at \$1.20 (\$0.15 × 8).

Part (a) (ii) common errors:

For parts such as these, the layout of workings is of high importance. For some candidates, this still needs improvement and too many candidates showed no workings at all, and just entered incorrect figures into a cell, with no cell formula to support the figure(s), thereby making it extremely difficult to award marks for workings.

Part (a) (iii) common errors:

Whilst there were some good comments and recommendations, too many candidates simply did not do enough for the 3 marks on offer.

Many comments were simply mentioning that each ratio had gone up or down without stating if it was good or bad for the company, thereby failing to demonstrate FM knowledge.

Too many gave a one line answer stating that based on the ratios they should pick loan notes or rights issue without any justification or further explanation. Several responses incorrectly recommended both options when a choice was recommended.

Part (b) common errors:

Weaker responses did not develop points made or gave very brief answers, such as a list of short points when a discussion was required. Some answers did not directly address the requirement, for example just covering theories of capital structure and therefore could only gain marks on the high gearing aspects.

Part (c) common errors:

Too many candidates did not develop points or gave very brief answers, such as simply stating two types of Islamic Finance (IF), often just two words, when a discussion was required.

Furthermore, some answers discussed IF in a more general manner such as a discussion about the eligibility of the business activities (the case states that the Gamgee's proposed activities are eligible) and/or discussion about the prohibition of the payment of interest. Neither of these points address the requirement.

Section 7

SPECIMEN EXAM QUESTIONS

SECTION A

1 Which of the following actions is LEAST likely to increase shareholder wealth?

A The weighted average cost of capital is decreased by a recent financing decision

B The financial rewards of directors are linked to increasing earnings per share

C The board of directors decides to invest in a project with a positive net present value

D The annual report declares full compliance with the corporate governance code

2 The following financial information relates to an investment project:

	$000
Present value of sales revenue	50,025
Present value of variable costs	(25,475)
Present value of contribution	**24,550**
Present value of fixed costs	(18,250)
Present value of operating income	**6,300**
Initial investment	(5,000)
NPV	**1,300**

What is the sensitivity of the NPV to a change in sales volume?

A 7.1%

B 2.6%

C 5.1%

D 5.3%

3 Governments have a number of economic targets as part of their monetary policy.

Which TWO of the following targets relate predominantly to monetary policy?

A Increasing tax revenue

B Controlling the growth in the size of the money supply

C Reducing public expenditure

D Keeping interest rates low

4 The management of Lamara Co has annual credit sales of $20m and accounts receivable of $4m. Working capital is financed by an overdraft at 12% interest per year. Assume 365 days in a year.

Calculate the annual finance cost saving if management reduces the collection period to 60 days (to the nearest dollar).

$ ____________

5 The following is an extract from the management accounts of Gohar Co:

	$000
Revenue	60,000
Cost of sales	(50,000)
Operating profit	10,000
Interest expense	(4,000)
Profit before income taxes	6,000
Tax	(4,500)
Profit for the year	**1,500**

60% of the cost of sales is variable costs.

What is the operational gearing of Gohar Co?

A 5.0 times

B 2.0 times

C 0.5 times

D 3.0 times

6 The following information has been calculated for Asani Co:

Trade receivables collection period	52 days
Raw material inventory turnover period	42 days
Work in progress inventory turnover period	30 days
Trade payables payment period	66 days
Finished goods inventory turnover period	45 days

Calculate the length of the working capital cycle.

____________ **days**

7 The home currency of Acaba Co is the dollar ($) and it trades with a company in a foreign country whose home currency is the Dinar. The following information is available:

	Home country	**Foreign country**
Spot rate	20.00 Dinar per $	
Interest rate	3% per year	7% per year
Inflation rate	2% per year	5% per year

What is the six-month forward exchange rate?

A 20.39 Dinar per $

B 20.30 Dinar per $

C 20.59 Dinar per $

D 20.78 Dinar per $

8 **Which of the following statements concerning capital structure theory is correct?**

A In the traditional view, there is a linear relationship between the cost of equity and financial risk

B Modigliani and Miller said that, in the absence of tax, the cost of equity would remain constant

C Pecking order theory indicates that preference shares are preferred to convertible debt as a source of finance

D Business risk is assumed to be constant as the capital structure changes

9 Skava Co has paid the following dividends per share in recent years:

Year	**20X4**	**20X3**	**20X2**	**20X1**
Dividend ($ per share)	0.360	0.338	0.328	0.311

The dividend for 20X4 has just been paid and Skava Co has a cost of equity of 12%.

Using the geometric average historical growth rate and the dividend growth model, what is the market price of a Skava Co share on an ex-dividend basis?

A $4.67

B $5.14

C $5.40

D $6.97

10 Gurdip plots the historic movements of share prices and uses this analysis to make her investment decisions.

Oliver believes that share prices reflect all relevant information at all times.

Match the level of capital markets efficiency that best reflects each of Gurdip and Oliver's beliefs.

Efficiency	Name
Not efficient at all	Gurdip
Weak form efficient	Oliver
Semi-strong form efficient	
Strong form efficient	

11 'There is a risk that the value of our foreign currency-denominated assets and liabilities will change when we prepare our accounts.'

To which risk does the above statement refer?

A Translation

B Economic

C Transaction

D Interest rate

12 **Which TWO of the following statements are features of money market instruments?**

A A negotiable instrument can be sold before maturity

B The yield on commercial paper is usually lower than that on treasury bills

C Discount instruments trade at less than face value

D Commercial paper is often issued by companies to fund long-term expenditure

13 **Which of the following are usually seen as benefits of financial intermediation?**

1 Interest rate fixing

2 Risk pooling

3 Maturity transformation

A 1 and 2 only

B 1 and 3 only

C 2 and 3 only

D 1, 2 and 3

14 Which TWO of the following statements concerning working capital management are correct?

A The twin objectives of working capital management are profitability and liquidity

B A conservative approach to working capital investment will increase profitability

C Working capital management is a key factor in a company's long-term success

D The current ratio is a measure of profitability

15 Identify, by clicking on the relevant box, whether each of the following statements concerning financial management is true or false.

It is concerned with investment decisions, financing decisions and dividend decisions	**TRUE**	**FALSE**
It is concerned with financial planning and financial control	**TRUE**	**FALSE**
It considers the management of risk	**TRUE**	**FALSE**
It is concerned with providing information about past plans and decisions	**TRUE**	**FALSE**

SECTION B

The following scenario relates to questions 16–20.

Par Co currently has the following long-term capital structure:

	\$m	\$m
Equity finance		
Ordinary shares	30.0	
Reserves	38.4	
		68.4
Non-current liabilities		
Bank loans	15.0	
8% convertible loan notes	40.0	
5% redeemable preference shares	15.0	
		70.0
Total equity and liabilities		**138.4**

The 8% loan notes are convertible into eight ordinary shares per loan note in seven years' time. If not converted, the loan notes can be redeemed on the same future date at their nominal value of \$100. Par Co has a cost of debt of 9% per year.

The ordinary shares of Par Co have a nominal value of \$1 per share. The current ex-dividend share price of the company is \$10.90 per share and share prices are expected to grow by 6% per year for the foreseeable future. The equity beta of Par Co is 1.2.

16 The loan notes are secured on non-current assets of Par Co and the bank loan is secured by a floating charge on the current assets of the company.

Arrange the following sources of finance of Par Co in order of the risk to the investor with the riskiest first.

Finance source	Order of risk
Loan notes	1st
Ordinary shares	2nd
Redeemable preference shares	3rd
Bank loan	4th

17 **Calculate the conversion value of the 8% loan notes of Par Co after seven years (to two decimal places).**

\$ ___________

18 Assuming the conversion value after seven years is $126.15, what is the current market value of the 8% loan notes of Par Co?

A $115.20

B $109.26

C $94.93

D $69.00

19 Which of the following statements relating to the capital asset pricing model is correct?

A The equity beta of Par Co considers only business risk

B The capital asset pricing model considers systematic risk and unsystematic risk

C The equity beta of Par Co indicates that the company is more risky than the market as a whole

D The debt beta of Par Co is zero

20 Which TWO of the following are problems in using the price/earnings ratio method to value a company?

A It is the reciprocal of the earnings yield

B It combines stock market information and corporate information

C It is difficult to select a suitable price/earnings ratio

D The ratio may need adjusting when valuing the shares of unlisted companies

---

The following scenario relates to questions 21–25.

Zarona Co, whose home currency is the dollar ($), took out a fixed-interest peso bank loan several years ago when peso interest rates were relatively cheap compared to dollar interest rates. Zarona Co does not have any income in pesos. Economic difficulties have now increased peso interest rates while dollar interest rates have remained relatively stable.

Zarona Co must pay interest on the dates set by the bank. A payment of 5m pesos is due in six months' time. The following information is available:

	Pesos per $
Spot rate	12.500 – 12.582
Six-month forward rate	12.805 – 12.889

Interest rates which can be used by Zarona Co:

	Borrow	**Deposit**
Peso interest rates	10.0% per year	7.5% per year
Dollar interest rates	4.5% per year	3.5% per year

---

21 Calculate the dollar cost of a forward market hedge (to the nearest dollar).

$ ___________

22 Indicate, by clicking on the relevant box, whether each of the following statements relate to interest rate parity only, to purchasing power parity only or to both.

The currency of the country with the higher inflation rate will weaken against the other currency	**Interest rate parity only**	**Purchasing power parity only**	**Both interest rate and purchasing power parity**
The theory holds in the long term rather than the short term	**Interest rate parity only**	**Purchasing power parity only**	**Both interest rate and purchasing power parity**
The exchange rate reflects the different cost of living in two countries	**Interest rate parity only**	**Purchasing power parity only**	**Both interest rate and purchasing power parity**

23 What are the appropriate six-month interest rates for Zarona Co to use if it hedges the peso payment using a money market hedge?

Interest rate options	
1.75%	2.25%
3.5%	3.75%
4.5%	5.0%
7.5%	10.0%

Interest rate to be used for:	
Borrowing rate	Deposit rate

24 Which TWO of the following are possible ways for Zarona Co to hedge its current foreign currency risk?

A Matching receipts and payments

B Currency swaps

C Leading or lagging

D Currency futures

25 Zarona Co also trades with companies in Europe which use the euro as their home currency. In three months' time Zarona Co will receive €300,000 from a customer.

Which of the following is the correct procedure for hedging this receipt using a money market hedge?

A Step 1 Borrow an appropriate amount in euros now

Step 2 Convert the euro amount into dollars

Step 3 Place the dollars on deposit

Step 4 Use the customer payment to repay the loan

B Step 1 Borrow an appropriate amount in dollars now

Step 2 Place the dollars on deposit now

Step 3 Convert the dollars into euros in three months' time

Step 4 Use the customer payment to repay the loan

C Step 1 Borrow an appropriate amount in dollars now

Step 2 Convert the dollar amount into euros

Step 3 Place the euros on deposit

Step 4 Use the customer payment to repay the loan

D Step 1 Borrow an appropriate amount in euros now

Step 2 Place the euros on deposit now

Step 3 Convert the euros into dollars in three months' time

Step 4 Use the customer payment to repay the loan

The following scenario relates to questions 26–30.

Ridag Co operates in an industry which has recently been deregulated as the government seeks to increase competition in the industry.

Ridag Co plans to replace an existing machine and must choose between two machines. Machine 1 has an initial cost of $200,000 and will have a scrap value of $25,000 after four years. Machine 2 has an initial cost of $225,000 and will have a scrap value of $50,000 after three years. Annual maintenance costs of the two machines are as follows:

Year	**1**	**2**	**3**	**4**
Machine 1 ($ per year)	25,000	29,000	32,000	35,000
Machine 2 ($ per year)	15,000	20,000	25,000	

Where relevant, all information relating to this project has already been adjusted to include expected future inflation. Taxation and tax allowable depreciation must be ignored in relation to machine 1 and machine 2.

Ridag Co has a nominal before-tax weighted average cost of capital of 12% and a nominal after-tax weighted average cost of capital of 7%.

---

26 In relation to Ridag Co, which TWO of the following statements about competition and deregulation are true?

A Increased competition should encourage Ridag Co to reduce costs

B Deregulation will lead to an increase in administrative and compliance costs for Ridag Co

C Deregulation should mean an increase in economies of scale for Ridag Co

D Deregulation could lead to a decrease in the quality of Ridag Co's products

27 What is the equivalent annual cost of machine 1?

A $90,412

B $68,646

C $83,388

D $70,609

28 Is each of the following statements, about Ridag Co's use of the equivalent annual cost method, true or false?

Ridag Co cannot use the equivalent annual cost method to compare machine 1 and machine 2 as they have different useful lives	**TRUE**	**FALSE**
The machine which has the lowest total present value of costs should be selected by Ridag Co	**TRUE**	**FALSE**

29 Doubt has been cast over the accuracy of the year 2 and year 3 maintenance costs for machine 2. On further investigation it was found that the following potential cash flows are now predicted:

Year	**Cash flow** ($)	**Probability**
2	18,000	0.30
2	25,000	0.70
3	23,000	0.20
3	24,000	0.35
3	30,000	0.45

Calculate the expected present value of the maintenance costs for year 3 (to the nearest dollar).

$ __________

30 Ridag Co is appraising a different project, with a positive NPV. It is concerned about the risk and uncertainty associated with this other project.

Which of the following statements about risk, uncertainty and the project is true?

A Sensitivity analysis takes into account the interrelationship between project variables

B Probability analysis can be used to assess the uncertainty associated with the project

C Uncertainty can be said to increase with project life, while risk increases with the variability of returns

D A discount rate of 5% could be used to lessen the effect of later cash flows on the decision

SECTION C

31 VIP CO

This scenario relates to five requirements.

Vip Co, a large stock-exchange listed company, is evaluating an investment proposal to manufacture Product W33, which has performed well in test marketing trials conducted recently by the company's research and development division. Product W33 will be manufactured using a fully automated process which would significantly increase noise levels from Vip Co's factory. The following information relating to this investment proposal has now been prepared:

Initial investment	$2 million
Selling price (current price terms)	$20 per unit
Expected selling price inflation	3% per year
Variable operating costs (current price terms)	$8 per unit
Fixed operating costs (current price terms)	$170,000 per year
Expected operating cost inflation	4% per year

The research and development division has prepared the following demand forecast as a result of its test marketing trials. The forecast reflects expected technological change and its effect on the anticipated life cycle of Product W33.

Year	**1**	**2**	**3**	**4**
Demand (units)	60,000	70,000	120,000	45,000

It is expected that all units of Product W33 produced will be sold, in line with the company's policy of keeping no inventory of finished goods. No terminal value or machinery scrap value is expected at the end of four years, when production of Product W33 is planned to end. For investment appraisal purposes, Vip Co uses a nominal (money) discount rate of 10% per year and a target return on capital employed of 30% per year.

Note: Ignore taxation.

(a) **Calculate the following values for the investment proposal:**

(i) **Net present value** **(5 marks)**

(ii) **Internal rate of return; and** **(3 marks)**

(iii) **Return on capital employed (accounting rate of return) based on average investment.** **(3 marks)**

(b) **Briefly discuss your findings in each section of (a) previously and advise whether the investment proposal is financially acceptable.** **(4 marks)**

(c) **Discuss how the objectives of Vip Co's stakeholders may be in conflict if the project is undertaken.** **(5 marks)**

(Total: 20 marks)

32 FROSTE CO

This scenario relates to five requirements.

Froste Co has a dividend payout ratio of 40% and has maintained this payout ratio for several years. The current dividend per share of the company is $0.50 per share and it expects that its next dividend per share, payable in one year's time, will be $0.52 per share.

The capital structure of the company is as follows:

	$m	$m
Equity		
Ordinary shares (nominal value $1 per share)	25	
Reserves	35	
		60
Debt		
Loan note A (nominal value $100)	20	
Loan note B (nominal value $100)	10	
		30
		90

Loan note A will be redeemed at nominal value in ten years' time and pays annual interest of 9%. The cost of debt of this loan note is 9.83% per year. The current ex interest market price of the loan note is $95.08.

Loan note B will be redeemed at nominal value in four years' time and pays annual interest of 8%. The cost of debt of this loan note is 7.82% per year. The current ex interest market price of the loan note is $102.01.

Froste Co has a cost of equity of 12.4%.

Note: Ignore taxation.

(a) Calculate the following values for Froste Co:

(i) Ex dividend share price, using the dividend growth model (3 marks)

(ii) Capital gearing (debt divided by debt plus equity) using market values; and (2 marks)

(iii) Market value weighted average cost of capital. (2 marks)

(b) Discuss whether a change in dividend policy will affect the share price of Froste Co. (8 marks)

(c) Explain why Froste Co's capital instruments have different levels of risk and return. (5 marks)

(Total: 20 marks)

Section 8

ANSWERS TO SPECIMEN EXAM QUESTIONS

SECTION A

1 B

Cash flows better correlate to business value (which can be calculated as the present value of the company's future cash flows) than profit. If the financial rewards of directors are linked to increasing earnings (profit) per share, for example, through a performance-related reward scheme, there is an incentive to increase short-term profit at the expense of longer-term growth in cash flows and hence shareholder wealth.

If the WACC decreases, the present value of the business's cash flows rises and the business value rises.

Positive NPV projects add directly to business value.

Declaring full compliance with the corporate governance code would boost the company's share price in a semi-strong efficient market.

2 D

Sensitivity to a variable that affects cash flows = NPV/present value of the cash flows affected if that variable changes × 100

In this case, a change in sales volume will affect both the sales revenue and the variable cost cash flows. Together, these become contribution.

Sensitivity to sales volume = NPV/present value of contribution × 100

Sensitivity to sales volume = 1,300/24,550 × 100 = 5.3%

3 B and D

Monetary policy relates to the size of the money supply and the price of money (interest rates).

Tax and government expenditure are aspects of fiscal policy.

4 $85,479

Receivables financing cost = receivables balance × interest rate

Therefore, the current financing cost is $4m × 12% = $480,000

New receivables = receivables collection period/365 × credit sales

New receivables = 60/365 × $20m = $3,287,671

New finance cost = $3,287,671 × 12% = $394,521

Finance cost saving = $480,000 – $394,521 = $85,479

Note: this calculation could be done in alternative ways:

Receivables collection period = receivables/credit sales × 365

Current receivables collection period = $4m/$20m × 365 = 73 days

73 days to 60 days is a reduction of 13 days' worth of sales sat in receivables, so the change in receivables is $20m × 13/365 = $712,329 and the finance cost change is $712,329 × 12% = $85,479.

Alternatively, take the existing finance cost that relates to a 73 day receivables collection period and pro rate it to 13 days' worth:

$480,000 × 13/73 = $85,479

5 D

Operational gearing can be calculated as contribution/operating profit

Contribution = sales revenue – variable costs

Contribution = $60,000,000 – ($50,000,000 × 60%) = $30,000,000

Operational gearing = $30,000,000/10,000,000 = 3 times

Note: alternative methods of calculating operational gearing, such as using fixed costs divided by total costs, would produce a percentage figure rather than the 'number of times' required for this answer, so are not appropriate here.

6 103 days

Operating cycle = receivables collection period + inventory holding period – payables payment period

Operating cycle = 52 + 42 + 30 + 45 – 60 = 103 days

Note: where the inventory holding period is broken down into periods for raw materials, work in progress and finished goods, they are all added in the calculation.

7 A

Using the formula from the formula sheet for interest rate parity theory:

$F_0 = S_0 \times (1+i_c)/(1+i_b)$

S_0 is the current spot rate: 20.00 Dinars per $1

i_c is the interest rate of the counter currency. In this case the counter currency is Dinars (it is the currency that does not have a value of 1 in the exchange rate): 7% per year

i_b is the interest rate of the base currency. In this case the base currency is dollars (it is the currency that does have a value of 1 in the exchange rate): 3% per year

You may think that the calculation is therefore 20.00 × 1.07/1.03

However, as the interest rates given are annual rates, we need to pro-rate the calculation to predict a forward rate in only six months' time. To do this we take each interest rate and multiply it by 6/12ths before putting it into the calculation:

7% × 6/12 = 3.5% and 3% × 6/12 = 1.5%

The calculation of the forward rate becomes:

20.00 × 1.0.35/1.015 = 20.39 Dinars per $

Note that an alternative method is to take the (1+i) elements of the calculation to the power of 0.5, but an ACCA technical article has confirmed that the above (simpler) method should be used for risk management questions when interest rates need to be pro-rated.

8 D

Only the statement about business risk is correct. The theories look at how changing **financial** risk (gearing levels) affects the costs of capital.

In the traditional view, the cost of equity grows non-linearly as financial risk (gearing) grows, i.e. it appears as a curve on a graph of cost versus gearing levels rather than a straight line. It rises gradually at low levels of gearing and then more steeply at higher gearing levels.

Modigliani and Miller said in their no-tax model (and in their with tax one) that the cost of equity rises proportionally with increases in gearing.

Pecking order theory suggests that directors choose the 'path of least resistance' when choosing a source of finance, preferring to raise funds internally at first, turning to external finance when internal funds run out. For external funds, debt is chosen before equity, so convertible debt would be preferred to preference shares.

9 C

$g = (D_0/D_n)^{(1/n)} - 1$, where D_0 is the current dividend, D_n is the dividend from n years ago and n is the number of years between the two dividends.

$g = (\$0.360/\$0.311)^{(1/3)} - 1 = 0.05$, or 5%

$P_0 = D_0(1+g)/(r_e - g)$, where P_0 is the ex-dividend market price of the shares, g is the growth figure just calculated and r_e is the company's cost of equity.

$P_0 = (\$0.36 \times 1.05)/(0.12 - 0.05) = \$5.40$

10 GURDIP – NOT EFFICIENT AT ALL. OLIVER – STRONG FORM EFFICIENT

Gurdip is basing her investment decisions on technical analysis, which means that she believes the stock market is not efficient at all, not even weak form efficient.

Oliver believes markets are strong form efficient.

11 A

The statement refers to translation risk.

Transaction risk is the risk of exchange rates changing and affecting the value of an individual transaction. Economic risk is the long-term version of transaction risk, where many such transactions are affected, and the value of the business may therefore be affected. Interest rate risk is the risk that the business is exposed to changing interest rates.

12 A and C

Negotiable instruments can be sold before maturity and discount instruments are traded at less than their face value (the difference being the discount).

Treasury bills are safer than commercial papers, so will offer a lower yield (return). Commercial paper is a relatively short-term rather than long-term money market instrument.

13 C

Intermediaries can pool risk by lending to a wide variety of individuals and businesses, reducing the risk of a single default resulting in total loss of assets. They engage in maturity transformation by bringing together many lenders (who generally prefer to lend for short periods) and borrowers (who generally prefer to borrow for long periods) and managing the different maturities by pooling the funds together.

Intermediaries such as banks may provide fixed rate loans or hedging instruments to help fix interest rates, but these are not considered an intermediary function, more as a provider of those instruments.

14 A and C

The twin objectives of working capital management are profitability and liquidity. Companies need to find an appropriate balance of these to manage their working capital effectively.

Working capital management is a key factor in a company's long-term success. Inadequate working capital management can put a company's survival at risk. For instance, running out of cash could lead to a company being put into administration.

The current ratio is a measure of liquidity rather than profitability.

A conservative approach to working capital management prioritises low risk levels over profitability. Such an approach will involve offering long credit periods to customers, holding plenty of inventory and paying suppliers on time.

15 TRUE, TRUE, TRUE, FALSE

Information about past plans and decisions is a function of financial reporting, not financial management.

SECTION B

16 1ST ORDINARY SHARES, 2ND REDEEMABLE PREFERENCE SHARES, 3RD BANK LOAN, 4TH LOAN NOTES

Debt is safer for the investor than equity, as it comes with legally binding agreements for repayment. The loan notes, which are secured on non-current assets, are safer than the bank loan, which is secured on assets that will fluctuate in value.

Redeemable preference shares are safer for investors than ordinary shares as, when there is limited cash for dividends, the preference dividends will be paid before any ordinary dividends. They are also prioritised above ordinary shares in terms of payment upon liquidation.

17 $131.12

The conversion value will be the value of eight shares in seven years' time.

Future share price in seven years, with 6% growth in value each year:

$\$10.90 \times 1.06^7 = \$16.39$ per share.

Conversion value = $16.39 × 8 = $131.12

18 B

Market value of loan notes = the present value of the future interest and conversion value, discounted at the investors' required return.

The cost of debt to the company and the investors' required return are not the same when tax is present. However, as only the cost of debt has been given in the question, we must assume that tax is not an issue and that this represents the investors' required return also.

Future interest = $100 × 8% = $8 per year, for seven years.

PV of this interest, discounted at 9% = $8 × 5.033 = $40.264

PV of the given conversion value of $126.15, at 9% in seven years' time = $126.15 × 0.547 = $69.00

Market value = $40.26 + $69.00 = $109.26

19 C

Beta factors represent systematic risk levels. The risk level of the market as a whole is represented by a beta of 1. A higher beta represents higher systematic risk and a beta lower than 1 represents lower systematic risk.

Equity betas consider both business risk and financial (gearing) risk. It is asset betas that only consider business risk.

The capital asset pricing model uses beta factors and only considers systematic risk. It is assumed that investors have diversified their investment portfolios to eliminate unsystematic risk.

A beta factor of zero would represent risk free debt. Company debt is unlikely to be risk free, so will not have a value of zero. Do note, however, than in calculations of beta factors for the FM exam, we do make the assumption that the debt beta is zero, for simplification purposes.

20 C and D

The price/earnings (PE) ratio is the reciprocal of the earnings yield, but this does not cause a problem in using it.

Valuations using stock market information as well as corporate information are appropriate, as it is market forces that determine share prices.

It is difficult to select a suitable PE ratio. For an unlisted business, a proxy from another company will be needed. Even if a suitable company is found, the ratio may need to be adjusted as shares in unlisted companies are generally lower in value than those of similar listed ones.

Even for listed businesses, using the company's current PE ratio will simply calculate the current share price. Adjustments must be made to better reflect the company's future position for valuation purposes.

21 $390,472

The six-month forward rate will be used. To determine whether to use the low or high rate, one approach is to consider what the bank will be doing with the counter currency (the currency in the exchange rate that does not have a value of 1). In this case, the counter currency is pesos, and the bank will be selling pesos to Zarona Co so that Zarona can make its interest payment. The bank buys high and sells low, so the low rate will be offered to Zarona: 12.805

Translating the 5m peso interest at this rate: 5m/12.805 = $390,472

22 PURCHASING POWER PARITY ONLY, BOTH INTEREST RATE AND PURCHASING POWER PARITY, PURCHASING POWER PARITY ONLY

Purchasing power parity (PPPT) theory incorporates inflation rates, whereas interest rate parity theory incorporates interest rates. Under PPPT, the country with the higher inflation rate will weaken against the other currency (which effectively cancels out the difference in purchasing power caused by the difference in inflation).

Both theories hold in the long-term rather than the short-term.

Purchasing power parity theory uses the difference in inflation rates to predict future spot rates. Inflation rates are a way of reflecting the different costs of living between two countries.

23 DEPOSIT RATE 3.75%, BORROWING RATE 2.25%

Under a money market hedge relating to a liability in a foreign currency, the hedge must be set up with an asset in that currency. In this case, with a peso liability, a peso deposit (asset) must be set up, so the peso deposit rate will be used. This rate is 7.5% per year, but the liability will be settled in only six months' time, so the rate needs to be pro-rated

Peso deposit rate for 6 months = 7.5% × 6/12 = 3.75%

As an asset has been set up for pesos, a liability will be needed for dollars, so the dollar borrowing rate will be needed, which is 4.5% per year. This will also need to be pro-rated for 6 months:

Dollar borrowing rate for 6 months = 4.5% × 6/12 = 2.25%

24 B and D

Currency futures could be used to hedge the transaction risk on the payment. As the payment relates to interest on a loan, currency swaps could also be used.

As payment must be made on the date set by the bank, leading or lagging are not appropriate. Matching is also inappropriate as there is no peso cash inflow to match the payment against.

25 A

When the Euros are received in three months' time, they should be used to pay off a Euro denominated loan. By doing so, there will be no need to translate the receipt into dollars at that time.

The correct procedure therefore is to borrow Euros now, sell them immediately for dollars and put those dollars on deposit for three months.

26 A and D

Increased competition should encourage Ridag Co to reduce costs. If they don't do this, they may find it harder to remain competitive.

Deregulation could also lead to a decrease in the quality of Ridag Co's products. With higher competition, the need to cut costs could lead to a temptation to compromise on quality.

Deregulation will lead to a decrease rather than an increase in administrative and compliance costs for Ridag Co. Economies of scale come from growing the size of the business. Ridag may find it harder to do this with increased competition in the industry.

27 A

Before calculating the EAC, the present value of the costs of an ownership cycle for the machine should be calculated.

As taxation is being ignored, the nominal before-tax weighted average cost of capital of 12% should be used to discount the cash flows.

	Cash flow	**Discount factor 12%**	**Present values**
t0 Outlay	(200,000)	1	(200,000)
t1 cost	(25,000)	0.893	(22,325)
t2 cost	(29,000)	0.797	(23,113)
t3 cost	(32,000)	0.712	(22,784)
t4 cost and scrap value	(10,000)	0.636	(6,360)
Total PV of costs			(274,582)

EAC = PV of costs/annuity factor for the length of the cycle

Annuity factor at 12% for four years = 3.037

EAC = $(274,582)/3.037 = $(90,412)

28 FALSE, FALSE

The calculation of the equivalent annual cost removes the issue of the machines having different useful lives. The machine with the lowest equivalent annual cost should be purchased, not the one with the lowest total present value of costs.

29 $18,868

Expected present value means a present value should be calculated using the expected values of the cash flows.

EV of year 3 cash flow = 23,000 × 0.2 + 24,000 × 0.35 + 30,000 × 0.45 = 26,500

PV of year 3 expected cash flow, discounted at 12% = 26,500 × 0.712 = $18,868

30 C

Statement C is true.

Sensitivity analysis only looks at the effect of changing one variable at a time, so ignores the interrelationships between variables.

Probability analysis can be used to assess risk rather than uncertainty.

A lower discount rate increases the effect of later cash flows rather than lessens them. This is because a lower discount rate increases the present value of the cashflows, making them more important to the overall PV.

SECTION C

31 VIP CO

(a) (i) Calculation of NPV

Year	0	1	2	3	4
	$	$	$	$	$
Investment	–2,000,000				
Income		1,236,000	1,485,400	2,622,000	1,012,950
Operating costs		–676,000	–789,372	–1,271,227	–620,076
Net cash flow	–2,000,000	560,000	696,028	1,350,773	392,874
Discount at 10%	1	0.909	0.826	0.751	0.683
Present values	–2,000,000	509,040	574,919	1,014,431	268,333

Net present value: 366,723

Note that if the Net cash flow figures were produced in a spreadsheet in cells B7 to F7, the =NPV formula could be used to produce an NPV of $367,515 (=NPV(10%,C7:F7)+B7). The difference in value is due to a lower level of roundings if the formula is used. This does not affect the marks given for either method.

Workings

Calculation of income

Year	1	2	3	4
Inflated selling price ($/unit)	20.6	21.22	21.85	22.51
Demand (units/year)	60,000	70,000	120,000	45,000
Income ($/year)	1,236,000	1,485,400	2,622,000	1,012,950

Calculation of operating costs

Year	1	2	3	4
Inflated variable cost ($/unit)	8.32	8.65	9	9.36
Demand (units/year)	60,000	70,000	120,000	45,000
Variable costs ($/year)	499,200	605,500	1,080,000	421,200
Inflated fixed costs ($/year)	176,800	183,872	191,227	198,876
Operating costs ($/year)	676,000	789,372	1,271,227	620,076

Alternative calculation of operating costs

Year	1	2	3	4
Variable cost ($/unit)	8	8	8	8
Demand (units/year)	60,000	70,000	120,000	45,000
Variable costs ($/year)	480,000	560,000	960,000	360,000
Fixed costs ($/year)	170,000	170,000	170,000	170,000
Operating costs ($/year)	650,000	730,000	1,130,000	530,000
Inflated costs ($/year)	676,000	789,568	1,271,096	620,025

(ii) **Calculation of internal rate of return**

To use linear interpolation, a second NPV should be calculated using a different discount rate. Here, a discount rate of 20% is used. If using this method, you may choose any rate, but it is a good idea to use a higher rate if the original NPV was positive and a lower one if it was negative.

Year	0	1	2	3	4
	$	$	$	$	$
Net cash flow	–2,000,000	560,000	696,028	1,350,773	392,874
Discount at 20%	1	0.833	0.694	0.579	0.482
Present values	–2,000,000	466,480	483,043	782,098	189,365
Net present value	–79,014				

Internal rate of return (%) using the linear interpolation formula:

IRR = L + (H – L) × (NL/(NL – NH)

IRR = 10 + (20 – 10) × (366,723/(366,723 + 79,014)) = 18.2%

Note that if the net cash flows are presented in a spreadsheet in cells B7 to F7, the =IRR formula could be used (=IRR(B7:F7)) to give a value of 18.0%. When using the =IRR formula, no second calculation of the NPV at a different rate is needed. This can be a substantially quicker approach than using the linear interpolation method, and is more accurate. Full credit will be given for either method in the exam.

(iii) **Calculation of ROCE**

Total cash inflow $2,999,675 ($560,000 + $696,028 + $1,350,773 + $392,874)

Total depreciation and initial investment are same, as there is no scrap value

Total accounting profit $999,675 ($2,999,675 – $2,000,000)

Average annual accounting profit $249,918.75 ($999,675/4 years)

Average investment $1,000,000 ($2,000,000/2)

Return on capital employed 25.0% ($249,918.75/$1,000,000)

Marking scheme			
			Marks
(a)	(i)	Inflated income	2
		Inflated operating costs	2
		Net present value	1
	(ii)	IRR	3
	(iii)	ROCE	3
Total			**11**

(b) The investment proposal has a positive net present value (NPV) of $366,722 and is therefore financially acceptable. The results of the other investment appraisal methods do not alter this financial acceptability, as the NPV decision rule will always offer the correct investment advice.

The internal rate of return (IRR) method also recommends accepting the investment proposal, since the IRR of 18.2% is greater than the 10% return required by Vip Co. If the advice offered by the IRR method differed from that offered by the NPV method, the advice offered by the NPV method would be preferred.

The calculated return on capital employed of 25% is less than the target return of 30%, but as indicated earlier, the investment proposal is financially acceptable as it has a positive NPV. The reason why Vip Co has a target return on capital employed of 30% should be investigated. This may be an out-of-date hurdle rate which has not been updated for changed economic circumstances.

Marking scheme		
		Marks
(b)	Discussion of findings	3
	Advice on acceptability	1
Total		**4**

(c) As a large listed company, Vip Co's primary financial objective is assumed to be the maximisation of shareholder wealth. In order to pursue this objective, Vip Co should undertake projects, such as this one, which have a positive NPV and generate additional value for shareholders.

However, not all of Vip Co's stakeholders have the same objectives and the acceptance of this project may create conflict between the different objectives.

Due to Product W33 being produced using an automated production process, it will not meet employees' objectives of continuity or security in their employment. It could also mean employees will be paid less than they currently earn. If this move is part of a longer-term move away from manual processes, it could also conflict with government objectives of having a low rate of unemployment.

The additional noise created by the production of Product W33 will affect the local community and may conflict with objectives relating to healthy living. This may also conflict with objectives from environmental pressure groups and government standards on noise levels as well.

Marking scheme		
		Marks
(c)	Maximisation of shareholder wealth	2
	Conflict from automation of production process	2
	Conflict from additional noise	1
Total		**5**

32 FROSTE CO

(a) (i)

Dividend growth rate 4 % per year ((52/50) – 1) × 100

Share price using DGM $6.19 (0.50 × 1.04)/(0.124 – 0.04)

(ii)

	$m	
Number of ordinary shares	25	
MV of equity	154.75	(25m × $6.19)
MV of loan note A issue	19.016	(20m × $95.08/$100)
MV of loan note B issue	10.201	(10m × $102.01/$100)
MV of debt	29.217	($19.016m + $10.201m)
MV of capital employed	183.967	($154.75m + $29.217m)
Capital gearing	15.9%	($29.217m/$183.967m)

(iii)

WACC 11.9%

((0.124 × 154.75m) + (0.0983 × 19.016m) + (0.0782 × 10.201m))/183.967m

Marking scheme			
			Marks
(a)	(i)	Dividend growth rate	1
		Share price using DGM	2
	(ii)	Capital gearing	2
	(iii)	WACC	2
Total			**7**

(b) Miller and Modigliani showed that, in a perfect capital market, the value of a company depended on its investment decision alone, and not on its dividend or financing decisions. In such a market, a change in dividend policy by Froste Co would not affect its share price or its market capitalisation. They showed that the value of a company was maximised if it invested in all projects with a positive net present value (its optimal investment schedule). The company could pay any level of dividend and if it had insufficient finance, make up the shortfall by issuing new equity. Since investors had perfect information, they were indifferent between dividends and capital gains. Shareholders who were unhappy with the level of dividend declared by a company could gain a 'home-made dividend' by selling some of their shares. This was possible since there are no transaction costs in a perfect capital market.

Against this view are several arguments for a link between dividend policy and share prices. For example, it has been argued that investors prefer certain dividends now rather than uncertain capital gains in the future (the 'bird-in-the-hand' argument).

It has also been argued that real-world capital markets are not perfect, but semi-strong form efficient. Since perfect information is therefore not available, it is possible for information asymmetry to exist between shareholders and the managers of a company. Dividend announcements may give new information to shareholders and as a result, in a semi-strong form efficient market, share prices may change. The size and direction of the share price change will depend on the difference between the dividend announcement and the expectations of shareholders. This is referred to as the 'signalling properties of dividends'.

It has been found that shareholders are attracted to particular companies as a result of being satisfied by their dividend policies. This is referred to as the 'clientele effect'. A company with an established dividend policy is therefore likely to have an established dividend clientele. The existence of this dividend clientele implies that the share price may change if there is a change in the dividend policy of the company, as shareholders sell their shares in order to reinvest in another company with a more satisfactory dividend policy. In a perfect capital market, the existence of dividend clienteles is irrelevant, since substituting one company for another will not incur any transaction costs. Since real-world capital markets are not perfect, however, the existence of dividend clienteles suggests that if Froste Co changes its dividend policy, its share price could be affected.

Marking scheme		
		Marks
(b)	Dividend irrelevance	4
	Dividend relevance	4
Total		**8**

(c) There is a trade-off between risk and return on Froste Co's capital instruments. Investors in riskier assets require a higher return in compensation for this additional risk. In the case of ordinary shares, investors rank behind all other sources of finance in the event of a liquidation so ordinary shares are the most risky capital instrument to invest in. This is partly why Froste Co's cost of equity is more expensive than its debt financing.

Similarly for debt financing, higher-risk borrowers must pay higher rates of interest on their borrowing to compensate lenders for the greater risk involved. Froste Co has two loan notes, with loan note A having the higher interest rate and therefore the higher risk. Since both loan notes were issued at the same time, business risk is not a factor in the higher level of risk.

Instead, this additional risk is likely to be due to the fact that loan note A has a greater time until maturity, meaning that its cash flows are more uncertain than loan note B. In particular where interest rates are expected to increase in the future, longer-term debt will have a higher rate of interest to compensate investors for investing for a longer period.

A further factor is that the total nominal value (book value) of loan note A is twice as large as loan note B and therefore may be perceived to be riskier.

Marking scheme		
		Marks
(c)	Discussion of equity	1
	Debt and recognising business risk is not relevant	1
	Time until maturity of loan notes	1
	Different value of loan notes	1
	Other relevant discussion	1
Total		**5**